Managing by Projects for Business Success

T0305318

To Lilian, Jean and Rupa
with gratitude for consistent support and patience
over many years.

Managing by Projects for Business Success

John Parnaby

Stephen Wearne

and

Ashok Kochhar

**Professional
Engineering
Publishing**

Professional Engineering Publishing Limited,
London and Bury St Edmunds, UK

First published 2003

© 2003 J Parnaby, S H Wearne and A K Kochhar

ISBN 1 86058 341 5

A CIP catalogue record for this book is available from the British Library.

Typeset by H Charlesworth & Co Limited, UK.

For the extensive range of titles published by Professional Engineering Publishing contact:

Marketing Department
Professional Engineering Publishing Limited
Northgate Avenue, Bury St Edmunds
Suffolk, IP32 6BW, UK
Tel:+44 (0)1284 724384 Fax:+44 (0)1284 718692
e-mail: orders@pepublishing.com Website: www.pepublishing.com

About the Authors

The three authors of *Managing by Projects for Business Success* bring a complementary set of experiences to the task.

Dr John Parnaby CBE is a Fellow of the Royal Academy of Engineering. His extensive business and industrial experience covers over 40 years. He has worked in the Iron and Steel, Chemicals, Machinery, Aerospace, Automotive Systems, Software and general industrial sectors at all levels, including Main Board Director. For 15 years he was with Lucas Industries plc, initially as Group Technology Director and latterly as the Chief Executive of an international portfolio of aerospace electronics, control systems, defence, automation and automotive businesses. He has extensive experience in the USA, Europe, UK, Japan and India. During this period he directed a major programme of group-wide competitiveness improvements including the introduction of Toyota- developed Japanese methodologies via a taskforce project approach covering over 100 business units around the world. He has been a Director of Scottish Power plc, Jarvis plc and Molins plc, and is currently Chairman of three companies.

He also created a successful systems engineering consultancy business, which carried out service and industrial business redesign programmes for many international businesses. He worked at the Universities of Durham, Glasgow and Bradford over a period of 14 years, and was a university Professor of Manufacturing System Design working on systems engineering R&D projects with a variety of companies. It was during this period he met the other two authors. He has published many papers and books on process control, systems engineering and business management.

Professor Stephen Wearne has fifty years' experience of industry and academia. He has worked extensively with a wide range of international companies and professional institutions to develop training and case studies in the management of projects and contracts. His research has concentrated on emergency projects, project teams, joint ventures, contracts, project management problems and the management tasks of engineers. He was Professor (Emeritus) of Technological Management at the University of Bradford, and is now a member of the Centre for Research in the Management of Projects at the University of Manchester Institute of Science and Technology (UMIST).

Professor Ashok Kochhar is a Fellow of the Royal Academy of Engineering and is Professor of Manufacturing Systems and Management and Head of the School of Engineering and Applied Science at Aston University, Birmingham. He has previously been Lucas Professor of

Manufacturing Systems Engineering and Head of Department of Mechanical Engineering at UMIST, and Professor of Manufacturing Systems Engineering, University of Bradford.

He has carried out research with a variety of companies on process systems and manufacturing systems over 30 years, and published several books and a large number of papers on manufacturing strategy, process control, manufacturing planning and control systems, cellular manufacturing systems, knowledge-based manufacturing management systems and Japanese manufacturing systems. He has, in particular, carried out industrially collaborative projects with a range of major companies including 600 Group plc and Lucas Industries plc. In collaboration with Lucas he ran some major applied research programmes and contributed to the introduction, via taskforce project teams, of Japanese manufacturing systems practices and cellular team organization design. He also ran senior management training programmes.

He has made a number of industrial systems and business practices research study visits to Japan and other countries, and has provided several advisory reports to the UK Department of Trade and Industry.

Contents

Organizing for Project-led Strategic Innovation   1

Support Tools and Techniques Section 1
Definitions and Acronyms

Applications of the Project Process   2

Support Methodology Section 2
The Professional Project Management Body of Knowledge

Support Tools and Techniques Section 2
Design for Implementation

Management of The Project Process   3

Support Methodology Section 3
Project and Programme Management Procedures

Support Tools and Techniques Section 3
Specifications and Contracts

The Order Winning and Product Introduction Process   4

Support Methodology Section 4
Customer Account Development and Management

Support Tools and Techniques Section 4
Tools for Competitiveness Improvement

Project Management Applied to the Change Process   5

Support Methodology Section 5
Planning and Control

Support Tools and Techniques Section 5
People and Organization

Making it Stick 6

Acknowledgements

John Parnaby would like to acknowledge the dedicated enthusiasm and support provided by previous senior colleagues in industry. As ever, when change is required, not everyone involved is supportive, and in large companies in particular, there can be politically engineered opposition to the change agent.

It is essential, therefore, that there is a large enough core of like-minded people, who have the interests of the company at heart, to ensure that beneficial change happens over a broad front.

Very many people cooperated wholeheartedly in the development and application of multidisciplinary task force change project management activities during a period of difficult industrial recession. Some were, however, particularly supportive and involved, over a long period, and contributed greatly to the many ideas used, and these must be mentioned.

Thanks go particularly to Lucas Industries colleagues Sir Anthony Gill, Bryan Mason, Ken Strangward, Peter Johnson, Phillip Barrington, Ian Guttridge, Mike Francis, David Friday, Colin Hull and John Garside.

Stephen Wearne would like to thank all who gave him early responsibility for major projects, and all who have collaborated since in developing individuals and the expertise and skills for them to apply to succeed in managing their projects.

Ashok Kochhar is grateful to Tony Sweeten, Chief Executive of 600 Group plc, David Brown, Neil Burns, David Edgeley, Mike Hollwey and Keith Oldham with whom he has collaborated on many projects over a number of years.

Foreword

This book is designed for the businessman, the Chief Executive, the Technical Director, the Manager, and everyone who has a transformational leadership role with a mission to create step changes in business performance, and to make them stick.

The authors also believe that the book will provide valuable teaching material for University Business Schools and Faculties of Engineering, Accountancy, Information Technology and Construction. It will support justification of modern strategic management principles, as well as the importance of the application of best-practice project management methods. The wide variety of case examples provided is designed to be particularly useful in MBA and undergraduate courses for helping students to acquire new core competences and effective business management skills.

The reasons why such a book was felt to be very timely are varied and compelling. Modern economic and competitive pressures grow ever more aggressive, and established practices become less capable of meeting the new demands placed on them in all areas of the enterprise organization. Customers have become more demanding, discerning and less loyal with continually increasing requirements for quality, performance, service and reduced prices. In addition, the number of competitors with well-educated and trained management is growing remorselessly.

In this environment, a practical, holistic or total systems approach to the management of innovation is necessary. Balanced business strategies for all core business processes are important, but also essential is educated and strong-disciplined management with the attention to detail necessary to deliver these strategies and maintain the effectiveness of new processes, core competences and procedures.

In order to survive, businesses have to develop a performance culture where the setting of targets for performance in total quality style, for every business process, coupled with an enthusiastic and dynamic no-compromise disciplined attention to delivery of performance milestones on time, becomes a way of life, the 'Company Way'. The authors believe that many young senior managers are frustrated with the superficial, corporate strategies and financial restructuring practices of recent years, and wish to take a more hands-on approach but they do not have the knowledge. This book aims to help fill a gap on the basis of *first educate then innovate* through team projects.

This can be perceived to be a tall order in the modern social environment, which has become like quicksand. Traditional behavioural disciplines, the foundations upon which reliable step-by-step progress is built, have been disappearing rapidly. Industries such as engineering and manufacturing, medical service providers, critical public services and others, which now have similar requirements for change, enormous attention to detail and strong operational disciplines, are under great threat. We are suffering badly from sloppiness and a lack of societal concern at a time when required rates of change in products, businesses and competitiveness are intense. The need for major problems to be solved systematically and carefully is visible all around us, in public service enterprises as well as in manufacturing and service industries. A new, modern approach to managing by projects for adding value through continuous innovation has become essential.

A general consequence of these features of modern life has been a massive growth in the insecurity of businesses and individuals in the developed countries. It is also increasingly common to see innovative and successful rapidly growing businesses start to falter when they become complex and sophisticated but unable to maintain their innovation and operational leadership disciplines and the associated attention to detail.

It is from this overview of our business environment, characterised by a ceaseless demand for innovation and change, supported by extensive attention to persistent and detailed execution, that the need for a book entitled *Managing by Projects for Business Success* was born. Project Management is the core competence required for managing large numbers of projects of all sizes in a variety of organizations, solving major problems and getting things done economically, quickly and professionally. For such a book to be of practical use to its target audience of hands-on Chief Executives and their teams, it is essential to combine the numerous underlying principles of the systems approach. This integrates all activities to control, develop and operate a business system with an extensive sprinkling of practical case examples. These examples represent proven experiences from leading international companies, and integrate applications of modern best practices and methodologies for organization design and operation.

The methodologies, tools and techniques used in this book are not new in concept, although a number have been adapted or modified and improved. The total packaged systems approach is the main new contribution made.

The authors hope that their efforts in compiling the work will make life a little easier and much more fulfilling for many well-intentioned managers determined to make an educated impact. They will discover that managing by projects is a serious business, which is hard, detailed work yet extraordinarily rewarding if taken seriously by combining top–down strategic direction with bottom up implementation.

How to use this Book

Managing By Projects has to be a detailed and disciplined process with a right-first-time philosophy, and the devil really is in the detail. It is vital that modern managers can absorb and apply the elements of the approach developed in this book in order to meet the modern business challenges of strategy implementation and avoid serious failures. In this modern approach to managing innovating enterprises, vision, flair, entrepreneurialism, generic principles, strategic frameworks to coordinate direction, and knowledge adaptation and transfer are all of critical importance.

The approach used in this book combines general strategy with detailed implementation practice which means that the reader will have to work hard to become a practitioner. However, mastering and applying the practices described will lead to considerable job satisfaction, success and pride in doing a quality job.

To help the reader make effective progress, the architecture of the book has been designed to facilitate rapid understanding of the broad picture presented, expedite choice of a rapid route through the contents to first trial application, avoid pitfalls and develop competence, interest and enthusiasm.

The architecture is provided in a chart at the front of Chapter 1 which is repeated at the front of each subsequent chapter.

1. The book develops along a backbone of six core chapters, from an initial definition of the strategic context for managing by projects, through explanation of a standard but flexible project process and then through specific application areas of generic importance to many organizations and enterprises.
2. Running in parallel with the core chapters are two sets of supporting modular sections, each colour coded:

   five supporting methodology sections
   five supporting tools and techniques sections.

Some of these sections relate to specific core chapters and others, such as Support Methodologies Section 3, relate to all chapters.

The methodology sections relate to methodologies, organizational practices and concepts for improving the way teams work. They provide an introduction to aid access to authoritative and more substantial published reference works. The tools and techniques sections are generally more detailed and specialized than the methodology sections and aim to provide hands-on techniques to help transform the concepts and ideas presented into workable practical designs.

3. Substantial reference literature lists are provided that support the use of a total systems approach across the core chapters of the book, coordinating the way in which many aspects, including ideas, concepts, experiences have been adapted to provide an integrated generic system of Managing By Projects. The reference lists are grouped into two sets for the convenience of the reader:

Set 1 – *A primary source group at the end of each chapter that are particularly relevant to that chapter, as well as to the supporting methodology and tools and techniques sections.*

Set 2 – *These references have general back-up bibliography to enable the reader to follow up on particular specialized topics. All references have a cross-referencing index to the chapters, methodology and tools and techniques sections.*

Chapter 1 is intended to be read thoroughly by Chief Executives and senior colleagues. It aims to give a generic stand-alone system overview of all the topics covered in the book and develop a business-need strategic approach. The intent is to help managers *to do the right things*. Following chapters then aim to help them *to do things right first time*. Organizational requirements with supporting case examples and definitions are introduced. After studying Chapter 1 thoroughly, readers may then move on by initially fast tracking, choosing chapters that focus on their job in their enterprise. Some important concepts are repeated in context in different chapters in order to ensure that a fast-track reader obtains a systems view.

Chapters 2 and 3 lead the reader through simplified case examples. The associated methodology section is a second generic section, although more specialized in that it deals in detail with the basic core competencies of the project process and its associated project management support system. It is intended as a detailed application guide essential to successful operation.

For senior managers, suggested example initial fast track routes through the book are:

Chief Executive – Chapters 1, 2, 3, 6
Operations Director – Chapters 1, 2, 3, 5
Sales Director – Chapters 1, 2, 4
Product Development Director – Chapters 1, 2, 3, 4

The authors hope that the particular architecture and style of the book as described will fulfil many of the support needs of managers who passionately want to get moving, get things done and get them right first time.

For academic staff and students involved in programmes with Business Schools, Engineering, Economics, Accounting and Computing Faculties:

Chapter 1 provides an overall experience-based insight into modern achievement-oriented general management business practices and leadership principles, with case examples introducing the skills required to deliver results. Chapter 2 provides a wide range of simplified and focused case examples for a variety of business scenarios to encourage student discussions for the development of experienced judgement. Chapter 3 provides a base for the teaching of project management practices to be applied by students to their own project activities. Chapter 4 provides an illustration of industrial business process operational practice in the winning of orders and delivery of new products. It provides useful examples of practical organization design principles to meet modern market demands. Chapter 5 provides an introduction to change management with a wealth of case examples of the detailed application of best practice methodologies from many sources. These can be selected to support courses such as those on Total Quality Management, Manufacturing, Operational Management and Organization System Design.

The methodology, tools and technique sections, including such elements as commercial contract writing and working in teams, can be used selectively to help students move into professional practice and make an immediate impact, even at junior levels.

The reference bibliographies will be helpful for supporting manager training, to support undergraduate and postgraduate project work and continued personal professional development.

Reader's Guide

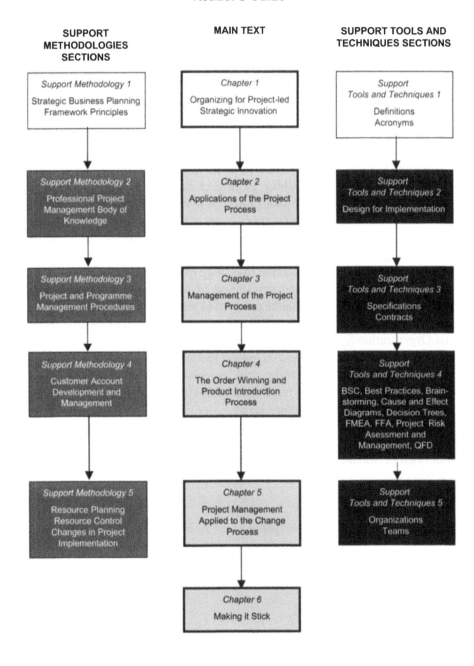

SUPPORT METHODOLOGIES SECTIONS

Support Methodology 1
Strategic Business Planning Framework Principles

Support Methodology 2
Professional Project Management Body of Knowledge

Support Methodology 3
Project and Programme Management Procedures

Support Methodology 4
Customer Account Development and Management

Support Methodology 5
Resource Planning Resource Control Changes in Project Implementation

MAIN TEXT

Chapter 1
Organizing for Project-led Strategic Innovation

Chapter 2
Applications of the Project Process

Chapter 3
Management of the Project Process

Chapter 4
The Order Winning and Product Introduction Process

Chapter 5
Project Management Applied to the Change Process

Chapter 6
Making it Stick

SUPPORT TOOLS AND TECHNIQUES SECTIONS

Support Tools and Techniques 1
Definitions Acronyms

Support Tools and Techniques 2
Design for Implementation

Support Tools and Techniques 3
Specifications Contracts

Support Tools and Techniques 4
BSC, Best Practices, Brainstorming, Cause and Effect Diagrams, Decision Trees, FMEA, FFA, Project Risk Asessment and Management, QFD

Support Tools and Techniques 5
Organizations Teams

Organizing for Project-led Strategic Innovation

1.1 Introduction – 'what's this all about' managing by projects, an overview

The first task of a book proposing the universality and importance of business management by projects must surely be to examine the underlying justification for changing from traditional business management models to a model based on management by projects. Therefore, in this chapter, the relevant aspects of supportive business experience will be assembled first, followed by an overview of the main features that managers need to introduce into their business. This will be expanded in the more specialised chapters that follow, together with a set of parallel cross-referenced sections describing the necessary supporting methodologies in more detail.

All modern public companies have a common aim, the creation of shareholder value. Every Chief Executive is very keenly aware of the penalties of failure to demonstrate actual growth and potential for further growth in shareholder value.

The most visible indicator of shareholder value is growth in the share price of the company. The two criteria mostly used to determine share price growth potential are:

- Underpinned potential for sales revenue growth over the coming years, backed up by evidence of recent growth.
- Actual and potential positive cash flow growth.

Share price, in effect, reflects the net present value of good growth in these two indicators. There have been some notable exceptions to the supremacy of these two simultaneous criteria in the so-called new economy companies with e.com after their name. Here, expectations of reduction in losses, plus naïve expectations for sales revenue growth, appeared to replace positive cash flows. However, the vulnerability of these measures has been dramatically demonstrated. Very fast growing businesses making low or negative returns also destroy value very fast since the returns on shareholder assets are lower than the cost in interest payments of borrowing cash for those assets invested. Such businesses clearly require operational management, cash control and development competencies, plus the value-adding applications and market knowledge, as do traditional businesses, on which to build growth.

There are two dominant means for achieving business growth:

1. Good management to achieve steady organic growth in sales and market share, by adaptively meeting customer needs with the right cost and quality.
2. Mergers or acquisitions.

The first of these requires highly professional management capable of continued innovation and a disciplined attention to detail coupled with a focus on making the return on investments significantly exceed the financing cost of those investments.

The second method is fraught with risk, particularly if the new partner or acquisition requires time and effort that overloads management and takes their eye off the demanding task of managing their original business for organic growth. Unless they can become more effective in managing their business for growth, performance falls and they also fail to quickly integrate and rationalize the new addition.

Over the ten years from 1990 to 2000 there has been an exponential growth in the volume of mergers and acquisitions. However, it is quite well known that an analysis of many of these demonstrated that 75%–85% of large acquisitions actually reduced shareholder value. This is because the acquiring management did not have the capability or project management competence to:

- integrate and restructure the acquisition rapidly enough;
- exploit synergies and other cost-saving opportunities along the value chain;
- exploit any added core competencies for creating new capabilities to utilize with a larger customer base;
- or merge the cultures quickly enough.

Many managements feel much more confident about the requirements to tightly operationally manage and control costs in their current company business where they are very experienced in the existing processes, practices and operational procedures, than they do about defining and managing the new factors necessary to achieve growth.

The most successful acquisitions are those where the potential growth and shareholder value from an acquisition were well defined by capable management in advance and the plans were clear to rapidly implement the changes and utilize the factors which positively provide growth. The acquisition price bid for the acquisition recognised the potential for value growth. The acquiring management were careful to list and quantify all of the factors of opportunity to increase shareholder value. Immediately on acquisition they put a trained transition project team in place to deliver value, managing this in a very tight and disciplined manner against clear targets and a defined time scale, with a clear carefully researched understanding of customer needs. Achievement of subsequent high growth as well as enhanced cash flow targets resulted in dramatic share price growth.

A Chief Executive who achieves high growth is seen as a star performer by institutional shareholders and corporate financial analysts and this example of professional acquisition selection and integration provides a first illustration of managing by projects for business success.

It also implies that many of the factors that have to be tackled to increase value from an acquisition are likely to be present in the situation where organic growth of an existing business is the aim. Some additional factors obtained through the acquisition can be combined to create dramatic additional growth. One example of such a factor is the availability of a larger customer base into which enhanced capabilities can be channelled.

1.1.1 Organic growth requirements

If we return briefly to the important opportunity of organic growth, which is the area with which many operational managements feel most uncomfortable, we have to determine why this is perceived to be so difficult to systematically develop. For many managers used to the repeatability of day-to-day, well-used operational disciplines, the levers for organic growth are perceived as ill-defined, loose and uncertain in terms of the methods required and having no reasonable guarantees of success. They do not know how, or are not competent, to achieve growth and so they are ineffective. They hide in day-to-day operations where they can make an impact, and create tremendous frustrations for the Board of the company as well as for the institutional shareholders by a collective failure to grow the share price and value of the business.

The missing links here are usually:

1. Operationally oriented managers do not appreciate the additional levels of improvement possible in many areas of the business. They are limited by their experience, and need education to stimulate and define opportunities for innovation.

2. They are not aware of relevant new organizational concepts, methodologies, supporting technologies, tools and techniques. Again, education and training-led innovation are the keys.
3. They do not have the necessary dedicated organizational levers to drive change and development strongly.

Potential areas for driving value growth through market expansion, market share and sales growth are:

- Introduction of new and improved platform products and services;
- Increased organizational effectiveness, supported by R&D and technology transfer, of the core business processes through organizational restructuring and simplification and the sharpening of core competencies;
- Improved customer interfacing and a clearer definition of the product and service needs of each customer;
- The application of world-class procedures in every area;
- Opportunities for effective outsourcing and synergy utilisation;
- Avoiding commoditisation of products, processes, services and organizational practices;
- Development of sophisticated commercial and pricing policies;
- Creation of low-cost-effective support infrastructures and elimination of wasteful organizational activity;
- Alliances to fill competency gaps and increase the scope of the value potential.

Managers need to have the knowledge to be able to define the internal and external resistors, drivers and critical success factors for value growth. They have to know how to quantify the value growth potential from each in order to define strategies and prioritize action plans and value-delta targets. However, plans and targets on paper by themselves are by no means enough. A strong, powerful and competent organizational mechanism is required to drive performance improvement and growth. A 'do-it' culture has to be created that systematically pulls all the levers for growth, in all of the areas present in most organizations, that is 'no-compromise' achievement oriented.

The proven mechanism for this is management by projects in which a hard-nosed, properly educated project approach is used to attack the areas listed above in order of potential to realize the opportunities in every part of the organization. No area must be immune. This approach to change management and development, when applied to acquisition integration and internal organic growth, has a great deal in common for both tasks, it is generic. Together they can create impressive value growth if properly sustained and driven.

A detailed appreciation of the approach to practical application is developed in the follow-on sections of this book.

1.2 Background to the genesis of a managing by projects philosophy

The concept of managing by projects may appear a strange one to business managers educated in the predominant principles of management which were practised in the period 1955–89 in the Western world. This was a period of relative stability with almost a steady state in organizational and management practices being taught and applied. Bureaucratic rigid organizational infrastructures divided into tightly defined and controlled specialized functional departments were commonplace. The consequential company territorial politics, over-high departmental operating costs, boundary problems, which fragmented natural business process flows, and complacency, led to stagnation of innovation. This was aggravated by Trade Union behaviour and practices, which mimicked those of management by insisting on time-honoured practices, protocols and procedures as their way of achieving political power in organizations and the powers of veto and control. There were many historical contributing cultural factors to this situation, which led to a lack of flexibility, an absence of dynamism and low levels of innovation. Management were as much a source of restrictive practices as were Trade Unions, due to their unwillingness to learn and to introduce modern methods. This type of behaviour indicates short-term thinking.

Many businesses had held on to their market position for a long period without having to make sophisticated innovations in what they did or how they did it. They were only just starting to feel uncomfortable from the pressures of emerging competition from companies where major investments had been made in the provision of modern educational infrastructures for engineers and managers.

Emerging economies had recognized that, to break into markets traditionally dominated by established suppliers, they had to focus on providing products or services with improved cost, quality, reliability, value, and on increased variety, to better meet the needs of niche customer groups. This required them to think outside the box of conventional practice and put intellectual and physical effort into rapid innovation.

To do this is not a simple task. A considerable and wide-ranging set of new knowledge, tools, techniques and methodological practices need to be embedded in the organization culture. People have to be persuaded and trained to move away from ineffective organizational practices. The changes required are very widespread, affecting every operational process, and are difficult to carry out without endangering the stability of delivery to customers unless excellence in change management is an organizational core competence.

Many companies had settled into a cultural form of collective behaviour which was primarily routine operational in style. The jobs and actions people took each day and the procedures they followed were virtually the same as they had performed the previous day, week, month or year. In many companies, the pace was slow, productivity was poor and the important entrepreneurial innovative and development skills had been dulled. The skills of risky, rapid commercialization of new products and services had been stifled. Taking entrepreneurial risks is much safer when underpinned by a platform of best practices and organizational competencies.

To respond to changing requirements, healthy organizations must maintain a good balance between a tightly disciplined standardized operating culture and a systematically managed innovative or development culture. Once a development culture has been lost, it is very difficult and time consuming to regenerate it without discipline, lots of energy and persistence. Change is difficult and is perceived as threatening to the status quo of people who have become comfortable and secure in their routines.

A culture in which the majority of people are routine operations oriented is often a very restrictive culture; even to what may be beneficial change from the business point of view.

While organizations with a steady state operations culture may have recognized the need to set up projects focused on product development, albeit not well organized at times, many never set up projects to redesign and develop their organization and its culture. They did not have the knowledge base to improve effectiveness and to achieve calibrated bench-marks for world-class levels of performance of their business processes. This was just not seen to be an important issue.

Commonly, where managers set up product development projects, acknowledging these as special difficult to manage cases where outcomes were difficult to predict with certainty, they often tolerated the inadequacies of specialized departmental structures and poor project management practices. They simply did not know what best practice was or what world-class project management competencies were.

The consternation and demoralization, which occurred in many companies in the period 1960–1980, can be imagined when excellent competitors appeared in their market-places. These competitors used breathtaking new practices and procedures such as those associated with business process systems engineering, a concept pioneered on a large scale by, and central to, for example, the excellent Toyota Production System.

Well-led companies open to new ideas gradually started to appreciate that in order to meet the new high standards required for survival in an increasingly global market-place, they had to change and develop every value-creating element of their organization, not just their products, while eliminating a lot of traditional non-value-adding practices.

This led to recognition of three vital and mutually supportive requirements:

1. To set up a programme of change projects covering every aspect of the business and its organization, starting initially with major restructuring and business redesign projects, and leading on to a follow-on set of continuous improvement projects.
2. The use of cross-functional task-force teams from across multiple departments. These provide the development project capability, using cross-discipline experience and viewpoints to provide higher quality solutions. They also break down departmental barriers, politics, secrecies and bureaucracy, to make change happen and make it stick in the shortest possible time scales.
3. Installation of a best practice training support programme and a project management infrastructure to ensure well-disciplined systematic progress in extremely demanding and complex situations while reliably maintaining business as usual, so far as delivering products and services day-to-day is concerned, facilitated by good communication with the customers and suppliers.

Such a leadership approach then created the environment which had as its natural outcome the concept of managing development and change by projects to distinguish it from the traditional functional line management approach used for repetitive routine operations.

The flexible co-existence in an organization structure of a total development process and an operations process is an essential requirement for survival. The wide-scale recognition of this critically important principle accelerated in all kinds of organizations, both public and private, during the period 1990–2000.

If a management team wish to simultaneously improve their organizational effectiveness and the range, quality and cost of their products or services, they must set about tightly and professionally managing their innovation approach simultaneously across many areas of the organizational system.

As an example, consider the case of reducing the delivered cost and improving quality of a manufactured product. This requires the whole operational delivery value chain process to be analysed and flow-charted, from procurement of materials to delivery of the product. It is necessary to list the opportunity areas and then set up resourced and monitored project activity to redesign the process to meet the improvement targets set. Two examples of mutually supportive projects illustrate this:

1. *A manufacturing system or service delivery system redesign.* Catalogue all sources of delay and confusion along the process which increase the lead-time, i.e. non-value-adding activities such as waiting, storing, inspecting, rectification, transporting. Then rearrange the process sub-systems into simpler cell team structures to eliminate these non-value-added activities and reduce the overall process time. Reducing overall process lead-time reduces costs since time is money, i.e. reducing time lost by all resources involved takes out considerable expense. Also simplification eliminates unwanted variations, errors and mistakes and so improves quality of performance. Reduced lead-time and waste also reduces inventory and work in progress levels, reducing financing costs and improving reliability of delivery to customers.

2. *Redesigning the product using a 'design for manufacture' project to reduce the number of component parts and make assembly easier.* This reduces manufacturing cost and improves quality. It also reduces component supply costs and the number of supplier quality problems and associated costly administration.

Expecting busy operational managers to find the time in a hectic work schedule to make major changes and improvements in such processes, as well as introducing new methods and practices, is unrealistic unless an executive development mechanism supported by training is integrated in the organization structure to help them.

The most effective mechanism is a project team structure in which task-force team projects are set up in priority order linked to the aims of the business competitiveness achievement strategy. These teams will professionally design the project and then hand over and train the operational staff to run the new systems and make change stick.

In this way, improvements across the whole organization, and the development of new products and services, progress in an orderly, managed and systematic way via a sequence of projects in priority order, to achieve the targets of the business competitiveness achievement plan.

This is exactly how the leading international companies manage innovation to maintain an effective, target-driven, entrepreneurial culture. Studies of world-class Japanese companies, such as Toyota, Hitachi and Honda, showed that the number of projects running at any one time ran into hundreds, ranging from large new product project teams through operational process effectiveness improvement task-forces, to small Kaizen continuous improvement teams. The driving principle was 'train–do–train–do' applied continuously, i.e. setting world-class stretch targets, training teams in new methods and then immediately setting them to work to apply the training to deliver the results required to meet the targets in a highly professional and effective manner. This is true innovation leadership and, when persisted with over time and with wide staff involvement, creates a stimulating buzz and high level of motivation across the company.

All areas requiring change, development and improvement in any organization are amenable to a disciplined project management approach. This is the executive lever that management can pull to deliver change and development.

There is a clear question which this book aims to answer:

'**How do you manage a company which runs hundreds of changing projects continually to maintain global competitiveness – what form of organization is used, how are the targets aligned to business strategy, who sets the specifications or targets, how are they all reviewed, who implements the results and how are these audited and checked out, against the strategic framework, the targets set, and the results expected?**'

There is also another dimension to managing by projects which most senior managers will recognize. In addition to delivering innovation by the use of various kinds of targeted task-force project teams to create improved business process effectiveness and efficiency, and then continuously improving these, there are elements of the various resulting business processes, which, in their routine operational mode, also deliver through projects. Clearly the change management process is one of these. Others are, for example:

1. The new product introduction process (PIP). Multi-functional development teams are used to deliver new products or services and their required manufacturing or delivery processes in the shortest possible time.
2. The order winning process. Customer account development or order winning bid project teams are used to identify and specify an opportunity to 'sell a solution' to a specific customer problem or requirement. They then systematically target the decision makers and their advisers in the

customer organization to secure an order or request to develop a product or service. They then transfer ongoing responsibility to a PIP project team and the routine operational function of customer account management.

3. The maintenance process, e.g. in a chemical, iron and steel, or utility company. Here an annual major reconstruction or overhaul of a blast furnace or a sulphuric acid effluent gas cleaning electrostatic precipitation plant, or the review and update of a complex IT support network, would be carried out against a short time scale by a project team combining company personnel and process plant sub-contractors integrating all necessary skills.

1.3 The critical business success factors summarised

1. The contemporary Chief Executive has to be aware that, due to the same logic that requires him to carefully put in place a line operations organization which expertly responds to command and control requirements to deliver the goods, there has to be a similarly carefully and intelligently designed and integrated development or change project line organization. This must be just as controllable to meet strategic requirements by systematically delivering a competitive overall performance project-by-project. A focused core full-time team is essential with identified supporting part-time members.

2. Managing by projects fails if it is not properly organized and resourced by professional staff of high calibre. Delivering change and making it stick are very difficult to achieve because the change agent has enemies who see themselves, and their part of the organization, threatened; in addition the change process is non-routine with no standardized solutions and with new problems to be solved, making planning difficult and risky.

3. Training and education in new ideas, methodologies and technologies has to be part of the support infrastructure to help the change project teams to innovate. The training of project teams in new methodologies and immediately facing them with demanding targets to achieve against tight time scales, in effect forces them to apply their new training to deliver. Online training in this way is much more effective than offline training provided 'in case it may be useful in future'.

4. New mechanisms must be operationally embedded in the company infrastructure and culture to set and communicate specifications, audit progress, support the teams, review and monitor regularly, and align all

implementation actions with the strategic business plan and its demanded time scales.

5. No part of the organization must be exempt from a professional approach to beneficial change, which makes it better able to meet the needs of customers and shareholders, economically and competitively, particularly if the organization is to survive and grow.

6. There is need for a standardized and auditable project management system supported by common training, terminology and procedures; however it must be flexible to meet the requirements of all types of project needed for success, and their auditing, reporting, and implementation tracking needs.

7. By facing his team with stretch targets based on real measures of competitor performance and utilizing opportunities such as failure to meet budgets, losses of market share, and lost bids, the clever leader creates 'significant emotional events' to galvanize change and focus attention.

8. In modern business, routine operations functions are very hard pressed to meet the increasingly sophisticated demands of modern markets with increasingly sophisticated services, and do not have the time or knowledge to carry out complex and demanding development projects.

1.4 The creation of a standardized tight–loose project and programme management framework

The term 'tight–loose' means using a carefully specified, flexible, well-ordered standard working approach, which is not bureaucratic and obstructive. Using standard familiar support infrastructure frameworks and design methods, standard working solves problems that are business specific, with selections from common tools, techniques and methodologies to suit the task; by setting business-specific goals and targets, trained teams are empowered to innovate.

For many years in many organizations an amateur approach to project management was rife. Frustrated Project Managers operating in progress chaser mode, with no line responsibility for staff involved, for time milestone achievement and for cost budgets and benefit targets, used persuasion to try to get dominant operations functions to provide a little of their time to help deliver innovation and development. These functions always had the get-out excuse that they were too busy on other priorities.

This stemmed from organizational stagnation and the lack of status and lack of executive power of the development role in the organization and the consequential poor rewards and low capability of the people willing to accept the associated poor career prospects. In fact, since many projects were doomed to failure from the outset, the powerless Project Manager found him or herself in a high risk occupation since he/she was often blamed for failures and fired. It could be said that only those people of insufficient ability to recognize that they were taking on an impossible task took on such unprofessional project management roles.

Typically, only a very small percentage of the energies of the dominant operational line management group were devoted to putting world-class practices and procedures for innovation in place. This is not sufficient to ensure the excellence essential for an effective operational organization. Ironically they usually had the operational skills to pursue an incremental continuous improvement role once a major change or development was completed in substance, to provide a new supporting driveable organization platform.

The contemporary company is now in a very different situation with very many demands for improvement and change in all its areas of activity. A steady flow of new products or services, cost base reductions, lead-time reductions in all processes, and improvements in product and service quality levels, measured in low parts per million, are essential for survival in the face of global competition.

This has resulted in a whole new set of requirements and expectations of very high standards for professionalism in innovation and change.

Some Chief Executives have realized that the first crude stage of change – involving the reduction of staff, the elimination of organizational levels and layers within the current organizational structure, and the withdrawal from unprofitable products or services or markets – was actually the easiest stage. It is a lot easier to get out of a business than it is to create one. They also discovered that cutting capability within existing old fashioned organization structures created major problems eventually. Two of these problems are:

- Eventually a department shrinks to such a low level that it can no longer complete its tasks and out of control fire-fighting results.
- The easy targets go first and these are often future value-adding activities such as training and development. The business becomes commoditised rapidly.

A parallel common mistake in some companies, exemplified by General Motors' approach in the 1980s, was to spend large capital sums on IT systems and automation without first simplifying and redesigning to create more effective organizations to reduce the need for such expenditure. The result was a failure to improve performance and a failure to complete, and effectively operate and support, such highly complex systems.

The second stage of change is now widely recognised to be much more difficult. It involves the creation of new types of flexible, innovative organization structures capable of increasing value-adding effectiveness, delivering balanced short-, medium- and long-term economic value-added (EVA), and of rapidly commercializing truly new products and services to ensure long-term growth and survival.

1.5 The evolution of the focused modern approach

In the late 1980s and early 1990s leading companies around the world started systematically looking for best practices that they could adapt and apply to create a non-bureaucratic supporting infrastructure for change and innovation.

Central to this approach was the creation of the core competencies of programme and project management to manage the change and development process and deliver results in the shortest time scale. The status of these core competencies became elevated in seniority. They were recognized as being important and change and development line management capability was integrated with the organization structure.

Manufacturing engineering companies such as Lucas Industries, General Electric, Rolls Royce Aerospace, and service companies such as utilities (e.g. Scottish Power) and retailers (e.g. Walmart), banks and insurance companies made determined attempts to achieve world-class levels of competence in project and change management. They sent task-forces around the world to bench-mark, search out best practices, write operational manuals, and set up training programmes for all levels of staff, to provide up-to-date skills and create an on-time innovation achievement culture. This enabled them in turn to implement a practical and rapidly effective 'management by projects' philosophy, which resulted in impressive business value growth and performance.

Widespread management by projects evolved with an increasingly common philosophy across different segments of industry. Change management became increasingly focused and accepted as the professional approach to restructuring, improving and developing businesses. As this happened it was discovered that the project process and the support systems

Table 1.1   Core competencies – managing by projects

Programme Director	Project Manager
(a) Qualifying competencies	**(a) Qualifying competencies**
• Technical understanding of the principles underlying the technologies and products of the business obtained from a relevant degree. • Experience of managing a range of successful projects and of at least one business process. • Broad understanding of business market information and business practices. • Understanding of business customers and their business process needs. • Logical and systematic. • Numerate and with financial control and business ratio appreciation. • Computer literate. • Appreciation of shareholder value contributors and aims of business strategy.	• Technical understanding underlying the principles of the activities and technologies of the area of focus of the project gained from a relevant degree. • General understanding of the relevant areas of the project application and business need. • Understanding of the project customers and his business processes. • Product and service understanding. • Understanding of general planning tools and techniques. • Computer literate and able to use advanced PC tools. • Basic financial and cash control knowledge.

All at one * level minimum – Four stars is exellent; one star is basic

---

Competencies requiring demonstrated exceptional capability

Drive for excellence	****	Drive for excellence	***
Concern for order and detail	****	Concern for order and detail	****
Leadership and team-building	****	Leadership and team-building	***
Self-confidence	****	Self-confidence	**
Managing stress and pressure	****	Managing stress and pressure	***
Commercial intuition	****	Commercial intuition	**
Conceptual thinking	****	Conceptual thinking	***
Problem solving and decision making	****	Problem Solving and decision making	****
Influence and communication	****	Influence and Communication	**
Customer orientation	****	Customer orientation	**

required in very different types of businesses had very much in common, i.e. they were generic.

Table 1.1 shows a single summary example of the results of a best practice survey by Lucas Industries to support the recruitment and training of Programme Directors and Project Managers by defining those elements of competence that such staff had to be very good at and those they particularly had to excel in. Such careful assessments have led in recent years to various project management societies and university research groups around the world, working together to share knowledge and ideas in order to create a common view of the generic body of knowledge (BoK) associated with programme and project management. The USA-based Project Management Institute and the UK-based Association for Project Management (APM) each introduced versions of their BoK in the period 1985–1995. These enabled professional requirements to be defined in detail to support best practice training although there were differences in focus between the two BoKs.

The UK version had a broader orientation to business general management and business strategic requirements and has recently been updated incorporating the views of 117 companies interviewed by the University of Manchester Institute of Science and Technology (UMIST) who were sponsored by the APM and industry to design an updated BoK. A more detailed discussion of this APM body of knowledge definition is provided in the Support Methodology section for Chapter 2.

In summary, therefore, the important common requirements of businesses of all kinds when faced with major needs to innovate for survival over the past 15 years, have resulted in consensus on a best practice approach to project management for all kinds of projects, large and small.

There is no question that perceptive business managers now recognize project management as a critical core competence for the achievement of their vision for their business. They have also come to recognize how effective project management is as a career development role for young managers with its no compromise focus on achievement of results within cost, time and quality constraints.

1.6 Organizing for project-led strategic innovation – lessons from recent history

Through the 1990s, very considerable changes took place and continue to take place in the way businesses operate and compete, whether selling products, services or, increasingly, both.

Competition from developing countries such as India, Singapore, Malaysia, Indonesia, Korea, Taiwan and China developed fast in most markets. This was driven by very low manpower costs, and their creation of support infrastructure, including good education systems that produce graduates and technicians of high quality, educated in modern practices.

In parallel, the innovative Japanese put enormous pressure on Western countries in the 1980s and early 1990s through intelligently focused market development approaches in areas such as automotive and electronics market segments. Their intelligent re-thinking and simplification of organizational principles and the associated practices, combined with new value-adding methodologies and careful analysis of target market needs was supported by an underlying philosophy focused on reduced cost of products and services, linked to orders of magnitude improvements in quality. This resulted in a value for money approach that successfully took away large market shares from slow to respond Western countries, indirectly reducing progressively the underlying cash flows and balance of payments of their economies.

The side effect of the progressive reduction in market share of manufactured goods, the traditional, internationally tradable wealth generation area of Western countries, meant less money was available for the purchase of services. A single manufacturing sector supports a large number of service companies ranging from consultancy to corner shops as well as the direct employees in that sector.

This ultimately led to cost reduction activities in service sectors such as banking and insurance which in turn led to job cuts, rationalizations, restructuring, and mergers; in addition increased efforts to reduce costs and improve the competitiveness of services resulted. Businesses such as textile products retailing were affected because there was less money in the pockets of consumers, who were suffering the impact of widespread staff redundancies and early retirements. This put pressure on prices and customer service so forcing these businesses to innovate.

The result has been a rapid increase in pressures for change and innovation. Executive Managers in all types of businesses learned the hard way that their products, services and organizational practices had become commoditised and easy to copy by fast-footed emerging competition. Indeed, many businesses have not survived and many Executive Managers have lost their jobs as a consequence. Chief Executives learned to their cost that wide-ranging innovation in their businesses was essential, and that new approaches were required for meeting the very sophisticated modern market requirements. *In short, the amateurism of outdated contemporary approaches was a recipe for disaster. Cleverness and education-led innovation had come of age. No business was immune to the need to change dramatically.*

It became clear to many businesses during the 1990s that, in order to survive and prosper, it was essential to strategically redirect their resources in the enterprise and innovate very rapidly; this required a highly professional structured approach at the heart of which was the management of a programme of innovation projects in each enterprise. To support such a wide-ranging and urgent strategic approach required new high standards of programme definition, and programme and project management, as well as a clear consensus and commercial understanding at every level in the business that the development and change project programme was essential to the future survival of the business.

Because of the size of the task, its costs and benefits, and its impact across all functions of a business, a more sophisticated, modern, sound strategic framework and business plan was also required to give sustained clear direction over a long period; within this period the project programme had to be carefully selected and embedded. There was no room for mistakes, tardiness and the retention of old fashioned practices. *The writing was on the wall in large capital letters, and the project management of development and change became a central core competence of many management teams.* This was true even for product development, well established in the best companies, because existing practices were seen to be uncompetitive, i.e. they took too long to deliver and the quality of performance benchmark comparisons against the leading companies were poor.

1.7 The competitiveness achievement plan

Chief Executives were faced with two priorities:

1. The introduction of the concept of an integrated total systems approach to change across the whole business system through the strategic design of a Competitiveness Achievement Plan (CAP) and a three to five year delivery programme with clear world-class objectives and targets based on wide ranging bench-marking (Figs 1.1a and b).
2. Application via the CAP of new organizational principles, including organization of the core business processes and of the management of change led by best practice project management.

Figure 1.1a shows how the strategic vision of a senior management team is developed in detailed stages and strategies, and finally delivered into every sub-unit of an enterprise by projects with clear objectives. Figure 1.1b is a master eight-module block diagram showing how, by starting in the top

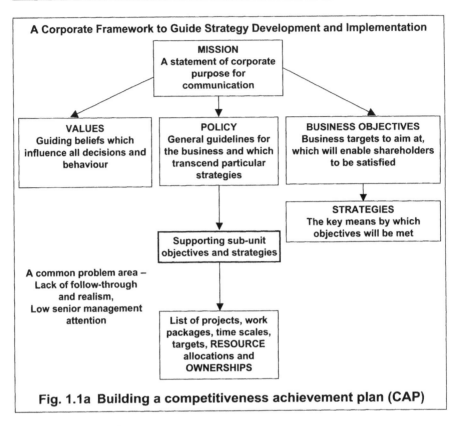

A Corporate Framework to Guide Strategy Development and Implementation

MISSION
A statement of corporate purpose for communication

VALUES
Guiding beliefs which influence all decisions and behaviour

POLICY
General guidelines for the business and which transcend particular strategies

BUSINESS OBJECTIVES
Business targets to aim at, which will enable shareholders to be satisfied

STRATEGIES
The key means by which objectives will be met

Supporting sub-unit objectives and strategies

A common problem area – Lack of follow-through and realism, Low senior management attention

List of projects, work packages, time scales, targets, RESOURCE allocations and OWNERSHIPS

Fig. 1.1a Building a competitiveness achievement plan (CAP)

left-hand corner, a company with a portfolio of business divisions develops a strategy for each business in Sections 2 to 5, to match its role defined in Section 1.

A detailed 3-year business plan is then developed in Section 6 through an operational plan based on forecast sales supported by project plans for development, change and the associated capital expenditure.

The financial plan, which provides the 3-year budgets for each business, derived from the integration of costs, benefits and revenues, is then constructed in Section 7 supplemented with financial measures of performance.

Section 8 defines the important non-financial measures of performance which have to be met.

The Support Methodology Section 1 summarizes in more detail the logical background to the preparation of a CAP. A typical summary of grouped headings for a 3-year CAP document used in practice is given in Table 1.2. These illustrate the breadth and sophistication of the challenge as

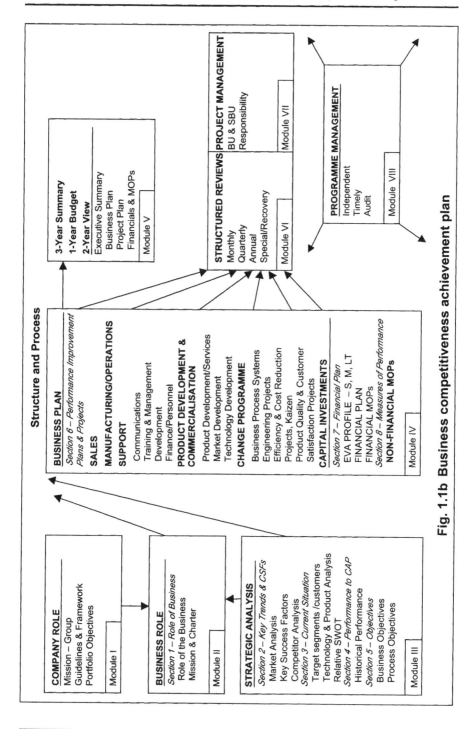

Structure and Process

COMPANY ROLE
Mission – Group
Guidelines & Framework
Portfolio Objectives

Module I

BUSINESS ROLE
Section 1 – Role of Business
Role of the Business
Mission & Charter

Module II

STRATEGIC ANALYSIS
Section 2 – Key Trends & CSFs
Market Analysis
Key Success Factors
Competitor Analysis
Section 3 – Current Situation
Target segments /customers
Technology & Product Analysis
Relative SWOT
Section 4 – Performance to CAP
Historical Performance
Section 5 – Objectives
Business Objectives
Process Objectives

Module III

BUSINESS PLAN
Section 6 – Performance Improvement Plans & Projects
SALES
MANUFACTURING/OPERATIONS
SUPPORT
Communications
Training & Management
Development
Finance/Personnel
PRODUCT DEVELOPMENT & COMMERCIALISATION
Product Development/Services
Market Development
Technology Development
CHANGE PROGRAMME
Business Process Systems
Engineering Projects
Efficiency & Cost Reduction
Projects, Kaizen
Product Quality & Customer
Satisfaction Projects
CAPITAL INVESTMENTS
Section 7 – Financial Plan
EVA PROFILE – S, M, LT
FINANCIAL PLAN
FINANCIAL MOPs
Section 8 – Measures of Performance
NON-FINANCIAL MOPs

Module IV

3-Year Summary
1-Year Budget
2-Year View
Executive Summary
Business Plan
Project Plan
Financials & MOPs

Module V

STRUCTURED REVIEWS
Monthly
Quarterly
Annual
Special/Recovery

Module VI

PROJECT MANAGEMENT
BU & SBU
Responsibility

Module VII

PROGRAMME MANAGEMENT
Independent
Timely
Audit

Module VIII

Fig. 1.1b Business competitiveness achievement plan

Table 1.2 Typical CAP control document structure

1. Executive Summary and Description of role of the specific strategic business unit within the Group.
2. Specific Vision, Mission and detailed objectives of the business

   Exhibit 2.1   Performance and variances against previous years budget and CAP, together with forecast forward variances.
3. Strategic Analysis and Market trends

   Exhibit 3.1   Market attractiveness and product sales growth analysis. Products and services life-cycle analysis.

   Exhibit 3.2   Forward view of core competencies and product/service development required. Strategy for each process.

   Exhibit 3.3   Key market trends by individual product and service.

   Exhibit 3.4   Summary of critical success factors.

   Exhibit 3.5   Competitor analysis and ratings versus bench-marks.

   Exhibit 3.6   Market relative share, market attractiveness, and competitive position of all product and service groups.

   Exhibit 3.7   Strengths, Weaknesses, Opportunities, and Threats Analysis (SWOT), top-ten issues.

   Exhibit 3.8   Supporting technology roadmap and service tool map to meet forward product and service development and commercialization.

   Exhibit 3.9   Financial and non-financial bench-mark targets for each business process and the business overall.
4. Business Action Plans

   Exhibit 4.1   Make versus Buy and facility outsourcing plan.

   Exhibit 4.2   Response to SWOT analysis for business and all suppliers/sub-contractors.

   Exhibit 4.3   Human resource and team development strategy and communication plan.

   Exhibit 4.4   Product and service and quality development objectives, including support requirements.

   Exhibit 4.5   Delivery process development objectives.

   Exhibit 4.6   Customer satisfaction, product and service quality analysis and forward development plan.

   Exhibit 4.7   Order winning and commercial process development plan.

   Exhibit 4.8   Detailed product and service development project plans and cost/benefit structure – rolling 3 years.

   Exhibit 4.9   Detailed change programme project plans and cost/benefit structure – rolling 3 years.

   Exhibit 4.10 Alliances and acquisitions plan.

Table 1.2 *Continued*

5. Integrated Three year financial performance plan.
    Supporting financial schedules:
    • Summary
    • Sales and profit variance from previous CAP
    • Sales and margins and segment/product profitability
    • Cash flow
    • Risk and opportunity analysis
    • Profit and loss account
    • Balance sheet
    • Impact assessment of price changes
    • Direct material purchase performance
    • Non-payroll overheads
    • Payroll costs
    • Product development and change programme costs
    • Capital expenditure
    • Stocks profile
    • Debtors profile
    • Non-trading items impact
    • Year-on-year comparison with bench-mark targets

well as the need for systematic structure and discipline to fit into good established practices.

1.8 Delivering a new vision

Project management is not just the province of engineering companies or associated only with the installation of engineering equipment and computer systems in non-engineering businesses. Indeed, a number of well-managed non-engineering businesses are more professional than many engineering companies in applying a disciplined project management methodology.

Managing by and through projects has become a common approach in many high quality companies that have settled into a mode of continuous change and innovation to maintain competitiveness. This has been a natural evolution from the originators of the total systems approach of Japanese world-class companies such as Toyota, developed while they were evolving into a powerful force during the 1960s to 1980s, with rapid growth and subsequent dominance of world automotive markets. Toyota created an organizational, directional control model, shown in Fig. 1.2, for driving and auditing strategic change into every corner of the business, which has been

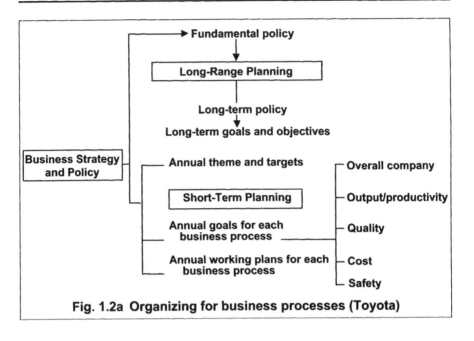

Fig. 1.2a Organizing for business processes (Toyota)

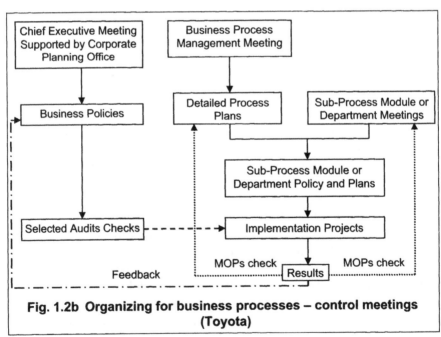

Fig. 1.2b Organizing for business processes – control meetings (Toyota)

an inspiration to many companies. This pioneered the concept of managing whole business processes from end to end as distinct from focusing only on managing fragmented departmental organizations, and will be discussed again later.

Best practice project and programme management are essential core competencies applied in modules vi to viii of Fig. 1.1b to control the delivery of the CAP to meet strategic objectives. They support and audit cost effective short lead-time innovation through a set of projects with calculated costs and benefits in each year of the three-year plan, over a wide range of activities of a developmental nature in many organizations:

- product and service development and introduction,
- customer account development and solution selling,
- bidding for orders and sales,
- change management for changes to organizations, business processes, practices, procedures, methodologies, and for continuous improvement (Kaizen) activity,
- maintenance and repair activities,
- acquisition and transition team application to rationalise, integrate and extract value from mergers and acquisitions,
- divestment and restructuring of businesses,
- plant and building construction,
- collaborative academic research projects,
- software development projects.

In addition, while there is a single generic framework of principles and essential disciplines associated with project and programme management, and the effective utilisation of natural group project team groups, this is very flexible, and many variants are applied, e.g. for:

- large complex projects,
- clusters of small projects,
- coordination of distributed sub-contractors by a main contractor or tier one supplier, e.g. in the automotive, aerospace and construction industries,
- continuous improvement project teams.

However, in each case these activities must be clearly communicated to and integrated organizationally, with:

- specialist functional support departments or critical mass skill groups,
- routine operational management functions,
- change programme management and change control structures across multi-divisional enterprises,

- administrative staff support groups,

and supported by:

- clear organizational ownerships,
- resource allocation tracking and administration,
- planned job rotation,
- training and personal development.

in order to provide a competitive and effective organizational system recognizing the needs of the business and of the individual.

Examples of world's best practice can be clearly perceived currently in organizations as diverse as hospitals, banks, insurance companies, engineering manufacturing companies, construction companies and utilities.

Therefore, often for the first time, senior managers in such organizations have had to completely bench-mark all aspects of their business and specify a carefully detailed set of targeted, costed and resourced change and development projects. These range from new or modified products and services development to the reorganization of their company around new business process models to improve operational effectiveness to world-class levels, and the introduction of new practices, procedures and methodologies. The resulting programme of projects was thus central to the delivery of the whole business strategy and to the competitiveness achievement programme. The budgeted benefits from the programme were calculated by reference to the difference between current levels of performance and world-class bench-mark levels of performance; one of the important roles of Programme Managers is to track progress in the financial and non-financial measures of performance to ensure budgeted performance is achieved.

1.9 Focusing management attention – payment by results

The generic form of the now widely applied practical CAP structure, shown in Fig. 1.1 and Table 1.2, has a modular inter-dependent structure. The plan control document is used in practice for a three-year programme. This includes the 3-year budget financial schedules as working documents and by use of a standardized format of exhibit tables can be typically of only 30-40 pages in length. Make no mistake, this is not a dusty report, it is a live

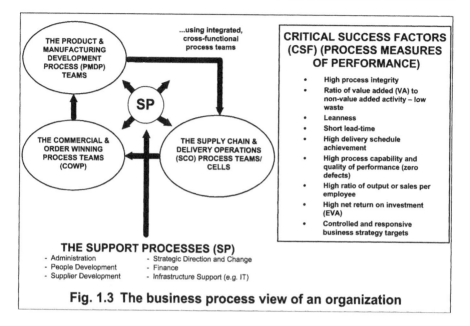

Fig. 1.3 The business process view of an organization

working document at the right hand of every General Manager of an innovating business, reviewed by the Chief Executive each month. The engine, which drives this, is the combined product and service development and organizational change project programme with its costs and benefits incorporated in approved annual budgets of teams of business managers. When successfully followed through, it delivers the emerging financial performance plan, the programme costs and the resulting financial performance improvements which must be built into the annual operating budget of the business. It is this budget upon which management performance incentive payments are based to grab management attention over the full period. This link between achievement of performance improvement milestones and reward is absolutely essential: (a) to ensure full attention to and commitment from the business team and (b) to the growth of shareholder value and customer satisfaction.

The deliverables from each project run each year must, in turn, be linked to the critical success factor and bench-mark targets set for each core business process; a typical example is shown in Fig. 1.3. These are driven through and cascaded in more detail via supporting related subsidiary targets set for the typical natural team groups sub-processes; as shown in the example in Table 1.3. These measures of performance are discussed in more detail in Chapters 4 and 5. The Appendix to this chapter provides a more detailed outline summary of the important modern organization concept of business processes.

Table 1.3 Typical business processes

(a) Top-level processes

1. Product Development and Introduction Process (PIP)/PDIP.
2. Delivery Operations Process (DOP).
3. Supply Chain Process (SCP).
4. Commercial and Order Winning Process (COWP).
5. Support Process (SP).
6. Change and Innovation Management Process (CIMP).

(b) Subsidiary sub-process team natural group modules – manufacturing business example

1. Marketing process for future product and service specification.
2. Front office – sales and account development process.
3. Customer interface, inside sales-support office process and despatch management.
4. Bidding and order winning process.
5. Distribution process.
6. Spare parts supply and customer service after-market process.
7. Project team (PIP and task force).
8. Manufacturing operations process and the cell multi-disciplinary natural group team.
9. Materials flow master scheduling and management process.
10. Materials acquisition and supplier development process (supplies module).
11. Materials kitting process (part of supplies module).
12. Process quality audit and Kaizen support process.
13. Tool management process.
14. Facilities management and asset maintenance process.
15. Invoicing and commercial administration process.
16. Cash management process.
17. Human resource recruitment, development and job rotation process.
18. Waste management process.
19. Plant acquisition process.
20. Strategic planning and review process.
21. Corporate finance and treasury process.
22. Specialist support function management process, including skills outsourcing management – Engineering, IT, Consultancy.
23. Technology development and acquisition process.

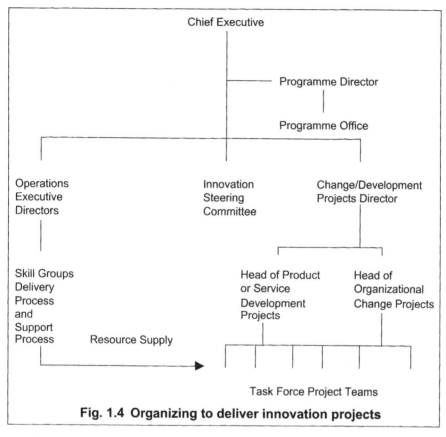

Fig. 1.4 Organizing to deliver innovation projects

The important areas of core competency and team support roles, which are required to be incorporated in the business organization, are shown in a practical case example in Fig. 1.4. The role of the Programme Director in Fig. 1.4 is summarized in Table 1.4, and integrates with the role of the Programme Office and project team roles shown later in Figs 1.5 and 1.6. The generic Toyota total business strategy direction and control framework in Fig. 1.2 applies to the single business unit organization of Fig. 1.4 just as much as it does for a corporation consisting of a group of businesses.

Once the strategic planning framework is completed in detail and all projects have been agreed and put in priority order, the organization for delivery projects can be properly initiated as shown in Fig. 1.4.

The key features of the organization example of Fig. 1.4 are as follows:

1. All development and change activities are perceived as central to the business strategy and their importance is communicated.

Table 1.4 Role of the programme director

- Take initiatives in facilitating change and provide support action, including support for project start-up.
- Be proactive in establishing priorities.
- In the early stages of project management maturity development provide close hands-on support, professional advice and guidance for Project Managers to ensure all projects embody best practice control and organizational principles.
- Propagate standards including the Company Programme and Project Management Standard Working Manual, and develop and distil new concepts for practical application.
- Plan, facilitate and support training in best practices in Project Management, and the use of Project Management software systems for information supply.
- Champion professional change and development in environments with strong operational demands, and support CAP project programmes.
- Work closely with Managing Directors and General Managers. Provide commitment, confidence and shared problem responsibilities. Help by timely action to protect the organization from risks resulting from project non-conformance.
- Provide a high quality responsive reporting and hazard management support to senior management.
- Maintain close contact with project reviews and monitor cost benefits via initiated audits where necessary.
- Issue weekly, monthly and timely hazard identification/recovery reports.
- Develop, network and propagate business process systems engineering methods and the elements of the Company way.

2. All projects have a budget, a set of target deliverables or specification, and a time scale.
3. All projects have a Project Manager or task-force leader who is line responsible and runs the budget for his/her project as well as taking responsibility for delivering to all target deliverables.
4. All internal change projects have an owner who signs off specification approval and receives the result of the completed project, sits on the innovation steering and review committee, and signs off acceptance for satisfactory project completion. Other names given to the steering committee commonly are 'Total Quality Council' and 'Change Council'.
5. The Programme Director who effectively acts as an arm of the Chief Executive, is the audit conscience of the organization, and has a

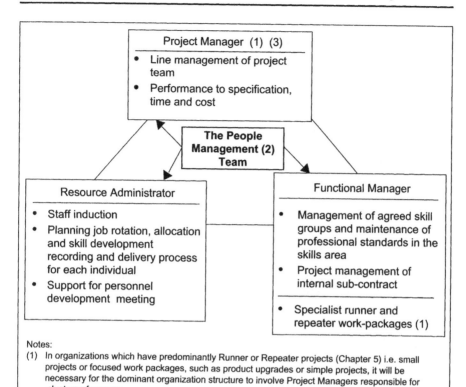

Notes:

(1) In organizations which have predominantly Runner or Repeater projects (Chapter 5) i.e. small projects or focused work packages, such as product upgrades or simple projects, it will be necessary for the dominant organization structure to involve Project Managers responsible for clusters of runners.

(2) An information requirements analysis of each project meeting and the people management team will be needed to focus the standard paperwork support form designs.

(3) Distinguish carefully between the Programme Manager and the Project Manager. The latter is the line manager responsible for achieving time, budget and specification requirements.

Fig. 1.5 Three elements in partnership in a team and matrix organization

supporting programme office with the roles shown in Fig. 1.6. The club rules referred to here relate to the agreed standard best practice methods, CAP frameworks, procedures, tools, techniques and practices which have been promoted by training and project start-up workshops, i.e. '*The Company Way*'.

6. The Programme Director, Projects Director and Executive Directors responsible for the operational and support processes, all sit on the business executive board and a representative group of these comprise the top-level steering and review committee for the critical change programme projects.

Note that, in a small company a single Projects Director or Senior Change Projects Director/Manager might combine the Programme Director, Projects Director and the heads of projects roles. Larger companies might

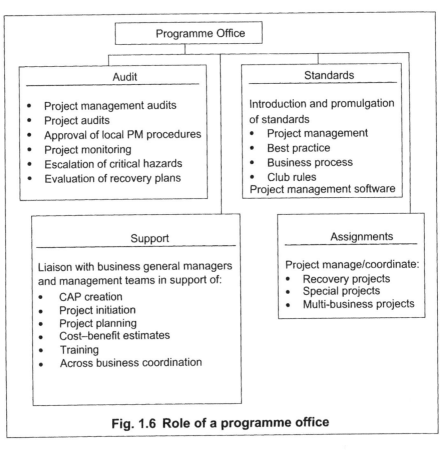

Fig. 1.6 Role of a programme office

have a separate Product Development Project Director role.

7. The programme office provides the Executive Board with information each month on progress of the programme, including also the flagging up of the programme hazards and the necessary recovery plans. The Programme Director also audits projects and provides task-force project team training support, both at project initiation and through its life, i.e. through the design phase and the implementation phase. He or she reports progress on category 1 (see below) projects to the Board.

For planning and selective review purposes, projects can be categorized into three categories:

Category 1
- Top strategic priority.
- Major impact on the business.
- Life threatening if not successful.

- Must be completed on time.
- Requires a monthly review and report to the Executive Board, which is also the approval level for each major work-package and initiation of category 1 projects.

Category 2
- Basic building block of a local business or product unit plan in a focused business unit area, contributing significantly to medium-term improvements.
- Reviewed regularly at local level for their implementation approval.

Category 3
- Part of a set of small-scale quick-hit continuous improvement projects advancing on a wide front, each requiring small-scale resource and a shared training and facilitation support.
- Flexible, and requiring quarterly progress summary reports.

The Programme Director maintains visibility on his overall change programme schedule of all three categories of project, and provides support as well as regularly attending reviews and reporting personally to the Executive Board progress each month. He/she ensures each category is properly supported throughout the project life-cycle.

The best practitioner companies distinguish carefully between the general overall facilitation role of Programme Director, and the project-specific line management role of Project Manager; supplemented by a definition of the project owner role, as the customer of the Project Manager. The Resource Administrator supporting role shown in Fig. 1.5 is essential for managing the inevitable conflicts of priority and project demands in multi-project organizations and for ensuring sound personal development of staff via systematic job rotation.

Important features of the role of Project Manager need to be carefully specified, for example:

1. Responsible for delivering the specification and all targets, meeting the needs of the customer on time – 'delighting the customer'. The specification must match the needs of the business and its CAP.
2. Responsible for the financial budget and meeting the planned expenditure profile.
3. Responsible for meeting all project delivery milestones.
4. Line responsible for the core project team of cross-functional staff and for managing work-package sub-contractor interfaces whether these are internal or external sub-contractors.

5. Responsible for any commercial interface with the customer, sometimes in partnership with colleagues from the order winning process in Fig. 1.3.
6. Responsible for providing timely information/communication to all interested parties.
7. Responsible for operating to the agreed company standard, computer supported, planning, control and reporting system incorporating typically the following elements:

   • a thorough process for developing good detailed specifications and targets;
   • minimum number of standard control meetings and reviews and recorded outcome action lists;
   • top-level and linked work-package planning Gantt-chart bar diagrams for progress monitoring against top-level milestones required by the customer or project owner; (see Support Methodology Section 3)
   • monthly work-package resource utilization plan – forecast and actual;
   • monthly cash flow plan, forecast and actual;
   • agreed specification change approval process and control plan;
   • hazard identification and recovery plans;
   • sub-contractor specifications and control plans;
   • delivery documentation plan and administrative control files, including minutes and allocated action plans from all meetings;
   • hand-over plan and acceptance sign-off requirements;
   • training plan for project owner receiving staff to operate new practices;
   • monthly top-level traffic-light red, amber, green upward milestone tracking report to the Programme Director;
   • quality control plan;
   • Project organization plan and responsibilities definitions.

Chapter 3 provides more comprehensive coverage of the generic project process.

1.10 Information support

To minimise organizational confusion and other non-value-added activity across the project programme, as well as to support effective communication and enhance participation across a company, a well-designed information system matching the project process is essential. Also, the utilization of the minimum number of effective control meetings, well designed, requires sound project data and information support. This should provide a facility for ease of networked computer access to agendas, meetings, minutes, action lists and project progress reports, including interfaces to the sub-contract suppliers. It should also communicate to customers for new product and service development or service development project owners for internal services as well as customers of the service.

The computer system should be standardized for ease of communication using a set of standard report spreadsheets with which staff become very familiar and to increase the efficiency of the review process. This is particularly important where multiple projects in a programme are running, with many sub-contractors and also with a consequential need for very effective resource management and job rotation across projects for staff development. In such cases a supporting Programme Administrator appointment is essential to ensure high quality administration, financial monitoring and meeting monitoring. This will avoid heavy administrative loads on the Project Manager and support team leaders, giving them the maximum time availability to run the project.

This topic will be covered in more detail in subsequent chapters. However, important specific requirements of the IT support system for Programme Directors and Project Managers are:

- Networking capability.
- Portability, i.e. laptop based as well as PC based.
- Capable of handling multiple projects in a programme and consolidating costs versus budget, project earned value versus planned work in progress, and resource plans and needs across projects to support weekly resource allocation meetings.
- Use in computer format of a basic standard set of project control spreadsheet report forms used by all participants (see Support Methodology section, Project and Programme Management Procedures, in Chapter 3).
- Availability of standard training materials and intranet access to case studies and experience knowledge bases for all participants and supporting toolkits.

Chapter 3 discusses project process control and support methodology in more detail. Support Methodology Section 3.3 provides typical samples of control spreadsheet forms widely tested in practice.

1.11 Summary of chapter 1

The two most common driving aims of an innovation programme must be to enhance the value-adding capabilities of an organization and improve its competitiveness. The starting point is a detailed analysis of strengths, weaknesses, opportunities and threats. With hindsight, what now appear to be amateur approaches to implementing change and developing businesses in the past have been considerably improved and refined in the last 10 years by leading companies. The new approaches have been tested and added to in order that company managements can compete with very aggressive and professional global competition.

This is a very sophisticated challenge particularly if time scales are short. The use of a disciplined and determined approach based on 'managing by projects' is becoming a well established and very effective practice as management teams gain the necessary knowledge, experience and understanding. The main driving forces have been fear of competition, the speed of global industrial change and the need to survive, supported by pressure for shareholder value growth.

Attempts to improve businesses by very basic short-term approaches to cost cutting and leanness creation has led in many cases to the widespread cutting out of value-creating development activities and over commoditization of products, services, technologies, operating methodologies, and organizational practices. It is now perceived as the road to eventual ruin once the early short-term gains have been realized.

The challenge which is slowly becoming recognised is to use the more intelligent approach of developing higher value-adding competencies, coupled with the avoidance of commoditization, by exploiting the multiple sources of potential improvement as follows:

1. Give equal management attention and resourcing weight to product or service development, business process development and organization effectiveness development instead of focusing only on short-term steady state operations management.
2. Pull all the levers associated with the strategically focused development of a difficult-to-copy combination of competencies:
   - clever operational procedures and methodologies;
   - clever lean organization designs for supporting team groups;
   - clever service delivery process designs;
   - flexible service delivery systems or manufacturing systems focused by 'make vs buy' analysis for scarce resource application with complementary outsourcing of low-cost commodity services and technologies;
   - clever service delivery technology or manufacturing process technology;

- clever software and hardware modifications to standard production or delivery equipment to create uniqueness;
- an embedded continuous improvement-achievement culture;
- close to the customer stance;
- embedded 'train/do' training support for innovation projects, regularly upgraded with evolving best practices.

Even 'make-to-print' commodity product or service companies can, via a professionally managed three-year change programme, have an opportunity to succeed by applying a selection of the above practices.

The best-led companies have acquired sets of best practices by learning from studies of other companies, not just in their own industry sectors, and have packaged a composite 'Company Way' delivered through management by projects using a CAP directional framework.

The resulting disciplined implementation procedures for managing the necessary comprehensive company-wide set of projects is quite essential for creating a dynamic action culture.

The basic supporting generic elements and frameworks which now include management best practice are:

1. A value-growth, strategically driven Competitiveness Achievement Plan with bench-mark targets for operational and development activities.
2. The application of new world-class organization practices to provide both operational and development excellence focused on teams in business processes.
3. Selective use of new methodologies and best practices.
4. The embedding of programme and project management competencies to drive effective change and development with disciplined regular review of progress against target.
5. A widespread communication structure.
6. Modern training practices for all levels including senior management using a train–do philosophy:
   - top management awareness and leadership executive workshops to educate and focus;
   - task-force and project team start-up workshops to provide direction;
   - skilled support and facilitation from business process systems engineers based in the Programme Office, expert in modern methodologies.

7. A strategic direction, audit, and review framework as in the Toyota model to ensure that change happens and is made to stick.
8. A Management Steering Group to control direction, educate, ensure wide involvement and cross-functional support, and to participate in reviews and decision making on project implementation.

These elements integrate with, and are supported by, a delivery project process enveloping short- medium- and long-term target requirements set by comparison with world class performance bench-marks.

The project process must be well supported by good communication and training, to ensure education-led innovation. A well-embedded project process greatly aids the achievement of a dynamic performance and *can-do* achievement culture.

Two case examples follow below, for very different types of business. These illustrate in broad terms the necessary organization designs for management by projects and the approach to innovation. Detailed underpinning of the practices and methodologies required is developed further in Chapters 2 to 5.

1.12 Case example 1 – service business change project

1.12.1 Overview profile

Company role and location
NHS Teaching Hospital, UK

Area of focus
A change project to introduce best practices for the organization and effective operation of core operational processes in a large city hospital.

Situation analysed initially
An admissions process for patients, which cancelled one-third of elective (planned) admissions. Excessive wait by patients for operations. Initial focus on Urology Speciality.

1.12.2 Critical issues

- Dysfunctional behaviour shown through the use of undisciplined, informal systems.
- Lack of identification of a staff team with the admissions process.
- Poor use of scarce resources such as beds and diagnostic support.

Reasons

- Lack of detailed process flow planning. Excessive non-value-added activity.
- No overall ownership of the admissions process – excessive fragmentation.
- Distrust of formal systems.

The change programme gave them the capability to:

- Use scarce resources properly, through simple planning and scheduling by an admissions natural team group responsible for the whole admissions process.
- Be able to change new systems to match changing demand.
- Train, and design training plans for, those working within new systems.
- Focus diagnostic services to match clinical specialty needs.

Estimate of measurable results

- Urology specialty – follow-on enthusiastic roll out (across all specialties).
- 500 bed nights saved – equivalent to two wards saved over whole hospital.
- Released bed resource capable of generating £90,000 p.a. – annual ward budget approximately £750,000.
- The ability to reduce waiting list through implementation of good process redesign and management practices.

1.12.3 Project specification

To improve the effectiveness of the admissions process and the medical materials supply chain process by 50%, while introducing new knowledge and culture

1.12.4 Project initiation

There were two stages:

1. The Chief Executive, Clinical Director, Director of Pharmacy and the management team were given a three-day training workshop on benchmarking and generic best practice business process systems engineering methodologies. These were based on world's best practices applied in the automotive industry and were found to be directly relatable to service industries. This culminated in the definition by the top team of their requirements for performance improvement.

As part of the workshop training, they were trained in basic change programme task-force project organization principles. They then chose a Change Programme Manager and allocated cross-functional staff to a task-force. They also designed a structured multi-level communication plan and specified the objectives of their change programme.

2. The Task-Force Project Team attended a five-day training workshop. This was opened by the Managing Director with a presentation summarizing the requirements for the task-force to categorize and then redesign business processes in a priority order. The targets were to reduce process lead-times by 50%, process costs by 30%, and to improve process quality of performance against a set of quality criteria by between 20 and 50%.

The criteria were related carefully to patient care, e.g. reduced waiting time, speed of service and clarity of diagnosis. A time scale of three months was given for the design phase of all deliverables.

The task-force team was trained in business process systems engineering, similar to the top management training, but with more emphasis on detailed tools and techniques and on the process to be carried out by the task-force. They also had to construct a top-level project and work-package plan to meet the specification; this was previewed by the Managing Director and his top team at the end of the workshop.

A Consultant Manufacturing Systems Engineer from an automotive industry engineering company was included in the task-force to facilitate transfer of automotive industry knowledge and experience.

The Task-Force Project Process was defined as having five stages:

Stage 1. Data collection
The collection of the fundamental data describing the operational activities and their associated job structure, paperwork systems, use of materials, their controls, requirements, deliverables and workloads. Basic flow-charting of the flow of patients, information and materials was used to identify non-value-adding (NVA) activities, which were then listed for elimination.

Stage 2. Data analysis and core business process definition
The core business operational processes were identified by flow-charting with their sub-processes, in three categories:
(a) Service Development and Introduction Process;
(b) Patient Operational Care Process;
(c) Support Processes, e.g. Purchasing and Supplies, Administration.

Stage 3. Steady state design

Steady state design of business process modules in priority order detailing the natural team group of staff to operate the process, their equipment, inventory and training requirements, and the best practice design measures of performance (MOPs) to operate to, on average, with minimized NVA activities.

Stage 4. Dynamic design

This was based upon an analysis of sources of variation in workload, historical assessment of peak loading, variations in patients diagnosis data and shift and holiday patterns.

Stage 5. Process control systems design

This required the definition of the information support systems required for each operational team responsible for multi-function process team modules. It was also essential to achieve a design requiring minimum support paperwork, with clear allocation of authority levels. Finally to ensure that changes to the operational practices were embedded in new standard procedures, it was important to design a minimum number of standing control meetings, their standard agendas, deliverables and attendees. Also, MOPs were defined for each team.

1.12.5 Project results

1. A new organizational model was put in place for the hospital which was based around natural process teams, and which embodied 60% less NVA activities.
2. The overall operational service delivery process for patient care was defined as five interfacing team groups:
   * Diagnosis
   * Admission
   * Treatment
   * Discharge
   * Aftercare

   The first of these included external members of the team such as General Practitioner professionals.
3. The admissions process was greatly simplified by putting all functions into a single team, and the initial 69 changes of patient flow ownership identified from workflow charts were reduced to 20, i.e. a 70% reduction. This resulted in over 50% reduction in each of lead-times, waiting times, patients waiting in bed, and a 25% increase in bed utilization productivity.

4. The materials supply process redesign project had two main phases. Phase 1 reviewed the whole supply chain process, i.e. performance, pareto analysis of spend by supplier and commodity, operational cost and NVA activities, such as excessive paperwork and unclear lines of authority. There were 1621 suppliers supplying 14,702 products at a total cost of £17M. The spend was spread over seven functional commodity groups.

Phase 2 was concerned with supplier rationalization into a reduced number of suppliers with a move towards 'just in time' (JIT) ward supply philosophies and the design of a natural group team approach, supported by good electronic information with allocated authorities by category of purchased item.

Phase 1 provided very large savings due to much reduced administration and invoicing, and the introduction of process quality management, coupled with strategic supply sourcing negotiation with preferred suppliers for increased volume per supplier. Money was removed from budgets in line with the savings defined by the task-force, and a reduction of over 20% was achieved. Nursing staff combined with purchasing staff to propose clinically acceptable product supply rationalization. A materials management team was made responsible for consolidating total hospital requirements. High volume requirements were procured on a call-off basis or an open contract agreed price basis. Simple 2-bin kanban systems were operated at each ward by nursing staff to control flow of materials JIT with a small well-organized 'hi–lo' bin storage area on each ward. A regional supply centre used regular time phased delivery drops around the hospital. The requirement for multiple signatures on low-cost materials ordering paperwork was removed giving nurses more authority and reducing lead-times.

The total reduction in materials procurement process costs from all sources was £1M within 12 months and growing.

1.13 Case example 2 – new product development

Area of focus
The winning of an order for the development, design and supply of digital electronic control systems for a new jumbo jet aircraft.

1.13.1 Project overall specification

To win the order and supply a new electronic controller at a 30% lower product development cost, 50% lower price, twice the reliability with doubled functionality of previous versions, and to meet a tightly defined set of time milestones.

1.13.2 Project initiation

Because of the very stretching targets it was concluded that the traditional project organizational approach, involving a project coordinator for major work-packages across large departmental functional groups, could not be used. The senior management were trained in business process systems engineering and the principles of using co-located simultaneous engineering team groups to operate the product introduction process, as developed in the Japanese automotive industry. This resulted in a new approach based on four main new elements of innovation.

The four main innovations were: (a) the design of a best practice standard product introduction process; (b) the use of co-located natural group cross-functional teams; (c) the integration of a well-managed control process; and (d) the design of a standard minimum number set of management control meetings to reduce proliferation and improve effectiveness of control meetings.

The modules of a total business process operated by natural team groups in phases, followed a defined standard product introduction process from concept development and bidding through to entry into manufacture. Specialist functional support was by formal sub-contract, with clear cost and specification definition to support groups, internal and external to the business. This included new technology problem solving development.

1.13.3 Phase 1. – Concept definition and bidding process

This phase involved a co-located cross-functional team including finance and marketing staff in a bid office, with all functions represented including customer personnel, and with a Project Manager totally line responsible for delivering to time and to target specification, including cost and reliability.

The bid team applied a document management system to improve the quality of bid proposal, using standard modules from previous projects, together with bid-specific elements, and to reduce the level of NVA administrative workload on the individual bid team engineers.

The result was that a bid was prepared in half the previous best time and with 20% fewer staff. Also, the detailed specification was of considerably higher quality due to the inclusion of customer personnel in the bid team, who effectively networked in their own organization in order to achieve quickly a right-first-time consensus.

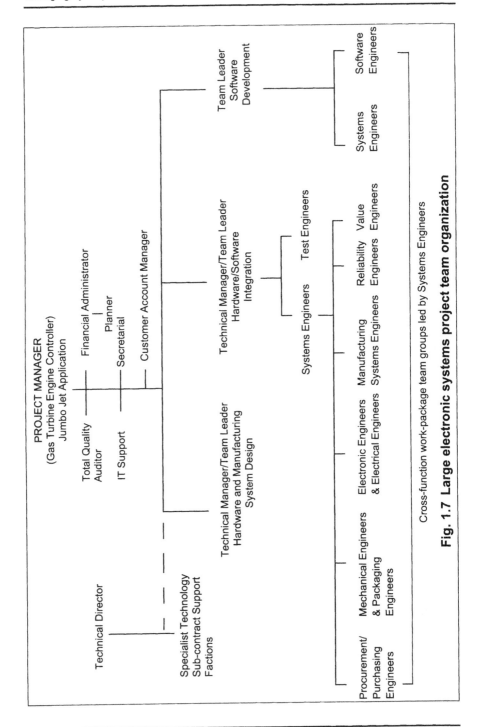

Cross-function work-package team groups led by Systems Engineers

Fig. 1.7 Large electronic systems project team organization

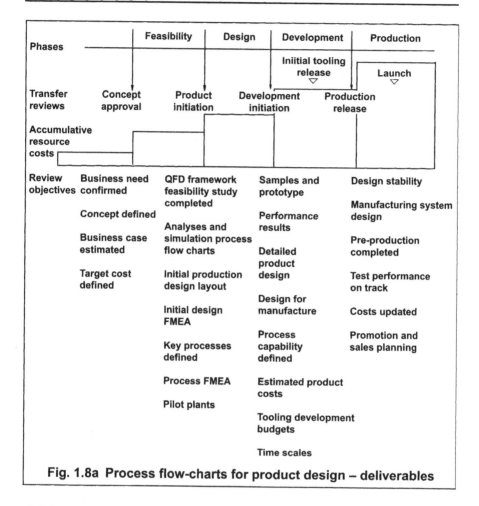

Phases		Feasibility	Design	Development	Production
				Iniitial tooling release ▽	Launch ▽
Transfer reviews	Concept approval	Product initiation	Development initiation	Production release	
Accumulative resource costs					
Review objectives	Business need confirmed	QFD framework feasibility study completed	Samples and prototype	Design stability	
	Concept defined	Analyses and simulation process flow charts	Performance results	Manufacturing system design	
	Business case estimated		Detailed product design	Pre-production completed	
	Target cost defined	Initial production design layout	Design for manufacture	Test performance on track	
		Initial design FMEA		Costs updated	
		Key processes defined	Process capability defined	Promotion and sales planning	
		Process FMEA	Estimated product costs		
		Pilot plants	Tooling development budgets		
			Time scales		

Fig. 1.8a Process flow-charts for product design – deliverables

1.13.4 Implementation phases

Following acceptance of the bid and placement of an order, a new cross-functional project team was set up, including members of the original team, reporting to a Project Manager.

The Project Manager was line responsible for the project, achieving the customer specification at target cost and delivering to all the project top-level time milestones, and to target development cost. The project team organization is shown in Fig. 1.7 and included over 100 personnel. The team was co-located in one purpose-built building and was provided with integrated support systems, including CAD, product data management and computers linked with the customers to support the extensive software

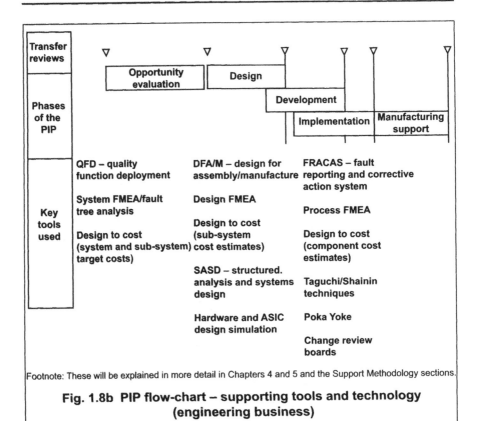

Footnote: These will be explained in more detail in Chapters 4 and 5 and the Support Methodology sections.

Fig. 1.8b PIP flow-chart – supporting tools and technology (engineering business)

transfer development and testing. Special-purpose hardware test rigs were provided for the sole use of the project to avoid queuing problems and priority confusion.

Particular features of the team design for the product introduction process (Fig. 1.8) were:

1. Training in modern support tools and techniques, as shown in Fig. 1.8a was provided.
2. Electronic, mechanical, software, quality and manufacturing systems engineers were included with automotive electronic sub-system design experience, particularly associated with design for low cost and minimum parts count, and with Japanese product quality standards measured in parts per million.
3. Careful attention was paid to simplifying organizational control methods and minimizing NVA and administrative activities to give engineers more time to focus on the product development and to ensure directional clarity:

(a) A financial administrator was included in the team. He sat in at all meetings and provided prompt minutes and action lists. He administered the budget and handled administrative links to the customer.

(b) A standardized project support software system was used. This integrated resource and cost management, using eight standard control forms for all aspects of work control; sub-contractors also used the same control forms.

(c) A set of standard meetings with standard agendas, defined deliverables and attendees was set up as follows:

- monthly project review meetings, chaired by the customer Programme Manager to ensure full openness and cooperation;
- monthly change control meetings, including customer personnel to facilitate change cost minimization through bundled modification package approval;
- monthly commercial meetings, to ensure commercial implications did not compromise technical discussions at the project management meetings;
- weekly Project Manager review;
- weekly quality review meeting to monitor the quality and reliability standard growth data;
- weekly resource management and allocation meeting;
- weekly technology liaison meeting with specialist functional groups outside the project team, responsible for carrying out sub-contract advanced technology work-packages;
- weekly supply chain process meeting;
- daily ten-minute stand-up meeting for each work-package team to facilitate rapid communication of plans and priorities;
- a project communication newspaper.

This approach reduced the wasteful proliferation of meetings so common with big projects, and ensured much greater clarity of direction and control.

1.13.5 Results

- A team with 15% fewer people than previous bench-mark projects, carried out 25% more work.
- The overall project lead-time was reduced by 35% compared with previous functional demarcation group organization approaches.
- The project met every top-level customer milestone and achieved first flight with time to spare for refinement. The customer awarded an excellent performance rating.

- The very ambitious product target cost was met, and part of the reason was a 60% reduction in the number of component parts in the product, compared with the previous generation jumbo jet engine controller.
- The mean time between confirmed changeovers of the product in service was increased to 30,000 hours, compared with the previous standard of 13,000 to 16,000 hours, including competitor products comparisons.

APPENDIX

Business processes – introduction

The implementation of true business process organizational architectures in manufacturing industry, outside of Japan, is very much in its infancy. Very limited experience of practical operation exists, many companies are not aware of the concepts, and few have even considered how to balance the need for excellence of core functional and technological competencies with effectiveness of processes.

In many organizations the management style commonly used for business process control is one of fire fighting based upon supervision of the outputs from each process. When the outputs are unsatisfactory in some way, a witch-hunt, followed by the use of temporary tight controls, is the mode of attack by autocratic management. However, typically once attention is removed the original problems return.

World-class organizations, by contrast, look at the total process, reorganize it around a process team then control all aspects of the process work flow through the team with the aid of a process flow-chart to facilitate monitoring. The team are given measures of performance to help them continually check and control their own performance. This approach avoids many output failures and also enables rapid overall control and improvement to be exercised continuously throughout the process because the process team has full ownership.

The best way to visualize a business process is to consider the group of skills and competencies which have to be brought together to develop or deliver a product or service. *Such a group is a natural process group* and is implemented physically in the form of a cross-functional team. It is supported by means for maintaining sharpness of functional skills, and represents the basic building block of a highly effective organization. It also operates and represents a practical matrix concept. The alternative of a traditional functional organization, in which concentrated single-functional skill groups reside in separate departments, fragments the natural process work flow and information flow. Such traditional arrangements are now becoming uncompetitive in a global market-place. They take longer to carry out tasks, have higher costs, produce a lower quality performance and create very narrowly focused people who then become vulnerable to change.

There are many obstacles to the creation of business process organization structures, not least of which is the resistance of vested interests and culture, the latter being changeable through new developments in education and training.

Current approaches to business process organization design are primarily *ad hoc* and often superficial. A systems engineering approach is essential even for a relatively small process module of an organization. A body of knowledge is required to support the implementation of business process concepts.

Tools and techniques, sharpened by semi-empirical application, must be developed for the first phase of design, to create the basic business process architecture. These must be supported by a further increasingly detailed second phase of development of methodologies for designing and supporting controls, team working practices, continuous improvement and system maintenance capabilities. Finally best practice and competitiveness studies must be continually carried out to determine measures of performance, which cascade in increasing detail from those which apply at the top of the organization across all business processes to those which are used to drive the performance of every process module, cell or team. There is typically a set of five generic measures of performance (MOPs):

- Quality.
- Customer satisfaction.
- Financial.
- Process lead-time or delivery time.
- Level of work in progress.

Some processes in manufacturing businesses depend heavily on the development of technological materials-forming processes and the associated machines and electronic control systems to carry out the processes and to test the products.

A great deal of multi-disciplinary R&D is required, therefore, to fill the gaps in methods, tools and techniques for design, practical operation and monitoring outlined above as well as for the development of education and training courses. Any suggestion that such work is not essential, or is not intellectually demanding and complex, cannot be defended.

Supporting frameworks for development

To guide a careful, systematic and structured approach for defining necessary R&D topics, logical frameworks are needed, which also ensure a systems approach.

A business process model

When viewed from the highest level there are only three core value-adding processes in a manufacturing business:

1. The development or innovation process.
2. The operational delivery process.
3. The support operations process.

In order to create these there is the need for a temporary further project managed process:

4. The change process.

The last eventually becomes integrated by evolution as a Kaizen or continuous improvement process within the first three processes.

It is necessary for practical application to sub-divide and add more manageable shape to the first three processes, and to recognize also that in large organizations these are implemented in the form of modules or process cells, linked by matching inputs and outputs and customer supplier relationships within a framework of measures of performance. A typical sub-divided generalized set of processes is given in Table 1.5.

Table 1.5 Business process framework

A. The strategic planning and strategy direction process.
B. The new product introduction process incorporating the marketing process, research, development, design, design for production, design of the production system.
C. The sales or order winning process.
D. The materials flow logistics management, manufacturing operations and delivery process.
E. The supply chain process.
F. The distribution process.
G. The financial control process.
H. The debtors control process.
I. The creditor control process.
J. The maintenance process.
K. The learning support process.
L. The technology support process.
M. The change management process.
N. The procurement process.

All processes must be supported by integral quality support systems, change control systems, continuous improvement Kaizen activities and planning systems.

A six-element framework for identifying and specifying R&D tasks in an integrated way, is given in Table 1.6.

As each process module is created organizationally and the management systems are developed, it is necessary to treat each module as a system within itself, and develop the necessary supporting elements. An illustration for a manufacturing cell process is given in Fig. 1.9, which applies equally to an office-based process cell.

Table 1.6 Identification of development areas for each business process

A. Organization of the business process for teamwork.
B. Development of process analysis and design tools.
C. Development of support tools, techniques and sub-system infrastructure for process operation.
D. Development of process technologies.
E. Control and monitoring systems development to meet bench-marks and measures of performance.
F. The integration of process-focused IT and its linking to shared infrastructure IT.

The principles of cellular process team structure, design and operation in offices and factories are covered in more detail in Chapter 5.

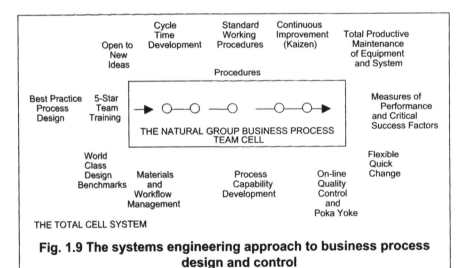

Fig. 1.9 The systems engineering approach to business process design and control

Figure 1.10 illustrates a practical business process integration example, see also Chapter 5, where examples of process module design are provided. In Fig. 1.10 the order winning process for standard products and special products is supported by a project management process for special product design and development and a materials procurement and kit assembly

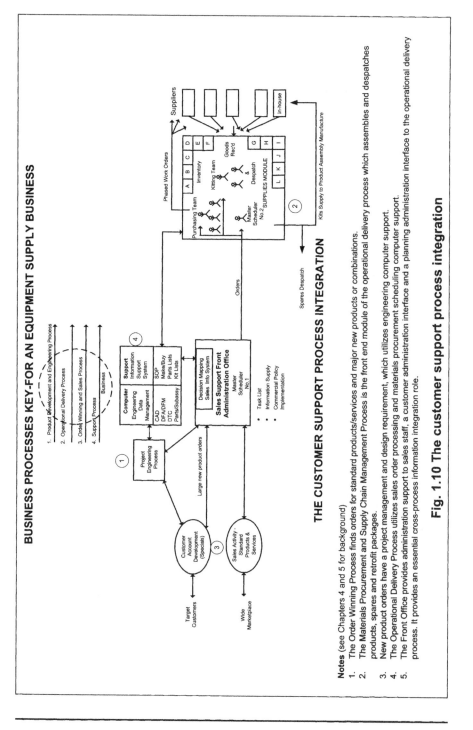

BUSINESS PROCESSES KEY-FOR AN EQUIPMENT SUPPLY BUSINESS

1. Product Development and Engineering Process
2. Operational Delivery Process
3. Order Winning and Sales Process
4. Support Process

THE CUSTOMER SUPPORT PROCESS INTEGRATION

Notes (see Chapters 4 and 5 for background)

1. The Order Winning Process finds orders for standard products/services and major new products or combinations.
2. The Materials Procurement and Supply Chain Management Process is the front end module of the operational delivery process which assembles and despatches products, spares and retrofit packages.
3. New product orders have a project management and design requirement, which utilizes engineering computer support.
4. The Operational Delivery Process utilizes sales order processing and materials procurement scheduling computer support.
5. The Front Office provides administration support to sales staff, a customer administration interface and a planning administration interface to the operational delivery process. It provides an essential cross-process information integration role.

Fig. 1.10 The customer support process integration

process for both types of product. The Front Office provides a sales support administration and customer interface capability as well as scheduling production to meet order requirements.

Further reading

Akao Y. (editor) *Hoshin Kanri – Policy Deployment for Successful TQM*, 1991, (Productivity Press).

Briner, W. *et al.*, *Project Leadership*, 2nd edition, 1996, (Gower).

Conway, B. *Project Management Today, Choosing the Right Projects*, pp.10–14.

Dauphinais, G. W. and **Price C.**, (editors), *Straight from the CEO,* 1998 (Nicholas Brearley Publishers).

Goold, M. and **Campbell, A.**, *Strategies and Styles,* 1987 (Blackwell Publishers).

Haspeeslagh, P. C. and **Jemison, D. B.** *Managing Acquisitions*, 1991 (Free Press).

Hamel, G. and **Pralahad, C. K.** *Strategic Intent*, The McKinsey Quarterly, 1990, pp. 36–61

Hammer, M. and **Champy, J.** *Re-Engineering the Corporation,* 1994 (Harper Business).

Heller, R. *The State of Industry*, 1987 (BBC Books).

Knight, C. F. Emerson Electric: Consistent profits, consistently, *Harvard Business Review,* 1992, Jan/Feb.

Kotter, J. P. *Leading change: why transformation efforts fail, Harvard Business Review*, 1995 March/April, Reprint 95204, 59-67.

Parnaby, J. *Business process systems engineering*, Int. J. Tech. Mgmt., 1994, **9**, (3/4), 497-508.

Parnaby, J. Systems engineering for better engineering, Presidential Inaugural Address, *Engng Mgmt J.* 1995, **5**, (6).

Parnaby, J. Factory 2000 plus, *Int. J. Manuf. Technol. Mgmt,* **4**, (1/2).

Parnaby, J. *et al.*, *The Lucas Manufacturing Systems Engineering Handbook,* 2nd edition, 1989 (Lucas Industries Publishers)

Rappaport, A. *Creating Shareholder Value,* 1986 (Free Press).

Rosandu, A. C. *The Quest for Quality in Services*, 1989, (Quality Press).

Slater, R. *Get Better or Get Beaten,* 1994 (Irwin Inc.).

Womack, J. P. and **Jones, D. T.** *Lean Thinking,* 1996, (Simon & Schuster).

For Chapter 2 go to page 81

The Strategic Business Planning Framework Principles – General International Examples

SM1.1 Background

It is a very logical assumption to make that every business needs a strategic business planning framework to guide, communicate and monitor implementation of the desired direction of the business. *The basic issue is that, if you do not know where you are going and properly manage the journey, you will probably never get anywhere.* This does not mean that all businesses have installed such a framework. Consensus over the logic requires cross-functional thinking at senior management level in a company. This is because an effective strategic management framework integrates and reviews, as a whole system, all the elements of the organization. However, such common sense cross-functional thinking has not been all that common. This stems partly from mistakes of the past, of which the most important was the approach in functionally structured organizations of creating specialist strategic planning departments. These were bureaucratic staff functions, which produced strategy reports without involving, in a project-managed fashion, staff and other employees from all levels in the line organization in the necessary ideas generation process and the implementation planning. As a natural consequence, strategic planning documents, after a rubber-stamping ritual, lay unused on dusty shelves.

In the 1980s and 1990s the more progressive companies, such as Emerson Electric, Lucas Industries, Hewlett Packard, and General Electric, all developed, with significant cross-reference to each other's best practices, integrated modern strategy implementation structures simultaneously with the introduction of business process effectiveness improvement projects. As would be expected, they used a change project programme as the platform to roll-out their structures with wide communication, training and personnel involvement.

As would also be expected from a study of best practice innovation in business over the period 1960–1990, Japanese managers and operations management educators also packaged integrated strategy direction and implementation practices. These were very detailed and very soundly based in systems engineering and control logic. A classical example is the so-called Toyota Production System organizational model (see Chapter 1).

In the UK and USA such strategy delivery frameworks operated under promotional labels such as Competitiveness Achievement Programmes (CAPs), Breakthrough Programmes (BPs) and Performance Excellence Programmes (PEPs). These had two important common principles:

1. They were promoted as a single long-lasting innovation initiative.
2. They were target oriented and based on bench-marking of world-class performance for all business processes, covering financial and non-financial performance targets.

In Japan, a single generic label, Hoshin Kanri, was applied as the end result of an evolution process starting from a low-level Statistical Process Control (SPC) focus that progressed through to a wider Total Quality Control (TQC). Hoshin Kanri embodies the Japanese word for compass needle and can be literally translated as a methodology for strategic direction. This label was subsequently refined into a Japanese description with the English translation, Policy Function Deployment (PFD).

The implications of the words in this label are as follows:

- Policy – strategy, target and means of achievement.
- Function – area for focus.
- Deployment – implementation,

and the spirit of this is embodied in the phrase 'making strategic requirements happen'. This triggers exactly a major source of frustration for many Chief Executives and senior managers, i.e. finding operational levers to pull to make changes happen. It integrates with, typically, a three year rolling business budget approval process by integrating the measurable costs and benefits of each improvement project in every budget year. The budget financial schedules approved each year are integrated with the CAP working document.

The critical business performance targets which are broken down into the detailed supporting targets at every process and sub-process level in the whole organization include the shareholder value targets of revenue and cash flow growth.

To avoid the short-term, asset stripping approach that has destroyed some previously good companies, the CAP includes two framework levels.

1. The business transition breakthrough, strategic restructuring level for products/services, business processes, organization structures, organizational practice – targeted by medium-term and long-term development bench-mark measures of performance (MOPs). These will be stretch targets, e.g. 50% improvement.
2. The month-to-month operational planning and management, short-term target level, supported by structured focused Kaizen continuous improvement project activities, which follow naturally and build upon the more effective organizational structures created progressively through the level 1 project programme.

It will be obvious that delivery, in an interactive step-by-step manner, of the requirements of the two levels in the CAP framework, requires two clearly defined, accountable and cooperative executive line management organization elements:

- an operations organization, for 'routine' process operations;
- a change and development organization with an approved, targeted, widely communicated and agreed-by-consensus, programme of carefully sequenced projects.

Many companies have destroyed their value-adding capability by cutting out the resource required to manage the second of these elements, arguing misguidedly that they cannot afford it. By thinking short-term they have unwittingly or deliberately cut out a future source of major value-adding improvement in the interest of achieving short-term financial results. This phenomenon is very typical of companies, which have a dominant and restrictive operational culture with transactional leadership which is short-term bonus payment oriented.

It is essential to the success of the CAP that the Chief Executive ensures a managed balance of the two styles of leadership, that is:

- transactual leadership
- transformational leadership

and to reinforce this desire in many detailed ways such as designing Board and Executive Committee agendas around the two item headings: development and operations. The Chief Executive also has the tricky task of communicating this intent to the Board, shareholders and city analysts, and winning their support.

SM1.2 Supporting features of policy function deployment (PFD, CAP)

The following provides an outline appreciation of a practical implementation framework.

1. A well-managed CAP ensures that the purposeful and focused pursuit of objectives is not lost in the bureaucracy, complexity and politics of an organization and that the responsibility and accountability for target delivery via specific projects is clear. It is an integrated step-by-step structured planning, implementation and review process for delivering strategy across the whole organization via every business process with clear financial monitors of performance being applied.

2. It provides a systems approach to integrate all personnel efforts towards a common purpose.

3. It is generic and applies to all types of organization, whether manufacturing or service, public or private, and allows management to enhance value-adding, growth and financial performance in a practical step-by-step way with total workforce involvement without anarchy and confusion.

4. It is the only way to make Total Quality Management (TQM) work, i.e. achieving total quality in all aspects of product and process performance to meet clustered targets under the three generic headings – Cost (C), Quality (Q) and delivery (D).

5. It embodies the fundamental logic of business process systems engineering principles applied to an inter-related set of business processes by integrating the elements of control
   - Inputs (Targets).
   - Control actions applied to the system via project management.
   - Monitoring and audits of outputs (deliverables).
   - Feedback tracking and corrective action day-by-day, month-by-month, and year-by-year, to ensure developing business targets are achieved.

6. It cascades top-level short–medium–long-term strategy business targets into every level of the organization, spelled out in locally relevant measures of performance aligned to a programme of change projects for every business process. This combines top-down direction with bottom-up process-specific implementation. Too often the latter is missing.

7. It enforces a systematic definition and process flow analysis of every business process to identify sources of ineffectiveness and waste or non-value-added activity using modern analysis tools, to focus project activity on prioritised sources of opportunity and problems requiring solution.

SM1.3 Some supporting methodologies – to support bottom-up implementation

The primary core supporting competencies required are those of project and programme management with a complementary computer-based planning and control document support system. A selection of some of the other generic methodologies is as follows:

1. The Plan (P), Do (D), Check (C), Action (A) methodology, which results from the business process systems engineering control concept, can readily be incorporated into a routine for use by all levels of personnel after training.
2. Process flow analysis – at top level for management awareness and at detailed level for solution design and team training, (see Fig. SM1.1). All elements of the process should have mutually supportive measures of performance to ensure that the total process target measures are achieved (see Fig. SM1.2).
3. Cause and Effect Action Planning – application of the Ishikawa fishbone diagram to define the potential causes of problems in achieving targets and then acting to eliminate these causes (see Fig. SM1.3).

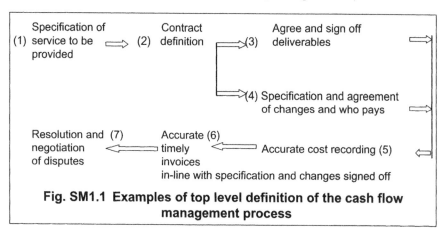

Fig. SM1.1 Examples of top level definition of the cash flow management process

4. Structured target and MOP setting (Fig. SM1.4).
5. Regular reviews (see Fig. SM1.5).
6. Supporting planning and control documentation structure.
    There are six generic and related documents typically, in the overall framework [labelled (a) to (f)].
    (a) Business situation analysis and data collection
      • Performance bench-marking.

- Market segmentation and share analysis.
- Competitor analysis.
- Product or service maturity and cost, quality, function competitiveness analysis.

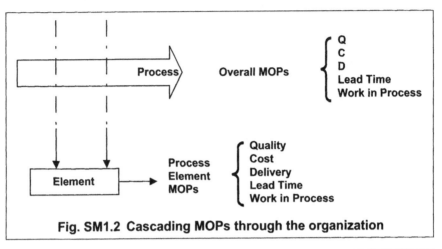

Fig. SM1.2 Cascading MOPs through the organization

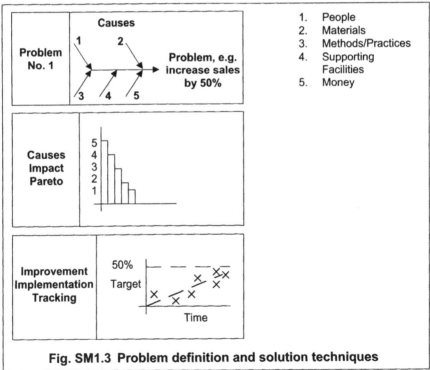

Fig. SM1.3 Problem definition and solution techniques

  - Strengths, weaknesses, opportunities and threats analysis.
(b) Plan summary
  - Core objectives and supporting target MOP cascade to each business process element.
  - Goal summary – short- medium- and long-term target deliverable milestones, grouped focus of improvements under Quality, Cost, Delivery, Lead-time, Work in progress.
  - Management owner of each task and target linked to bonus.
(c) Action plan – list of change and development projects, owners, costs and benefits.
  - Implementation plan – work-package and timing plans.
  - Implementation review plan and review teams.
  - Annual budgets and financial schedules plan incorporating costs and benefits.
7. Overview summary of the management process elements

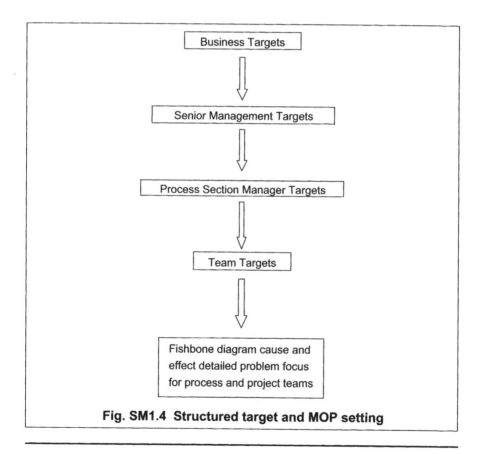

Fig. SM1.4 Structured target and MOP setting

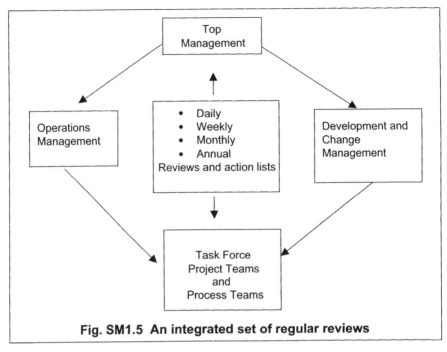

Fig. SM1.5 An integrated set of regular reviews

There are three primary elements as shown in Fig. SM1.6. The importance of building understanding and consensus throughout the company cannot be over-emphasised while, at the same time, installing a practical implementation mechanism, to embody all sub-system elements of the CAP system as shown in Fig. SM1.7.

To facilitate the creation of the CAP process and its controls, via a change project, a convenient basis for the project plan can be provided in the PDCA plan–do–check–action format of Fig. SM1.8. This helps with the progressive rapid definition of the detailed implementation work-packages essential for practical implementation by project teams.

The overall purpose is to create systematically a more effective and durable organizational capability, architecture and action culture capable of achieving much higher levels of performance, to break away from the status quo. This is built upon a sound analysis of current and future problems, opportunities and external environment pressures to support a leap forward in meeting the needs of the customer and the constraints of the total business environment.

By focusing on a few core top-level objectives each year, underpinned by supporting actions at process and department level in a non-confusing single initiative framework, major progress can be made.

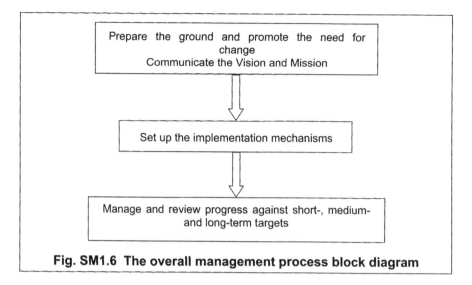

Fig. SM1.6 The overall management process block diagram

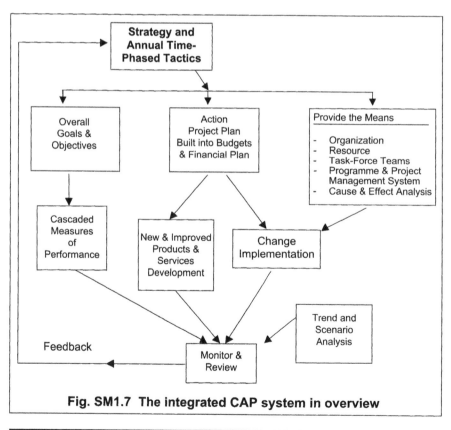

Fig. SM1.7 The integrated CAP system in overview

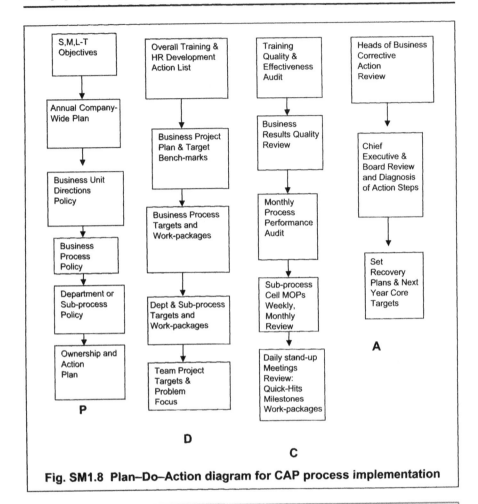

Fig. SM1.8 Plan–Do–Action diagram for CAP process implementation

Table SM1.1 Definition of policy function deployment

- Persistent dissemination and deployment of the vision, strategy, required direction, targets and plans to all levels of management and the workforce.
- Enabling all levels to act powerfully in an integrated way on a set of analyses and systematic implementation actions in priority order across all business processes.
- Based soundly on a cause and effect analysis of opportunity, a delivery means supported by project management and with disciplined regular feedback, consistently applying PDCA logic supported by trained application of modern tools, techniques and methodologies. Embodied in 'The Company Way' culture for conducting its business.

Ownership of the new model

Problem

The Development Director reported to his Projects Leader that the Managing Director had ended the Board meeting with an enthusiastic word of praise for the successful testing of the prototype. All we have to do now is make it and sell it.

The Projects Leader was therefore delighted to be able to send her already prepared details to brief the Production Department on the design of the new model, and with this notes on customers' expected delivery, quality and works testing requirements. Two weeks later the Project Leader phoned the Production Director's office to ask if there were any queries. After some delay about who was dealing with it the Project Leader was told that there was no provision in Production's budget for a new model this year, and in any case all staff were busy on the bottlenecks caused by the variants ordered on current models. Production's plans were to optimize material stock and throughput to suit production of the established current models. They were unaware of the new model until this moment. It was not their project.

Principles

- The corporate planning process should cover the planning and budgeting for new models through their life cycle to production and after. For every project it should produce a strategic plan and budget agreed by the executive team and Board. All relevant functions should then allocate resources according to the strategic plan and define their work packages and deliverables in line with the agreed programme and specification. Design for implementation should be part of the approved project plan from the beginning, with target costs agreed.
- An executive working party should be formed to review and then plan the implementation of the new model, and this example should become the precedent for establishing a programme management system of multi-project management in the company in which all functions would 'own' all projects from birth and so agree the future allocation of resources.

Lesson

- The immediate need was to rescue this new model, but also to do so in a way that would establish how future projects would be brought out successfully.

Support Tools and Techniques Section   1

TT1.1 Definitions

Some words and phrases used in project management mean different things to different people, particularly in different industries and different countries. This list states the definitions which are used in this book.

Word	*Meaning*
Project	Any substantial task which uses resources to innovate or improve the production of goods or services. A project causes changes and can be the means of achieving changes. A project is usually defined by objectives, a budget, a programme. A project is complete when it has achieved its objectives.

Typical projects produce:
- A new or re-modelled product.
- A new or re-modelled production system.
- A new or re-modelled factory, office or any support facility.
- The termination and decommissioning of any of the above at the end of their economic or permitted use.

Equally important as projects are:
- Changing the culture, practices and habits of an organization.
- Re-engineering a business.
- Rationalising and integrating an acquisition.
- Re-locating established systems and services.

And important to any of the above are sub-projects such as:
- Refurbishing plant and services.
- Trial projects, prototypes.
- New and improved information systems.
- Developing an operational cell with a new team structure.

- Human resourcing, training, redundancy and redeployment programmes.

Projects can thus be 'soft' and 'hard', large, small, multi-stage, multi-project, multi-site.

Activities	Identifiable items of work for a project. See also Work-package.
Alliancing	Arrangement between two or more organizations to manage a contract between them jointly – see also Partnering.
Approvals	Within an organization the formal approvals of specifications, budgets for expenditure or proposed terms for a contract.
	During a contract the customer's agreement to a supplier's proposed design, programme or other information submitted to the customer or his representative for 'approval' but the approval usually not relieving the supplier of liability for the satisfactory performance of the contract.
	Also the acceptance that a supplier has achieved the contract specification, deliverables and other terms.
Battery limits	The boundary at which the deliverables from a project meet existing organizational boundaries, plant, services, utilities etc.
Battle of the forms	A process of offer, counter-offer, counter-offer, etc. of proposals for the terms of a contract, often consisting of exchanges of printed forms which have conditions of contract or terms of sale printed on their reverse side.
Bid	Offer to enter into a contract, indicating costs, time, etc.
	Also within a company a proposal for expenditure on a project.
Bought-in bought packaged equipment	Complete module, work-package or unit of equipment to achieve a performance requirement.
Change	Change from the project scope originally agreed between the customer and supplier which occurs during design development, construction or commissioning of a project. See also Variation order.

Client	= Customer
Commissioning	Preparation and start-up of new or modified project. See also Mechanical or process completion.
Completion of equipment	Technical readiness for testing or commissioning. Hand-over may be another stage in a contract. In either case a contract may specify that customer and supplier formally 'sign off' that the stage has been achieved.
Conceptual engineering	Design work to study possible schemes and options for project. Some use the phrase to mean design to provide the basis for a feasibility study. Others mean by it the next stage of design.
Conditions of contract	In English law 'conditions' means all the terms of a contract which are fundamental to the intentions of the parties, so that failure to comply with a condition is a serious breach of contract, but in engineering and other industries in the UK documents often called 'conditions of contract' are sets of general and commercial terms comprising conditions and warranties. See also Model conditions of contract.
Consequential losses	Costs incurred due to a breach of contract, for instance sales lost because of late completion of a project.
Consideration	In contracts made under English law 'valuable consideration' means payment.
Consortium	Contractual collaboration or formation of a joint subsidiary by two or more organizations, usually for one project, sometimes for a series of projects. See also Joint venture.
Consultants	Advisers on projects, design, management, best practices, techniques and technical or other problems.
Contract	Agreement enforceable at law.
Contractor – see also Supplier, Vendor	Supplier of goods or services (may include consultancy services, technical design or management services) to a customer. 'The contractor' means a party to a contract, as distinct from any contractor. The word 'the' is important in English practice as identifying the particular contractor. In some other countries where the English language is used in contracts the practice is to write 'Contractor' or <CONTRACTOR>. The contractor may be a consortium or a joint venture of two or more companies.

Contract price	Amount to be paid a supplier for performance under the terms of a contract, as distinct from what the work cost the supplier.
Contract price adjustment or fluctuation	Payment by the supplier to a supplier for changes in national costs of materials or labour. See also Escalation.
Critical path activity	An activity for a project in the sequence of activities (the critical path) which governs the total time expected to be required for a project.
Crucial activity	An activity which if not completed satisfactorily is a serious risk to achieving the objectives of a project.
Customer	The organization or individual who will own and/or operate the facility at the completion of the project.
Damages	Compensation for loss. See also Liquidated damages terms.
Deliverable	The useful product promised from a project or a work-package.
Detailed design	Production of the drawings, specifications and other information needed for the procurement of equipment and services, demolition and site preparation, construction, testing, commissioning, plant operation and maintenance.
Determination	Termination of a contract by completion of all obligations, or by agreement, frustration or breach.
Deviation	Used by process industry suppliers to mean a change to the quantity, nature or timing of the deliverables agreed at the start of a contract. See also Variation.
Earned value	Value of work completed at any time during the progress of a project (usually compared with the value of the work which it was planned should have been completed by that time).
The Engineer to a contract	Person nominated the role of 'The Engineer' as specified in the contract, usually as the channel of communications between customer and supplier. In more recent contracts the person is called 'The Project Manager'. In some countries use of the title 'Engineer' is controlled by law.
Engineering	The work of designing a project, specifying all

	procurement, and planning construction, installation, testing, and commissioning.
Engineering definition or Engineering specification	Documents detailing the technical requirements for a proposed project. It is typically produced to form the basis for estimating project cost sufficiently accurately for submitting the proposal for sanction.
Enquiry	Invitation for tenders.
Equipment	The process and control items required to form an operational unit.
Escalation	Changes in contract price due to inflation, i.e. rises or falls in national or regional wage rates or materials costs *and/or* Changes in contract price due to variations or claims.
Estimate	Calculation of the predicted cost, resources or time required for the future work required for part or whole of a project.
Express terms	Written terms in a contract, i.e. expressed, not implied.
Facility	The completed system or capability resulting from a project.
Fast track (or 'fast trak')	Not a precise phrase, but usually meaning a plan to implement a project faster than at minimum capital cost.
Feasibility study	Engineering, estimating, marketing and other work carried out on a proposed project or alternatives to provide the basis for deciding whether to proceed.
Firm price	Varies in its meaning, but is often used to indicate that a tendered price is offered only for acceptance within a stated period and is not a commitment if it is not accepted within that period.
Fixed price	Usually means that a tender price will not be subject to escalation, but it may mean that there is no variations term. Like other words used in contract management, 'fixed price' has no fixed meaning. What matters in a contract are the terms of payment in that contract.
Flow sheet	Drawing showing the flow of product, deliverables, materials, energy or information between the components of a project.
Force majeure	Overwhelming event beyond the control of the parties to a contract, such as war or earthquake.
Forms of contract	In the UK means model forms of agreement and

	performance bond published with sets of general conditions of contract. See also Model conditions of contract.
Frame agreement	Agreement between two or more companies stating the terms for Alliancing or Partnering.
Free issue	Materials purchased by a customer and issued to a supplier without charge to use for a project.
Functional engineer	Engineer employed in a specialist engineering discipline, for instance control engineering or civil engineering.
Gantt chart	Bar chart form of time schedule.
Gate	A formal stage in a project where its expected worth, progress, cost and execution plan are reviewed and a decision is made whether to continue with the next stage of the project.
General conditions of contract	See Model conditions of contract.
Guarantee	In finance a guarantee means an undertaking by a bank or other third party to recompense a party to a contract for a specified fault by the other party *or* In engineering a guarantee can mean a warranty from a seller to a customer for the performance and safety of a design, system, equipment or whatever.
Hand-over	Handing over of the ownership of part or all of a project. See also Taking over.
Implied terms of a contract	Terms which are part of a contract by law but are not expressed. In contracts under English law they can include:

- The duty to exercise skill and care.
- Fitness for purpose (where the purpose has been made known to supplier and is not overridden by an imposed specification).
- Responsibility of a supplier for his sub-contractors.
- Compliance with statutes (viz. EC Regulations, Factories Act, Construction Regulations, Health & Safety at Work Act etc.).
- Furtherance of purpose – both parties will do their best to perform the contract.
- Liability of a supplier to carry out his work at reasonable speed.

In-house	Within an organization.
Joint venture	Collaboration between two or more organizations, usually for one project, sometimes for a series of projects. See also Consortium.
Lead supplier	= Main supplier = Prime contractor.
Level	Used to mean the amount of detail shown or available – see Level One plan.
Level One plan	The master plan for a project. For all but small projects progressively more detail is given in Level Two, Level Three, etc. plans.
Line manager	Classically a manager responsible for part or all of the resources needed for production. Now used to mean the person with management responsibility for an individual whether or not also responsible for the tasks which that individual may be carrying out – for instance if the individual is temporarily seconded to a project team.
Liquidated damages terms	Liability in a contract to pay a specified sum for a specified breach of contract such as being late in completing construction.
Long lead item	Item to be ordered at the start of a project because of the time the supplier requires to obtain materials and/or do his work.
Lump sum payment	Single payment for all the work done under a contract *but* often used to mean fixed price.
Main supplier	A supplier who enters into a contract to supply a defined deliverable but in turn employs others to supply some of the services and goods required. Also known as a Lead, Prime or Tier 1 contractor.
Making a contract	Entering into a contract. The agreement to enter into a contract may include a term that the contract does not come into effect until some later date or action. Or that the work is not to start until the supplier is instructed to do so.
Mechanical or process completion	Equipment/systems are complete, inspected and checked as correct to design and specification *or* Equipment/systems are complete, inspected and checked as correct to design and specification, and pre-commissioning tests and trials are complete.

	In either case mechanical completion can be a milestone when a payment becomes due to the supplier and can also be the time for contractual hand-over to the customer.
Milestone	Event of significant value or change of risks during the progress of a project.
Model conditions of contract	Sets of contract terms on general matters likely to be required by customers in any contract for a class of work, usually defining words used, the responsibilities of the parties, procedures, liabilities for damage and injuries, mistakes, failure of supplier or sub-contractors, delays, changes in legislation such as taxation, frustration of contract and termination. These general terms are designed to be used with a specification, drawings, schedules and other documents which state the particular terms of a contract. They are also called 'general conditions of contract', 'model forms' or 'standard forms'.
	Sets of model conditions for various types of business or classes of project are published by government agencies, trade associations and professional bodies.
Offer	See Tender.
Order	See Purchase order.
Ownership	Used to mean commitment to the objectives of a project, as distinct from legal ownership.
Partnering	Arrangement between two or more organizations to manage a contract between them cooperatively – as distinct from a legally established partnership. See also Alliancing.
Parties	The 'persons' who offer and accept the terms of a contract. (A company or corporation has legally the status of a person.) 'Third parties' are any others who are not parties to that contract.
Payback period	Time taken for the investment in a project to be paid back by the cash it earns in use.
Penalty	Under English law what is called a 'penalty' in a contract may not be enforceable. See Liquidated damages terms.
Performance of a contract	Completion of all obligations in a contract.

Plant	System of equipment and services which comprise an operational unit.
	Also used by suppliers to mean equipment used in demolition and construction work.
Practical completion	The project or a section of it is sufficiently complete for the customer to take it over or begin to use it.
Price	See Contract price.
Prime supplier	= Main supplier.
Procurement	Purchasing of services, materials or equipment.
Produit en main	The supplier remains in control of what he has supplied.
Program	In the US = Programme, see below.
	In the UK means computer software.
Programme	Diagram or table showing proposed dates for starting and completing activities, see also Schedule *or* A set of related projects.
Project breakdown structure	= Work breakdown structure.
Project champion or 'owner'	Manager with the authority to represent the investors and customers for a project.
Project data book	A collection of the relevant project information handed over to the customer at the end of a project.
Project Engineer	An engineer responsible for one or more work-packages for a project, responsible to the project manager.
	See also Project Manager.
Project execution plan or Project implementation plan	Document stating the project programme and who is to be responsible for all the activities necessary to carry out a project.
Project Manager	Person responsible for establishing and achieving the objectives of a project.
	See also Project Engineer.
	In some contracts a person is nominated by the customer as the 'Project Manager' to be the sole channel of communications between customer and supplier.
Project post-completion	The process of collecting and examining data and experience on a completed project from those involved

review or report	in the project, to be used as learning for the future.
Project sponsor	The investor in a project.
	See also Project champion or 'owner'.
Promoter	= Customer *or* Client.
Punch list	List of outstanding activities to be completed before work will be accepted.
Purchase order	Contract for smaller purchases.
Qualified acceptance	Limited, modified or restricted acceptance of an offer to enter into a contract, and therefore a counter-offer, not an acceptance.
Qualified bid	Limited, modified or restricted offer, not compliant with all the terms proposed in an invitation for tenders.
Quotation	A 'quotation' may be an offer to enter into a contract or only an indication of price.
Retention = Retention money	Part of the payment due to a supplier for progress with the work which is not paid until he has discharged liabilities to remedy defects for a period after the taking over or acceptance of the works.
Sanction of a project	Decision by the appropriate body in the customer organization to authorize expenditure of resources on a project.
Schedule	See (Time) Schedule.
Schedule of rates	List of approximate quantities of items of work to be done by a supplier with prices ('rates') per unit quantity of each item.
Selective tendering	Inviting tenders only from selected suppliers, usually those considered to be qualified by their resources and their performance of previous contracts or chosen following a first stage of qualifying bidding.
Seller	= Supplier.
Sign off	Formal process for project stakeholders or contract parties to sign a document to establish their agreement to it, for instance:
	• Within a company the signing off of a definition of project objectives and deliverables.
	• Between customer and supplier signing a certification of the completion of a commissioning test.
Simple contract	Under English law a contract not under seal and made orally or in writing by:

	• Offer
	• Acceptance
	• Valuable consideration (usually payment)
	• Identity of intention
	• Intention to make a legal relationship
	• Possitility
Speciality contract	In England a contract made under seal.
Standard forms of contract	See Model conditions of contract.
Start-up	The commissioning (see Commissioning) of a completed system or facility *or* A formal process of making a new project team effective.
Statute law	Law made by the European Union of Parliament.
Steering committee	Group formed usually for larger projects to guide the project manager on behalf of all stakeholders in a project.
Sub-contract	A contract between a Main contractor and a supplier for part of the work for the main contract. Also a contract between that supplier and another in the supply chain.
Sub-contractor	Company providing services, goods or management services to a main supplier and not in contract with the customer.
Sub-letting	Employment of a sub-contractor by a main supplier.
Substantial completion	= Practical completion.
Supplier	= Contractor, Vendor *or* Sub-contractor.
Supply chain	The sequence of contracts customer → main supplier (Tier 1) → sub-contractor (Tier 2) → materials suppliers (Tier 3, etc.) and the subsequent reverse flow of deliverables.
Take-off	Calculation from drawings of the quantities of materials, etc. required for work.
Taking over	When the use or the ownership of the works passes from supplier to customer, usually formalized by approval and acceptance procedures specified in the contract.
Tender	See Bid.
Termination of	See Determination contract.

a contract

Terms of a contract	All the obligations and rights agreed between the parties, plus any terms implied by law. In English contracts the terms may consist of conditions and warranties.
Terms of sale	= Terms *or* Conditions of contract. Terms of sale are the words, more typically the phrase, used for small contracts such as in purchasing materials or plant.
Test schedule (also sometimes includes Acceptance tests)	A list of the tests and inspections necessary to indicate that the project has met the agreed performance requirements. Acceptance tests are those which a customer may want to witness before accepting hand-over of the project.
Third parties	See Parties.
Tier 1 supplier	Main supplier. See also Supply chain.
(Time) Schedule	Bar chart, diagram or list showing the proposed starting and completion dates for activities.
Turnkey contract	Comprehensive contract in which the supplier is responsible for the design, supply, construction and commissioning of a complete building, factory or process plant, usually with responsibility for fitness for purpose, and perhaps also to train customer's staff and pre-commission and commission the plant.
Valuation	Calculating the amount of payment due under the terms of a contract, at stages in larger contracts and at completion.
Variation	Change to the quantity, quality or timing of deliverables ordered by the customer's representative under a term of a contract.
Variation order	Instruction from the customer or his representative for a variation.
Vendor	Company or person contractually committed to providing goods (either direct to the customer or through a supplier).
Vendor information	Design information from a vendor that is essential to the customer or supplier for the design of the project.
Work breakdown	Division of the work for a project into defined

| structure | packages or sub-projects, showing the responsibilities for the management, reporting and control of each package. |
| Work package | A particular piece of work for a project as defined in a work breakdown structure, usually consisting of a set of related activities. |

TT1.2 Acronyms

Acronym	*Meaning*
ACWP	Actual cost of work performed to date
AFC	Anticipated final cost
APM	Association for Project Management
APMP	Accredited Project Management Professional (awarded by APM)
BCWP	Budgeted cost of work performed
BCWS	Budgeted cost of work scheduled
BDEP	Basic design and engineering package
BDP	Business deployment planning
BM	Bench-mark or target performance
BPR	Business process redesign/re-engineering
BSC	Balanced score card
CAD	Computer-aided design
CAE	Computer-aided engineering
CAP	Competitiveness achievement programme
CIM	Computer integrated manufacturing
CIMP	Change and innovation management process
CoC	Conditions of contract
COTS	Commercially available off-the-shelf
CPA	Critical path analysis (in network planning) *or* Contract price adjustment or fluctuation (in contracts)
CPC	Collective product commerce
CPD	Continuing professional development
CPI	Cost performance indicator
CPM	Critical path method of project planning *or* Certificated Project Manager (awarded by APM)
CS^2	Earned value technique
DFM / A	Design for manufacture/assembly
DOP	Delivery operations process

DTC	Design to cost
ECR	Engineering change request
EFC	Estimated final cost
ETC	Estimated/expected time of completion
EV	Earned value
FFA	Force field analysis
FMEA	Failure mode and effects analysis
FRACAS	Fault reporting and corrective action system
GAO	General Accounting Office (USA)
IAI	International Alliance for Operability
ICT	Information and communications technology
IJPM	International Journal of Project Management
IMF	International Monetary Fund
IPMA	International Project Management Association
IPR	Intellectual property rights
IPT	Integrated project team
IRR	Internal rate of return
ISO	International Standards Organization
IT	Information technology
JIT	Just-in-time delivery (of components, materials or services)
JV	Joint venture
KPI	Key performance indicator
LDs	Liquidated damages (in contract liabilities)
LoB	Line of balance
LTPA	Long-term purchasing agreement
LQM	Local quality manual
MOPs	Measures of performance
MPM	Modern project management *or*
	Multi-project management
MSD	Manufacturing system design
MTBF	Mean time between failures
NAO	National Audit Office
NPV	Net present value
NVA	Non value adding
OWP	Commercial and order winning process
PDCA	Plan–Do–Control–Act
PE	Project Engineer
PEP	Project execution plan
PERT	Program evaluation review technique
PIDCAM	Plan–Implement–Do–Check–Action/Assess management

	process
PDIP	Project development and introduction process
PIP	Process improvement plan/project *or*
	Product introduction plan *or*
	Project implementation plan
PM	Project Manager
PMI	Project Management Institute (USA)
PMJ	Project Management Journal
PMP	Project Management Professional (awarded by PMI)
PMT	*Project Manager Today* (magazine)
QA	Quality assurance
QFD	Quality function deployment
QS	Quantity Surveyor
RoI	Return on investment
SAS	Society for acronym suppression
SASD	Structured analysis and systems design
SCP	Supply chain process
SHE	Safety, health, and environment
SP	Support process
STEP	Standard for the exchange of product data
SWOT	Strengths–Weaknesses–Opportunities–Threats analysis
TIC	Total installed cost
TQM	Total quality management
VA	Value adding
VO	Variation order
WB	The World Bank
WBS	Work breakdown structure

Reader's Guide

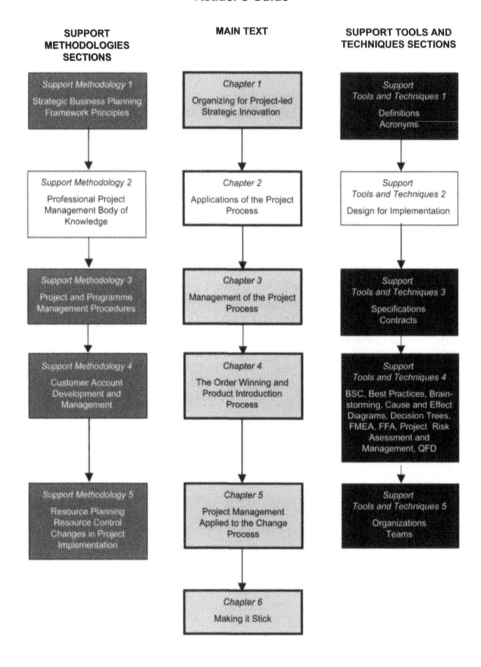

SUPPORT METHODOLOGIES SECTIONS

MAIN TEXT

SUPPORT TOOLS AND TECHNIQUES SECTIONS

Support Methodology 1
Strategic Business Planning Framework Principles

Chapter 1
Organizing for Project-led Strategic Innovation

Support Tools and Techniques 1
Definitions Acronyms

Support Methodology 2
Professional Project Management Body of Knowledge

Chapter 2
Applications of the Project Process

Support Tools and Techniques 2
Design for Implementation

Support Methodology 3
Project and Programme Management Procedures

Chapter 3
Management of the Project Process

Support Tools and Techniques 3
Specifications Contracts

Support Methodology 4
Customer Account Development and Management

Chapter 4
The Order Winning and Product Introduction Process

Support Tools and Techniques 4
BSC, Best Practices, Brainstorming, Cause and Effect Diagrams, Decision Trees, FMEA, FFA, Project Risk Asessment and Management, QFD

Support Methodology 5
Resource Planning Resource Control Changes in Project Implementation

Chapter 5
Project Management Applied to the Change Process

Support Tools and Techniques 5
Organizations Teams

Chapter 6
Making it Stick

Applications of the Project Process 2

2.1 Introduction

The concept and techniques of managing by project apply to all sorts of businesses, public services and private interests such as charities. Managing by projects is simple in theory: agree what is wanted; understand why it is wanted; provide the resources to implement it; agree the deliverables; put together the natural project team; delegate authority to the Project Manager; anticipate the risks of changes; inspire people to deliver maximum value; assess what is really happening; improve from experience; and give credit to all who helped.

Practice does not always seem so simple. The objectives of the project may be seen differently by different stakeholders. Many of the organizations and people involved in a project may also have other interests. Communications between them can be complicated, imperfect and influenced by previous events and future prospects. Objectives may change during the project, or expected resources fail to appear. Progress may be hard to measure. And all this may feel unique. These problems are not unique. The real problem is that effort and discipline are needed to apply the principles set out in this book. This chapter uses simplified examples to show how these principles can be applied in the circumstances that can arise at stages through real projects. Chapter 1 has referred to examples in manufacturing and health services. In this chapter we look in more detail at stages of different projects large and small in various sectors of industry.

2.2 Capital projects

2.2.1 Facilities for business and services

All businesses and public services depend upon the facilities produced from projects such as new buildings, factories and communications systems. These assets form the fixed infrastructure for producing products and services. They require significant capital expenditure, and hence are known as capital projects. They take time to create from new or to adapt from previous uses and hence demand planning and control.

The construction of a new building or road is what many people assume is meant by the word 'project'. Certainly those are projects. Construction projects have a long history, and abundant techniques for planning, cost estimating and procurement have been developed for managing them. That does not mean that construction projects are good examples for all others. Many continue to cause anxieties about delivery on time, to quality and within budget, though often almost repeats of previous projects. Civil engineering and building projects have long had problems of adversarial attitudes between their promoters and the contractors and these organizations and their representatives have shown only limited commitment to tackle the problems because of their wide use of untrained and temporary staff. Only recently have US and UK customers and others supported national campaigns to study their experience of construction systematically and apply the lessons to try to achieve continuous improvement.

Who initiates a project as its promoter, who invests in it and who uses the resulting facility varies greatly from project to project. The users range from once-in-a-lifetime novices to sophisticated capital-intensive businesses, but most users buy or lease the facilities from suppliers such as contractors who with design consultants, specialist sub-contractors and materials suppliers specialize in delivering these projects.

2.2.2 Stakeholders

In capital-intensive industries, the prospective user is often the promoter of a project, for instance in the process industries where the users have the operating experience and the new facility usually has to be designed to fit with existing systems. The same is characteristic of many projects, commercial or public. These are promoted by national and local government authorities, though with the recent innovation that the financing and operation of their projects such as new hospitals is now often franchised to contractors. The promoter of the construction of an office block or other commercial buildings is often a developer or a contractor who invests in building the project in order to sell or lease the completed facility.

For its promoters a project is only a means to an end – the business or a public service. For designers and contractors, projects are their business.

Promoters, owners, users, designers, contractors and other suppliers may thus all be distinct stakeholders in a project, each taking different risks and having different criteria for the success of the project. Whether the project is large or small, planning and coordinating the contractual and informal relationships between all these interested parties is often the most important task for its managers.

At its start a project must promise to meet a market or social demand. The 'Community Chest' case described below is an instance of a small project but one involving a variety of stakeholders.

2.2.3 Project initiation – the Community Chest project

The quality of life in a small town was threatened by the closure of all the branch offices of national 'High Street' banks and also a reduction of post office counter services. The banks' branch offices were quite busy with cash and credit services for private customers and small traders, but calculated that they earned no profit from that work. They considered that the presence this gave them in the town was no longer worth its cost. Because of the growth in the size of companies, the potentially valuable and risky work of loans and other services for businesses was now conducted by regional or national offices. One bank had already left the town. Closure of one of the two building society branches was also rumoured.

After a series of public protests the Parish Council Chairman called an informal meeting of representatives of the banks, building societies, the post office shop owner, other traders and members of the community. At this meeting the banks and building societies indicated that most of them expected to be leaving the town within a year or so. Strong criticisms of this and remarks about profits made nationally led to a long and fractious meeting. The main argument from the locals was that the banks and building societies had a duty to continue providing personal cash services. Further amalgamations of the banks was suggested to save their costs of staying in the town, but in response to this it was stated that they doubted whether further amalgamation was a basis for survival and success.

Discussion continued, in effect on how to try to force the banks to maintain their current services. Amidst this someone joked that all these organizations should instead be partners in setting up a single cash handling centre in the village, a 'Community Chest'. This was taken up as a positive solution to the problem. After a short discussion all agreed to consider the idea of establishing a single cash counter service operating for all the banks, building societies, social security and the post office, operating six days a week, and in a building with a secure outer lobby for cash dispensers and night safes.

The meeting agreed with the Chairman's suggestion that he would invite some councillors and representatives of the traders, banks and building societies to form a steering group to develop the proposal. At the suggestion of a retired bank services manager, the Council's former Chairman agreed to chair the steering group. The retired bank services manager agreed to be their Project Manager.

2.2.4 Lessons from the Community Chest project

The birth of the 'Community Chest' project as described above follows several of the recommendations that experience shows are vital for a successful project. The stakeholders were involved from the start, and indeed the project was conceived by them collectively. The proposal met all the local requirements, and indeed appeared to offer a better service than previously without any organization having to sustain unacceptable costs. This was an encouraging beginning.

Whether all the stakeholders were equally committed to the project was not so certain. In Chapter 1 projects were classified into three categories of importance. Applying these classifications, the 'Community Chest' example is a Category 2 project for the local community, but only Category 3 for the national organizations who traditionally provide cash handling services to the community. Because of these differences in the importance of the project to the different stakeholders, all parties needed to be committed to the project formally. The recommended means of doing so was by an incorporated joint venture. A first task for the sponsoring committee and Project Manager was therefore to obtain the support to establish this commitment, and on that basis obtain agreement on how decisions would be made on the scope, financing, launch, development, implementation and delivery of the project.

A theme of this book is that every project needs a Programme Director to define in consultation with stakeholders' representatives what is really wanted. And it needs a Project Manager to define in consultation with resource providers how best to deliver it. One task of the Programme Director is to make sure that resources are allocated to the project to achieve the business objective. In this case the chairman of the sponsoring committee would have to establish that role, by agreement with all the interested parties. The role of the Project Manager is to manage the risks of delivering the project. Both roles are not necessarily full-time jobs. They are required however small the project. They are needed throughout a project, one to maintain attention to the business objective, the other to see that resources are being used to deliver maximum value. Projects are a flash in the pan. Their demands for information, decisions, communications and resources are transient. By contrast, the functional departments in businesses, manufacturing companies and public services ideally seek to optimize regular tasks. Managing a project therefore demands the managerial knowledge and skill to link project dynamics and functional continuity.[1]

In the Community Chest case a prospective Programme Director and a Project Manager were in place, but the two individuals chosen needed professional support and training in order to be able to understand and manage their tasks. To understand what would be expected of her, the start for the Project Manager was to read the *Standard Terms for the Appointment of a Project Manager* published by the Association for Project Management.

2.3 Launch of a project

2.3.1 Project definition

There is most flexibility to change a project very early in its development. Once in use the asset can be the least flexible element in the user's business.

Even if using standard systems or components, the information used to decide to invest in a project can have changed by the time the resultant facility is ready to use. The success of a project therefore depends upon the quality of the initial attention to what is needed, why, and to how these answers may change.

Sophisticated and novice promoters can help themselves think what they want to achieve by using systematic but simple checklists of questions to consider before starting a project, for instance:

1. What performance and characteristics are required from the project?
2. Why?
3. What are the criteria for success?
4. How may the answers to the above change during the project?

Answers to the above four questions are needed to guide the Project Manager in decisions on how to use resources to implement the project. To avoid muddle, the answers should be understood and agreed at the start. They should also be kept under review, as objectives and priorities change during all but very brief repeat-work projects.

If no Programme Director is providing guidance on the above questions, the Project Manager may need to answer them alone, particularly to anticipate how changes may affect the project plans.

---

[1] See also Support Methodology Chapter 2 *Professional Project Management Body of Knowledge*

2.3.2 Quality, time and cost

A project can have more than one objective. These different objectives can make conflicting demands, most typically in requiring a trade-off between quality, time and cost. To plan a project a decision is therefore needed as to where the project is in the triangle of these variables, as shown in Fig. 2.1.

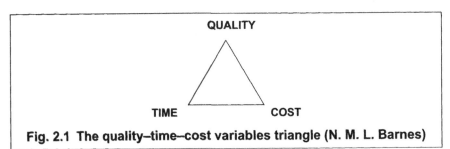

Fig. 2.1 The quality–time–cost variables triangle (N. M. L. Barnes)

A project can be planned to be implemented at maximum speed, and so incurring the costs of using resources uneconomically. Or at minimum cost, using resources as economically as possible and therefore more slowly. Or between the two. For the typical project expected to earn a financial return, the total time to be allowed for its implementation should be decided after estimating the likely cost of the project over a range of possible rates of implementation and selecting the time at which the net present value of extra income obtained earlier by faster completion equals its extra cost.[2] The priority between time and cost therefore tends to be different for commercial projects from those for public services.

The objectives of a project should state whether it is to be completed at minimum initial cost, or whether in a faster economic time, or as emergency work, in order to guide the planning of the use of resources. Skills and techniques for planning what to do when to deliver a project are well established. Planning the planning is required to ensure that the planning of the use of resources is designed to meet the priorities between quality, time and cost.

The following case describes the time taken to choose a novel system of organization designed to help achieve the priorities for a major project.

2.3.3 Project launch case – alliancing

Two oil marketing companies formed a joint venture company to promote and operate a large offshore project to develop an as-yet untapped offshore

---

[2] See also Support Methodology Chapter 5 *Resource Planning*

oil and gas field. The field extended over three sea exploration areas and the licenses to plan to extract from these areas were held by the two companies. The reservoir was deep and required a major offshore installation. The two companies therefore decided to develop the project jointly rather than follow the usual practice of one being leader and manager for a project on behalf of other partners.

Their first estimate of the capital cost of the project was based upon cost data from previous projects adjusted for project size and for price inflation. For the gas and oil to sell in the increasingly competitive world market the companies calculated that the capital cost had to be 20% less than this estimate. Without evidence that this reduction could be achieved there would be no project. A report from the industry had stated that improvements in project cost and delivery could be achieved by a change of culture in using the experience of contractors and suppliers. As mentioned earlier, the culture governing contracts for engineering and construction had been characterised by adversarial relationships and mistrust at almost every level and interface. The report advocated changing the culture of contract relationships to one of teamwork and openness.

To study this and the evidence from other current projects the companies formed a joint working party of seconded senior staff which was given time to recommend a procurement strategy for the project. The working party and others consulted in the companies all agreed that a prime engineering contractor should be selected to join the two companies to form a project alliance. Drawing on experience of others, the companies agreed that the objective of the alliance would be to build '... upon the client and contractor skills and align them to work together towards the common goals of creating safe and quality facilities, below cost targets, sharing the profits of success.' As an alliance between two companies and a contractor was novel to the companies, the working party prepared detailed presentations of their strategy to their Boards. The result of this thorough study was that the concept of a step change in culture to an alliance with a contractor was fully accepted.

The contractor was chosen in a competition judged on the basis of reimbursable cost payment terms plus consideration of alliance philosophies and safety performance. The three parties then appointed one member each to an Alliance Board whose unanimous decisions were to be binding on all of them.

A second major step was that the Alliance Board appointed a Programme Director with the authority over all three parties' decisions on how to execute the project. A director from the contractor was selected as the most appropriate person.

The advantages hoped for by 'alliancing' were achieved by:

- Forming a single team of staff of all three companies, the 'natural' multi-functional team.
- Making the team responsible for all functions including operation of the completed facility.
- Seconding all staff for the team from their parent companies but planning for their future employment (the few not happy with secondment were returned direct to their companies).
- Locating all the team together in their own separate building.
- Team induction, training and sustained team building.
- Sharing of all data and reporting.

A third major step was to extend the alliancing to include the contractors chosen to engineer and supply the heart of the project, the set of complex process, power and service modules for the facility. What became the 'process' alliance consisted of seven companies in one alliance. For all of them the alliancing was the basis for:

- Aligning goals and objectives.
- Commitment to aggressive reduction of the project capital and operating costs.
- Shared incentive contracts.
- Removal of contract interfaces and duplication of functions of clients, prime contractor and others.
- Sustained attention to the operation of alliancing, particularly open sharing of ideas, problems and solutions.
- Encouraging publicity, reports and lectures on the experience and lessons for other projects.

The project was completed early and within the reduced budget. The two oil companies continued with the joint venture to operate the completed facility.

2.3.4 Lessons from the alliancing case

Total cost reduction was the priority for this project, and for this reason alliancing to align different commercial interests was adopted for the project despite the risks of the novelty of the relationship. The three companies were able to accept these risks as for all of them it was a Category 1 project which would not have proceeded without showing those innovations which would promise to achieve that priority.

This case shows what was possible in a change of culture in planning and managing the contractual relationships between companies and with their major suppliers. The project demonstrated that our daily human experience that a small number of people can work together is also possible on a large scale if everyone is located in one team and they have a common purpose, unified leadership and shared information, even if only temporarily.

The team working for this project was judged to be successful by individuals and the companies, but it was agreed that sustained attention to purpose and relationships had been required to maintain this throughout the project as problems arose and as roles in the team changed or ceased to be required.

2.4 Bidding for funding

2.4.1 Planning a bid – a research project case

Dr Robert Hugh of Ware University was keen to respond to the government's initiative in inviting bids for research to define the lessons of the successes and failures of computer-based manufacturing systems.

The invitation for research bids stated that the funding would favour proposals which would demand high levels of collaboration with industry, with significant input of resources, in cash and kind, from the industrial partners, and in the research team collaboration between manufacturing engineers, management scientists, psychologists and computer scientists. The final research proposal had to be submitted within four months.

Dr Hugh's expertise was occupational psychology. He had worked in industry, and since joining the university had undertaken a number of research projects on team building in companies in telecommunications, mining, the media and food processing. In recent years, he had started to take an interest in the problems in the manufacturing industry. His challenge was to form a suitable project team with the requisite skills and create an industrial consortium consisting of companies in manufacturing which would provide a significant amount of resource input.

2.4.2 Organizing a bid – the research project case

Dr Hugh contacted Jo King, IT Manager in an automotive systems assembly company, with whom he had worked previously on a project in the media industry. Jo was receptive. His company had had little success with the implementation of computer-based manufacturing systems. His company believed that many of the problems were human rather than technical. He gave his wholehearted support to the project. Working together, they prepared a draft two-page outline summary setting out the project objectives, the main features of the project, the associated methodology, the resources required, the project deliverables and the potential benefits. Jo agreed to bring the proposal to the attention of his colleagues in other manufacturing companies. They also agreed to meet at two-week intervals to review the progress on the preparation of the detailed project proposal.

Formation of an industrial consortium was one aspect of the project. A related significant challenge was to form an academic team requiring expertise from four different areas. Hu had to find willing partners in the Department of Manufacturing Engineering, the Management Centre and the Department of Computer Science. He asked for advice from his Head of Department and the University Industrial Research Consultant, Mo Bray, who was a walking knowledge base of the expertise of the university staff. Between them they identified two individuals in each department who may be interested in joining the project team. Bray also agreed to help find suitable industrial partners. Dr Hugh gave Bray a copy of the outline proposal for circulation to potential industrial partners.

Dr Hugh had separate meetings with the identified individuals. He received a lot of encouragement and ideas for the project from his meetings. One member of academic staff from the Management Centre had the requisite expertise and agreed to join the project team. Both of the individuals from the Computer Science department, while indicating interest in the project, declined to be part of the project team since the work was of a practical nature while their interests lay in theoretical aspects of computing. One of the individuals in the manufacturing engineering group had a high level of expertise in the application of information technology to manufacturing enterprises. It was felt that he could provide the computing expertise required to carry out the project in a professional manner. The second academic from the manufacturing engineering department had the necessary expertise in the area of integrated manufacturing systems. A meeting of the whole academic team followed meetings with the individuals. All of the individuals were very interested in the project and contributed a number of ideas to refine the proposal. Through his networking Robert Hugh had formed a very competent project team.

At the next meeting between Jo King and Robert Hugh, Jo reported a high level of interest in the project among 6 out of 10 companies contacted. Three were partners in his company's supply chain, while others were big players in other industrial sectors. All were interested in the project because they had made significant investments in computer-based manufacturing systems, which had not lived up to expectations. They were interested in finding out the real causes of the lack of effective implementation and how they could improve the situation. Mo Bray, who later joined the meeting, reported that 5 out of 12 companies he had contacted were willing to help with the project. Robert was very encouraged. He felt that he had the making of an excellent project proposal.

During the next four weeks, Robert had separate meetings with the potential industrial partners to discuss the project, their interest in it as well as their suggestions for improving the quality of research work, and what they would contribute to the project. He followed up by having meetings with his academic colleagues and Jo and between them they revised the outline proposal. This was followed by the preparation of a detailed academic case for research, including a critical state of the art review of the subject area, the need for research, the research aims and objectives, research methodology, project plan, work packages, the resources required, milestones and deliverables, and the exploitation route.

A joint meeting of all the academics and the potential industrial partners was arranged to discuss the detailed proposal. A large amount of discussion took place during the meeting. Much of it related to the practical aspects of the project, in particular the tools and techniques to be used, the cash and in-kind contribution of the individual partners, the project management arrangements, the role of partners, the collaboration between the partners, milestones and deliverables. One partner decided that their company could not take part in the project because of the financial difficulties it was facing and could not provide the necessary time and effort. The other partners came on board and agreed to provide letters of support confirming their contributions. The total cash and in-kind contribution of industrial partners added up to £950,000 over the three-year duration of the project. This compared to a request for £560,000 of governmental research funding. Following the meeting, the proposal was revised again to take account of the comments made.

The final draft was e-mailed to all the partners with a request for any final comments to be sent within two days along with formal letters of support. Some further suggestions followed, which were considered by the academic team and led to some further refinements. Formal letters of support were received from nine of the ten partners by the deadline date. The tenth company failed to respond, in spite of repeated requests. This necessitated a further refinement of the proposal in order to modify the figures relating to the contribution to be made by the industrial partners. In spite of this disappointment, the proportion of the industrial contribution was far greater than that specified in the call for research proposals. Robert Hugh, his academic colleagues and industrial partners were satisfied that they had been able to prepare an excellent proposal and they expected that it would be funded.

Four months later Robert Hugh received a letter indicating that their research proposal had been very well received and that it would be funded. He heaved a sigh of relief and took a deep breath. The real work on the project was about to start !

2.4.3 Lessons from the research project case

Universities, in common with industrial organizations, have witnessed very considerable competitive pressures. Government funding for teaching and research has been squeezed. Much academic long-term research has given way to projects designed to provide results in the short- and medium-term. Increasingly, the research grants have been targeted at work involving collaboration and significant input from industry. Research evaluation exercises have been used to provide different levels of funding to university departments depending upon the level of their research excellence.

Dr Hugh's university had a good record in attracting research grants from different funding bodies. Research-related income provides 55% of the university's income. It has been able to spin off a number of companies, involving venture capital funding, to exploit the results of its research. From its successes so far the university considered that successful completion depends upon many factors common to all sorts of projects, the most critical ones being:

- Realism of the original aims and objectives.
- Agreed measures of performance.
- Project champions – academic and industrial.
- Calibre of staff working on the project.
- Commitment – job satisfaction.
- Continuity.
- Team working (effectiveness).
- Challenge of the research project.
- The quality of collaboration between the members of the research consortium.
- Resources.
- Technological constraints.
- Quality of project planning, monitoring, review and control.
- Supportive culture.
- Guidance to all parties based upon the lessons of past successes and problems.

2.5 Delivery process design

2.5.1 *Work breakdown structure and procurement strategy*

An avoidable cause of unexpected costs and delays to projects is a lack of early attention to the choices in how and when to employ who to provide services, software and hardware, including project management services. Anyone initiating a possible project should therefore follow the example of the alliancing case and start to plan how to procure these services at the same time as the first attention to defining the project.

The first choice is whether to build, buy or to lease the facility and the supporting services for its management, hand-over and operation. There is as yet no standard way of allocating the work for a project among in-house departments and outside suppliers and contractors which is right for all projects. Some promoters of projects incur avoidable costs by laying down an inflexible way for executing all their projects. Some novice promoters incur avoidable costs because they stumble by trial-and-error and rediscover known answers too late to make best use of them. Its promoter needs to study choices in how to procure a project, drawing on experience and ideas from previous projects.

The work breakdown into work packages should therefore be designed for each project, depending upon its size, complexity, urgency, novelty, risks and the capacity, interests and motivation of all parties. Work breakdown is more than deciding who can best do what. It should state agreed responsibilities in terms of the delivery of systems and the whole project as a useful facility.

2.5.2 Implementation risks

Projects are obviously investment risks. Most projects are what Morris has classified as a 'single shot' risk. The project is the prototype, without the opportunity for testing before moving into implementation. The implication is that user, sponsor and all who could contribute experience and ideas to a project need to work as a team to plan ahead in order to get the product right first time, and on time.

Many publications state the lessons learned from investment in projects. Despite all the lessons acknowledged by companies and individuals, wasteful habits are repeated, particularly in poor decisions at the 'front end' of projects. Most of the cost of a project is determined by the early decisions on its scope. The greatest risks to the successful delivery of projects are in delays due to poor timing of decisions which affect scope. The recurrent wasteful habits are:

- Initial haste and lack of sufficient resources to study project objectives, alternatives and risks.
- Initial interest only in the scope of the project without thinking how best to procure it.
- Changes avoidably late in the project caused by:
  - Lack of a single point of authority over the project.
  - Failing to consult and commit stakeholders.
  - Failing to anticipate changes in markets and priorities.
- Expecting potential suppliers of services such as consultants and contractors to price their proposals for the project in a short time and with little information, causing them to take relatively big risks and then concentrate on obtaining extra payment rather than delivering what their customers wanted.
- Choosing between bid prices without first selecting who is fit to do the work, resulting in poor work which has to be repeated.
- Asking for a special design when a standard would be good enough.
- Not supervising how everyone starts their tasks, resulting in reports of lack of preparations and progress received too late to avoid delays.
- Taking over before the new facility is proven and understood.
- Failing to require a formal audit and sign-off procedure to check each stage against the project objectives.

The lessons are clear: organizational cultures need to change, by change programmes as set out in Chapter 5 designed to establish disciplined management of the start of every project that devotes resources to detailed planning, faces the risks and makes decisions based upon facts. From all this should come the best possible definition of the project and a risk management strategy. Project delivery can then be planned to meet the priorities between quality, economy and urgency.

2.5.3 Delivery process design Case Study I – an urgent project

Geographical changes and urbanization were increasing the probability of recurrence of the severe flooding of the low areas of the country experienced 10 years earlier. Action to increase the protection was now agreed to be urgent. A new regional protection system was the eventual answer, but it would take 5 years to be effective. To provide interim protection the local and national authorities agreed to proceed with temporary raising of the waterfront walls and river banks, as an urgent project.

A Project Manager was appointed for this urgent interim project under a system established for projects dependent upon inter-departmental collaboration. The Project Manager called together a steering group representing all the authorities and their departments involved, to define, agree and coordinate all work for the project.

To do the physical work required access to some 800 riverside properties such as private houses and their gardens, parks, historic buildings, offices, bonded warehouses, industrial yards, wharves and public utilities. Some were abandoned and derelict. In many the investigation and construction work had to be coordinated with the occupiers' daily use of their properties, the handling of goods, their security, etc. Obvious characteristics of the project were the geographical spread of the properties, lack of freedom to do the work in them and the comparatively minor scale of much of the work. Decisions on the design and construction of the bank strengthening and raising depended upon contacting the frontagers to explain the need for the work, and arranging with them access to investigate the state of the banks and to construct the raising agreed as suitable and least inconvenient to all concerned. Investigations in detail had not been carried out for the feasibility studies, because of the limitations of time. Rapid design decisions and agreement were required simultaneously in order to achieve the programme of construction.

The project team was therefore decentralised into sections. Staff to man these teams were borrowed from consultants. The public authorities concerned took the unusual action of delegating cost decisions to borrowed staff. A Deputy Project Manager was appointed and was leader of a programme support office responsible for design coordination, planning, monitoring of costs and progress, and contract administration.

Contractors were employed for the construction work following the authorities' established rules. Contractors already approved for the class of work tendered competitively, but contractors' views were first obtained on the programme and terms of contract suitable for the uncertainties and speed of the proposed work. Standard terms of contract with flexible terms of payment were used and the established procedures for awarding the contracts were followed, to save time in asking the authorities for exceptions. For the same reason, a proposal to be allowed to offer contractors a bonus for early completion was not pursued.

This urgent project was completed within the time set and the small budget.

2.5.4 Lessons from the urgent project case

For the community at risk and the public authorities the urgent project described above was in Category 1 in our classifications of importance, as recurrence of the previous large scale of flooding would have been costly and a severe political embarrassment. The need for urgency was therefore widely accepted in the public authorities concerned. This contributed directly to agreement that temporary staff should be employed whose decisions would be the chief influence on costs, that construction contracts could be placed based upon uncertain information and that this strategy could be executed straightaway simultaneously over the whole project.

Establishing the project delivery plan quickly was possible because the concept of a Project Manager was already established with appropriate terms of reference accepted by all departments.

Time was saved by making use of established procedures and not asking for exceptions, particularly exceptions to the rules on contracts.

The programme support office was valuable for providing coordination and a single point of reporting on what was physically widely dispersed work. It also checked a research team's review of the management of the project.

2.5.5 Delivery process design Case Study II – technology transfer

F&C, a traditional family owned manufacturing company was facing severe competition from imports from lower cost countries. The company was introducing new models, but most of these were engineering-led rather than market-led, and the manufacturing processes and techniques used by the company were out of date. It was fighting a losing battle. In an effort to turn around the company, the family owners decided to appoint a new Chief Executive, Dr Roger Knight, with experience of turning around loss-making operations.

Roger Knight conducted a thorough review of operations. He made some short-term changes to stem the losses. At the same time, he concluded that the long-term survival of the company depended upon achieving a high level of change. Most of the managers had been with the company for more than twenty years, which had seen relatively little change.

He needed some agents of change, probably bright individuals who had not worked in the company previously.

Financial constraints ruled out the employment of management consultants. In a previous company Roger had had peripheral involvement with a 'Teaching Company' programme with the local university for technology transfer. He had been impressed by the practical and speedy results achieved by the graduates recruited to carry out the programme. He decided to investigate the possibility of a Teaching Company Programme with the local University of Ware. He telephoned the university, and was put through to the business development unit. The business manager arranged an appointment between Knight and the university's Industrial Research Consultant, Mo Bray. Bray had worked in industry most of his life and had successfully increased the university's links with commerce and industry. They discussed the company requirements and quickly established that the company needed to become a market-led organization, improve its product introduction process, and make significant improvements to the operation of the manufacturing system. On his return to office, Mo drafted a one-page summary of the requirements for a Teaching Company Programme and e-mailed it to Roger Knight and his academic colleagues in the management centre and the manufacturing engineering department.

2.5.6 *Organizing the technology transfer case*

Roger was generally happy with the outline of the proposed programme and suggested that he and his colleagues would like to visit the university to meet the academics interested in working on the programme. Following some preliminary meetings and discussions with colleagues it was agreed that Billy Mitchell from the Management Centre and Stephanie Walker from the Manufacturing Engineering Department should be the university academics on this particular teaching company programme, with Walker being the academic leader.

Bray arranged a meeting at the university between the academics, Knight and his recently recruited Marketing Manager, the long-serving Design Manager and the Manufacturing Manager. The company personnel made a presentation during which they outlined the main problems faced by the company and the need for change. The academics responded by outlining their previous experience of working with industry and how their expertise could help resolve the problems. There was a considerable amount of discussion. They concluded that they had the makings of a good partnership, which would benefit the company as well as the university and that they should proceed further with the development of the detailed programme. At this stage Bray suggested that before proceeding further it would be wise to arrange a visit by the Teaching Company Directorate (TCD) Consultant assigned to the University. Bray, who had previously sent a copy of the one-page outline of the programme to him, arranged the visit. During his visit to the company, the TCD Consultant made his customary check about the financial health of the company. He also asked a number of questions about the company's approach to product design, marketing and manufacture. He was particularly interested in the management's commitment to change and the company's ability to work with the academics. While he was concerned that the company had not embraced much change during the previous 20 years, he was satisfied that the new management in charge could achieve the objectives it had set itself. He concluded that Bray and his academic colleagues should proceed further with the development of the proposal.

The academic and industrial partners hammered out the details of the Teaching Company Programme involving the employment of two Teaching Company Associates, each for a two-year period, but spread over a three year period. The formal application was submitted just three months after Knight had made the first contact with the university. The application was considered by the TCD, who raised a number of minor queries. The academic and industrial partners jointly responded to the queries. The TCD was satisfied with the response, and agreed to award a grant covering 60% of the cost of the three-year programme.

The programme was run over the following three and half years – the additional six months being accounted for by the difficulties associated with the recruitment of the second Associate. There was a high level of cooperation between the academic and industrial partners. Any difficulties were resolved during the regular meetings between the partners. The academics visited the company regularly to work with the Associates and the company personnel. In fact for all practical purposes they became a part of the company. There was a high level of commitment on the part of the Chief Executive and his senior colleagues. A number of valuable achievements were realised.

1. The machine shop was transformed from a functional layout to a full cellular structure. This improved the machine shop efficiency by 35%. Cell leaders were trained and developed to reduce set-up-times, develop teams, plan and manage workloads, etc. Greater flexibility of skills was introduced.
2. A lean manufacturing approach was implemented. This resulted in a 50% reduction in inventory levels.
3. The assembly areas were reorganized using a task-force approach headed up by one of the Associates.
4. Appropriate procedures were set up to introduce simultaneous engineering concepts into the company, which resulted in a significant

reduction in the company's time-to-market. A new range of products was introduced, which resulted in a 25% increase in market share.

5. Financial benefits included a once only increase in profit of £100,000 with a recurring profit increase of £250,000 per annum.
6. The programme allowed the university staff to be involved in practical and applications-related work in real manufacturing environments. It provided rich, first-hand experience of the difficulties involved in the practical implementation of advanced manufacturing techniques.
7. Both of the Associates were registered for MPhil degrees, which they completed successfully. It also provided very valuable teaching and case studies material.
8. Two papers were published in refereed academic journals.
9. The collaboration between the company and the university continued after the teaching company programme had been completed.

2.5.7 Lessons from technology transfer projects

During recent years, governments have put an increasing amount of emphasis on partnerships between academia and industry in order to improve the competitiveness of the latter and provide real life experience for academics. Universities have been encouraged to transfer the results of their research to companies. Many different approaches have been used for this purpose. One of the most successful is the Teaching Company Programme. The University of Ware has been very active in this, and based upon its experience has concluded that the success of Teaching Company projects depends upon the following factors:

In the Company:

- Chief Executive's commitment to the project.
- High level of visibility of the project in the Company.
- Continuity of management and direction.
- Time commitment at all levels in the Company.
- Capital resources to exploit the technology.
- Stable economic and industrial prospects.
- No disruptive change of company ownership.

and in the research team:

- Good quality trained Associates.
- Facilities available.
- Good understanding of the Company processes.

- Good project management.
- Retention of the Associates.
- Synergy with other research projects, MSc, and undergraduate projects.
- Understanding the benefits in commercial/financial terms.
- Prospect of publication of papers in academic journals and at conferences.

and between all parties:

- High commitment of all stakeholders.
- Personal understanding and regular contact between all partners.
- Technical and interpersonal skills and support.

2.6 Procurement processes

2.6.1 Contracts

Practice in procuring goods and services for projects is well developed in all Western countries, but is not always satisfactory to the suppliers and to their customers. As in all purchasing, supply and demand tend to be out of phase, and there is a sellers' market when a technology is developing, a buyers' market when a technology has matured.

Only recently in the UK have model terms of contract been developed for engineering and construction projects with regard to market forces and designed to establish the relationships needed to deliver success for all parties. Traditional practice in some industries and in bureaucratic organizations has been rather to follow standard practices for all their projects regardless of differences between them in objectives and risks. For instance, in civil engineering the tradition has been to separate design and construction responsibilities and to link them by contracts which emphasize the control of payment to the contractor. Traditions in the building industry have been much the same. By contrast, for new factories the promoters usually employ many specialist engineering and construction firms in parallel, and with little concern for contractual risks. In the process industries the promoters usually employ a single prime contractor made responsible for all decisions and work to deliver an agreed performance from the completed facility. For new software systems public and business organizations have tended to tell the supplier to decide what to supply. Any of these alternatives may be appropriate for any project, depending on the priorities and risks of the project.

Three questions can help to design a strategy for procurement of the services and goods for a project:

1. Who is to be responsible for what?
2. Who is to bear which risks?
3. What terms of payment will lead to achieving the project objectives?

The answers to these questions should provide the basis for deciding on the scope and number of contracts for the work for a project.[3]

A performance specification is appropriate when the purchaser wishes to make the supplier responsible for the satisfactory performance of the deliverables. A purchaser who decides to specify how a supplier is to achieve the specified performance takes the risk of relieving the supplier of responsibility for the results.[4]

As for a whole project, every purchase should be planned to balance quality, time and cost. The choices for a promoter for each procurement are to buy:

- Cheap, standard and quick, or
- Bespoke, tailor-made, value for money or expensive, or
- Cheap, standard and slow.

The result of a contract is commitment by project but between organizations which have other projects in hand or in prospect. Most these organizations should be project-minded, particularly the designers and contractors whose work is projects. But these are multi-project businesses, as are the suppliers of materials and other services. They want a balanced flow of work, which means work over a continuing series of projects which they get only by commitment to projects for different customers each wanting first call on the supplier's resources. All these businesses thus need their own strategies for survival, success and growth through change and management by projects – as already argued in Chapter 1.

The promoter of a project should therefore plan whether to obtain the services and goods needed from one or many organizations, and whether in parallel or in series or both. In other words to choose a contract strategy for each project depending on its objectives and risks.

2.6.2 Procurement chains

Traditionally the procurement of projects has been based on employing equipment suppliers, engineering consultants and prime contractors with many sub-contractors and suppliers in an extensive procurement chain. All these are specialists in what has to be procured. No-one traditionally

---

[3] As reviewed in Support Tools and Techniques Chapter 3 *CONTRACTS*.
[4] See also Support Tools and Techniques Chapter 3 *SPECIFICATIONS*.

managed the whole project. Only a contractor who manages a 'turnkey' contract gets experience of delivering a complete facility fit for use.

The resulting separation of responsibilities in traditional procurement and the concern for control of payments has tended to lead to disputes and delays of no value to any party. Losses of production or services due to delay in being able to start to use a new factory, office or system can be much more costly than the differences between the prices bid by one supplier and another. Contract practice and attitudes have not linked the interests of stakeholders and suppliers. Many promoters of projects have employed contract and legal experts to control procurement as a separate function, rather than to be part of teams for planning and managing projects as a contribution to the core business. As a result of this separation of roles, good advice and experience is not well used, often because applied after it could have been used to avoid problems. Functional expertise and project needs should be partners in choosing the contract strategy which should best achieve each project's objectives.

Attitudes towards contracts for public construction and other projects in many countries have reflected political emphasis on employing the cheapest consultants and contractors and on terms of contract which specify detailed control of payment to contractors and suppliers. These attitudes are changing. Buying cheap and courting claims for extra payment do not produce successful projects. Public and private stakeholders in industrial countries now expect the promoters of their projects to achieve whole life value from investment in a project. In the last 25 years in the US and UK, the concepts of Partnering and Alliancing – as in the previous case study – have been developed for customer and supplier to work together to deliver a project, and governments are increasingly developing Public–Private partnerships with businesses to design–build–operate public services. All these indicate recognition that procurement should be only a means to an end and that the objectives of the project require sustaining through to completion of all the partners' liabilities.

2.6.3 Procurement risks

Cost and delivery risks in a project can be predominantly placed with the contractor. Public and private promoters are increasingly expecting contractors to finance projects.

Contractors reduce their cost risks by:

- Letting most and perhaps all the work to sub-contractors.
- Joint ventures.

It is up to promoters to enter into contracts that ensure that sub-contractors and suppliers remain liable for satisfactory delivery.

The following case illustrates actions by a contractor to enter a new market while continuing mainly with an established business.

2.6.4 Project procurement case – a supplier's business

Big Steel Ltd are one of several long-established companies in the UK who bid for contracts to design and supply steel structures for buildings and other large projects. They are usually employed as sub-contractors to general civil engineering companies, but recently they have enjoyed a distinct success in undertaking a large and novel structure in steel and new materials.

Most of their competitors have now been acquired by general contractors. Big Steel decided on a 5-year strategy to move themselves into contracting to undertake complete projects which will include large or novel structures. They decided in this new business to develop, make and offer to erect on hire temporary stadia for major social and athletics events. To acquire know-how in selling such services, Big Steel bought two smaller companies which had specialized in scaffolding and in marquee erection for large events. The company was now four businesses. The structural sub-contracting, scaffolding and marquee businesses each continued in its own market. Undertaking complete projects was a new business that was intended to draw on the expertise of the others. For this new business Big Steel set up a wholly owned company Total Steel.

Big Steel moved the CEO of the marquee company to be CEO of Total Steel. When Total Steel obtained its first contract to supply a complete stadium it in turn placed an internal order for the main work on the established Big Steel structural business and also internal orders on the acquired small companies for services for erecting the structure. This contract for a complete stadium was from a new customer, not a previous Big Steel customer.

Part way through its work for the stadium contract a regular customer sent direct to Big Steel an order for a large amount of work. Big Steel's Works Director gave the work for this order priority. Total Steel's CEO heard about this from a Big Steel Production Engineer. With her he established that it would delay completion of the stadium parts well beyond critical dates and therefore run the risk of losing money under the liquidated damages term of the contract.

The Total Steel CEO took the problem to the Big Steel Operations Director, on the basis that Big Steel was his sub-contractor. The Operations

Director answered that we are all the same company and that Total Steel was only a service to help bring work into the factory.

2.6.5 Lessons from the suppliers' business case

The trading roles and commitments between Total Steel and the established Big Steel business had to be established systematically. The company had three options:

1. Total Steel to be an agent of Big Steel, there to bring in work at times and prices agreed by Big Steel. In this arrangement Total Steel would be a cost centre, not a separate profit centre.
2. Total Steel and Big Steel to be separate contractors. Total Steel would be free to negotiate contracts with customers and then negotiate with Big Steel. In this arrangement both Total Steel and Big Steel would be profit centres.
3. Total Steel to be the only contracting arm and employ the rest of the company. In this arrangement Total Steel would be the only profit centre. The rest of the company would be cost centres.

The first option would limit the freedom of Total Steel to enter new markets. The third option would stop Big Steel continuing to trade directly with well-established customers.

The second option was chosen. It required all parts of the company to accept that to be competitive in its market Total Steel would have to be free to ask Big Steel to bid for work in competition with other companies in the industry.

In making this choice the company stated that they required Big Steel and Total Steel to use internal 'contracts' to define commitments to each other for every work-package, but they expected all staff of the two organisations to establish good relationships and cooperate to anticipate problems as was already practiced in Big Steel in their relationships with outside customers. In other words, whether they were departments within a company or were formally wholly owned companies, commitments between them for each work-package should be defined as if contractual but communications should be open and constructive.

Following this decision the company formed a working party of middle-level staff from all four businesses to design a knowledge management system to enable all to gain from sharing contacts, market information, specialist expertise and common lessons. A change programme was also needed to establish a new culture of communications and commitments.

2.7 Implementation of projects

2.7.1 Organization of resources

The number of people working on a project rises rapidly for its implementation. Within the suppliers and often also the promoter's organization a project may be one of several sharing resources. If so, a matrix system of organization is commonly used to allocate resources among the projects while maintaining expertise of specialists in the various functions, as discussed in later chapters. In these arrangements the Project Managers are rarely the line managers responsible for the quality and longer-term development of the resources. Their minimum role is coordination, but this demands skills and support in leadership to direct all resources towards achieving the objectives of their project.

Traditional management of projects grew from experience of the need for attention to the delivery and cost of what has to be procured. Now successful projects are recognised as demanding thorough attention to project definition, risks and relationships up-front and through a project. Projects one by one are transient and make discontinuous use of resources. Continuous improvement therefore demands corporate attention. In this way a project can be the hidden vehicle for a longer-term change, for instance to strengthen the role of project management, as illustrated in the following case.

2.7.2 Project implementation case – joint venture and consortium

A joint venture 'ES' was formed by two manufacturing companies, Company E experienced in electrical and control systems, Company S in factory services. Their objective in the joint venture was to work together when needed to be able to undertake to design and supply complete power plants. Company E's additional objective was to take the opportunity to gain experience of undertaking 'turnkey' contracts and then consider acquiring Company S or a similar company so as to become a turnkey contractor in the power market.

The two companies' staff working full-time in the joint venture were re-located to be together in one building. Their staff working on other projects continued in the two companies as before.

The joint venture's research, development and bidding costs were shared 60:40 between the two companies. Bids by the joint venture to offer to prospective customers to undertake a project were presented by company E as the lead contractor, with company S named as sub-contractor. When a bid led to a contract, relationships between E and S changed from being a joint venture. This change was not clear to staff in the two companies, particularly because they continued to share offices. Terms of sub-contract between E and S were drafted in order to define responsibilities, but when the joint venture received its first contract, several staff meetings were needed to resolve questions on how to continue to work as a single team.

The second turnkey contract ES obtained was to design and supply a complete power plant to another industrial country. One condition of the contract was that ES would use local suppliers in that country as much as possible. ES therefore agreed with a set of the local appropriate suppliers that they would form a local consortium which would be the sub-contractor undertaking all the work for the project in their country.

The responsibility for the second project within the joint venture was the task of the Project Manager in company E. Within that company the project competed with the first project for technical and commercial manpower, especially those required to define the scope and terms of the sub-contract packages and to agree and supervise procurement through company S. Detailed dates for technical and contractual information had to be agreed with all the suppliers in both countries. Neither company E nor company S had previous experience of such complex requirements. The Project Manager concluded that his team should take the lead in the planning needed for all parties' resources. Because this was unusual the Project Manager proposed that the two companies should form a steering committee consisting of all their line managers which would be the joint authority for committing resources to all their projects. Problems of resources were already being experienced on the joint venture's first contract. This persuaded the two companies to establish the steering committee.

Formally the local consortium was sub-contractor to the company E, the main contractor. For other projects in their country the local companies in the consortium had direct trading links with the customer. Communications between the local companies and company E, and between the customer and company E therefore tended to leak to the other parties. This disturbed company E's managers. In fact it aided the project. Contract commitments were honoured without problems leading to disputes because all parties were aware informally of each others' plans, progress and problems.

As a result of the success of the project, company E decided that they would appoint a Director of Development who would chair a permanent steering group of line and project managers to plan and commit resources to all future work. The company's system of organization was thus changed to what is known as a 'strong' matrix.[5]

2.7.3 Lessons from the joint venture and consortium case

The joint venture was appropriate for the two companies as a means of working together to develop new technology and integrated project proposals that would attract new business. The transition at bidding for a contract for one of the companies to be the main contractor and the other a sub-contractor kept the contract structure simple and clear for the two companies and for the customer. It was confusing to employees of the two companies until explained to them in a series of briefing meetings followed by the establishment of detailed terms of sub-contract between the companies.

The steering committee function formalised how decisions should be made to plan resources and commit them to projects. In the process it achieved a change of culture in company E to accept that Project Managers were the company's profit earners and that functional departments were cost centres there to provide the resources needed to attract and deliver projects. Undertaking a second project provided a useful opportunity for company E to move towards the managing by projects concept.

The consortium of local suppliers for the second project was a success because of its members' longer-term interest in satisfying the customer. In the operation of the consortium, past relationships and longer term interests between the local suppliers and the customer resulted in leaks of their communications with the middle man – the main contractor. This unusual experience for companies E and S was in fact of benefit to them and all parties in avoiding or resolving problems on the project. The contracts between them were valuable in defining their responsibilities for the project. The results were successful for the project and the companies because of good communications and shared wider interests.

Companies E and S were later merged, together with others, as is often the trend after joint ventures between contractors who have been competing in developed markets.

2.8 Handover and post-completion lessons

2.8.1 Completion planning

Reviews of completed projects often include the recommendation that the potential users and their staff who have the experience of starting up,

---

[5] See also Support Tools and Techniques Chapter 5 *ORGANIZATIONS*

operating and maintaining previous projects should at least be consulted in the first discussions on new projects. A frequent lesson from experience is that how a project will end should be planned from the start, at least to define responsibilities and priorities on how it will be tested and handed over. But under pressure to make quick decisions and limit costs this recommendation often remains a good intention to apply next time.

Decisions at the start of a project thus tend to be concentrated on the immediate choices and problems, for instance the task of defining the scope and design concepts of the project. The result may be lack of sufficiently early attention to effects on the completion and hand-over of a project, resulting in delay because of problems which might have been foreseen, as was the risk in the following case.

2.8.2 Hand-over and post completion case – systems replacement

Nobody in the company really wanted to replace the data processing systems, at least not yet. They had to be replaced because of age and to respond to one customer's standards. A time limit had been set by that customer. The company operated two identical parallel data processing systems. One was normally dedicated to a special customer's work, for security. The other served all other customers, but in an emergency work could be alternated between the two systems.

The replacement project was planned by a project team consisting of the Marketing Manager, Systems Manager, Office Manager, Buyer, Services Engineer and Maintenance Supervisor. The replacement work was expected to take 4 months per system. In planning the project the project team considered whether to replace both at once or in turn. The advantages and risks foreseen of these two choices were:

- Replacing both at once should limit the period of interruption of normal work, concentrate attention on the project, make more economic use of the system supplier's resources and reduce the risk of over-running the time limit.
- Replacing the systems in turn would enable all services to continue, though with some restrictions, and all concerned could apply lessons and resources from the first to the second.

They chose to replace the two systems in turn, and to sub-contract ('put out') some of the non-security work if necessary during the project.

The Buyer then invited the supplier of the existing systems to meet the project team to discuss being appointed to supply and install the replacements. The supplier stated that a new system already in use in their own business would be suitable, and that they would commit themselves to completion for the company on time in order to use this success to attract future customers. On this basis the project team agreed to proceed.

The project team met the supplier's representatives again as and when questions or changes arose, and then arranged to meet the supplier every two weeks to see the supplier's plans, review progress and resolve any uncertainties and problems. The company's project team met together only for these meetings with the supplier, including when discussing contract matters such as whether to allow the supplier an extension of the completion date for the first system because of changes requested by the company. In the event the first system was late but the second completed by the original date set. Greater delay to full operation was caused by the company's staff not being released from current work to learn how to use the new system, but this was reduced by the supplier lending staff to the company. The supplier was paid additional amounts for this and the costs of the changes. The new systems operated satisfactorily but were not effective for several weeks because of the lack of trained company staff.

2.8.3 Lessons from the systems replacement case

The company's project team involved the managers with operating and maintenance experience from the start. Their attention was therefore concentrated on the relationship between the project and operations but they failed to anticipate the need to train their staff on the new systems.

The project team agreed to the supplier's proposal to buy a system already in use. They were perhaps reluctant to ask for a totally new system tailor-made for them because of the pressure of time. A few changes were made, but these caused only an intermediate delay to completion of all the work. The results were technically satisfactory.

For both parties this was an important project, in our Category 2, so all were dedicated to delivering it. The future users were represented from the start of the project, but the company's project team did not appoint a Project Manager, and the supplier's representatives attended all their meetings including discussions about the contract with the supplier. The project was thus run quite informally. The company's lack of project and commercial experience was compensated by the contractor's expertise and wish to deliver a model project. The project was supplier-driven, successfully, but the company learnt little about managing future projects.

2.9 The project process – conclusions

Projects are transient work but they are the essential foundation of businesses and public services. Individuals are employed on them project by project. Corporate action is needed to learn lessons from them and apply the lessons to future projects.

The project life-cycle of decisions and actions provides the common basis for us to apply the best of experience and ideas from all projects to others. As illustrated in Fig. 2.2, projects of any sort proceed from first ideas on the demand leading to the first concept of the project, feasibility studies to decide the economic worth or other justification for launching it, progressively more detailed technical and planning decisions, orders for the procurement of resources, implementation, acceptance and so into use. The stages are similar in nature whether the project is grand and novel, or small rebuild or upgrading work.

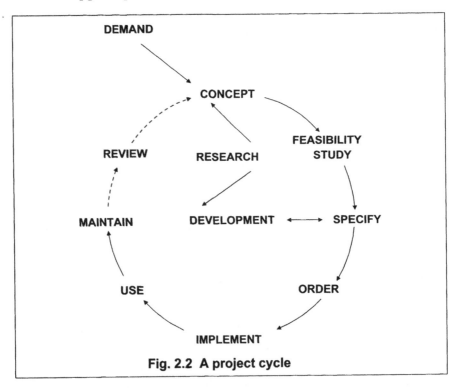

Fig. 2.2 A project cycle

Each stage in the cycle has a distinct objective. It should be planned and managed to achieve that objective. Success depends upon meeting the needs of the investors, users, suppliers and other stakeholders. Projects depend upon the commitment of resources, used with drive and leadership based upon good information. Their progress should be reviewed through each stage and in terms of earned value. The risks need managing by someone who has the authority to decide how to use resources to deliver maximum value. Changes should be controlled on the basis of how certainly they improve the achievement of objectives.

The cases were typical in that the projects involved only temporary and perhaps never repeated relationships between investors, users and suppliers. Contracts are too much expected to be the only link needed between all parties. Terms of contract can be used which motivate all parties to shared success, but the whole project process should be planned and managed in a strategy which recognises all parties' wider interests and cultures.

The cases also illustrated problems of achieving teamwork between all parties to a project within a company. Because the needs of a project are transitory the principles of contractual commitment can be applied within a company to work to be done as a service by one department to another. By this practice who is to be responsible for delivering the performance required from every work-package should be agreed.

Some of stages in the project process can be merged when the risks and size are minor, for instance repeat projects, or if the project is truly urgent. If the risks are great some stages may have to be repeated. For instance, the decision to launch a project may have to be reviewed later if problems arise in implementation or if the market demand for the product changes. Thus the speed of the work stage by stage can vary, depending on complexity, novelty or the relative importance of quality, time and cost, but all projects have a similar life-cycle and thus logical principles and experience of previous projects can be applied to the management of every new project – as discussed in Chapter 3.

For Chapter 3 go to page 125

Further reading

Association for Project Management, *Project Management Body of Knowledge*, 3rd edition, 2000.

Association for Project Management, *Standard Terms for the Appointment of a Project Manager,* 1998.

Barnes, N. M. L. and **Wearne, S. H.** The future for major project management, *Int. J. Project Mgmt.,* 1993, v **11** , (3), 135–142.

Dieter, G. E. *Engineering Design: A Materials and Processing Approach!,* 2000 (McGraw Hill).

Morris, P. W. G. *The Management of Projects,* 1997 (Thomas Telford).

Morris, P. W. G., **Patel, M.** and **Wearne, S. H.** Research into revising the APM project management Body of Knowledge, *Int. J. Project Mgmt,* 2000 **18**, (3), June 2000, 155–164.

2

The Professional Project Management Body of Knowledge

A survey of people in UK industry and public services showed that there is a core of knowledge and skill required for managing any project.[1] This skill and knowledge is increasingly important today as a core competence for all managers to manage the projects and the many internal changes required in companies to survive and succeed against competition.

SM2.1 Professional competence

The data obtained in the survey produced a new basis for the Association for Project Management (APM)[2] to re-define their 'Body of Knowledge' (BoK) for the management of projects. The APM BoK defines the topics in which APM considers professionals should be knowledgeable in order to be competent. The BoK is the document that the APM uses as the normative document governing its examinations, certification and accreditation. The BoK provides a basis for assessing competence in the management of projects and for benchmarking best practice and performance.

A professional is someone who is considered by society as being competent to practice without supervision. To do so, he or she needs to:

- Understand the relevant body of knowledge.
- Have appropriate experience.
- Be appropriately certificated/licensed to practice competently.

---

[1] The survey was sponsored by the APM and six companies, and carried out by the UMIST (University of Manchester Institute of Science & Technology) Centre for Research in the Management of Projects (CRMP) led by Professor Peter Morris.

[2] The APM is the second largest professional project management body in the world, currently with over 12,000 members, and is the UK member of the International Project Management Association.

- Maintain a programme of continuing professional development and education.
- Subscribe to the code of ethics of the profession.

The Body of Knowledge as a criterion of professional competence is thus crucial.

SM2.2 The survey

The aim of questioning people in industry and public services was to:

- Identify the topics that project management professionals – practitioners, educators and others – consider need to be known and understood by anyone claiming to be competent in the management of projects.
- Define what is meant by those topics at a generically useful level.
- Update the body of literature that supports these topic areas.

In general the research showed that:

- The amount of difference in definition and usage of topics was less than anticipated.
- Broad acceptance of terms used is emerging.
- Different industries or supply chains tend to concentrate on different parts of the BoK.
- Most people accept that project management covers the total project life-cycle – including the vital front-end definition and the back-end hand-over and evaluation of the completed project.
- It is extremely difficult to find authoritative guides to many of the topics, and indeed to the BoK as a whole.

Most of the people in project management who were questioned in the survey stated that they believed that there is a generic discipline that is core to the practice of the management of projects across a very wide range of industries and applications, and that as a result it is worth trying to define what this core is.

Figure SM2.1 shows the scope of the revised body of knowledge published by the APM in 2000, which was derived from the survey. The topics fall into seven sections:

- The first section deals with a number of *General* and introductory items.

The remaining six sections deal with topics to do with managing:

- The project's *Strategic* framework, including its basic objectives.
- The *Control* issues that should be employed.

- The project's *Technical* demands for team competence.
- The *Commercial* features of its proposed implementation.
- The *Organization* structure that should fit the above.
- Issues to do with managing the *People* that will work on a project.

Underlying all these topics there has to be awareness and understanding of a project life-cycle, a process basis to the BoK, as shown in Fig. SM 2.1.

SM2.3 Best practice

One question discussed in setting out a BoK was should the APM follow or be prepared to lead in describing good practice?

In several instances in fact the research team and steering group took a lead in defining what they understood are best practices models of project management, using the research data to guide writing the new BoK, but not to dictate it. References to standards, and to documents issued by other professional bodies are a particularly important case. ISO type documents are important because of their perceived authority and general pervasiveness. Yet they do not necessarily reflect perfect practice.

2.4 Scope of BoK topics

In defining the topics in the BoK there are challenges in the use of some words. Should 'Requirements' be used, 'Briefing' or 'Specification', for example? In the new APM BoK definitions are therefore given for each topic.

To be generic to meet the needs of all kinds of businesses and industries we believe that the APM BoK definitions need to be interpreted broadly and should be extended to cover:

Strategy – include the Strategic Role of a Project, for a customer or supplier.
Project Management Plan – include Design of the Process Delivery System.
Work Content – include the Specification, Front-End definition of a project.
Design – include Design for Implementation of the Project.
Design, Modelling – include Prototype Product or Service.
Make, Build and Test – include Assemble.
Hand-over – include Supply, Deliver.

SM2.5 Conclusions

P. W. G. Morris in reporting on the research and new BoK comments that traditionally project management has been seen largely about completing a

APM Project Management Body of Knowledge

1 General

10 Project Management
11 Programme Management
12 Project Context

Strategic

20 Project Success Criteria
21 Strategy/Project Management Plan
22 Value Management
23 Risk Management
24 Quality Management
25 Health, Safety and Environment

3 Control

30 Work Content and Scope Management
31 Time Scheduling/Phasing
32 Resource Management
33 Budgeting and Cost Management
34 Change Control
35 Earned Value Management
36 Information Management

4 Technical

40 Design, Implementation and Hand-Over Management
41 Requirements Management
42 Estimating
43 Technology Management
44 Value Engineering
45 Modelling and Testing
46 Configuration Management

5 Commercial

50 Business Case
51 Marketing and Sales
52 Financial Management
53 Procurement
54 Legal Awareness

6 Organisational

60 Life Cycle Design and Management
61 Opportunity
62 Design and Development
63 Implementation
64 Hand-Over
65 (Post) Project Evaluation Review [O&M/ILS]
66 Organisation Structure
67 Organisation Roles

7 People

70 Communication
71 Teamwork
72 Leadership
73 Conflict Management
74 Negotiation
75 Personnel Management

Opportunity Identification	Design and Development	Implementation	Hand-over	Post-Project Evaluation
Concept/Marketing Feasibility Bid	Design, Modelling and Procurement	Make, Build and Test	Test, Commission, Start-up	Operation and Maintenance/Integrated Logistics

task 'on time, in budget, to scope'. This traditional view is understandable and reflects the task implementation purpose of project management. In order to accomplish projects on time, in budget and to scope you need to manage scope, schedule, cost, risk, etc. Defining the scope, cost and time targets should be a means to ensuring that the technical, commercial, business, environmental, and other factors are effectively aligned with organizational and control issues to ensure an optimum outcome. Morris comments that to many practitioners and observers, this view is not all that is needed for many projects. The factors that cause projects to fail or to succeed certainly include the traditional ones of inadequate planning and monitoring tools, teamwork, etc., but also include technical, commercial, external and environmental issues, and the way the initial requirements of the project are established, what in some industries is called the 'Front End'. As a result, the APM BoK is now broader than the previous two editions.

The BoK is important because it is one of the few general documents that gives a genuine cross-industry, authoritative view of what a professional in the management of projects should be expected to know. But a BoK should never be totally frozen. Practice changes. The BoK should be updated periodically.

Big shot in the foot

Problem

The Airport Chief Executive's PA phoned all of us for an immediate meeting on hearing that after two year's development the new processing unit for the central catering system had failed its acceptance test.

On the way I wondered what had failed, and thought as Project Manager what we might be able to do to minimize consequential delay to the whole project. I was fifth to arrive at the meeting, still before the Passenger Services Director, Technical Director, Quality Manager and several others. The Commercial Director had started to set out a twin strategy to pursue the supplier to move heaven and earth to rectify the problem with the unit while at the same time ensure that they remained contractually liable for our consequential losses. The Chief Executive suggested shifting the work to one of the specialist sub-contractors. The Quality Manager questioned whether that firm had TQM certification for all the work that might be needed, but he could go there that afternoon to start to re-assess them.

During this discussion the Food Technician arrived. His apology was cut short by the Chief Executive stating that he wanted a top-level working party appointed to start that afternoon to assess all the options. The Food Technician dared speak again to say that he was late for the meeting because he had phoned the Inspectors for detail of the failure. They stated that the unit had not failed the test. Not believing the results they had checked the instrumentation. They had repeated the test overnight. The unit had passed the test, without question.

Principles

- The Project Office should be seen and used as the centre of project information.
- The Project Manager should take the lead in assessing a problem, in analysing the facts and in calling meetings to define actions.
- Check facts.
- Listen to all knowledgeable individuals.

Lesson

- Don't lose face by jumping off your high horse in mid-stream.

Support Tools and Techniques Section 2

Design for Implementation

All business projects involve the design of a product, service, process, system or operation. Design must be followed by implementation. A product, system, service or process, in general, can only be said to be well designed if it is easy to implement. This principle applies equally to engineering companies as well as public services, for example the handling of passengers at airports. A poorly-designed airport passenger handling system will lead to higher costs as well as frustrated customers and employees. Supermarkets design their checkouts to minimise the time taken to process the purchases made by individual customers as well as to reduce the checkout operator idle time. Automotive assembly lines and the associated supply chains are designed to maximise the production rates, minimise non-value-adding activities including the stock levels, thereby minimising costs.

During the last three decades, a number of approaches have been developed by engineering companies to help with the product design process. These include:

- Design for manufacture.
- Design for assembly.
- Design for maintenance.
- Design for use.
- Design to target cost.
- Design for reuse.

The basic principles associated with these approaches are equally applicable to the design of systems, services and processes. Clearly the design process will vary, depending upon the type of project. In all cases, the design process can be improved by following some very simple principles.

TT2.1 Design for Manufacture and Assembly (DFMA)

The first two of the above listed approaches, namely design for manufacture and design for assembly are often combined to form the 'Design for Manufacture and Assembly' (DFMA) approach. It is used to analyse a product design, at an early stage, for its ease of manufacture and assembly. For maximum benefit, it is essential to use this approach at the concept design stage since this is the only stage at which the design can be influenced without incurring significant additional costs. In a wider context, for example the design of processes, systems and services, the design for manufacture and assembly can be translated into a design for implementation dimension. Design for implementation requires the product, system, process or service designers to think about the consequences of their design on its realisation.

TT2.2 Design for maintenance

All products, systems and processes have to be maintained over a period of time. It is essential that the maintenance issues be considered at the design stage. A system or product, which is configured using a number of modules, will simplify the maintenance process. A related issue is the ease of access to the module. A modular approach to system or product design will make it possible to take out the faulty module and replace it quickly with a fully functional module. This will reduce the downtime, which can be of crucial importance in many circumstances. The faulty modules can be repaired and reused.

TT2.3 Design for use

Many products, systems and services are designed without giving adequate consideration to usability. Many product manuals are very difficult to understand because technical specialists have written them. As another example, in an effort to reduce their costs, many banks have turned to call centres. There are some excellent examples of call centre services that have many satisfied customers. Equally there are numerous examples of poorly-designed call centre services with many frustrated customers. Frequently, the fault does not lie with the individuals manning the call centres. The main problem is with the design concepts used and inadequate consideration of the usability aspects. Computer software provides another example where the usability aspect can be crucial. The jobs of many individuals involve constant interaction with a computer. The use of computer program A that saves the user an average of 5 minutes per hour, compared with program B, because of its ease of use, will save the equivalent of one month's salary every year.

TT2.4 Design to target cost

In a highly competitive and quality conscious market-place, cost leadership is a major issue for many organizations. It is essential to consider, early in the design process, the life-cycle cost of the product or service. A basic principle that must be followed in all cases is to design a maximum amount of cost out of a product or service in the first place. The design to target cost technique involves an identification of the price that the customers are willing to pay for a product or service. This can then be used to determine the target cost, taking into account the expected profit margins. The establishment of a target cost must not be used to compromise the performance targets. The difficult challenge is achieving the required performance at a cost that will leave a good profit margin. This will require a multi-disciplinary approach and an iterative process. In real life, it is hardly ever possible to achieve the target cost the first time round. Targets will need to be set for each of the major cost elements and kept under constant review.

TT2.5 Design for reuse

The cost of many products, systems or services can be reduced significantly by a modular design approach. The same module can be used in a number of products or systems thereby spreading costs. Many complex software systems are built up from a number of modules that are used in more than one application. Another example is the use of the modular approach in universities. Increasingly, the same module is used to teach students on a number of degree programmes. Successful application of this approach requires that the modules be carefully designed so that the modules meet the real requirements of students on different degree programmes.

TT2.6 Summary

Design is an essential aspect of all business projects. Careful consideration of the implementation, usability, maintenance, target costs and reusability issues, early in the design process, should lead to better value and lower costs without compromising the performance standards.

Further reading

Association for Project Management, *Project Management Body of Knowledge*, 3rd edition, 2000.

Association for Project Management, *Standard Terms for the Appointment of a Project Manager,* 1998.

Barnes, N. M. L. and **Wearne, S. H.** The future for major project management, *Int. J. Project Mgmt.,* 1993, v **11** , (3), 135–142.

Dieter, G. E. *Engineering Design: A Materials and Processing Approach!,* 2000 (McGraw Hill).

Morris, P. W. G. *The Management of Projects,* 1997 (Thomas Telford).

Morris, P. W. G., **Patel, M.** and **Wearne, S. H.** Research into revising the APM project management Body of Knowledge, *Int. J. Project Mgmt,* 2000 **18**, (3), June 2000, 155–164.

But it's always late

(With acknowledgements to Mr John Finegan)

Problem

A project management graduate was assigned the production of a new product as his first project with the company.

During the project he was asked for weekly updates on its progress. In his weekly reports he confirmed that the project was on time, within budget and on target for product cost.

The first 600 units were produced as planned. There was silence at the other end of the phone when he reported to Sales & Marketing that these were in the warehouse. Sales & Marketing were not ready for the new product. 'You asked for them in September, and now you have got them! I have updated you every week, how can you not be ready?' 'We know that you told us that everything was on target, but we are always told that and things are always late so we built in a bit of spare time. We cannot move them until January.'

As a result £180,000 worth of finished goods sat in the warehouse for 3 months and further stock bought in to the programme lay in the factory gathering dust.

Principles

- Plan for either a just-in-time or a low risk performance. Make clear which when agreeing dates.
- Involve all parties in decisions, plans and progress.
- Develop an achieving culture.
- Use a project as a means of changing a culture, but it has to be designed to do so.

Lesson

- Culture dominates commitments.

Reader's Guide

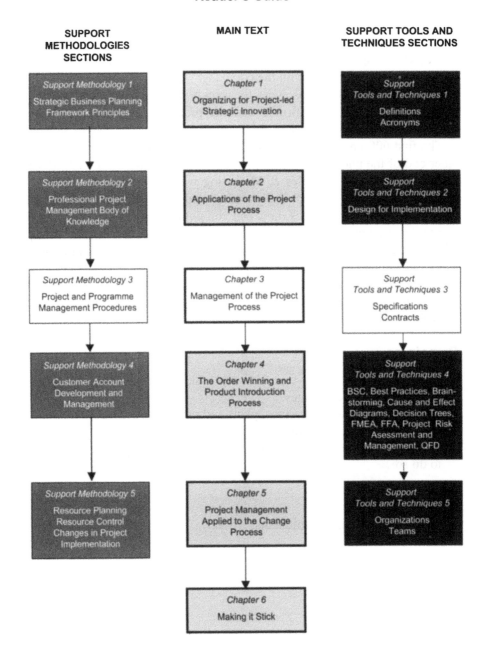

SUPPORT METHODOLOGIES SECTIONS

Support Methodology 1
Strategic Business Planning Framework Principles

Support Methodology 2
Professional Project Management Body of Knowledge

Support Methodology 3
Project and Programme Management Procedures

Support Methodology 4
Customer Account Development and Management

Support Methodology 5
Resource Planning
Resource Control
Changes in Project Implementation

MAIN TEXT

Chapter 1
Organizing for Project-led Strategic Innovation

Chapter 2
Applications of the Project Process

Chapter 3
Management of the Project Process

Chapter 4
The Order Winning and Product Introduction Process

Chapter 5
Project Management Applied to the Change Process

Chapter 6
Making it Stick

SUPPORT TOOLS AND TECHNIQUES SECTIONS

Support Tools and Techniques 1
Definitions
Acronyms

Support Tools and Techniques 2
Design for Implementation

Support Tools and Techniques 3
Specifications
Contracts

Support Tools and Techniques 4
BSC, Best Practices, Brainstorming, Cause and Effect Diagrams, Decision Trees, FMEA, FFA, Project Risk Asessment and Management, QFD

Support Tools and Techniques 5
Organizations
Teams

Management of The Project Process 3

The project process is a particular case of a generalised framework for operating specific product development and enterprise change/development business processes.

3.1 General features of the business process system concept

The systems view of a business is relatively modern. In the systems view a set of well-designed and integrated core organizational processes, supported by relevant technologies, systematically deliver their outputs and collectively deliver the business strategy and objectives. Table 3.1 provides definitions of a system and a business process.

The most successful early application of the systems engineering approach for the creation of a highly effective and competitive organization was the Toyota Production System developed from the 1950s to the 1970s. This highly intelligent Toyota approach led to very rapid growth of its automotive sales and to world domination. *Consequently, the idea of building organizational teams around core processes has gained ground in all areas of industry, with considerable beneficial innovation completed or in progress in many companies.*

The concept of a balanced flow process with integrated controls is well established in the education of control systems engineers, chemical engineers and metallurgists. For many years in the chemical and pharmaceuticals industries, processes were carried out in a series of specialist functional steps or stages. As each stage completed its specialized work, the batch of material was stored as work in progress and then transferred to the next stage for a further quantum of a different specialized element of work to be done. This approach suffered from a number of disadvantages.

1. Very considerable handling and movement of the work, often over long distances from stage to stage.

2. High inventory of work in progress at each functional stage awaiting progressing. Low visibility of the location of the work and its stage of completion. Difficult to manage. No overall control responsibility.
3. Variable quality of work done from batch to batch for different orders resulting in the risk of considerable scrap or re-work. This prevents a right-first-time capability being achieved.

Table 3.1 Definitions of a system and a business process

A system
- A system is an integrated combination of elements designed and combined to follow a common purpose.
- Systems engineering takes a total view. Two levels are involved: (a) the macro level concerned with the design and control of a business organization; (b) the micro level concerned with the design of a set of standard working routines for a team.
- Applies pragmatically the principles of control systems engineering.

A business process
- A business process consists of a seamlessly linked and integrated natural group of skills and competencies and has clear interfaces with other processes.
- Starting from a set of customer requirements it delivers a high quality product or service to a competitive target cost in a competitive lead-time – its product or service is as required to meet the needs of an internal customer or an external customer.
- A business process has a set of inputs and it processes these in an integrated way to add value and produce a completed identifiable set of outputs.
- A business process is identified by a process flow-chart listing the sequence of value-adding activities or functions which make it up and which cut horizontally across a traditional vertical functional organization.
- A business process is managed as an entity via a natural group team and a clear set of control mechanisms and measures of performance.
- A maximum of five fundamental tasks or job roles are needed to operate a business process:
  1. Leading
  2. Controlling
  3. Skilled value-adding
  4. Materials and information moving
  5. Facilities maintenance and support

The chemical and pharmaceutical industries introduced continuous flow processes for their manufacturing operations many years ago. In these processes the material is worked on continuously with all stages collected together, interfaced in sequence, and fully integrated and controlled. This has the considerable benefit of shorter lead-times, much lower quantities of work in process, and consistently controlled high quality.

The business process concept extends the chemical process concept into office-based processes and other non-manufacturing areas where a series of stages or specialized functional activities are integrated under the total control of a dedicated cross-functional or cross-discipline team. Similar large benefits are achievable, plus the additional cultural, motivational and productivity benefits resulting from the clear ownership and responsibility of the team for the whole process operation and its performance. The problems encountered at departmental boundaries are eliminated. All business processes have generic features in common. These are:

- They can be represented for design and operational control purposes by work flow and information flow-charts through the chain of functional skills required for their operation.
- They have a range of inputs and produce outputs or deliverables to meet specifications of their particular customer need.
- They require, as an input, detailed specifications for the required deliverables to meet their customer needs.
- They require embedded distributed information collection and controls for their management.
- They require standardized working procedures to achieve consistent productivity and quality of performance.
- They are operated by teams of people with the natural group of skills required to meet the application specific role of each process.

Teams can be formed, in general, to operate two categories of process:

1. Short-term single-cycle processes, e.g. a project.
2. Steady state long-term continuous operational processes, e.g. the service delivery operations process or the cash management process in a company.

Both of these exhibit generic features of processes even though the application areas may differ from company to company and industry to industry. Category 1 encompasses project processes, where a problem is required to be solved once for the first time, e.g. the design of a new product or service to meet a requirements specification. Other examples would be:

- A task-force project with a short life set up to analyse and redesign a part of the operations of a business with a view to simplifying it and reducing the amount of inefficiency or non-valued activity in the operation. This would be called a business process effectiveness improvement project. Once completed, the new process design and the standard operational working methodologies would be operated by a new trained team as a steady state operations process on a continuous basis.

- A project team to install a new software package in a multi-site retail products distribution company. The software will provide access to the stock lists for all warehouses in a single standard format and facilitate on-line update when items are sold or new batches are received for stock. This project would flow-chart the warehouse material and information flow processes, specify the control requirements, install and test the software, populate the stock database, train the operating staff, hand over to the Operations Manager and his team. It would then cease, i.e. the project is a one-off or single-cycle activity. The Operations Manager and his team would then continue with steady state operation following standard working procedures supported by continuous improvement for the life of the package.

3.2 Structure, people and culture

In general, innovation projects can be categorized in two groups for convenience in planning.

Group 1 Research, design and development projects to create a new product or service and concurrently design and implement the new or modified manufacturing or delivery process for these.

Group 2 Change projects to redesign business processes, practices, and methods so as to eliminate wasteful or inefficient practices, improve business effectiveness and enhance performance of the employees.

Sets of projects in each category are called programmes, i.e. Development Programmes for products or services, and Change Programmes for business competitiveness improvement to meet or exceed world-class bench-mark targets.

A project process and its team organization can only be defined and organized in detail once the type of project is clear, and the application focus is defined. Case Example 2 in Chapter 1 (Section 1.13) illustrates this. The particular disciplines, procedures, practices and controls of project management on their own do not constitute a process, instead they represent a methodology or support infrastructure used to support a particular project process. Innovative companies have generally found that it is very important for maximum effectiveness to define a set of standard working procedures and control information charts to support their project management procedures. This creates a common language across the company and allows a single, shared, low-cost support training course to be used by all personnel. It enables standardization on terminology and software for use on PCs and laptops networked for ease of rapid communication. Because many projects of both categories are very complex, such a standardisation simplifies the project operation, makes it more reliable and reduces costs. It also makes it familiar, quicker, and easier for management to understand information presented to them and to carry out reviews. The Support Methodology section for this chapter, presents a best practice standard. Specifications of the general project Body of Knowledge statement are detailed in the Support Methodology section for Chapter 2.

Many companies have not implemented a best practice design of a project management support infrastructure, and the result is usually confusion and a failure to deliver reliably to specification, time and cost. Setting up a change project to design, install, and train employees in the practices and use of the embedded procedures, and associated simple IT system, is one of the best investments an innovating company could make to provide a foundation for effective delivery of Group 1 and Group 2 project programmes.

A further important requirement is to take very seriously the competencies of project and programme management; to define these, select staff with the right personal qualities and skills, and to support them with personal development programmes.

Unlike routine operational processes, projects, due to their temporary nature, carrying out the particular set of activities and solving the particular problem for the first time, are very demanding and difficult because they literally embark into unknown territory. There is no beaten track to follow and no guarantee that the targets and specifications set are achievable. Large projects with many team members are very difficult to plan and manage for high productivity and minimum cost since often the team and its sub-contractors are working together for the first time and are working on problems which have not been solved before in the particular form, therefore there is a great deal of uncertainty. While the use of standard supporting tools, techniques and methodologies in which the teams have been trained will provide a major benefit by ensuring good order and tight control, there is still, nevertheless, a great deal of uncertainty. Because of this, the jobs of Programme Director and Project Manager are very tough roles. Unless the roles are properly defined and built into company structures as mainstream important jobs with a regular career route, it will be impossible to recruit top-class ambitious staff. Running a big programme or project with full responsibility for on time, target cost and specification delivery is like being the General Manager of a temporary complex development company, with full accountability for results.

Project Managers can feel vulnerable, due to the very demanding nature of the job with very tight time milestones to meet and very long working hours, sometimes relying heavily on the support of temporary contractors. In addition, at the end of the project they may not have a job to go to. Change Project or Programme Managers suffer from the additional hazard that they encounter considerable hostility from their colleagues in operational roles. This is because their work often results in reorganisation and restructuring of the company so that people are made redundant and others are moved into new roles. Therefore, the Change Project Manager and his team are often seen as a threat to the security of individuals at all levels from the very senior director to junior staff. As a consequence many blocks and political manoeuvres are used to prevent the Change Manager from doing his job. Experienced support from his boss to outmanoeuvre the in-house politicians is essential.

Poor quality companies often do not recognize the significant requirements of managing by projects. A common mistake made is to use a Project Manager merely as progress chaser for tasks allocated across a fragmented set of specialist function departments, each of which may have its own agenda and view of business requirements and reports through a separate organizational line.

Many problems and obstructions occur at department interfaces. Information flow is confused, fragmented and filtered at the interfaces between departments and levels in the organization. It is said that the efficiency of information transfer across these interfaces or levels is only 25% at each interface, i.e. only one-quarter gets through intact. This means that, with three layers for example, only $\frac{1}{4} \times \frac{1}{4} \times \frac{1}{4}$ of the information or 1.6% of the information fed into the first layer emerges from the third layer.

The performance inadequacies discussed previously in the analogy of the batch chemical process are also generic to such organizations, but aggravated considerably by the fact that the progress chaser type of Project Manager does not have line responsibility for the people involved, the budget and the quality of specification delivery. He may be given responsibility for meeting the completion date, but clearly, under the conditions described, this is totally unrealistic. Therefore, such organizations find it impossible to recruit top-class Project and Programme Managers and often resort to giving the job to young staff who do not have the experience or training necessary for such demanding roles.

Managing by projects requires the design of job roles and the modification of organizational methodologies and structures to facilitate this highly effective and high potential approach. Such changes necessitate the setting up of change project task-forces to redesign the organization and group teams of people around ordered business processes. This should occur in a stepwise manner as each natural process module of the organization is designed. It also requires a difficult and time consuming culture change to get people out of old habits, customs and procedures; this leads to two important requirements:

1. Education-led innovation, i.e. training the project task-forces in best practices and training the new process operation teams in new standard working procedures to suit the requirements of new organizational process team modules which are to be created for operation by the teams.
2. Creating new organizational structures aligned to the business processes and involving employee teams, after training, in the implementation of these structures, not relying on external consultants to do it. This ensures that ownership, as well as practical knowledge of the new practices, is held in-house. It also facilitates culture changes.

Meeting such requirements means that Chief Executives and their senior managements must themselves learn new skills and take an intelligent approach. They must be prepared to install a change management organization structure as the lever to deliver the necessary changes on a project-by-project basis involving the operational management and their staff, in targetting, reviewing, implementing and, subsequently, running the new structures. They also have to be trained to understand the methodologies of change project management and business process systems engineering.

A traditional functional department organization structure with its cross-boundary politics and interface communication inefficiencies inhibits the achievement of world-class business performance that is so necessary in order to compete in the modern global economy.

3.3 Features of projects processes

A professionally set up management by projects style of operation of a business with strong educated leadership, develops a can-do achievement culture. Using the typical competitiveness achievement plan framework described in Chapter 1, business objectives are clearly defined, benchmark targets are set, and problems to be solved are communicated by team briefings and workshops. The whole organization responds flexibly to each new challenge by forming well briefed and directed, temporary project teams of many types and sizes, from new product teams to service delivery teams, to Kaizen groups, for delivering results on time. Instead of making excuses for not delivering results, actually getting things done, identifying hazards to the project plan and implementing recovery plans becomes a way of life and a stimulating performance delivery culture results.

Because each team and its leader control the process they are responsible for, the responsibilities are clear and the roles of the participants are obvious. In addition, the good project management principles of writing clear specifications, holding weekly and monthly reviews of progress against detailed project plans, and allocating responsibilities for actions, provides the necessary intelligent pragmatic degree of empowerment and freedom of action, but within disciplined orderly constraints.

Operational teams responsible for process modules such as a manufacturing cell or a front office process are set short- medium- and long-term targets to meet for quality, work in process turnover rate, process lead-time, output schedule achievement, productivity, cost and continuous improvement, and are monitored on progress. They are supported by easily accessible training mechanisms such as open learning units and have specialist support groups they can call on to help them.

Temporary change project task-forces take on defined operations process restructuring, waste elimination and best practice introduction projects in priority order in line with the business plan. They are reviewed regularly against progress in achieving their targets, closed down on completion and reformed for the next projects so widening the involvement across all of the workforce. Everyone gets a piece of the action.

Development project teams running such endeavours as product or service development activities, customer account or marketing development projects or warranty problem investigations are regularly being formed, trained, reviewed for progress and disbanded on completion. This requires a modern management infrastructure for setting targets, agreeing project priorities, reviewing progress, allocating resources and enforcing standard working disciplines as outlined in Chapter 1.

A very important underlying principle is the importance of creating customer – contractor/supplier relationships through the organization and between teams.

- Every problem or task has a defined owner or customer for whom the team leader or Project Manager is delivering a solution or solving a problem.
- Specialists inside or outside the organization are regarded as sub-contractors to the teams, and are required to formally quote a cost and delivery time to meet the project plan requirements for the supply of specific work-packages to each operations process team or project team. They are regularly reviewed by the team leader, attending main project review meetings. This involves everyone in the organization, in an orderly way supported by good information flows, in the process of delivering the competitiveness achievement plan and ensures clear visibility of requirements.

In this type of environment, support methodology tools such as Quality Function Deployment (QFD), Failure Modes and Effects Analysis (FMEA) and Concept Conversion become very powerful aids and catalysts for team working and brainstorming across the individual specialisms in each team.

All sub-contractors, whether internal, external, part-time or full-time members of a project team, know exactly where their work packages fit. They have signed-off to deliver, into the overall work-package breakdown structure, that work-package required to meet the project specification, and the delivery date milestones to enable the whole project to meet the immovable customer delivery milestones. They are each required to regard their work-package as a project in itself, and produce project plans for review and control, in standard format.

All participants learn in this way the critical importance of the project management discipline of right-to-left planning which is so central to an achievement culture. Right-to-left planning recognises that the end date is sacrosanct, and the project managers must work back from this date to plan the necessary work breakdown structure. They determine the order and dependencies of activities, the critical bottleneck path and the resource and cost requirements to decide the latest start date, enabling the end customer delivery date to be met. Any threats or hazards to the completion date must be tackled by the production of a recovery plan for presentation at the next project review.

The action culture and can-do attitude is thereby networked throughout the organization and into the supply chain by tight synchronisation of all work-packages. All parties learn the need to be competitive in their offerings and to strive to delight their customer.

3.4 Filling in the project process structure

As has been mentioned, the project process can only be totally defined in depth and detail when the application area of the project is specified, even though the disciplines, methodologies and controls involved in project management are generic. The degree of complexity is a function of the size and degree of difficulty of the application requirement. Thus, the process of a product development project will vary considerably in detail and work-package structure from that for a small Kaizen continuous improvement project.

However, there is advantage in defining the basic principles and generic elements in some detail to facilitate the application of the powerful concept of standard working procedures, and to provide common training workshop packages and common terminology so essential to improved effectiveness of the whole organization. A simple view of the process is shown in Fig. 3.1 in input–output format.

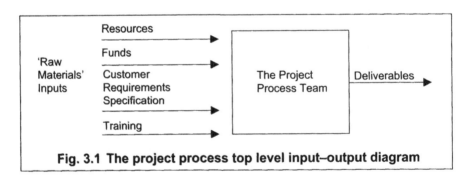

Fig. 3.1 The project process top level input–output diagram

A more comprehensive but still high-level approach to defining the process in relation to the strategic plan embodied in the competitiveness achievement plan is shown in Table 3.2.

Table 3.2 follows the broad route of opportunity identification, specification, bidding, implementation approval, implementation hand-over review, and sign-off, in a linear way, but does not show the many concurrent interactions which occur simultaneously and naturally within the cross-functional project team or its sub-process teams.

Table 3.2 Overall description of the project process

Stage	Description
1	Justification of projects to match the business plan: • change and innovation programme definition to protect the future, • product and service development programme definition, • three-year integrated rolling programme definition, • estimation and approval of budget.
2	The initiation, specification, and customer bidding or owner agreement sub-process project plan overall definition, work-package structure definition, deliverables, milestones, and customer interfacing strategy for each project.
3	Set-up a visible organization chart for the natural cross-functional skill group teams for the project.
4	Communication, team training, business awareness creation and team roles and responsibilities definition.
5	Provision of supporting frameworks, tools, techniques, and controls.
6	Development and supervision of detailed bid and delivery project plans.
7	Initiation of the delivery project sub-process, its project management, controls and customer/sub-contractor or supply chain requirements.
8	Definition of specification change control and hazard recovery team activity reviews, the management and commercial control requirements.
9	Commissioning, completion, owner/customer sign-off, user training and hand-over.
10	Post-completion audit and financial performance review, lessons learned analysis and Intranet case study writing for use by future teams.

3.5 Project and programme management support systems

To create and install the necessary support systems requires a very detailed definition of the project management process so that all of its report information and control requirements can be met. However, developments over the past 10 years, initially related to new product development projects, with considerable market-driven progress by automotive and aerospace equipment manufacturing companies, have led to convergence on a relatively generic world-class format. This is a consequence of their requirements to introduce major new products with increasing frequency, shorter total introduction time, and reduced resource costs, in order to compete in their market-places. The initial stimulus came from the performance of the Japanese car manufacturers who, by careful flow-chart analysis of their product introduction process, followed by its subsequent improvement, were able to produce a new model in half the time taken by their Western competitors and at 20–40 per cent lower cost.

In essence, best practice involves the use of co-located multi-discipline project teams supported by a system of standard organizational controls, standard procedures, and standard working protocols. Because of the demanding and detailed nature of project activities, a degree of disciplined management control and formality is essential for effective performance.

There can be many differences from business to business resulting from varieties in type, size and scope of projects. However, in practice, there is a great deal in common so far as generic standard practices are concerned.

Project Managers have learned the hard way that '*doing the right things*' and '*doing things right*' go hand in hand. Also it has transpired from innovative leading service companies' experiences that the standard procedures are directly transferable from other industries with great benefit.

While smaller companies may not require some of the elements, there nevertheless is benefit in them utilising many of the procedures. In particular, the disciplined approach to detailed planning and reviewing for managing the achievement of target milestones on time, which is the foundation for an action-led achievement culture, is totally transferable.

3.5.1 Fundamental project management issues

Some specific important requirements are listed below.

1. Build into the planning process a clear view of where the project deliverables fit into the customer-needs time scale. This requires visibility of the customer's top-level right-to-left plan and its delivery milestones, and then matching to these the critical supply project milestones, highlighted for project phase review purposes.
2. Usually significant preparatory work by an initial core team is required to confirm an expanded detailed specification and the means for delivering it. From this they then need to estimate the work breakdown structure required in the form of a work-package list covering the total estimated work plan, together with a specification for each work-package and a time phased task matrix, resource and cost estimate. The work-package assembly-tree structure will need considerable iterative

working in detail to define the critical path interdependency sequencing and to refine the time scales and cost estimates against a target cost for viability purposes. This work can only be done efficiently by a co-located cross-functional team, supported where necessary by geographically remote colleagues' teams responsible for specialised work-packages, utilising networked IT support and project data management. By on the job brainstorming aided by standard support tools and methodologies, they ensure all aspects are considered. By pooling their diverse skills and experiences, sitting around the same project table, they communicate quickly and very effectively just by talking to each other. This is much better than separating them by department walls and linking them by expensive IT systems.

3. The work-package list is sequenced in order of anticipated execution, with an iterative eye on the team resource required over the allotted time period. This then allows the Project Manager to endeavour to level schedule the resource utilisation and provides the basis for:

   (a) A time phased plan of the work-package execution order with a view to paralleling of work-packages where possible to minimise the project lead-time. A right-to-left planning discipline is essential. At this stage it is very important to have a standardised project process flow-chart in view to ensure work-package sequencing is acceptable to meet time milestones for key stages or phases requiring approval, i.e. concept approval, budget approval, solution design sign-off etc.

   (b) As the work-package sequence plan is consolidated, this allows the necessary plan charts to be completed to form a basis for forward project control and in particular:

   • A project work-package bar diagram where the list of work-packages is laid out against a horizontal time scale showing the planned start and end times and the necessary paralleling of work to meet a lead-time target and any technical constraints.

   • A project work-package network diagram which links start and end times across work-packages and chains together the dependencies, i.e. where one work-package has to be completed before another can start. This network allows the critical path to be defined which is the linked set of dependent work-packages that control the total project time scale. This is called the bottleneck path and focusing on it allows the Project Manager to control the total project time by giving special attention to progress of work-packages and tasks on this path at his reviews.

   • a planned time-based expenditure profile;

- a planned time-based profile for achievement of key elements of the delivery specification to allow earned value tracking, i.e. relating the costs expenditure profile to the monitored work completed profile;
- a planned resource requirement profile, by skill category.

(c) There are other important elements which have to be included in the project control system in a structured way to allow systematic control which, if not controlled, can dramatically impact the cost and time scales. These include:

- A hazard warning of anything which is threatening the achievement of a work-package being completed on time, with a recovery action mechanism.
- Advanced notification of requests to change the specification, from all sources, so that the functionality impact, time, cost and responsibility for paying can be agreed early before major impact results. The management of specification change and its agreement often needs a supporting problem management IT system of its own called Fault Recording and Control Action System (FRACAS).
- The regular recording and filing, after sign-off approval, of all work completed and other relevant information to progressively build a reliable database accessible to the team and the customer. This requires good support facilities for data management ranging from an integrated networked computer system to providing adequate administration support in large projects. Without efficient organization of this, a considerable amount of the project team's time can be dissipated so reducing productivity and increasing the wasteful time spent working on the wrong problem or searching for information. Such no-value-added waste is a major disruptive and cost increasing factor in badly run projects. A disturbing statistic based on studies of a range of projects is that an average team member only spent 50% of their time on value-added work. Clearly, using one full-time trained administrator is more economic than having a 20- or 200-person team waste 50% of their time.

4. A project organization chart is required with people in natural groups allocated in sub-process teams. Teams should be identified by role on the chart, related to their ownership of particular groups of work-packages and tasks, co-located for most effective operation and open to access by those who will use the outputs of the project as it processes. The team leader network, the lines of ownership and communication, and the

formal communication mechanisms should be made very clear to avoid confusion and wasteful activity.

5. An overall control and approval system design for the project which provides a framework for constrained empowerment of the teams as well as:

   • the information needed for control and the feedback mechanisms to provide informed actions;
   • the means for providing control actions;
   • those control points which are internal to the project process;
   • those control points which require external agreement, e.g. by the customer or project owner, sub-contractors or for commercial or business reasons.

The control elements have a number of forms ranging from the important specification of the minimum number of fundamental control meetings, their standard agendas, attendee lists and required outputs, to the use of a standard set of plan spreadsheets matched to the project process and its phases. If this is not done, confusion reigns and excessive numbers of ineffective meetings result, together with a lack of visibility of critical items and a growth in fire-fighting and random progress chasing. These again are forms of non-value-added waste which cause productivity to plummet and costs to escalate.

In designing the project process flow-chart, its organization chart and its control system, substantial attention should be paid to the elimination of waste using the Toyota seven-deadly-wastes methodology. For example, the co-location of process or sub-process natural group teams automatically eliminates delays due to communication, excessive paperwork passing, difficulties of contacting or discussing topics with colleagues, multiple databases in non-standard format and many other non-value-adding impediments to progress.

Making it easy for staff involved in a project process to get together eliminates many inadequacies. A focused team is better able to deliver a right-first-time approach than a set of distributed individuals hiding behind functional departmental walls and non-aligned responsibilities, who perceive no common purpose. An organization built around a few natural team groups as distinct from a large number of individuals, finds communication and cooperation much easier so that productivity and quality of work grow rapidly. The lead-times are shorter and their flexibility in terms of the ability to change direction quickly is much higher. It is much easier to coordinate, inform and control a small number of teams with clear roles than a large number of dispersed functional specialists. The information has only to be directed to a small number of team leader nodes. Also, the IT support requirements are much simpler and cheaper as a consequence. The important message is '*first simplify before automating*' and do not simply make the waste circulate more quickly.

Clearly, the ideal would be a single co-located team and this is possible for small change projects or small product or service upgrade or development projects. For very large projects, including those which cross businesses, this is not possible and therefore a logical sub-division into sub-process team modules grouped around specific project phases and related sets of work-packages is the next best option, together with a good team leader-to-team leader communication network. This use of distributed team groups dispersed internationally is very necessary for international companies and supplier groups.

6. Provision of a modern best practice support infrastructure. There are two primary areas of need here.

   (a) Provision of the necessary equipment such as computer systems for supporting the design of the services or products and their delivery systems and provision of access to service delivery module lists or product design-for-manufacture capability. These generically can be grouped as CAD support and project data management or knowledge management systems. They may be very simple such as a small PC to support a continuous improvement group problem-solving activity to a large computer for simulating the design of a transport logistics system or a set of powerful work-stations used for simulating and designing electronic systems and their manufacturing system.

   (b) Provision of training in modern best practice methodologies. There is now a developed and proven set of methodologies for business system redesign and for new product and service development. Some are problem specific, related to the particular application area, and others are generic. For example, for change projects, flow-charting, non-value-adding activity analysis, natural group team design and the five-step business process design methodology used in Case Example 1, Chapter 1 (Section 1.12) are generic. For both change and product/service development, systems tools and techniques such as QFD (Quality Function Development) and FMEA (Failure Modes and Effects Analysis) are essential generic team tools. These catalyse team working because they only become effective when used by a cross-functional project team, as distinct from use by a single specialist, because of the broad knowledge base present in the team for brainstorming the necessary exhaustive set of alternatives required by these techniques.

FMEA is a process of listing, in a spreadsheet, all sources of potential failure to achieve customer satisfaction, to categorise these in order of seriousness, and then to design out the risk systematically.

QFD is a structured approach which takes the overall specification for the project and its performance quality requirements, and then breaks this down into a fully detailed set of requirements at the level of every individual project work-package and task.

Both techniques are easily used via simple computer spreadsheets, networked for ease of access. They are covered in detail in the Tools and Techniques section of Chapter 4.

Selecting the relevant methodologies, making them available via the Programme Office and ensuring that every project team is trained in them at the project initiation workshop improves performance massively. This will lead to major gains in productivity and quality of performance by the whole team.

7. The project team will evolve from the preliminary specification and concept development stage into the full blown production stage. It is then very necessary to ensure that the teams are fully briefed on the specification of customer requirements, the standard planning and control system, the top-level milestones, the critical path, their roles and place in the organization, the administrative controls and the work-package assembly-tree structure as well as the work-packages they are involved in, in carrying out tasks. A start-up launch briefing session and methodology standards workshop, followed by regular update and review sessions in line with the project phases, are essential.

3.5.2 Putting the management support system elements in place

One of the secrets of the Japanese success in a number of industries, particularly the automotive manufacturing industry, was the use of a process standard working methodology. This is not to be confused with the traditional US and European bureaucratic approach to work study and method study which was highly specialised and focused on individuals in a highly rigid way. The latter approach was carried out by old style Industrial

Engineers and Managers who assumed they knew best what was required to execute tasks, examined in isolation from the overall process system effectiveness. There was also over-detailed focus on prescriptive job design leading to serious labour demarcation issues and loss of flexibility.

In contrast, the Japanese approach to standard working focuses on the cost and quality of the operation of the total process system and team effectiveness; the approach is flexible and subjected to educated continuous improvement. It involves the team members in the development and improvement of the standard working methods via structured continuous improvement change projects. This approach is formalised and documented at every stage of development leaving a clear audit trail. This factor, plus the involvement of the user team, brings a tremendously powerful discipline to the practice of increasing the effectiveness of business processes. The combination of standard working with the application of process flow-charting to the design of simpler and more effective low waste, lean processes without sacrificing value-adding innovation capability, indeed it is enhanced, provides a very powerful competitiveness drive. The practice underpins the reliable achievement and development of performance quality standards and productivity. This applies not only to product quality where quality measured in a few parts per million can be achieved, but also in the quality of performance of all processes. Quality of process performance can be measured in such MOPs as errors per invoice, time taken to respond to customer telephone calls, delivery on time, output per employee or the many other detailed MOPs typically used throughout the business processes. This characteristic of an almost automated operational approach combining people, equipment and world-class practices to achieve excellence in performance has been named Autonomation by the Japanese.

Combinations of people, technology, equipment and business systems can be designed and operated to achieve continually a high, and consistently reliable, performance, even in high-variety product and service businesses, and any changes for improvement are made to stick by being integrated with standard working. There has been a growing tendency in well-led companies to apply the best practice standard working idea to the project process. The usual approach has been to set up a cross-functional project team to travel and study best practices in other companies and then to consolidate these in a set of standard procedures for the overall process approach. This approach is then implemented through the roll out of training for project teams and the induction training of new recruits to the company. Two important underpinning practices applied in this to make it stick are:

1. The production of a process procedures flow-chart and associated operating manual, regularly updated by Kaizen continuous improvement activity, post-project debriefings, learning from others and from internal case study experience exchange or knowledge capture. The growth in the use of in-company intranets has increased the ease and potential of this practice.
2. The provision of standard generic training courses at two levels, the awareness level and the expert practitioner level.

A brief summary of the main elements typical in the standardisation of process team practices will now be presented item by item.

3.5.2.1 Company standard project process flow-charts

(a) Overview level, focused on the main phases and the approval milestone phase-gates. Note that, in a team project there is considerable interaction and iteration between stages as the elements of the concept, design of the product/service, design of the delivery system and its support system, evolve and become firm. This happens naturally in a co-located team, and is called concurrent engineering; however, the complex interaction and overlapping are difficult to show on a simple linear flow-chart. Figure 3.2 shows an overview example. Chapters 1 and 5, and the Support Methodology section in Chapter 3 provide others.
(b) More detailed 'from-to' flow-charts for material flows and information. Typical flows within each phase and each team using standard detailed flow-chart symbols for NVA and VA activities. This is covered in Chapter 5 in more detail.
(c) Input–output diagrams for whole team activities or project stages listing all required inputs and outputs, and connecting these to show a total stage-to-stage input–output flow-chart for all teams in a network.

3.6 Overview of activities supporting the project process phases

It is necessary for full implementation, to expand the ten-stage overview of Table 3.2.

1. Project definition

Appoint Project Manager. Define project opportunity, scope, objectives, risks, business and budget CAP requirements, review classification level, overall plan, competitiveness objectives.

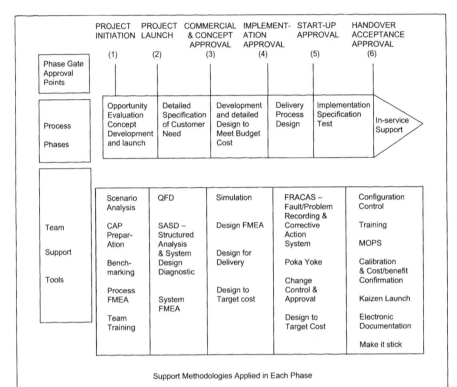

Fig. 3.2 Overall project process flow-chart into service hand-over and main phases

2. Create expanded draft specification

Create the first outline specification of customer requirements, the outline work package structure with those items which are now identified and the outline MOPs and cost–benefit analysis, for briefing the project team.

3. Project authorisation

Management workshop to prepare overall project plan and time scales, presentation for approval, plan for project launch and participation, provide market justification assessment, discussion of options and risks. Itemise cost structure versus target cost profile. The information base and definitions will be approximate at this stage and will rely heavily on the amount of analysis done and past experiences, until the detailed project work progresses.

4. Organization

Define the project team organization and publicise this, location, reporting lines of authority, support facilities and communication plan. Confirm project controls and standard procedures.

5. Develop the detailed specification

Form initial core cross-functional team to collect data, review experience and carry out analysis to develop the specification in full detail, including detailed performance measures as a basis for work-package structure definition, allocation, resource planning and cost profile calculation.

6. Project launch by management

Allocate full team members' names to the organization chart including agreed customer and sub-contractor representatives. Run a launch communication workshop to train the team. Agree the controls, the standard control meeting designs and owners, options approval, changes control, hazard management and recovery plan procedures, regular reports by destination and type required.

7. Work breakdown analysis

Define detailed work breakdown structure (WBS), work-package structure tree and dependencies, internal work-packages as well as sub-contract work-packages. Draw up a skill-group task-matrix for the work-packages to facilitate work-package allocation to sub-process natural group teams and sub-contractors. Construct the preliminary right-to-left project bar diagram plan (Gannt diagram) for subsequent refining as data becomes firm from the early work of the teams.

8. Work-package network definition

Draw up the dependency and bottleneck control path network including all necessary testing requirements, piloting or prototyping requirements.

9. Project detailed planning and scheduling

Construct the full schedule timing, cost profile and resource profile plan and finalise time phased resources requirement. The schedule should be in layers or levels, that is:

Level 1. Master- or top-level schedule for project phases linked to the customers top-level milestone schedule.
Level 2. Major work-package schedule bar diagram for each team.
Level 3. Task breakdown schedule for each work-package and grouped by teams. Provide a checklist of all standard procedures, key dates and standard meeting dates.

10. Resourcing

Levelled schedule week-by-week resource needs, part-time and full-time, finalise and approve budgets and reporting/audit, skill requirement/training needs. Define resource allocation management standard procedures. Provide a clear explanation of all infrastructure and facilities support including IT system.

11. Formal approval of full project plan

12. Plan execution, monitoring and reviews

Finalise in relation to customer and project top-level milestones the key review meeting dates, their internal and extended review groups, their roles and the phase gate approval dates. Operation of the process in line with standard working procedures and contracts approved. A forward review plan timetable is needed so that the project team know what is required, with all reports and their dates listed.

13. Final review meeting

14. Project final report

15. Formal project hand-over and customer/owner sign-off

3.6.1 Top-level (Level 1) milestone plan and work-package relationships

The activities of the project process fall into the following groups:

1. Overall project level – top-level plan, customer milestones and in-house milestones.
2. Major work group modular sub-divisions, e.g. internal project activity, sub-contract activity, pre-approval activity, design, implementation.
3. Module work-packages – integrated groups of skills/tasks.
4. Detailed tasks.

A critical task therefore, during the concept definition and planning phase, is the division of large projects into manageable sub-groups of work-packages, with their inter-relationships. In schematic form, these can be represented as shown in Figs 3.3 and 3.4.

3.6.2 Project controls

All projects require carefully attention to the design of their control system to ensure their objectives are met.

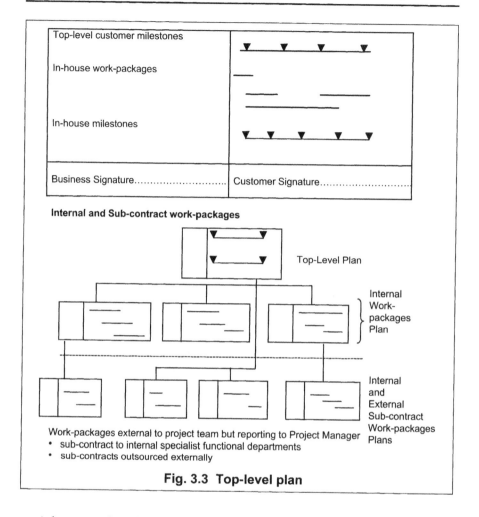

Top-level customer milestones	
In-house work-packages	
In-house milestones	
Business Signature............................	Customer Signature............................

Internal and Sub-contract work-packages

Top-Level Plan

Internal
Work-
packages
Plan

Internal
and
External
Sub-contract
Work-packages
Plans

Work-packages external to project team but reporting to Project Manager
* sub-contract to internal specialist functional departments
* sub-contracts outsourced externally

Fig. 3.3 Top-level plan

A best practice characteristic of many Japanese companies is that they spend a long time in the planning stage and in gaining agreement and consensus from all interested parties. As a result, contract documents are often simple. The project then proceeds in a very orderly and systematic fashion and the implementation time is short. In contrast, many Western companies rush in and spend only a short time on specification development and planning. The result is a high level of uncertainty at all levels in the team and an amateur implementation process, which takes a very long time with many mistakes, much re-working and high costs.

A project to redesign the front sales office process in a services company will be much smaller than a project to design a new jumbo jet aircraft. A

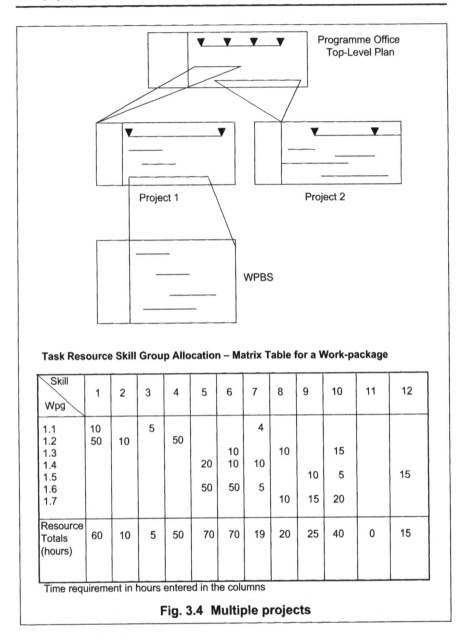

Programme Office Top-Level Plan

Project 1

Project 2

WPBS

Task Resource Skill Group Allocation – Matrix Table for a Work-package

Skill / Wpg	1	2	3	4	5	6	7	8	9	10	11	12
1.1	10		5				4					
1.2	50	10		50								
1.3						10		10		15		
1.4					20	10	10					
1.5									10	5		15
1.6					50	50	5					
1.7								10	15	20		
Resource Totals (hours)	60	10	5	50	70	70	19	20	25	40	0	15

Time requirement in hours entered in the columns

Fig. 3.4 Multiple projects

Kaizen programme involving several hundred continuous improvement projects will require reasonably complex plans and controls at the total company programme office level with a focus on resource planning and training to suit the varied areas of problem solving application knowledge required. An individual Kaizen problem solving project with a team of only three or four people will require a relatively simple planning and control framework even though the problem solution discipline requirements may be significant.

In principle, all of the points of control will be needed in all projects but their realisation will be more complex in large programmes than in small programmes.

Planning and control frameworks for multiple project, multiple site situations will be more complex and more demanding of programme and project management skills than single project single site situations, for example, in the difficulties of resource allocation management to match changing priorities.

Projects with very large numbers of work-packages and complex task allocation matrices will be more difficult to manage and control than a project with small numbers of work-packages and a small team.

In general, control of project progress to meet the specification and objectives is exercised via two mechanisms.

1. The range of control meetings, including top management reviews and customer reviews, supported by regular reports on carefully defined dates for designed purposes, e.g. top management monthly report. The basic discipline of insisting on clear agendas and the circulation of written minutes and actions lists with owners is critical to sound control, particularly so for commercial meetings with customers. Good quality administration recording and filing procedures are essential for resolution of disputes and cost claims for example.
2. Testing of prototypes, sub-systems, preliminary results testing and analysis, and the careful reviewing and monitoring of achieved building blocks in the implementation stages.

Therefore, there is always the risk of changes being required throughout the project process. If enough cross-functional effort was spent on the preliminary concept definition and specification development aspect and if good project management and controls are applied, then the amounts of change and uncertainty are less. Cost escalations and time losses will be lower, hazard recovery actions will be fewer.

All projects embody considerable risk of failure and the bigger the project the bigger the risk. If a carefully designed set of control meetings, with specified focused roles, is not put in place at the beginning, with minimum bureaucracy and tailored to the size and difficulty of the project, then time-wasting *ad hoc* meetings spring up quite rapidly as people search for answers, clarity of focus or reassurances that all is progressing to plan. These *ad hoc* meetings are usually not properly defined in terms of role, agenda and inputs needed. Staff attend but are not sure what is required of them and the result is much wasted time and reduced productivity. In badly run projects, meeting proliferation results and attendance at meetings becomes a substitute for real value-adding work. It can be very startling, when initiating a new business process design by flow-charting, just to audit and list the number of meetings taking place each week and see their costs in staff time and overlapping roles.

3.6.3 Control meeting design

1. To minimise the number of meetings, each should focus on a fundamental core area and should have a clear purpose and role. There should be a short written set of terms of reference and a role statement.
2. There should be a standard agenda but with space for any other related business.
3. There should be a list of named attendees and possibly agreed substitutes and a named Chairman.
4. To aid attendance planning there should be a fixed minimum frequency, venue, day, time and target duration for each meeting and the list of proposed meetings should be formally approved by the Programme Director and Project Manager.
5. Minutes should be circulated with allocated actions against names of attendees with dates for completion.
6. There should be a stated set of deliverables plus the input requirements such as reports, monthly data etc., needed for decisions.
7. There should be sign-off of the deliverables agreed by the Chairman.
8. Some meetings may benefit from having dual Chairmen, e.g. major monthly project reviews are likely to benefit from customer involvement and from having the customer chair alternate meetings.
9. Regular participation in the body of a meeting by customers and suppliers for specific meetings can be very beneficial in stimulating cross-boundary teamwork, gaining commitment and in obtaining helpful knowledge input or access to resources. This also considerably aids good communication and enlists support.
10. The projects administrator should maintain a centralised set of minutes and actions records with a regular weekly outstanding action list summary, and should chase actions. He, by regular contact with team leaders outside the meeting, should support an agenda item regularly reviewing actions lists items.

3.6.4 Example of a typical set of generic control meetings for a project

1. Daily 15 minutes stand-up coordination meeting of team leaders.
2. Daily 10 minutes work-package team meeting to review achievements, variances and priority short-term forward recovery plans.
3. Weekly project progress review meeting and weekly priority problem action list identification.
4. Weekly operations process (e.g. manufacturing) change acceptance and implementation planning meeting.
5. Friday morning weekly resource allocation meeting.
6. Monthly specification management and change request review meeting.
7. Monthly planning and scheduling meeting shortly before monthly project review.
8. Monthly technical meeting – to specify and tackle special technical feasibility problems off-line via specialist functions.
9. Monthly quality, process-capability and reliability meeting or agenda item on monthly project review meeting.
10. Monthly senior management project progress review including financial review.
11. Monthly business requirements and commercial meeting.
12. Programme office support meeting – monthly/quarterly.

Note

When the project is one of a portfolio as part of a programme, some of the above meetings may be general, across projects, e.g. for resource planning.

A separate business and commercial meeting is often required for new product projects in order to allow pricing and contract issues to be discussed off-line without compromising technical staff discussions on problem solution or specification change request implications.

3.6.5 Common needs for standardization across a company

A common project classification system into category 1, 2, 3, etc. in the CAP, by size or priority or degree of risk, for programme management and reporting level by the Programme Office will facilitate the definition of a standard set of report structures to suit the needs of Corporate level, Division level, Business unit level and project level reporting.

To achieve a well-run project, a central reference administration file incorporating the following items is advisable, where these are significant in relation to the size, focus, type, and scope of a project or programme:

(a) Draft project specification.
(b) Signed-off final specification.
(c) Project team organization chart (this should also appear on the team area notice board).
(d) Signed-off level one plan and phase gate review dates.
(e) Project launch agenda.
(f) Records of completed training packages.
(g) Records of training workshops run.
(h) Minutes of meetings and reviews with action lists and owners. It is particularly important for top-level milestone phase gate reviews to be disciplined and formalised with clear decisions noted and actions lists correctly specified, to suit all parties involved.
(i) Monthly progress reports.
(j) Hazard reports.
(k) Recovery plans.
(l) Project stage/work-package completion reports.
(m) Signed off hand-over documents.
(n) Project process and quality audit reports from the programme office.
(o) Budget and financial control documentation.
(p) Commercial agreements and customer correspondence.
(q) Change and quality problem solution requests from all sources, each with a reference number and date entered into the FRACAS action support system.
(r) Record of training or procedural/operating issues.
(s) Record of resource training carried out.
(t) Regular inputs to the business management executive monthly project reports and customer reports.

Good records, including e-mails and correspondence for major projects are essential to support the commercial interactions, which typically arise in business, such as negotiations over responsibilities for costs of specification changes.

For a very large single product or service development project, or major change or acquisition transition programmes these records will be located in the project or programme control office. For multi-project change or Kaizen programmes, a central programme office file system will minimise the costs. Each small single Kaizen problem solving group or small change project will only require a very small amount of administrative support. The main requirement will be to ensure openness, and to record the following: objectives, knowledge gained, results audits, names of full- and part-time members, the support training and review agendas as well as the implementation and hand-over, staff selection, training requirements and explanations of the new designs and practices – e.g. in an operating manual or handbook.

It is particularly important for review purposes for project budgets and the monthly costs to be fully itemised under such headings as people, training, travel, equipment, facilities, external suppliers, internal suppliers, as well as by work-package and project phase, to facilitate detailed management. This will also help in planning future projects as well as in subsequent audits of cost/benefits for change and Kaizen projects or true product or service costs, to support pricing policies.

The project hand-over and sign-off ritual needs to be taken seriously even for the smallest Kaizen programme in order to generate a business-like can-do and action achievement culture focused on delivering what was agreed, on time. Suitable senior people should be involved such as the Business Manager, Project Manager, Project Owner and User Team Leader, and the deliverables acceptance procedure should state clearly that:

- the project is complete with agreed changes noted;
- the agreed specification was met and the objectives are consistent with the original objectives;
- the customer representatives support the hand-over;
- the project and its results relate to specific tasks, targets and objectives in the competitiveness achievement plan and the agreed cost/benefit budget element.

In some situations such as the running of pharmaceutical, aerospace, and defence industry projects where safety-critical products or services are being developed, the documentation control procedures have necessarily to be very formalised to assure that standard procedures have been followed and to facilitate future traceability of data for investigation of any subsequent failures or accidents. In such cases an integrated networked electronic data management and document control system will be essential. In change projects such as business process systems redesign, cost reduction and productivity improvement projects, this will not be required to the same extent. There will, however, be a need in these projects to ensure that the standard working methods, operating manuals and training requirements for the new process operating teams, and the process control methods, have been properly embedded. A single Kaizen problem solving project associated with, say, the reduction of the number of paper forms used in a sales office sub-process may merely require confirmation that this was completed to a target of 50% reduction in the time allotted and the new procedures have been embedded.

3.7 Summary

Overall, managers need training in modern professional practices for business process organisation design. All participants in the management by projects approach need to be trained in the standard project process procedures, and roles and responsibilities. They should be committed to persistent action for achieving targets on time and understand the application of the six inter-related concepts:

- Plan
- Communicate
- Monitor
- Control
- Action/Implement
- Delight the customer

This will require a suitable level of formality and discipline in project management and control, which cannot be skimped if the objectives are to be reliably met of delivering the CAP in a hard-nosed no-compromise manner.

In driving culture change to deliver a dynamic can-do culture, top management will need to carefully create several significant emotional events to focus attention and catalyse persistent action. Central to this are the needs to:

1. Have a full-time Project Manager with budget and team ownership and clear project schedules and plans.
2. Have a core of full-time team members in each project and a clear definition of the roles of part-time members and work-package owners, supported by agreed standard best-practice working procedures.
3. Ensure senior management's visible commitment, sub-contractor's participation, and care in setting and justifying bench-mark targets.
4. Properly specify and launch every project emphasising the use of best practice standard working procedures and the use of

standard control forms to avoid confusion at reviews.

5. Set up a formalised line organization structure for change and development management with clear programme and project responsibilities defined. The Change Manager and Programme Director need to be business-executive level appointments to recognise their importance and status in order to attract high calibre people.

6. Ensure monitors, audits and controls are carefully designed and in place, properly supported for tracking performance, priorities and the requirements of the CAP.

Figure 3.5 summarizes the programme management roles and functions integrated to meet the CAP plan as defined in Chapter 1.

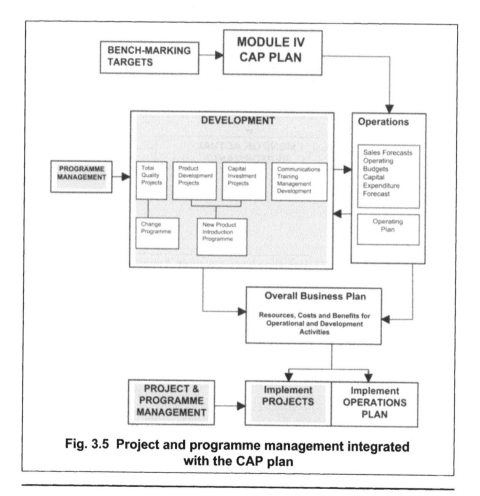

Fig. 3.5 Project and programme management integrated with the CAP plan

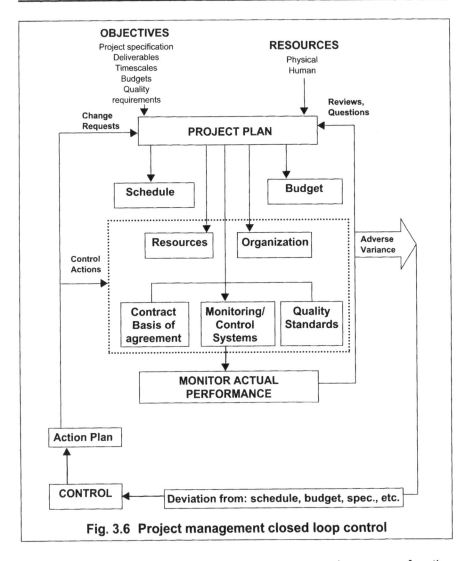

Fig. 3.6 Project management closed loop control

Figure 3.6 summarizes the closed loop control process for the business project process. A set of example plan control charts is provided in Support Methodology, Section 3.

For Chapter 4 go to page 197

Further reading

Association for Project Management. *Contract Strategy for Successful Project Management,* 1998.

Keenan, D and **Riches, S.** *Business Law*, 5th Edition, (Pitman Publishing).

Lawson, G. A. *et al., Project Management for the Process Industries,* 1998, (Institution of Chemical Engineers). Includes lists of abbreviations and definitions of words used in UK process industry contracts.

Miller, R. B. and **Heiman, S. E.** *Conceptual Selling,* 1987 (Warner Books N.Y).

Parnaby. J., *et al., The Lucas Manufacturing Systems Engineering Handbook,* 2nd edition, 1989 (Lucas Industries Publishers).

Project and Programme Management Procedures

Project Management practices are in their most advanced form of application in sophisticated safety-critical service industries such as aerospace and automotive. However, careful selection from, and in some cases simplification of, the set of practices involved, will allow their use with great benefit in all kinds of business applications. Examples from advanced companies are used in this section to illustrate the art of the possible.

To avoid confusion and ensure good communication and clarity of purpose, it is good practice to adopt common control and support documentation procedures across an organization.

It impresses project customers when their suppliers' team members operate in visibly disciplined and effective ways. These range from the procedures used for defining project objectives and specifications, to the control schedule standard forms they use in project reviews to clarify every aspect of progress with the minimum of paperwork.

All processes have a lead-time and a process capability or reliability, which can be optimised by careful design of standard working procedures, which embody common sense flexibilities, kept up-to-date by continuous improvement practices. The project management process is no exception to this sensible rule.

Standards and guidelines are beneficial in the following ways, preferably packaged together in a company reference handbook for use in process operations and training:

1. Carefully design and standardise the set of control meetings to eliminate the risk of proliferation of ineffective wasteful meetings.
2. Integrate related definition of measures performance cascaded to each level in the project work-package structure.
3. Standardise a generic project flow-chart, its phases, milestones and phase-gate transfer approval point requirements, capable of applying to all kinds of project. Relate to the project organization chart line responsibilities.

4. Standardise the set of paperwork control forms or their computer-based equivalents for planning, monitoring and control, to ensure all important information aspects can be covered for any type of project or multi-project programme.
5. Embed the mandatory use of a project launch workshop to communicate the objectives, provide training in relevant best practices where necessary, and communicate across all personnel groups affected.
6. Define clear project specification structure standard requirements.
7. Create structured project files.
8. Standardise the supporting procedures required to operate alongside the main value-adding core of the project process.
9. Provide a project Risk Analysis framework to guide preventative and recovery action planning.
10. Communicate clear authorisation, review and approval requirements, including change approvals.

Projects generally fall into two groups:

(a) Change, effectiveness and competitiveness improvement projects of a high variety, depending upon the type of enterprise.
(b) New product or service definition, development and introduction.

SM3.1 Example of meeting structure definition

SM3.1.1 Set of control meetings (see also Table SM3.1)

1. Project Manager's review meeting – weekly
Attendees:
- Project Manager
- Major work-package group owners
- Quality support staff
- Project Administrator
- Procurement Manager

2. Project owner/customer review
Attendees:
- Owner/customer steering committee
- Programme Director
- Project Manager
- Commercial Manager
- Heads of main project sub-teams

3. Change Control Committee – weekly/monthly
Attendees:
- Project Manager
- Commercial Manager
- Project Administrator
- Senior staff from delivery process and product development areas

4. Scheduling and resource planning – weekly
Attendees:
- Programme Director
- Project Manager
- Human Resources Administrator
- Scheduler/Planner/Buyer
- Head of support technical functions
- Project Administrator

5. Technical development review – monthly
Attendees:
- Project Manager
- Technical function heads/work-package owners
- Project Administrator

6. Commercial and financial control review – monthly
Attendees:
- Programme Director
- Project Manager
- Commercial Manager
- Finance Manager

7. Quick-hit problem action list progress review – weekly
Attendees:
- Project Manager
- Project Administrator

Note
It is good practice to involve customers or project owners and their staff in key meetings, to facilitate communications and take advantage of their knowledge and support, particularly when hazards arise in relation to time, cost and specification deliverables or where customer site assistance and cooperation is needed.

SM3.1.2 Meeting design example – weekly project review

Table SM3.1 Weekly project review meeting

Time	Agenda Item	Owner
20 minutes	1. Overview of progress on meeting action list.	• Project Administrator
10 minutes	2. Top-level project milestone schedule overview and customer/commercial meetings feedback. MOPs review, priorities.	• Project Manager
75 minutes	3. Work-package group owners reports versus schedules; forecasts and hazard recovery plans.	• Work-package group owner
15 minutes	4. Quality standards in-service statistics and problems report.	• Quality support
30 minutes	5. Technical problems progress review.	• Technical Manager
30 minutes	6. Product and Delivery Process Change Control Committee report.	• Committee chairman
15 minutes	7. Financial report.	• Project Administrator
15 minutes	8. Actions, priorities and quick-hit problem list allocations finalisation	• Project Administrator
3.5 hrs TOTAL TIME TARGET		

SM3.2 Measures of performance

There are five core groups of monthly measures of performance, which can be cascaded to each work-package owner, in their terminology. Top-level examples are:

1. Progress to achievement of specification and deliverables requirements (SDs).
2. Schedule milestone date achievement (SA).
3. Project and work-package cost versus budget and estimated cost to completion (C).
4. Number of dated change requests raised, outstanding, percentage approved, and number of resulting specification changes by source (CRs).
5. Delivered service or product cost evolution, by sub-system, versus target (TC).

For business process effectiveness improvement projects monitoring, there are other MOPs which can be used, selected to suit the nature of the business, its processes and sub-processes. Examples are:

- Bid process – orders as a percentage of bids made;
- Design – number of changes per drawing, or assembly efficiency;
- Delivery process – percentage of service modules delivered to schedule;
- FMEA score for service;
- Quality score achieved;
- Warranty costs as a percentage of sales;
- Number of FRACAS requests per month and percentage of total closed-out.

Chapter 1 includes example overview flow-charts for a product introduction project process (PIP), as well as a project organization structure, in the Appendix, for the operation of such a process. Chapter 4 develops the PIP concept of Fig. SM3.1 in detail.

SM3.3 Standard schedule forms for planning, monitoring and control

Standard planning charts and forms, applicable to both single projects and programmes of projects, with integrated resource and cost budget controls, should be available to project teams for networking between laptops, servers and the Internet.

Comparisons of best practices in leading companies have shown considerable synergy and that about seven standard report forms will cover all the likely planning and control requirements of all types of project, while eliminating the need for voluminous reports. Figure SM3.2 shows a typical set. These can be simplified for small projects.

These also cover the information supply and monitoring needs of the Programme Office, the Business Manager and the project team.

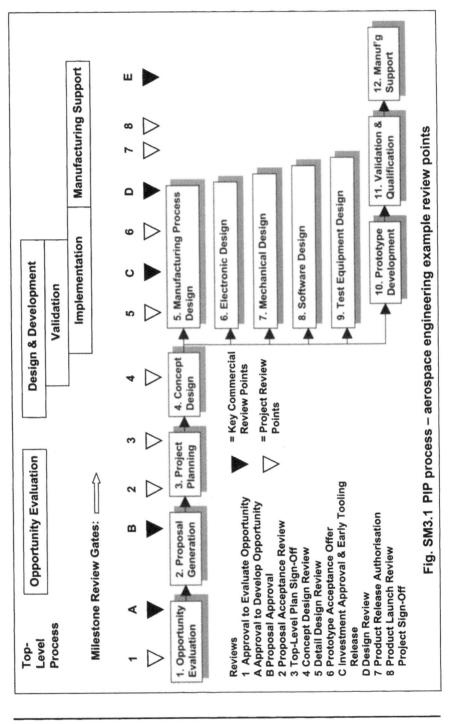

Fig. SM3.1 PIP process – aerospace engineering example review points

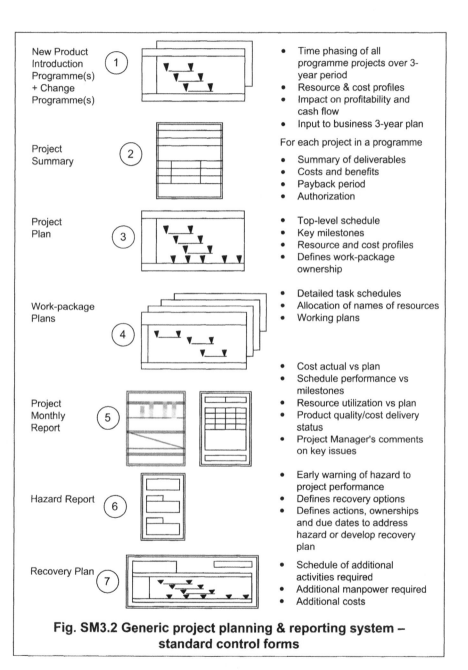

New Product Introduction Programme(s) + Change Programme(s) ①
- Time phasing of all programme projects over 3-year period
- Resource & cost profiles
- Impact on profitability and cash flow
- Input to business 3-year plan

Project Summary ②

For each project in a programme
- Summary of deliverables
- Costs and benefits
- Payback period
- Authorization

Project Plan ③
- Top-level schedule
- Key milestones
- Resource and cost profiles
- Defines work-package ownership

Work-package Plans ④
- Detailed task schedules
- Allocation of names of resources
- Working plans

Project Monthly Report ⑤
- Cost actual vs plan
- Schedule performance vs milestones
- Resource utilization vs plan
- Product quality/cost delivery status
- Project Manager's comments on key issues

Hazard Report ⑥
- Early warning of hazard to project performance
- Defines recovery options
- Defines actions, ownerships and due dates to address hazard or develop recovery plan

Recovery Plan ⑦
- Schedule of additional activities required
- Additional manpower required
- Additional costs

Fig. SM3.2 Generic project planning & reporting system – standard control forms

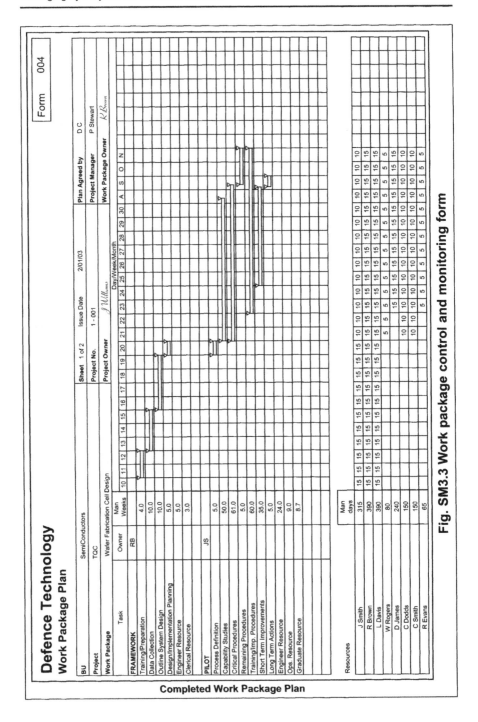

Fig. SM3.3 Work package control and monitoring form

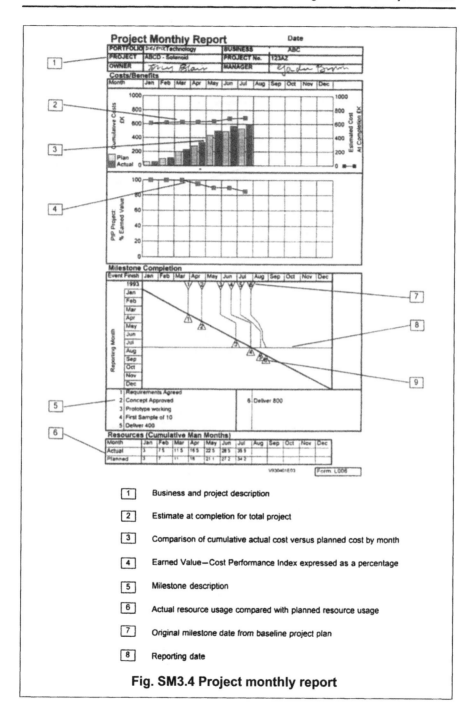

Fig. SM3.4 Project monthly report

1	Business and project description
2	Estimate at completion for total project
3	Comparison of cumulative actual cost versus planned cost by month
4	Earned Value—Cost Performance Index expressed as a percentage
5	Milestone description
6	Actual resource usage compared with planned resource usage
7	Original milestone date from baseline project plan
8	Reporting date

Fig. SM3.4 Project monthly report

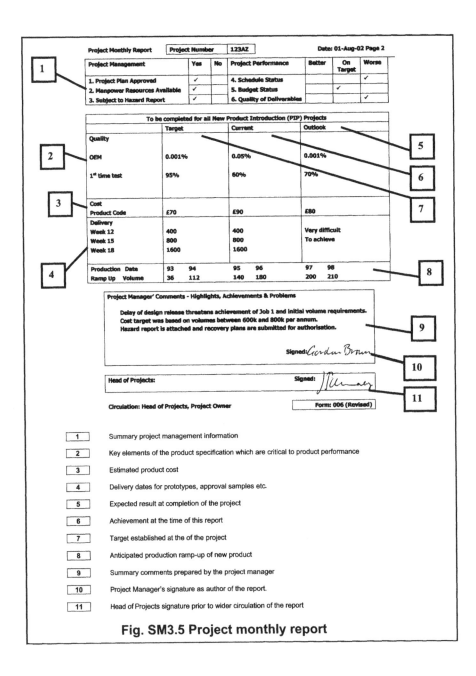

Project Monthly Report	Project Number	123AZ		Date: 01-Aug-02 Page 2		
Project Management	Yes	No	Project Performance	Better	On Target	Worse
1. Project Plan Approved	✓		4. Schedule Status			✓
2. Manpower Resources Available	✓		5. Budget Status		✓	
3. Subject to Hazard Report	✓		6. Quality of Deliverables			✓

To be completed for all New Product Introduction (PIP) Projects			
	Target	Current	Outlook
Quality			
OEM	0.001%	0.05%	0.001%
1st time test	95%	60%	70%
Cost			
Product Code	£70	£90	£80
Delivery			
Week 12	400	400	Very difficult
Week 15	800	800	To achieve
Week 18	1600	1600	
Production Date	93 94	95 96	97 98
Ramp Up Volume	36 112	140 180	200 210

Project Manager' Comments - Highlights, Achievements & Problems

Delay of design release threatens achievement of Job 1 and initial volume requirements.
Cost target was based on volumes between 600k and 800k per annum.
Hazard report is attached and recovery plans are submitted for authorisation.

Signed: *Gordon Brown*

Head of Projects: Signed:

Circulation: Head of Projects, Project Owner   Form: 006 (Revised)

1	Summary project management information
2	Key elements of the product specification which are critical to product performance
3	Estimated product cost
4	Delivery dates for prototypes, approval samples etc.
5	Expected result at completion of the project
6	Achievement at the time of this report
7	Target established at the of the project
8	Anticipated production ramp-up of new product
9	Summary comments prepared by the project manager
10	Project Manager's signature as author of the report.
11	Head of Projects signature prior to wider circulation of the report

Fig. SM3.5 Project monthly report

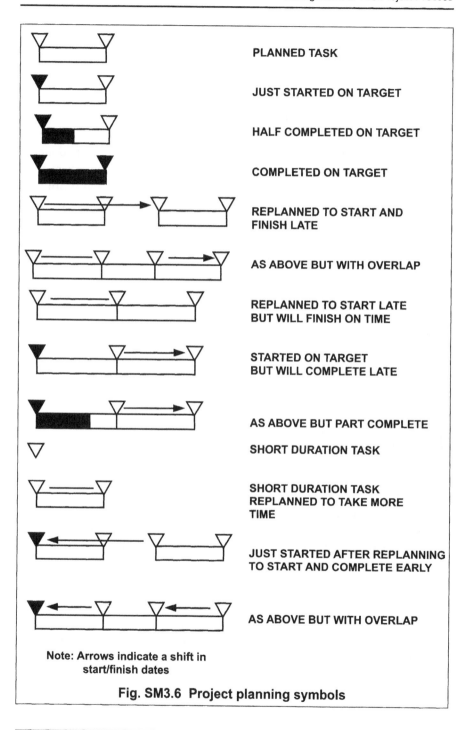

PLANNED TASK

JUST STARTED ON TARGET

HALF COMPLETED ON TARGET

COMPLETED ON TARGET

REPLANNED TO START AND
FINISH LATE

AS ABOVE BUT WITH OVERLAP

REPLANNED TO START LATE
BUT WILL FINISH ON TIME

STARTED ON TARGET
BUT WILL COMPLETE LATE

AS ABOVE BUT PART COMPLETE

SHORT DURATION TASK

SHORT DURATION TASK
REPLANNED TO TAKE MORE
TIME

JUST STARTED AFTER REPLANNING
TO START AND COMPLETE EARLY

AS ABOVE BUT WITH OVERLAP

Note: Arrows indicate a shift in
start/finish dates

Fig. SM3.6 Project planning symbols

As project and programme management is a core competence for any business which is managed by projects, the use of the standard schedule control forms should be built into training courses and project launch workshops, in order to embed best practice planning and control in the business culture.

A typical set of control and reporting standard forms is shown in an integrated manner in Fig. SM3.2. Some good practice working samples of the forms are provided in Figs SM3.3 to SM3.5. They include the double-sided monthly report form used to support project accounting where it is necessary to adhere to standard accounting principles for taking profit and sales revenue into monthly accounts in proportion to the earned-value profile versus the plan.

Note that the term 'earned value' for the project assesses the estimated value of work completed and relates this as a percentage to the project expenditure at the date specified. It is a very important control measure. Figure SM3.6 shows the project planning chart symbol conventions used to track actual versus planned progress. Note also that the critical path through a project is that interdependent sequence of work-packages whose total time required is the longest. This is often governed by a particular demanding work-package called a bottleneck.

SM3.4 Project launch procedure

The primary reason for a launch procedure is to ensure that the project team get off to a highly motivated unambiguous start, equipped with clearly understood objectives using some additional skills, relevant to their task, imparted by training.

It is particularly important that a senior executive initiates the launch and sets the objectives in the context of the CAP business strategy perspective and subsequently reviews the finalised project plan proposed for formal sign-off. The launch should include a briefing from all relevant stakeholders, e.g. customers and financial management.

A sample set of main headings for a launch agenda framework is:

1. Project background, business CAP context, aims, summary of elements, summary of previous similar project case studies.
2. Plan milestones and targets related to project process flowchart and standard control forms.
3. Overall guiding concept.
4. Commercial context and policy.
5. Relevant best practice training.

6. Project review dates and requirements, phase gate milestones.
7. Project owner hand-over requirements.
8. Authorisation and approval requirements.
9. Regular communication planning requirements.
10. Team location and infrastructure support facilities.
11. Validation audit requirements.
12. Detailed project specification, task list planning and execution.
13. Project document control, filing requirements, hand-over requirements data management, configuration control, change control and FRACAS.
14. Project overall budget structure.

SM3.5 Project specification structure documentation

This is a very important document package and, depending upon the stage the project is at, it may be relatively simple, e.g. for the production of a preliminary proposal as a basis for a bid, or very complex, as for the final detailed design and delivery stage.

Example main group headings are:

1. *Project summary.* This will define the area of application of the project, its title and reference number for configuration and document control, the customer or potential customers, and any critical customer requirements or contractural requirements. The customer key milestones should be identified, such as the target completion date.

   It will define the business need and the forward benefits expected, together with a statement on project funding and expected returns and target costs. It will list expected deliverables and dates, any prototypes and hand-over documents. It will itemise areas of risk and quantify these where necessary.

2. *Marketing summary.* This will explain the market need or background to the specification of the product or service and the expected product life curve with an associated revenue flow profile and net present value or internal rate of return. The post-completion support service requirements will be specified including life-cycle costs and benefits. All special contract or market conditions will be provided including competitor analyses where relevant.

3. *Technical specification and design brief.* This will describe the expected product or service, i.e. the deliverables, with performance requirements and measures of product performance in detail, whether a platform or variant, and for the latter the base platform product or service characteristics and any modular options required.

It will link in the specific requirements requested by the customer, including customer or market standard quality and initial and life-cycle cost requirements. It will define the production or delivery process requirements.

SM3.6 The project file

For most types of project, the maintenance of a well-structured detailed file of key documents, including the signed-off contract or authorisation to proceed, is very important indeed. For instance, in some industries where litigation and disputes are common, it is vital to retain signed-off copies of the specification from the customer, lists of agreed specification changes, and the approved responsibility for payment, also descriptions of problems encountered and their resolution.

In addition, all correspondence to and from the customer should be filed. The minutes of all meetings and actions lists, a risk management or FMEA file are other items likely to be required.

A configuration control document should be maintained, up to date and with approvals signatures.

The original negotiation paperwork, including the request for quotation (RFQ) and all agreed amendments and other correspondence, should obviously be filed.

In addition to these, the standard project, plans, work-package specifications and the monitoring schedule package should be filed, together with all progress reports, organizational structures and responsibilities and the actual performance records, by date of achievement.

For some types of project there should be a copy of the original cost estimating analysis, the budget and the monthly actual expenditure and resource tracking records, and all approval documents.

SM3.7 Supporting standard procedures

The use of a set of procedures containing generic best practice requirements to aid the performance of tasks or the operation of processes or systems is extremely helpful in maintaining standards of performance.

If badly done, these can be administratively bureaucratic. If done well, they can be short, clear, easy to read and extremely helpful for training staff in standard practice, while performing the role of helpful maps or guidelines and giving easy access to corporate know-how.

The best approach is to avoid wordy documents and for compactness use:

- flow-charts,
- input–output block diagrams,
- standard forms and worksheets,
- checklists,
- bullet points and short explanations.

These also have the advantage of making auditing of the processes very easy by selective sampling at flow-chart nodes. The following examples to guide standard procedure development are provided for illustration.

SM3.8 Risk and sensitivity analysis, procedural basis framework

All projects are prone to risk. In good project management practice, instead of just waiting for risks to happen, managers aim to reduce the amount of risk by careful analysis up-front of the likely sources of hazards and risk, and then include mitigation mechanisms in their plans, actions and controls. This will not eliminate all risks but can bring considerable beneficial reductions in risk. Sensitivity analysis is the logical estimation of the size of risk resulting from FMEA analysis and specific changes or errors and their listing in pareto order to aid decision making and corrective action.

It is useful to use a checklist of headings of potential areas of risk to guide systematic thought and analysis. For example:

1. Financial risks – e.g. factors affecting costs and returns.
2. Product risks in the market-place chosen and for the entry timing.
3. Commercial risks – e.g. from pricing policies, promotional and support plans.
4. Customer risks – support, capability, state of business.
5. Specification risks.
6. Technological risks – product/service and delivery process.
7. Business capability risks – lack of competencies, resources, funding.
8. Product plan and milestone schedule risks.

In some companies with very complex products requiring long, large, expensive product development projects, it is common practice to use a points score checklist standard risk analysis summary form attached to the front of a draft bid proposal. Such a procedure is often used prior to the customer bid submission stage to aid decision making and to help determine the development cost contingencies and the basis for the pricing policy used, with its separate development and supply cost structure plus estimates of warranty costs.

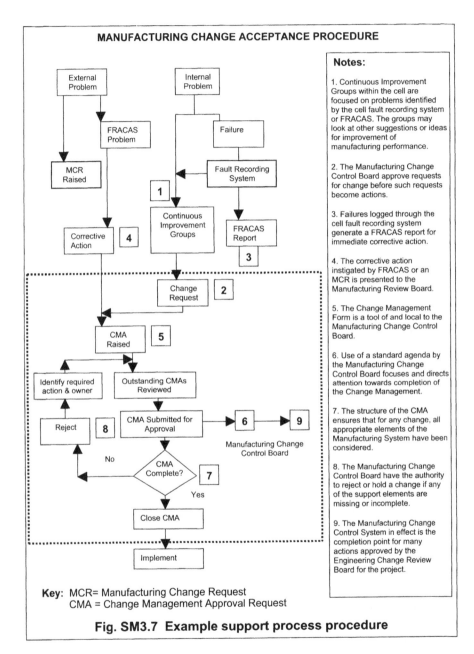

MANUFACTURING CHANGE ACCEPTANCE PROCEDURE

Notes:

1. Continuous Improvement Groups within the cell are focused on problems identified by the cell fault recording system or FRACAS. The groups may look at other suggestions or ideas for improvement of manufacturing performance.

2. The Manufacturing Change Control Board approve requests for change before such requests become actions.

3. Failures logged through the cell fault recording system generate a FRACAS report for immediate corrective action.

4. The corrective action instigated by FRACAS or an MCR is presented to the Manufacturing Review Board.

5. The Change Management Form is a tool of and local to the Manufacturing Change Control Board.

6. Use of a standard agenda by the Manufacturing Change Control Board focuses and directs attention towards completion of the Change Management.

7. The structure of the CMA ensures that for any change, all appropriate elements of the Manufacturing System have been considered.

8. The Manufacturing Change Control Board have the authority to reject or hold a change if any of the support elements are missing or incomplete.

9. The Manufacturing Change Control System in effect is the completion point for many actions approved by the Engineering Change Review Board for the project.

Key: MCR= Manufacturing Change Request
CMA = Change Management Approval Request

Fig. SM3.7 Example support process procedure

SM3.9 Configuration control and specification change control procedures

Projects always have the potential for variation and change. If this is not carefully controlled by validation, approval and an accurate negotiated cost allocation procedure to the customer, supplier or sub-contractor, project costs can escalate dramatically with 50% increases being quite typical. Extreme examples of this have been in such cases as railway system modernisation projects, the European Channel Tunnel construction project and some large government IT system projects. Disciplined and determined management of product, service and process change, and the maintenance of work-package, sub-system and component traceability will make a very substantial improvement.

There are two specific requirements:

1. The operation of a well-documented and well-managed configuration control system to ensure that every element of the developing product or service has a unique identifier with a corresponding up-to-date specification and a documented record of the modification history. At the very least, this ensures that customers can easily, for example, find the correct spare part or module when they have to carry out maintenance. The basis for the design and operation of a configuration control system is described in Chapter 4.
2. The definition and operation of a procedure to manage requests for changes (CRs) in product, service and delivery process specifications. These come from many sources and rapidly build up complexity and confusion resulting in cost escalation through loss of control. A system design is discussed in Chapter 3.

An example of a change control procedure is shown in Table SM3.2 and a flow-chart example for a manufacturing process change control procedure is shown in Fig. SM3.7.

SM3.10 Procedural checklists

Procedural process checklists represent an excellent way to build standard best practice working practices into the culture of an organization. As a final example, which pulls together the elements outlined in this methodology section, Table SM3.3 provides a simplified top-level reference checklist for project management.

Table SM3.2 Engineering change control process – best practice outline procedure

1. The process is coordinated to follow a standard flowchart by a cross-functional team, often called the 'Engineering Change Control Board/Committee' with a senior Chairman and representatives from marketing, sales, product design, R & D, manufacturing engineering, accounting, project management, and aftermarket.
2. A change process standard flowchart should be drawn up with fast track route sorting and approval gates shown. A standard process operations manual should be developed, including the duties specification for the process Committee.
3. The engineering change process must also incorporate a manufacturing acceptance process with sign-off to say that changes are manufacturable and that all tooling, drawings and operator training etc. have been provided to enable manufacture.
4. The Committee operates to a standard agenda, standard attendee list, and standard list of deliverables or sign-off requirements. They meet at a standard time every month. If there is a large, new product introduction project running, they may appoint a sub-committee to focus solely on this, and they meet weekly. Special arrangements will usually be needed at start-up to process, codify and catch up on the current backlog of change requests.
5. The Committee is supported by a Technical Administrator who convenes the meeting, maintains formal minutes, action lists, and specification agreement forms in a standard format, as well as the Committee records files. He should provide a standard checklist to guide the meeting procedures and decisions.
6. There should also be a target cost set for each design change, i.e. cost of change and cost impact (or cost reduction) on product.
7. The Committee is supported by an accountant who checks out the costs of any proposed changes, their price impact, and validates the reason for each change and 'who pays?'.
8. A standard change request form is used. This has the name of the originator, a reference number, date requested, date required. It gives full reasons for the change and a clear written specification of the change required. It requires the cost impact of the change and the ownership to be agreed for final completion prior to sign-off by the Committee.

Table SM3.2 *Continued*

9. Change requests are grouped by the Committee into categories based upon a runners, repeaters, strangers-type classification. Each type may follow a different approved route through the change process with the simpler changes following a 'fast track' and more complex 'strangers' requiring a project team and possibly R&D activity with a clear project plan and review gates for progress reviews.

10. All sources of requests for changes are channelled via a formalised FRACAS information and categorised database system (fault and change recording and corrective action system) i.e. a single database, with a standard form procedure for entering change requirements. Change requests entered into FRACAS may be originated by customers, design office, manufacturing, parts, and service organisation etc., using the same standard procedure.

11. Where possible, for maximum economic advantage and minimum disruption, multiple changes should be rolled up into 'mod-packs' to be consolidated and implemented en-bloc on defined mod-pack dates, with all necessary spares, catalogue, and specification update paperwork finalised.

12. A running project bar diagram plan should be compiled for all approved changes in the form of specialist work packages allocated to functional specialists or projects allocated to small teams and reviewed by the committee in a disciplined manner against target close-out dates, specifications, and costs.

13. The final approval sign-off should be by the Chairman, Accountant, Administrator, Marketing representatives.

Design process for change control
1. Flow chart the process, identifying any parallel routes, categorise change request into groups, and identify all non-value-added activities in each relevant branch of the process flowchart by using standard work study symbols for the detailed process definition.

2. Carry out departmental input-output analysis for all departments currently involved in the change process and validate those required.

3. Simplify and regroup the process for operation with the minimum of non-value added work, by a natural group team and to reduce lead-time by a target factor of typically ten.

4. Define measures of target performance improvement (MOPs).

Table SM3.3 Project management checklist

Project start

1. Produce and circulate a project organisation chart showing all reporting lines.
2. Train the project team and local management.
3. Ensure that there is a clear agreed project specification and top-level project plan, and that contractual obligations are understood.
4. Clearly specify all work packages both internal and external to the team, and ensure a clear resource and time plan aligned to top-level targets.

Project control

1. Set up control meetings and checklists, standard agendas and attendance lists, e.g.
   (a) weekly progress review against planned objectives,
   (b) weekly planning meeting and recovery planning for hazards,
   (c) daily half-hour stand-up meeting and exception reporting,
   (d) budget review meeting,
   (e) monthly review and resource planning with cross-functional resource committee.
2. Meet relevant local senior management regularly, at least once a week on major/high profile projects.
3. Carry out regular financial reviews.
4. Keep the customer informed.

Documentation

The following are a few key items to consider:

1. Create and maintain project file to include:
   (a) all meeting minutes, listing attendees,
   (b) standard action sheets for each meeting, numbered with dates and names against each action,
   (c) a log of all achievements and problems with relevant accountability,
   (d) all work package bar diagrams and high level plan.
2. Timesheets, checked weekly.
3. Where appropriate, for each completed work-package install an operational procedure with an owner and defined control procedure (e.g. meeting agenda and attendees to make change stick operationally).
4. Provide regular weekly reports in an agreed standard format with sign-off by senior project staff.

Table SM3.3 *Continued*

Targets
1. Insist on commitments and targets being met by all. Use a sign-off procedure.
2. Call on relevant consultants for help where needed.
3. Where a project is deviating from agreed targets, produce a recovery plan to bring it back in line.
4. Ensure a training programme is specified for ongoing operational staff, linked to a formal hand-over and sign-off procedure.

Project close
1. Were project objectives achieved?
2. Is all deliverable documentation with customers?
3. Ensure that a post-project review and report is completed and filed for reference.
4. Ask the customer to sign off the handover.
5. Formally record requests and reasons for extra charges.

Just in time

Problem

Spring high tides had unseated the only main gas supply pipe into the holiday centre and housing estate. The next spring tide could fracture it. The Maintenance Supervisor's adviser estimated that three weeks was enough time to design and build new pipe supports. But to do this approval for the work was first needed from the Centre Manager and the company's Operations Director, Assets & Maintenance Board, Contracts Officer, Safety Officer and Finance Committee, in that sequence, and also from the local statutory authorities responsible for roads, planning permission and environmental protection, also normally after the company has finalized its proposals.

The Maintenance Supervisor submitted his proposals to all the company officers and statutory authorities simultaneously, without any of them being aware that he was not following the customary lengthy practice of sequential approval for a project. He feared that the alternative of asking for agreement to changing the custom would have taken weeks. An unusual need was thus met by appearing to follow the usual channels.

If his tactics had been detected by any party, the Maintenance Supervisor's fall-back strategy would have been to rely on the obvious urgency of the work to obtain their immediate agreement.

Principles

- An emergency means time overrides cost control.
- Adapt procedures to serve company objectives.

Lesson

- The Maintenance Supervisor took a logical low risk justified by the objectives of the project.

Support Tools and Techniques Section

3

TT3.1 Specifications

TT3.1.1 Definition

The specification for a project, purchase or task defines the scope, quality and standards of what is to be provided. It can be for a service, a product, system or process, and can include the support required after delivery of the project.

A specification is also called a requirements specification, scope definition or requirements definition.

Standards are usually stated by specifying compliance with established international or national standards, and for lack of these, trade or company standards.

Delivery dates for a project or work-packages are sometimes stated in a contract specification, at other times in another part of a contract.

TT3.1.2 Performance and service specifications

A '*performance specification*' states what the project, purchase or task is to achieve. It leaves the supplier to propose how to achieve it. Many specifications also specify how the supplier is to achieve the specified performance. These are sometimes called '*service specifications*'.

Performance specifications are used when the purchaser wishes to make the supplier responsible for the satisfactory performance of the deliverables. A purchaser who decides to specify how a supplier is to achieve the specified performance incurs the risk of relieving the supplier of responsibility for the results.

The same principles apply to specifying work to be done as a service by one department to another within a company. Who is to be responsible for achieving the performance required should be agreed.

A specification may also define the scope of maintenance and other support required after delivery of a system, hardware or services.

TT3.1.3 Stakeholders

The scope and standard of work demanded by a specification determine most of the cost of a project. The basis of the specification should therefore be defined and agreed with all stakeholders.

Many customers tend to ask for what they think they can get. This may not be the same as what they really need. A systematic 'needs analysis' should distinguish between what they say they want and what they will really need when they get it.

Organizations speak with many voices. Not all of them think collectively across functions before they state what they want. Sometimes none of their representatives individually would agree with their collective answer to a question. Corporate received wisdom is often unwise. Penetrate to the eventual user, as far as possible. Ask for facts. Question, and when you have the answers ask what may change and why. Get written commitment. The proposed supplier of a service often has to do this.

Standard terms of contracts usually include a procedure for proposing, deciding and paying for changes. (This procedure should be omitted if the project is urgent and it is agreed that the project will proceed as first defined.)

Whether or not there is a contract, a customer who doesn't express clearly and precisely what is wanted and a supplier who doesn't challenge this deserve the limited success they enjoy.

TT3.1.4 The delivery chain

At the start of a project the customer or users may have only general ideas of what they want. They may be reluctant to be committed to a definition because it may have to be changed when they have obtained more information on their needs and on what can be supplied. Despite this, the first specification should be written down to provide an agreed basis for proceeding further, with notes on it stating the uncertainties and the possible need for changes. The initial specification is too often too brief, based upon limited study of the demand for a proposed project and drawing upon experience and ideas rather than much expenditure on studying ways of achieving the required result.

A clear and precise specification should be the basis of the internal financial bid or external contract bid for a project, and then developed stage-by-stage with expenditure on more detail. It is then usually broken down into specifications for each work package. The specification of a substantial package of work to be done by one organization, for instance a prime supplier, will require further sub-division and amplification to provide the specifications to define the work of each sub-contractor.

TT3.1.5 Checklist for specifications

In drafting or reviewing a specification for a product, system, service or change project check the following if relevant.

- Customer's requirements and expectations, function required and users' demands, in terms of payload, throughput, duty cycles, operating envelope, emergency capability, special safety risks, working environment, and parameters of performance, reliability and availability.
- Scope of supply, spares, manuals, technical data, responsibilities for preparatory work, installation, testing, commissioning and limits of scope.
- Whether standard, customised or special components are required, to British, EU, US, the customer's or other standards.
- Whether operation processes or procedures need to be adapted to suit location, local safety, contracting and other legal standards, maintenance conditions, access, relationships with other parties and services.
- System interfaces, standards and constraints.
- Software and IT protocols.
- Requirements for control and supervision of sub-contractors.
- Licensing, public approvals, reporting requirements, political climate and potential threats.
- Safety and emergency provisions.
- What support services the customer may need – training, help line, spares and extras.

TT3.1.6 Specifications for purchasing or selling

The specification for a purchase or sale is usually part of a set of documents. For a large contract the others required are usually:

- General conditions of contract.
- Programme for statutory approvals or legal equivalents in a country.
- Procedures and reporting manual.
- QA manual.
- The health and safety file (or equivalent national requirement).
- Communications guide: names, addresses, etc. of sponsor/customer's representative, the Project Manager and all managers and contacts in departments, contractors and other organizations responsible for work for the project.

The set of documents needs to be coordinated to ensure that they say all that is required, do not duplicate information and are consistent with each other. For a large contract this task is a project in itself.

TT3.1.7 *General principles for drafting specifications*

1. Assess confidence and risks in the requirements capture.
2. Define requirements in terms of what matters to the users.
3. Specify only what you can test. If you can't test it, you don't know you've got it.
4. Define acceptance and sign-off procedures.
5. Make maximum use of standard specifications.
6. Define what must also be specified in sub-contracts.
7. Plan and coordinate the drafting work.
8. Control changes.

Acknowledgements

The checklists used in this chapter were compiled with the aid of engineers, managers and others when attending project management courses run by the Institutions of Chemical and Mechanical Engineers and the UMIST Centre for Research in the Management of Projects.

Of course it's in the scope

Problem

Making their technical operations planning staff redundant had ended the Company C's anxiety that their specifications for purchasing new systems were too elaborate and too technically advanced for its needs, i.e. suffered from 'gold-plating'. 'We can always buy the expertise we need when we need it' was the policy.

Because of a market threat Company C then decided to hasten the start of three projects for systems replacement and expansion. They approached the consulting firm 'XCo' which had been established by Company C's own former Technical Manager and several of his assistants. XCo were asked to prepare design and contract detail for Company C to invite bids to supply and install equipment and services. XCo were already fully employed on a project for a larger customer, but offered to draft instructions to enable Company C to engage another consultancy. In response Company C asked XCo to employ other consultants as their sub-contractors. XCo complied, employed YCo, and sent YCo a performance contract for the design and contract work for the three projects.

Company C then appointed ZCon to supply and install the equipment and services in accordance with the design and contract documents provided by YCo. As installation started Company C noticed that ZCon were not providing instrumentation, spares, testing procedures or commissioning and operating instructions. ZCon stated that such work was not in their contract. XCo advised that YCo must take action to remedy these omissions as they had entered into a performance contract and therefore had responsibility for specifying whatever was necessary for the safe and efficient installation and operation of the three projects.

Company C had sent ZCon their records of operating systems needed for system shutdown, removal and new connections. The details were found to be incomplete and out-of-date. ZCon, YCo and XCo argued that the extra work this caused was not in their contract.

Principles

All parties had to consider three separate questions:

* Who is liable contractually?
* What is best for the project?
* What is best for future business with the other parties?

Lessons

* Don't expect others to know what you need. Don't expect to get what you don't specify.
* Agree the scope and responsibility for every work-package.
* Downsizing should be based upon benefits–cost analysis, not just on fashion.

TT3.2 Contracts

Contracts are the formal basis for defining an agreement between customer and supplier of services and goods, for instance for supply of the hardware, software and longer-term services for a project. A contract and the applicable law establish the parties' legally enforceable obligations and liabilities.

How to procure the services and goods needed for it should be part of the first thinking about every project. Procurement strategy should be a midwife at the birth of a project. It should develop with the risk strategy. For instance, whoever initiates a project should consider whether they know enough to decide whether the project could be economic and its product fit for its purpose, reliable, safe and lawful. If not, do they need to buy some market, engineering, legal or other advice? And if so, from who, and what is their liability if the supplier of this advice is late or gives poor information?

The same questions should be asked whenever you propose to purchase or hire any resources during a project. The questions are simple. The answers do not have to be complex. They demand that the promoter of a project should bring professional discipline to thinking about which goods and other services are better bought and which are better produced internally, when, what are the priorities and the risks, and how to buy them to achieve best value for the project.

TT3.2.1 What is a contract?

TT3.2.1.1 Purchasing, purchase order, procurement, sub-contract

All the above words mean one or more contracts in the contracting process. The single word '*contract*' is used here to mean all such agreements, whether in a company called a contract, order, purchase order or sub-contract, and whether for a small purchase of a service or materials or for large-scale physical work in manufacturing or construction.

TT3.2.1.2 Contract

What is a contract? The *Short English Dictionary* defines a contract as an agreement enforceable by law. In other words a party to a contract can refer a dispute about that contract to a court of law or other recognised system, depending upon the terms of the contract and the ruling law. Many commercial contracts include terms for resolving disputes, but disputes are not the intention of most parties to contracts, we hope. Designing an agreement to be enforceable at law is a way of playing safe. It should be secondary to the objective of defining what goods or services are to be supplied, when, how, and what is to be paid for them.

Personally we make and execute contracts daily, for instance to buy car fuel, food etc. So we all have experience to use to try to plan successful contracts.

TT3.2.2 Words

Many contracts for large or risky work include a list of definitions of some of the words used in them. This is wise and helpful, but unfortunately the definitions vary from contract to contract and so there are no standard meanings used consistently even within the English-speaking countries. As far as possible the most typical meanings are used in these notes. Here we state how some words are used.

TT3.2.2.1 Promoter, client, operator, owner, purchaser, buyer, company, employer

All these alternative words are used in different industries to mean what is most commonly called the customer for the project.

The word 'buyer' meaning the organization wanting the services or goods can be confused with the individual job title 'Buyer'.

In these notes we use the most general word *'customer'*.

TT3.2.2.2 Contractor, supplier, seller

These alternative words are used in different industries. The word 'contractor' can mean a construction company or a supplier of equipment. In these notes we use the more general word *'supplier'*.

TT3.2.2.3 Project Manager, Engineer, Purchasing Officer, Buyer

As noted above, the word 'Buyer' may be the job title of a person in a company. In some contracts the words 'Project Manager', 'the Engineer', 'Purchasing Officer', 'Buyer' and others are used to define the person representing the customer in communications with the supplier. If so defined, that one person is contractually the sole channel of communication with the supplier.

TT3.2.3 Planning a contract

TT3.2.3.1 Scope and terms of a contract

The obvious principle should be to plan a contract strategy which is likely to meet every party's objectives and therefore avoid conflict. Experience shows that this demands attention to the choice of number, risks and terms of payment of contracts and sub-contracts for a project. The ideal choice of contract terms varies from project to project, depending upon a customer's priorities between quality, economy, speed and flexibility, her public policies, the suppliers who are willing and able to do the work, and the ability of all parties to operate the preferred contract arrangement.

Different industrial cultures in different countries vary in their reliance on the legal enforcement of a contract. Opposite ends of this spectrum are presented by the USA and Japan. The latter rely much less on detailed contract terms, and more on common interests, partnership and trust. But in all but emergency conditions, satisfaction of all parties is most likely if time is taken to explore and define the purpose, scope, risks and best value of a proposed purchase before entering into a contract.

Before deciding to buy or sell anything therefore give attention to:

1. *Who is to be responsible for what?* – who is to be responsible for defining objectives and priorities, design, quality, operating decisions, safety studies, approvals, scheduling, procurement of hardware and software, construction and equipment installation, stores, spares, inspection, testing, selection and training of staff, commissioning, maintenance and other operational services, and managing each of these?
2. *Who is to bear which risks?* – who is to bear the risks of defining the project, specifying performance, design risks, approvals, selecting sub-contractors, productivity, mistakes and insurance?
3. *What are the appropriate terms of payment?* – for advice, information, design, equipment, construction, project services and management.

The resulting contract should specify *what* is to be done by *who*, *where*, *when*, *how* relationships between the parties are to operate, and *who* shall do what *if* changes seem necessary or other problems arise.

If a contract is the result of a series of proposals, discussions, letters and replies, what is known as offer and counter offers, one final document should state all that has been agreed. It should replace all previous communications so as to leave no doubt as to what has been offered and accepted. To avoid later doubts or disputes all parties should sign-off the complete final document.

TT3.2.3.2 Choice of the number of contracts for a project

The choices are between one comprehensive contract for all the goods and services for a project, and two or more contracts in series or parallel. Or a joint venture of suppliers. The customer can take the role of being the prime contractor and project manager, and employ many specialist suppliers as sub-contractors.

One of the above choices may be appropriate to only a part of a project. If so, an option for the customer is to employ one supplier for that part and one or more others for the remainder. Or a project might be so large that more than one supplier is appropriate to share the risks. For the equipment required for a new factory one supplier might be employed to install equipment supplied by others.

One choice is to give one supplier 'performance' responsibilities, that is to undertake to design and supply a complete project or systems to meet a specification which states the customer's requirements. Comprehensive contracts are variously called turnkey, engineer–procure–install–construct (EPIC), all-in, package deal or design & build contracts, for instance for construction projects. As these words do not define responsibilities precisely, we use the general term 'comprehensive contract'. Software system suppliers often act as prime contractors with such comprehensive responsibilities. Such a contract should ensure undivided responsibility for meeting the customer's requirements. To achieve this customers logically has to at least agree the performance, life-cycle economy, standards, approvals and all else that matters to them in design before agreeing such a contract. The customer should require the supplier to provide detailed information for approval, particularly on the operational and efficiency characteristics of what is to be supplied, and on how the supplier is planning to deliver a complete set of coherent work packages. In such a contract the customer usually has limited freedom to make changes ('variations') to the specification or the supplier's design. Similar principles can be applied in using a project approach within a company for a bid to specify and develop a new product.

Stage-by-stage contracts are logical if limiting the customer's commitments and risks, such as if cost has a greater priority for a project than early completion, as detailed and final design can be completed and priced before the customer is committed to the major costs of proceeding with the rest of the project. The most common example of stage-by-stage contracts is a design contract between a customer and a consultant or design supplier, and then a contract between the customer and a 'main' supplier.

Separating the responsibilities for stages and types of work for a project is logical if design requirements are uncertain at the start, the project team is newly formed, or suppliers have limited capabilities or knowhow relative to the size or type of work needed for a project.

Parallel contracts and direct management of the detail by customers is logical for work which is urgent or is interdependent with the operation of existing installations, because of the financial importance to them of maintaining services and production.

TT3.2.3.3 Supply chains

In all industries the main suppliers employ sub-contractors and suppliers of equipment, materials and services in parallel.

A common principle is that in a main contract a supplier is responsible to the customer for the performance of his sub-contractors. Practice varies in whether a supplier is free to decide the terms of sub-contracts or has to match their terms 'back-to-back' with his contract with his customer, choose the sub-contractors, accept their work and decide when to pay them. It also varies in whether and when a customer may by-pass a supplier and take over a sub-contract.

The potential advantages and disadvantages of the choices for customers in employing a supplier apply in turn to a supplier in planning the employment of a sub-contractor.

Main suppliers usually employ many sub-contractors in parallel, to use their expertise and resources when required, but in turn the sub-contractors employ others to supply materials and for specific work for a project. This hierarchy of contracting can form a long chain of procurement, starting with agreeing the main contract, then sub-contracts, and then sub-sub-contracts. The last are sometimes the source of information or materials which is needed first for a project. The supply chain is therefore a process consisting of a time-critical sequence of activities. The chain of payment operates in reverse, from the customer through the main supplier, and then to sub-contractors and onwards.

Parallel direct contracts between a customer and each specialist supplier are an alternative to one main contract, but in turn the specialist suppliers are likely to employ sub-contractors. In planning the use of suppliers a customer should therefore consider the effects of a hierarchy of contracts on critical activities and on motivation of sub-contractors to perform.

The word 'vendor' is used in some industries to mean a sub-contractor who is supplying his or her own designed equipment for a project.

TT3.2.4 Risks

TT3.2.4.1 Contract risks

The major risks of any contract are the customer's, in deciding to proceed with a project, and then stating or agreeing scope and specification, choosing the contract strategy, selecting and supervising the supplier, controlling changes and accepting the results.

TT3.2.4.2 Risk allocation

The options available to a customer in allocating the remaining risks are:

- *Avoid it* – by changing project design or timing, or by reducing dependence upon suppliers and others.
- *Transfer it* – to a main supplier, vendors or design suppliers, or partial transfer in a joint venture.
- *Reduce it* – by a combination of any of the above, up-front planning and insurance.
- *Absorb it* – by allowing for extra costs, delay or reduced performance.

The choice of terms of contract can motivate those who provide a service, design, write software, manufacture equipment etc., to be economical, quick or whatever are the customer's objectives for a project.

Contracts which place more than the above risks on suppliers are likely to be uneconomical and fail to achieve their objectives. The best suppliers may be unwilling to bid for high risk contracts.

TT3.2.4.3 Liquidated damages terms in contracts

A familiar but not necessarily satisfactory instance of transferring a risk is the inclusion in a contract of 'liquidated damages' terms which make the supplier liable to pay his customer a specified sum for a specified breach in performance such as lateness in delivery. This is an alternative to the supplier being at risk for damages at large, i.e. having to pay the actual consequential losses incurred because of late delivery, poor performance of a system etc.

A 'liquidated damages' agreement in a contract can be positively reinforced by also offering to pay 'bonus' extra amounts for completion on time or for recovery after delay. The intention of these terms in contracts is to encourage suppliers to avoid being late. In practice, the effectiveness of these types of deterrent may be limited because a supplier aware that he may be late can calculate whether it is cheaper for him to lose the sum specified rather than employ extra resources to recover lost time – especially as the latter usually requires using resources uneconomically. Such contractual liabilities may also be mitigated or unenforceable because the supplier can show that his work has been affected by the customer, third parties or risks excepted from his liabilities.

Many suppliers may be unwilling to undertake a contract which could make them liable for consequential damages unless the liability is limited, i.e. 'capped'. And there are customers who will take unfair advantage of such terms in a contract. Care is needed in agreeing such terms.

The more detailed the protectionary terms in a contract the greater the potential scope for disputes, and the greater the need for experienced project management by customer and supplier to anticipate and avoid all such problems. Elaborate contractual terms are no substitute for detailed attention to risks, early planning, allocation of quality resources to the work and energetic supervision by both parties to get it completed satisfactorily.

TT3.2.4.4 Partnering and alliancing

Partnering and alliancing between customer and supplier to manage their contract relationships cooperatively has been the subject of experiments, study and discussion in the USA and more recently in the UK. The objective of these arrangements is to move away from the disputes and confrontation that have been characteristic of many contracts. Trust is needed, at all levels. Achieving this depends upon agreement between the parties at the levels of management that can commit their companies to collaborate and share information.

In partnering for a series of projects or packages of work, customer and supplier can benefit from the continuity of knowledge of practices and people, scope for continuous improvement and savings in bidding costs and time.

In alliancing a single management team is appointed by all parties to the contract which has the power to anticipate problems, manage the risks and avoid disputes. This can extend to include major sub-contractors.

TT3.2.5 Terms of payment

Cost is a primary measure used by customers when selecting projects, assessing risks, comparing prospective suppliers' bids, and reviewing the immediate and the longer term results. But quality, reliability and the ability of a supplier to provide excellent service are very important to any customer competing with others in their market. Value for money over the life of the project is thus the concern of customers. The contract price is only one factor in this. Money for value over the life of a contract is the concern of suppliers, and therefore their major interest.

In planning a contract to purchase materials, a structure, design or other services a customer should therefore consider what terms of payment are likely to motivate suppliers to try to achieve the objectives of the project. The same applies to a supplier when planning to purchase from sub-contractors, so that all the following comments may be equally relevant to sub-contracts.

Fixed price terms of payment are preferred by many customers who place performance contracts, that is when a supplier is responsible for design, supply of equipment or fabrication work to a price, and the customer does not expect to have to specify further detail or changes.

Fixed price terms of payment are appropriate for projects which are fully specified before prospective suppliers are invited to bid and if completion of the chosen supplier's work on time or ahead of programme is more valuable to the customer than second thoughts on design or changes to any terms of what has been agreed.

The alternatives in other conditions are cost-reimbursable payments or agreement on a target cost and sharing of savings. For these alliancing is particularly appropriate to provide the framework for joint decisions.

Payment for stages of work completed, i.e. milestones achieved, is commonly agreed in larger contracts.

The words 'lump sum' mean that a supplier is paid on completing a major stage of work, for instance on handing over a section of a project. In practice 'lump sum' is also used in some sectors of industry to mean that the amount to be paid is fixed, based on the bid price but perhaps subject to change to compensate for inflationary effects on suppliers' costs. 'Lump sum' does not literally mean the price is fixed. If you mean fixed price, best say 'fixed price'.

TT3.2.6 Internal contracts

The internal commitments of departments within an organization to provide services for a project internally could be defined in the equivalent of internal contracts which specify the scope, standards and price of the work as if the departments were separate companies. This arrangement should have the advantage of making responsibilities clear. Except that disputes between the departments would be managerial rather than legal problems, these internal 'contracts' can be similar to commercial agreements between companies.

A joint venture can be formed by two or more companies which are owned by the same holding company. This is known as a 'family' joint venture. Depending upon the governing law, the relationship between the members of a family joint venture might be contractual, or an internal matter for the holding company, or both.

TT3.2.7 Lessons of contracts

* Say what you mean.
* Plan how it will end before you start.
* Specify only what you can test.
* Be aware of how a contract is created and how it can be discharged.
* Decide which terms of payment are effective.
* Define the obligations and rights of every party.
* Anticipate what can go wrong, applying risk management.

- Choose the terms of contract logically, depending upon the nature of the work, its certainty, its urgency, the motivation of all parties and other factors such as the relationship between an investment in new plant and systems already in use.
- As documents different in function are usually prepared by different groups of people, the set for a contract should be coordinated by one person.
- Contracts should be a means to an end.
- There is no such thing as a bargain.

Further reading for Support Tools and Techniques

Planning Contracts for Successful Project Management, 1998 (Association for Project Management).
Keenan, D. and Riches, S., *Business Law,* 5th edition (Pitman Publishing).
Lawson, G. A. *et al., Project Management for the Process Industries*, 1998 (Institution of Chemical Engineers). (Includes lists of abbreviations and definitions of words used in UK process industry contracts.)
Wearne, S. H. and **Wright, D.,** Organizational risks of joint ventures, consortia and alliance partnerships, *Int. J. Project and Business Risk Mgmt,* 1998, Spring, **2**(1), 45–57.

Two rights make a wrong

Problem

The new wrapping machine being developed was certainly novel. A customer had already ordered one, for urgent delivery. After the order had been placed for the machine various members of the customer's staff visited the manufacturers: their Project Manager had been to see the manufacturers' proposed programme of work; the Factory Services Manager to discuss the machine installation procedure; and a Control Engineer to obtain data on the start-up characteristics of the machine.

On returning to her office the customer's Project Manager phoned the manufacturers to state her concern that their programme lacked detail. She proposed visiting them again soon when they should present a programme showing dates and the resources to be used for all their internal work and for procuring the big forging and other critical components. The manufacturers stated that she had no right to demand to see this information. She stated that attention to detail was in the interests of both companies, and she reminded them of the 'penalty' clause in the contract for late delivery. The manufacturers replied to this stating that they were no longer liable for delivery to the contract date as the Control Engineer had asked for a design change. Also the Factory Services Manager had told them that installation of the new machine could not start on the date assumed by the manufacturers. They were therefore stopping work on the machine until these uncertainties had been resolved.

The customer's Project Manager suspected that the manufacturer's threat to stop work was a tactic to gain time. The Control Engineer was certain that he had only asked for information, and not asked for a design change. The Factory Services Manager confirmed that he likewise had only suggested a date for starting installation to see if that suited the manufacturers. The Project Manager therefore wrote to the manufacturers that under the terms of their contract the manufacturers had a right to be given instructions in writing but none had been given and therefore the manufacturers had no right to claim that the customer had affected the commitment to deliver to the date specified at the time of entering into the contract.

Principles

- A contract should be used to meet the objectives of all parties.
- Be aware of legal rights in a contract and the needs of the project.
- At the start of a contract set up regular integrated team meetings to anticipate scope, progress or cost risks.
- Establish an internal discipline for discussing possible changes and for managing communications with all parties to a contract.

Lesson

- Careless conversations can cause contractual chaos.

Reader's Guide

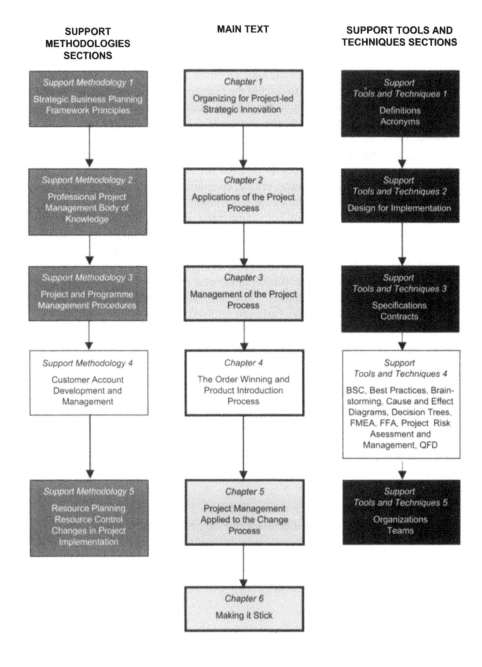

SUPPORT METHODOLOGIES SECTIONS

Support Methodology 1
Strategic Business Planning Framework Principles

Support Methodology 2
Professional Project Management Body of Knowledge

Support Methodology 3
Project and Programme Management Procedures

Support Methodology 4
Customer Account Development and Management

Support Methodology 5
Resource Planning Resource Control Changes in Project Implementation

MAIN TEXT

Chapter 1
Organizing for Project-led Strategic Innovation

Chapter 2
Applications of the Project Process

Chapter 3
Management of the Project Process

Chapter 4
The Order Winning and Product Introduction Process

Chapter 5
Project Management Applied to the Change Process

Chapter 6
Making it Stick

SUPPORT TOOLS AND TECHNIQUES SECTIONS

Support Tools and Techniques 1
Definitions Acronyms

Support Tools and Techniques 2
Design for Implementation

Support Tools and Techniques 3
Specifications Contracts

Support Tools and Techniques 4
BSC, Best Practices, Brainstorming, Cause and Effect Diagrams, Decision Trees, FMEA, FFA, Project Risk Assessment and Management, QFD

Support Tools and Techniques 5
Organizations Teams

The Order Winning and Product Introduction Process

Chapter 1 considered the business process organizational concept pioneered by Toyota in the 1960s, applied by some enlightened and intelligent companies through the late-1980s, and then partly reinvented by management consultants in the mid-1990s.

It was pointed out that some business processes are relatively permanent, often operate in a relatively steady state, and can be re-organized around relatively permanent, cross-functional team concepts, while others, usually development and change processes, are temporary. The development processes are particularly difficult to manage, and are usually run as transient projects, requiring application of the demanding management by projects skill set.

The case examples in Chapter 1 included a summary of a product development project team organization for the design of an electronic systems product, and its entry into production. This phase of design and introduction is often called 'The Product Introduction Process' (PIP), with the date of the start of production being referred to as the 'job 1' milestone.

The product introduction process is the second section or module of a larger process, which starts with the generation of an idea for a product, then research combines with market analysis until an attractive product specification gels and it becomes economically attractive to proceed further. Figure 4.1 provides a summary of common alternative forms of business process flow-chart for the whole product innovation process from idea to delivery. Note that the first common section represents the strategic direction process, or the CAP initiator for the business.

There are three distinct cases:

1. Where an entrepreneur or entrepreneurial company has an idea for a new platform product or service, checks it out by careful market analysis and decides to run a project to design and make it. This phase is shown on the left-hand side of Fig. 4.1. They then hire sales staff to sell the product or service, and for the first stage of this process, until sales revenues start to roll in, they are spending shareholders' money. They may offer a

standard generic product or a product of high volume potential for a niche market where the perceived combination of price, volume and available timescale to more than recover development start-up costs and make a good return, forms the basis for business success. Such companies often have a portfolio of products at varying stages of maturity or commoditisation. It is important to track where each is on a market penetration S-curve (covering the three phases of: initial growth, full growth and sales reduction), in order that a further redesign or update project can be run to re-life or cost reduce the product in a timely manner before sales fall away dramatically.

2. The second situation in the centre of Fig. 4.1 is where a standard platform product has been sold for a lengthy period during which time it has progressed through the market S-curve to the point where it is mature, has become commoditised. Competitors have copied or overtaken it, and its sales are falling. Managers must anticipate where a product development, or new geographical, niche or sector market account development project is required to redesign, upgrade, reduce the cost and include more attractive features, in order to re-life the product. The alternative is to discontinue offering the product.

3. Where a large company such as a motorcar or aircraft manufacturing company decides to produce an innovative brand new vehicle with a set of optional variants, they set up a large project to design their vehicle and ask a large number of first tier suppliers to bid against outline specifications to develop the specialized major sub-systems of the new vehicle. These tier 1 suppliers set up expensive, large, complex projects to develop and introduce a product specifically for one customer and, in turn, they set off a chain reaction by asking their tier 2 sub-system and tier 3 base component suppliers to bid against a requirements specification to provide elements of their sub-system. Such large programmes are very difficult to manage and require full application often in a globally dispersed manner of all the detailed elements of project and programme management, discussed in Chapter 3, if they are to be competitively delivered to the required target cost and time milestones.

The two sectors of industry, mentioned above, probably represent the highest pinnacle of achievement in terms of project and programme management expertise. The smaller companies at tiers 2 and 3 depend heavily on the vehicle manufacture and 'tier 1' suppliers for help in management, coordination and in learning best practices.

The bidding process, which precedes the initiation of the product introduction process, is also run as a project. This is because the tier 1

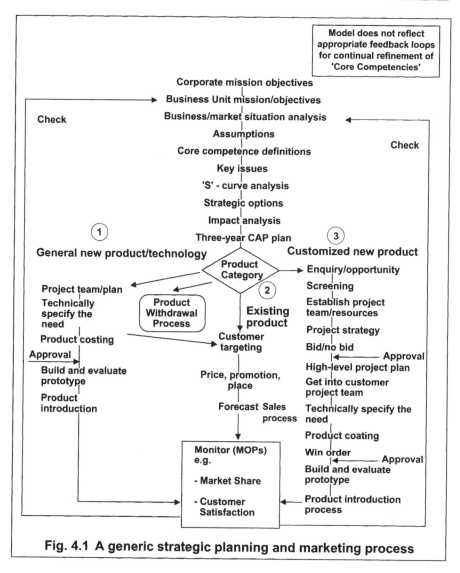

Model does not reflect appropriate feedback loops for continual refinement of 'Core Competencies'

Corporate mission objectives

Business Unit mission/objectives

Business/market situation analysis

Check

Assumptions

Core competence definitions

Check

Key issues

'S' - curve analysis

Strategic options

Impact analysis

Three-year CAP plan

(1) General new product/technology

(3) Customized new product

Product Category

(2)

Project team/plan

Technically specify the need

Product Withdrawal Process

Existing product

Enquiry/opportunity

Screening

Establish project team/resources

Project strategy

Product costing

Customer targeting

Bid/no bid ◄——— Approval

Approval

High-level project plan

Build and evaluate prototype

Price, promotion, place

Get into customer project team

Product introduction

Forecast Sales process

Technically specify the need

Product coating

Win order ◄——— Approval

Build and evaluate prototype

Monitor (MOPs) e.g.

- Market Share

- Customer Satisfaction

Product introduction process

Fig. 4.1 A generic strategic planning and marketing process

suppliers receive an invitation to bid with a requirement specification and target cost. They then have to set up a first phase multi-function project team to carry out enough detailed work, including technology route mapping, to determine how to meet the requirement specification and to be able to estimate all the many costs involved. This step is particularly important since such large project programmes may run for several years, prior to the introduction of a new vehicle model, and inaccurate costing can lead to large losses.

If a bid is successful then the process moves in close cooperation, including regular progress reviews, with the customer into the next phase of integrated detailed product development, design and design for manufacture, including design of the manufacturing system before entering the repetitive manufacturing operations stage in which many varieties, of basically the same platform product, with updates are produced over several years. A large market for spare parts and service develops in parallel, and continues long after vehicle production ceases on product maturity. Such major economic opportunities justify the high development costs, and allow profitability with a low target sales price due to standard product high volume economics.

Mid-way between the two examples above of a generic product and a product specifically designed for one customer, is the situation of a company which sells products or services, which have a generic common core, but which has to tailor the design or configuration of their product or service to meet the requirement of a particular sector. Usually such companies concentrate on a few large target sectors in order to gain good experience and understanding and accumulate detailed knowledge of the application area. It is necessary to reduce the costs of tailoring for each new order using clever combinations of standard and variant modules. In this way they partly specialise in order to increase efficiency, which is the usual aim of any standardisation of products and services, achieved by repetitive experiences. It is often the only way to ensure the company makes a profit, particularly if there is not a long repetitive manufacturing and delivery life over which to recover initial design project costs. An example of such a company would be an IT systems integrator supplier selling large integrated IT systems to banks and insurance companies. Here some of the modules of the product and services such as computers and maintenance support, are common to both sectors and others relate purely to the different particular business processes and practices operating in each sector.

Suppliers like this operate an order winning process in which a relatively small number of customer account development managers act as first phase project managers who target particular customers in a given sector, supported by a cross-functional team, to commercially penetrate that customer. They then make a bid to secure a large project order at which point a product introduction project team takes over. The account development manager maintains contact because he will usually have a target for revenue per order to achieve and will also have an account target revenue to aim for over several years from the same customer by bidding for other opportunities.

From the above examples, the following important principles emerge:

1. There is a complex total business process to be managed by projects, in modules, ranging from opportunity identification through customer account development and bidding to win the order and then moving into the product introduction phase.
2. In the type 2 and type 3 cases described above, managing by projects is necessary for both the bidding and account development phase, and the product introduction phase.
3. In the type 1 case, account development and bidding is replaced by a standard product sales operation process; often large numbers of sales staff interface with a large number of customers with common product or service purchasing requirements, to win a steady stream of orders. Examples would be mobile telephone or standard household equipment sales.

The above discussion makes it clear that the procedure for deciding what the boundaries of the business process are for a given business can appear confusing if not backed up by process analysis, as discussed again later in Chapter 5. It could be argued at an extreme that all businesses consist of just a single process. However, while this may be organizationally viable for a small company where everyone has multiple roles, it is just not acceptable organizationally for very large companies. In the latter, a careful sub-division into focused Business or Product Units, Processes and Sub-processes, plus synergistic shared support processes interlinked by a strategy and supporting control systems, which economically provide assistance to all other processes, represents a practical way ahead.

Note that there are natural phases in multi-function processes, which lead to a practical division into sub-processes, but be aware that specialist functional departments cannot be called integrated processes and connecting them together with IT is not a satisfactory way to create an integrated process as will be examined in detail in Chapter 5.

In this chapter we will consider in turn two such sub-processes divided at natural end-of-phase milestone points. These are:

1. The order winning Customer Account Development and Bid Project Process (OWP) – see also Support Methodology Section 4, for more detail.
2. The product introduction process (PIP) for which a simplified phased flow-chart is provided in Case Example 2, Chapter 1, Fig. 1.6 and the Support Methodology Section 3, Fig. SM3.2.

Before starting with the first of these, note that for reference, a further interrogation of the business process concept, building on the general introduction in Chapter 1 is provided in Chapter 3, to develop and consolidate understanding of this fundamental organizational concept.

4.1 The bidding and order-winning sub-process

4.1.1 Overview and Context

The bidding and order winning sub-process of a Company is a natural skill-group team activity, generic to the business needs for winning orders and delighting the customer. It is a sub-process in the sense that it is the front-end element on a time scale, of the product or service introduction process for a company. It begins with a sometimes loosely defined identification of a customer requirement and continues to a natural break in the time sequence where agreement has been reached on a specification with the customer to proceed with them to develop and deliver their requirements. On the completion of this sub-process the natural group bid team is likely to be reformed into a more comprehensive project team to design and deliver the customer's exact requirements, to a specified price, quality level, and time scale.

The team approach for operating the bidding process is easily justifiable in practice, as experience has shown, from a number of points of view.

1. It reduces the lead-time of the activity when compared to the traditional approach where separated functional departments try to coordinate and reconcile conflicts between needs as perceived by these fragmented functional specialists and the truly integrated business and customer needs. The fragmented approach also grows a wasteful and costly administrative and coordinating bureaucracy, spawning lots of meetings, e-mails and paperwork.
2. It reduces confusion, the team effectively 'sit around the same table' and talk to each other all the time. This is much more effective than writing letters or surrounding them with complex expensive administration IT.
3. It enables the bidding process to be run operationally as a distinct project using world's best practice project and programme management disciplines. This will deliver results, with clear lines of responsibility and authority, integrated team leadership, with visible time scales and targets, tight cost control and regular team progress reviews by management.
4. The customer can develop a clear line of single point contact and communication with the bid project manager and the team, which

reduces delay and confusion, and which enables tight change control by customer and management alike. It facilitates direct involvement of customer personnel.

5. The bid team is briefed and trained as a unit and has all the necessary cross-functional skills integrated. This enables all the knowledge and experience associated to be rapidly focused on the total resolution of problems by the Project Manager.

The nature of the bidding process varies in detail from industry to industry, as outlined earlier, but with considerable commonality of procedures and this can be illustrated in more detail by the following case studies:

Case Study 1 – the aerospace and defence industry

When a large company such as Boeing, British Aerospace, Airbus or Westland decides to develop and introduce a new aircraft, weapon or other piece of equipment, the process involved can extend in phases over several years and the costs involved are very high, necessitating excellence in project management of the process to ensure tight control.

It proceeds by asking its sub-contractors to make bids for the supply of sub-systems or components. There are often many sub-contractors involved, in industrial tiers from tier 1, full authority sub-system supply, through to tier 3, simple component part supply. To manage such complexity, effectively and economically, requires coherent bidding process project teams to be created by each main sub-contractor, often integrating their sub-tier supplier personnel.

Each main sub-contractor is supplied with a requirements statement. This is often defined in broad terms only, by means of a top-level project time-milestone plan, a target cost and an overall framework specification, including such elements as inputs and outputs, weight, definitions of interfaces with the other sub-systems, maintenance requirements, life-cycle cost targets and a target production readiness date.

To deliver a detailed bid prior to the carrying out of the follow-on stage of research and development, necessary for realising the full product definition and the associated manufacturing system design, requires the setting up of a skilled and experienced, full-time bid team with a good Project Manager. The team has to have on-line involvement of all necessary specialists including financial, purchasing, cost estimation, concept design and manufacturing systems engineering skills.

The team will be carefully trained and briefed at the project start-up, via a structured workshop, on all the customer and business requirements; the part-time team members will be designated as well as the full-time core members. They will be supplied with the necessary infrastructure support, including desktop publishing capabilities for bid document preparation. A large amount of support documentation is required by the customer and government agencies concerned with approval and safety criticality. Computer links and video conferencing facilities will also often be necessary. This is to ensure tight integration of customer, sub-contractors and suppliers.

They will operate in a high-pressure environment to tight time scales, and will be reviewed regularly as well as being subjected to tight project management disciplines. They will manage all necessary inputs required from materials and parts suppliers.

At the end of the bidding process, a formal and very detailed bid proposal document will be presented to the customer on the date required. After customer reviews and other interactions with the bid team and the business commercial management for price negotiations and specification development, the bidder will be formally informed whether they have won or lost the order. If the order is won, the bid team is modified and augmented, and embarks on the next project managed phase of development and design, including design of the manufacturing delivery system. The aim is to ensure that the product can be manufactured and delivered repetitively at the target cost to high standards for many years, together with any required spares and services.

Case Study 2 – the automotive vehicle industry

The automotive industry is progressively changing its traditional approach, following widespread introduction of the Toyota production system, and has operated a bid process project team approach with great benefit in a very similar manner to the aerospace and defence industries. When a new concept for a car, truck or other vehicle is defined, the vehicle builder companies such as Rover, GM, BMW, Volvo, Ford, send requests for quotations (RFQs) to their approved sub-systems suppliers for such items as brakes, diesel fuel systems, electronic control units, suspensions etc. A bidding process is necessary since these often have to be developed or modified and tested to suit the new vehicle even though they may have component parts that are standard with other vehicles. However, the automotive industry has recently moved to a standard platform concept for several different model vehicles, using standard sub-systems, such as engines, for each platform in order to achieve cost benefits similar to other industries, such as machinery suppliers, which have standard products.

From an overall organizational point of view, the top companies have found great benefit from the introduction of a simultaneous or concurrent engineering team organization in which staff are grouped into co-located product and service development teams. These are either focused on specific customers or on specific products linking via IT systems to sub-contract work-package teams for a variety of vehicle customers, with additional support from specialist functional groups on a sub-contract or part-time basis. In this situation, the bid process is often built into the regular duties of the relevant development team, so achieving the additional benefit of the detailed historic knowledge of the customer and product.

Case Study 3 – winning an order from a distributor of general goods and services

A typical example of this would be the situation where a product or service provider wished to target a large distributor. A bid would be prepared with a view to winning acceptance from the distributor of an agreement to advertise and promote the product or service in their general goods catalogue, distributed widely to thousands of customers.

Once a foot in the door was obtained, in the form of an expression of interest from the distributor, a Project Manager also fulfilling the role of the Customer Account Manager would be assigned. A core team, which may be quite small, would be designated. Some members would be part-time, but with clearly defined time allocations, priorities and responsibilities.

The team would just work with the customer to identify his requirements for a version of one of their standard products or services, e.g. special labelling, branding, patterns, alternative materials of construction etc., and would then systematically modify their product features specification to meet the requirements and house-style of the distribution company, together with any particular niche and volume pricing requirements. The bid team would arrange mock-up prototypes, their packaging, testing or evaluation, and progress through to the point where a formal quotation is presented to the distributor, who then agrees to place an order. The implementation follow-on leading to production of the variant would be via a project team of the necessary specialists to meet the time deadline and volume ramp-up requirements of the customer. They would supervise the initial deliveries, liasing with the customer to resolve rapidly any difficulties, which arose. They would also train and hand over to the production operations team after formal sign-off acceptance.

In all three cases above, there would be regular reviews of progress by the business General Manager and other senior staff such as the Commercial and Sales Directors, Finance Director and the Product or Service Development Director to ensure that decisions outside the scope of the project team can be made quickly and wider issues resolved. Also, the bid process Project Manager would meet regularly with the relevant senior customer contact staff to maintain close communications on any changes in requirements and to facilitate the necessary interfaces between team members on both sides. Integration, wherever possible, of customer representatives within the bid team, can be very beneficial. This maintains door-opening access to the customer organization, utilises the experience and knowledge of the customer's market and systems, and brings all necessary knowledge to bear on resolving obstacles and problematic issues via team brainstorming sessions, or when pre-contract evaluations turn up unforeseen problems. It helps to ensure the precise fulfilment of customer requirements. Loyalty, motivation and good ownership of the end result is achieved in both supplier and customer organizations.

In cases of companies where there is a high volume of bids or quotations required and the product or service variations required from the standard are relatively small, then one common approach is to operate a bid office with a bid preparation manager, who has a small core semi-permanent bid team, with temporary personnel regularly rotated in and out of the team to supply necessary skills and experience. This team processes all requests for quotations (RFQs) and produces all quotes.

4.1.2 Generic elements and needs of the bid process – thinking through the process design

It will have been deduced from the examples above that, by using a trained co-located cross-functional project team, the whole bid process is given a higher integrity, a clear line of authority and accountability, operates much more rapidly, and achieves stronger commitment than the traditional process of sending packages of paper and requirement lists around a fragmented set of specialist functional departments. The intensive and continuous interaction and exchanges, which take place within a trained and well-managed team, create very high levels of effectiveness and efficiency.

In the traditional situation, paperwork gets lost, sits on people's desks, priorities are unclear and communication is confused. The wrong problems are solved and the customer interface also becomes fragmented with no clear lines of control resulting in much confusing informal communication.

Many companies have created marketing departments staffed by marketing specialists who try to operate bid control independently and yet do not have all the skills and experience to make bids. Their role is often confused with the sales department leading to obstructive company politics. Engineering or other technical specialist departments trying to work with such groups are often not involved early enough or given full and accurate communications to enable them to understand the customer views and needs.

The critical issue here is that marketing has to be seen not as a self-contained activity but as a team process requiring a whole range of support skills to be utilised on-line and just-in-time as and when required. Engineers often become impatient with the time it takes customers to define needs and agree their requirements, and they can be sidetracked from target cost and commercial contract requirements by the excitement of tackling interesting new technical problems. They also often comment that sales staff 'sell products we don't have' or would like to give the product away at excessively low prices. Sales staff are often unclear of the role of marketing staff, see them as trespassing on their territory, and resent the fact that marketing staff do not directly generate immediate increases in sales. They also often appear secretive and do not communicate well with technical support staff, resent the way technical staff think that they agree impossible-to-meet requirements, and fail to get their colleagues to appreciate the requirements of the complex psychology of the customer interface. This may, as discussed in the Support Methodology section, often involve a wide range of individuals, functions and departments, all of which have differing perceptions of the supplier, his capability and his products and services. Clearly these problems get in the way of doing business and have to be resolved by a professionally operated team project process supported by modern tools and methodologies.

For these reasons, it is essential that business managers analyse and think carefully through the design and organization of the bid process from the way in which bid opportunities are discovered to the point at which the bid document is delivered and discussed.

The basic steps of process definition and design are as follows:

1. Draw a process flow-chart which lists the value adding elements and phases of the process.
2. List the personnel and infrastructure support necessary to meet the requirements of each value-adding element.
3. Define the natural group team required.
4. Standardise the project management methods, procedures and associated minimum set of control meetings, reviews and associated report forms, i.e. standard working procedures as discussed in Chapter 3 and amplified in Chapter 5.
5. Standardise the start-up workshop training requirements for each bid team and the mandatory supporting senior management attendance requirements for the team launch.

The basic stages of the process are:

A. Customer account development and management.
- Identifying and categorising target customers, the associated opportunities and potential follow-on opportunities.
- Staying close to the customer and identifying the set of customer personnel from all areas associated with defining requirements and making the purchasing approval decision. This element is called 'Decision Mapping', and is detailed in the Support Methodology section.
- Solution selling, i.e. getting customer personnel to identify their problems to be satisfied or 'pains' to be resolved for them to be satisfied that the bid and supplier are acceptable.
- Facilitating an account strategy and development plan for each target customer.
- Communicating the opportunity effectively and the state of progress, to all relevant staff.
- Clearly defining the key objectives and tactics.
- Obtaining the RFQ.
B. Set up the bid process team – choose and train the Project Manager and natural group team to support the bid.
C. Develop the top-level framework of the RFQ into a more detailed bid project time plan, an expanded specification, and the list of work-packages necessary to produce a design for the product/product variant or service to meet all of the customer requirements, including a target cost.
D. Carry out all work-packages for a design of the product or service and the delivery system to sufficient depth to allow the likely cost and performance to be determined in relation to customer requirements. Define the implementation requirements and time scales, while also listing areas of risk and uncertainty, sufficient to ensure an acceptable safety factor.
E. Prepare a professional quotation package and any necessary customer presentation package, and deliver the quotation on time to the customer.
F. Follow up and resolve any subsequent customer requests or needs until the order is placed. Throughout the process, follow up by targeting specialist personnel from the bid team on any concerns or controversial perceptions raised by customer personnel associated with the purchasing decision and uncovered in the decision mapping activity in item 'A' above. A good team communication system for tracking and communicating actions emanating from customer meetings is necessary to support this process.

In defining the natural group bid project team, the customer account manager should be a full-time or part-time member depending on whether he or she manages only one or several accounts. The full-time core team and part-time specialist sub-contract, internal or external, members, together with any components supplier and customer representatives are chosen to join the temporary bid process teams to carry out or contribute to work-packages identified in item 'C' above. Representatives of functions such as finance, commercial, quality assurance, and manufacture or service delivery operations should be included in the teams to ensure a truly cross-functional approach, not just a multi-discipline approach.

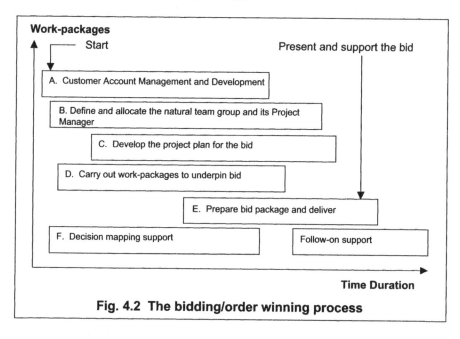

Fig. 4.2 The bidding/order winning process

4.1.3 Summary

The use of such co-located temporary project teams, allocated specifically for the process of making an order winning bid, has many advantages compared with the traditional alternative of a small group of administrators circulating task lists around functional departments and then progress chasing actions. The principal advantages are:

1. Speed of action and on-line team communication.
2. Very high motivation and goal seeking culture development.
3. Use of team members who have fresh knowledge and expertise of

implementations etc. from field application, development, manufacturing and repair operations.

4. Wider training of staff across functional skills and in application experiences from different points of view.
5. Enhanced quality of concepts and understanding of business needs through the wider vision obtained from continuous in-team brainstorming for problem solution and through single-minded focus on meeting a multi-dimensional customer specification.
6. Reduced preparation cost and lead-time and improved professional style and quality of the final bid.
7. Improved personal skills of team members and a broader appreciation of business targets, the customer viewpoint, and the supplier viewpoint.
8. More effective utilisation of the skills and knowledge base of customers and suppliers or sub-contractors targeted through project management methods on a common goal.

However, because the bid teams change continuously and come and go as the bid frequency varies, to ensure consistency of quality of performance some permanent infrastructure support is necessary for the process. The requirement is to very economically share such infrastructure, common to all bid project teams.

4.2 Infrastructure support requirements

4.2.1 Organization

The company organization design must reflect the needs of a modern business process management approach, as shown in the example of Fig. 4.3. Here the organization is set up as a set of core process and support process elements, which fit neatly together as a very effective system.

A brief clarification of the elements of the organization chart is as follows:

4.2.1.1 Bid Office/Bid Manager

A Bid Office or area managed by a permanent Bid Office Manager who, if not an accountant, is supported by a financial administrator to maintain focus on target cost, life-cycle cost and gross margin requirements of the product or service. Cross-functional bid teams are located in the Bid Office for the period of bid preparation and then return to their base unit. The Bid Office contains the necessary IT support system and team working support tools as well as other support equipment, company standard procedures reference manuals and codes of practice.

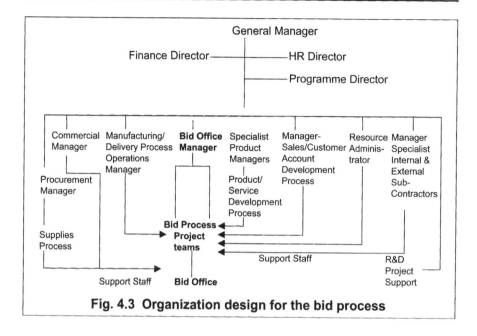

Fig. 4.3 Organization design for the bid process

4.2.1.2 Product Managers

These are responsible for leading the ongoing development of the knowledge and experience base of their product and providing application-specific reference support.

4.2.1.3 Manager Specialist Sub-contracting

Responsible for the residual specialist function groups that cannot be economically justified to work full-time in particular project teams. They share their time across several teams, which develop the general foundation specialist skills and technologies common to all products. Also responsible for procuring quotes for specialist external sub-contract work-packages, to supply to bid project teams.

4.2.1.4 Commercial Manager

Provides expertise in pricing policy, contracts design and the associated legal aspects.

4.2.1.5 Manufacturing/Service Delivery Process Operations Manager

Once the bid process and the total product or service development and introduction process is completed, this manager is responsible for accepting the designs and providing the delivery of the actual product or service for the customer.

4.2.1.6 Resource Administrator

Keeps track of the whereabouts of all staff and their experience in all business process teams, and supports the weekly resource allocation and planning meeting attended by all project heads and the General Manager. Ensures systematic development and utilisation of staff and rotation between functional roles, specialist roles and project team roles.

4.2.1.7 Manager Sales/Customer Accounts

Responsible for finding target customers and managing the implementation of the account development and sales management strategies. Once a lead is developed to the RFQ stage, hands over to the bid process team.

4.2.2 *Other support infrastructure items in the Bid Office*

- A database of all previous bid documents for reference.
- A standards database of re-usable bid document modules, bid illustrations etc, in a quality format which can be selected for use in final bid proposal documents to speed up the process of bid document preparation and house-style enforcement.
- Financial modelling software packages.
- In-service statistics.
- IT-based tools to support networked team working ranging from video conferencing and word processing packages to overhead slide presentation package generation and technical tools such as QFD, FMEA, or software development and simulation aids.
- All minutes of meetings and records of customer meeting decisions and agreed actions supplied by the Customer Account Manager from the decision mapping and solution-selling activities, as well as customer change requests, for change control.
- A mandatory standard meeting discipline to ensure that all project control meetings are well run and actions recorded and distributed with the minimum number of meetings, each with a standard attendee list and standard agenda and the associated database of minutes accumulated for an audit trail.
- Standard report forms on progress to the bid project plan.
- Decision mapping and solution-selling, networked information spread-sheet support software.
- A standard team training workshop capability for use when briefing and initiating a new bid team on the customer requirements, the bid document structure and responsibilities or ownerships, and the project plan, as well as how to use the bid office facilities and the company standard procedures.

These are just illustrations, and a well-designed Bid Office environment can provide great productivity benefits at low shared cost from a quality-assured, flexible working environment. The benefits achieved in competitiveness improvement can be immense. Typically, a well-designed bid process utilising well-trained teams has been shown to increase bid success rates from around two out of ten to seven out of ten, which leads to high sales and profit growth.

4.2.2.1 Relationship to the CAP

In the business CAP structure discussed in Chapter 1, Fig. 1.1a and 1.1b, the primary development activities in module IV are the change programme, discussed in detail in Chapter 5, and the product and service development process of the three core processes in any business, i.e.

* The bidding and product introduction process for winning and delivering orders.
* The product production and delivery process.
* The business support process.

The first two are those which should provide the most value enhancement and opportunity for growth. However, the third creates new opportunities via the customer order-winning process, and provides economically shared administration and other support for value adding providing they are well-designed and managed for effectiveness and leanness.

Within the support process is another sub-process, the corporate strategy facilitation process, shown in Fig. 4.1, which is led by the Chief Executive and which provides the catalyst and leadership for the creation of the CAP. The change process is a second important follow-on sub-process in the overall support process, since it provides the persistent systematic and energetic activity and focus to continually re-engineer, update, improve and make more capable all of the other processes. The change process is the subject of Chapter 5. The product or service development process provides a double opportunity both to enhance business performance and also protect the business future.

This is achieved firstly by searching out and qualifying market opportunities, and detailing customer needs for new products and services then developing and designing them or updating existing products and services, it creates the source of ongoing sales revenues.

Secondly, by being subjected to redesign and best practice introduction via the change programme within the overall rolling CAP project plan, its capability and effectiveness can be increased and then subjected to structured continuous improvement activity, as explained in Chapter 5.

In the current chapter, we will now examine all-embracing, modern approaches for applying team project management practices and organizing the product and service introduction process. Such an approach is often referred to as either Simultaneous Engineering, or Concurrent Development because of the dual operational consequence of using multi-disciplinary teams with continuous iterative and interactive consideration of all aspects of the customer requirements and the requirements for economic and productive delivery of these.

4.3 Project management of the product introduction process

Continual timely innovation in products and services to meet customer needs is an essential activity critical to success in all commercial businesses and many other organizations.

Industries such as the motor vehicle or aircraft manufacturing segment have to carry out very long, expensive and complex projects to introduce new vehicles to maintain their competitiveness and improve market share. They continuously innovate in such areas as styling, fuel efficiency, the introduction of new electronic technologies, the use of new materials, and the application of low cost manufacture and assembly methods, to produce improved products. They also have to continuously improve support services such as spare parts supply and vehicle repair.

Service organizations such as universities have to innovate in all their service provision areas, such as research and the development of new, relevant and attractive courses, in order to attract research funding and students.

Banks and insurance companies introduce new financial investment product offerings at a high rate, to meet competition, some of which have been stimulated by the availability of the Internet.

Construction companies take new design concepts for buildings and infrastructure, such as roads and railways, and translate these into physical realisation via manufacture and assembly of modular components, fittings and structures. These are one-off events of a demanding transient nature requiring a temporary project management organization, with all of the consequences which this entails.

In all cases, there is a generic process involved for conceptionalising and creating something new, which, therefore, creates the need for a dedicated, properly resourced, disciplined and trained project managed team approach. Modern market conditions demand competitive performance.

The potential economic and other types of benefit from forming cross-functional teams for project management come from a number of sources:

1. A reduction in the time, often by as much as 50%, required to deliver the project compared with the traditional departmental organization 'pass the parcel' methods.
2. Delivery to exactly meet the customer need specification.
3. Major cost reductions due to reduced lead-time and more efficient and effective management with minimisation of confused and wasteful activity, allowing productivity to increase and, hence, smaller team sizes.

Product or service development and introduction projects in different industries come in a wide range of sizes and complexities. All have, to a degree, to apply multiple skills because of the broad knowledge base usually needed. New knowledge from research is required together with custom and practice knowledge adapted to new requirements. Some projects require the use of a very large multi-skill resource team over a long period, and others may only need a small number of people. All types of project can benefit from a disciplined approach to definition, management of detail and control.

Generic phases, of which points 1 and 2 apply to all projects, are:

1. Definition of need, R&D. Requirements specification.
2. Design, introduction into a delivery implementation process, first-time manufacture or delivery.
3. Repetitive manufacture or delivery.

Not all of these phases will necessarily be fully confined within a single organization or business, hence management of the process across company and international boundaries may be very demanding. The phases are not followed totally consequentially, i.e, there are usually overlaps and much iteration as part of the concurrent engineering concept. This requires very good communication, review and control systems, and the clear definition of the position and timing of logical review phase milestones to ensure orderly progression, as discussed in Chapter 3.

As a business process, therefore, a large product and service development project can be divided into cross-functional team modular phases or cellular co-located work-package team groups. Some of the modules may be operated by sub-contractors, coordinated by a master project group or lead contractor, efficiently integrated internationally by the use of a standard project management system and integrated IT and data management.

4.4 Definition of the product introduction process (PIP)

The PIP process encompasses a set of skills and activities logically related to the design of the product or service and the design and creation of the realisation and delivery process. It is important to design the organization structure and management practices so that such innovation processes do not proceed in a linear sequence, but rather in cross-functional interactive clusters between natural phase gate milestones. This is essential to good performance.

An illustrative example of a typical set of activities, which are required for a business concerned with the design and manufacture of aerospace engine electronic control systems, as introduced in the case example of Chapter 1, is shown in Table 4.1. This has much in common with all kinds of development projects.

Table 4.1 Major Activity phases for electronic control systems projects	
1. Opportunity assessment and market analysis	Fit to market plan, potential sales volumes and market price target.
2. Proposal development and cost profile, net present value and internal rate of return calculated for the estimated sales volumes and target price	Bid team formed, proposal prepared and assessed. Approval to bid. Bid submitted. Bid information communicated to project team on project launch.
3. Project planning	Project team formed and trained, and project launched. Project plans and work-package structures prepared. Organization structure and controls defined.
4. Concept definition	Customer requirements defined in detail. Applications knowledge accessed, comprehensive product and process concept design agreed.
5. Functional detail design	Electronic circuit design, Mechanical Design, Design for assembly and manufacture, Design to target cost, Software Design and Build.

Table 4.1 *Continued*	
6. Manufacturing system design	Manufacturing process, manufacturing controls and manufacturing support tooling and equipment specification and design. Manufacturing cell system design, manufacturing control system and measures of performance, quality standards design. Team structures design.
7. Prototype development	Initial samples of sub-systems and components built and evaluated with feedback to functional design and manufacturing system design.
8. Test equipment design	Design and manufacture of all required test and quality assessment hardware and software, and test plans written to meet specification requirements and associated test strategy.
9. Design validation and qualification	Validation by (potential) customer of conformance to specification and duty. Approval certification from all relevant authorities for the product and manufacturing system and control procedures.
10. Introduction to manufacture	Train manufacturing cell teams, provide complete drawings, standard working and continuous improvement procedures, ramp up production and test all processes, controls and administrative/quality recording practices, quality problem definition and problem solving procedures and approvals required.

The ten activity phases in Table 4.1 have considerable managed internal team interaction, which has been alluded to previously, which does not just proceed in a sequential linear manner.

Also, the project is clearly a complex multi-disciplinary activity, which requires careful design of an effective co-located team organization as provided in the case example of Chapter 1. This ensures efficiency and high quality process capability using the methodologies described later in Chapter 5, where detailed methodologies for natural group team design are also described.

4.5 Project controls

Three important features ensure good control:

1. The use of a set of project control and planning forms on a computer information system, together with a document filing and control system, for wide access by the team and for reviews. The Support Methodology Section provides some examples for adapting to meet specific needs.
2. The use of a set of standard meetings for management, communication and control.
3. An integrated evolving product data management system.

The project planning and organizational design requirements follow naturally after compiling the project control charts as summarized in Chapter 3 and the Supporting Methodology Section 3.

There is usually a top-level macroscopic schedule plan, supported by the fully detailed work-package plans, covering the whole process and characterized by a set of major time milestones based upon right-to-left planning backwards from the introduction to market date. It is necessary to monitor conformance to these milestones and the planned costs regularly; involving customers in milestone reviews where relevant, for their ideas and to aid communication. This intermediate reviewing process is supported by the programme office, which also helps formulate and start up the project to maintain best practice continuity. It provides opportunities to ensure that the best product design and delivery processes are achieved with many opportunities to close out problems and provide detailed advice and steering from an experienced reviewing or steering group and the programme office.

The customer related, so-called top-level or macroscopic, progress milestone review and approval points in Table 4.1 are also augmented by a number of important additional process control approval points, as summarized in a typical set in Table 4.2. Together these help to eliminate

Table 4.2 Process approval reviews related to the Table 4.1 example

1. Approval for resource allocation to scope the opportunity and costs	This examines the fit of opportunities to CAP strategy, the size of the market, the potential value of the opportunity in relation to other opportunities in terms of sales and net present value, and agrees the necessary first stage budget required to define the scope and assess the risks, often in conjunction with a target customer.
2. Approval to bid	This provides executive approval for a team resource to develop a bid proposal document, including a project plan.
3. Proposal approval	The formal review of the specification and the proposal document in detail, either prior to presentation to a customer for contract negotiation or prior to starting the full project delivery process.
4. Post-proposal acceptance review	This follows customer acceptance of the bid regardless of whether the customer is an internal or external customer. It enables senior management to interpret and assess the final specification, prices, duration of contract, and contract conditions to be met. It marks the decision point to resource and start-up of the delivery project team.
5. Top-level project plan sign-off	This reviews the full specification, all project plan control forms, work-package structure and ownerships, the project team organization and resources, and the forward review timetable through to the delivery date.

Table 4.2 *Continued*	
6. Concept design review	This reviews the proposed product concept and the manufacturing process concept, including the fit to existing manufacturing system capabilities and the need to augment these.
7. Detail design reviews and commercial reviews	There are likely to be several of these as the design evolves, and the necessary iterations between software, hardware and manufacturing concepts are carried out, linked to sub-system prototype and device testing while focusing on target cost achievement. It is during this very detailed stage that the use of the best practice team tools and techniques, shown in the project flow-chart of Case Example 2 in Chapter 1, require intense application and are the most effective. Product modules and sub-assemblies may be approved and signed off at these reviews, subject only to change control, once the total product prototype takes shape, and feedback from manufacturing trials is provided. The effective control of iterative changes is essential and can have a major impact on project cost. The most effective approach is to avoid drip-feeding changes into the various activities of a project on a daily basis, since this is distracting and confusing. Instead, a FRACAS (Fault Recording and Change Action System) information system in which faults, problems or changes requested from all sources relating to product design and manufacturing process change

Table 4.2 *Continued*

	requirements are communicated, with their explanation and justification, into a project database. Then, at two- or three-monthly intervals a single 'Modpack' is defined for execution on a particular date and approved in a design review with the associated manufacturing change review approval. From this point, the product configuration control version number is changed to facilitate tracking and is held constant until the next 'Modpack' is defined and implemented. In between these stages, the design reviews incorporate a commercial review to assess the contractual and pricing consequences of 'modpacks' and identifies 'who pays'. The commercial reviews will involve customer commercial representatives, who will be required to formally agree to pay for their areas of responsibility in initiating changes. It is good practice to separate commercial reviews from technical reviews to avoid impeding technical progress from negotiation stances and customer–supplier trading policies intruding into debates.
8. Final product prototype acceptance approval DV1 (Design Validation)	This will be a joint customer–supplier evaluation review to ensure that all changes are satisfactorily completed and recorded, and that the product specification and performance is compliant with business requirements and that all testing has been satisfactorily completed on the final prototype version.

Table 4.2 *Continued*	
9. Production facility and resource approval (DV2)	This may involve several stages as each product sub-system is approved, to save time, and is the authorisation for the initiation of the production delivery process.
10. Final design approval and delivery launch (DV3)	This is a joint supplier and customer sign-off of their agreement to the product design and the production process, and it may coincide with product launch approval to authorise commencement of delivery. A formal sign-off by the customer will be required.
11. Project sign-off approval	This is a joint review meeting with the customer after the delivery process has been proved to be successful. It may be several months after delivery launch and usually triggers the final project payment by the customer. Repetitive ongoing product supply, the provision by the customer of an ISIR (Initial Sample Inspection Report) are integrated with the instruction to start post-job-1 repetitive production.

delays and confusion from problems, mistakes and uncertainty, They enhance project process capability and quality of performance. They also aid communication with and involvement of a wide cross-section of staff and so help to support a performance culture. The review group needs to be cross-functional and with wide experience ranging from technical to commercial, financial and operational matters.

It should be noted that the process teams carrying out the project activity are likely progressively to vary in both size and range of skills as the project process moves from phase to phase, as well as in the degree of specialist work-package sub-contracting both inside and outside the boundaries of the business unit. Sloppiness and lack of attention to detail in the face of workflow crossing business boundaries can lead to very expensive mistakes and considerable aggravation.

4.6 Organizing the product introduction process

Chapter 1 introduced an overall organization model into which the management responsibility for the product development process, supported by a programme office, is integrated. It also provides an example organization chart for a large project, cases of which have also been discussed earlier in the current chapter, as a framework for illustrating the application of the general project and programme management practices covered in Chapter 3.

However, when the organizational implications are examined for application of management by projects practices across the whole business, there are several complicating factors, which must be resolved to create a balanced and effective organization. The most important ones are as follows:

1. Small companies do not need and cannot provide large project support infrastructures. If small companies are involved in large company projects, they will generally provide small work-packages under the umbrella support of the large company project control infrastructure. In small companies, there is likely to be only a small core project team for each project with part-time members helping on a scheduled basis. The full-time core of as few as two or three people will generally have multi-skill capabilities in relation to the organization knowledge base.

2. Larger organizations will be likely to have a range of projects simultaneously running, from the very small and short-term to the large and longer-term project requiring a large core team with all the core skills needed.

3. There is still a need to retain some specialist functional groups that share their skill across a range of projects. It is important to make sure that these do not feel unimportant and left out of the mainstream by providing them with clear project work-package ownership responsibilities, on a pseudo-contractual basis, to maintain commercial pressure to perform, involving them in main project reviews and offering managed job rotation experience between project roles and functional roles. This is particularly advantageous for staff in research departments, who can feel isolated, to develop their experience and utilise their skills to the full, while providing enhanced job satisfaction.

4. Effectively organized and managed resource management across projects, functions and supporting administrative units is essential.

5. The necessary controls and synergistic support must be carefully integrated across the organization with distinct sub-business processes, well defined in terms of their roles, particularly the support processes.

Where multiple projects, ranging from very large to very small, are concerned, it is helpful to use a general classification process as given in Table 4.3.

Table 4.3 Classification process

Classification	Description	Description
Runner	Narrowly focused work-package and lying within specialist functions competence.	Functional Manager or subordinate.
Repeater	Work-package crossing a few functions only, or within a small local project team, with a narrow specification.	Lead function or local team leader.
Stranger	Large, demanding multi-functional project with a very broad complex task. Leadership.	Project Manager with support from Programme Office etc.

Cross-functional teams should not be restricted to technical staff from different disciplines. There is often a need for full- or part-time team members with skills in such areas as marketing, finance and purchasing/commercial functions.

Very large and complex projects will justify having their own product change and configuration control committee because of the large volume of work entailed, which would clog up the working of the overall business product portfolio change controls. On completion of the project, they would hand over responsibility for ongoing change control to the central change control committee, as the mass of new detailed work was completed (see Support Methodology Section 3 and Chapter 5).

4.6.1 PIP Organization design case example

Figure 4.4 shows the project and support organisation chart for the product and manufacturing development section of the organization in a medium-

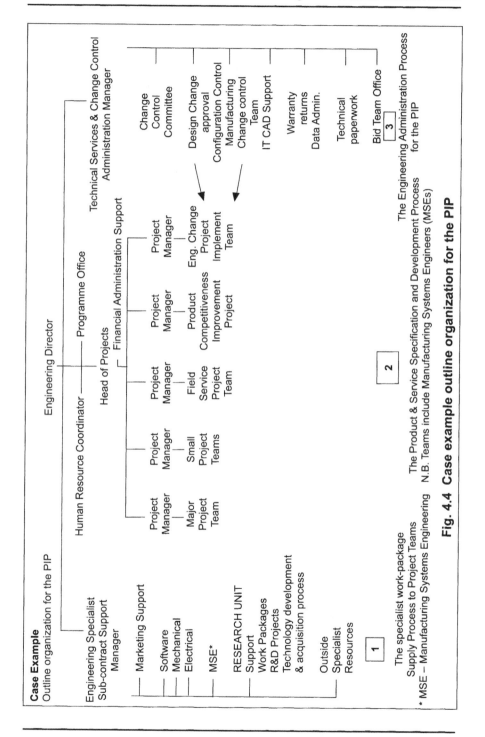

Fig. 4.4 Case example outline organization for the PIP

sized capital goods engineering company, which is in the process of developing a new complex standard machine for selling to a range of customers, while continuing to maintain other products in a range for different markets. This was a blend of best practice from several companies following reorganisation using an organizational change competitiveness achievement project programme. While a specific industry sector example is shown, over 70% of its features are generic to a wider class of businesses, and it provides a good starting point for managers to work from when planning an organization redesign project. Examples of competences and functions integrated are given below.

Product Introduction Process
- Marketing
- Research
- Purchasing
- Electrical and electronic engineering
- Mechanical engineering
- Software engineering
- Manufacturing systems engineering

Wider functions to be involved (basis for part-time support staff in team structures)
- Sales and field service support
- Manufacturing management
- Quality systems audit
- Finance
- Aftermarket, spares and service distribution

The main features of this major segment of a company organization are described below, there are three clear business sub-processes labelled 1, 2 and 3.

Sub-process 1
Provides integrated procurement and management of specialist work-package support to all projects from internal functions, as well as from external contractors. This maintains internal core competence requirements and also provides R&D technical capability to fill gaps in the technology route map for new knowledge and for troubleshooting advanced technical problems. In addition to the specialists illustrated, there may be a need for others such as professional reliability engineering for electronic/mechanical/software-integrated products.

Sub-process 2

This is the core project delivery process for new products and associated after-sales services. Each project manager is line-responsible for his/her core team and its project plan, controls the budget and delivers the project deliverables, i.e. specification, delivery date, project cost and target cost compliance. He/she also specifies and orders sub-contract work-packages and reviews their progress in his/her project reviews.

For the large project a dedicated project administrator is necessary to arrange meetings, minutes, correspondence and financial administration. For the smaller projects, a single Project Manager, with a line reporting team, will be responsible for a number of less demanding projects requiring a similar cross-section of skills. He may still, as in the large projects, need to sub-contract specialist work-packages where the specialist skill requirement is not a full-time one. His team will have a wide mix of skills these can be fully utilised by the number and requirements of all his projects. The total task may be just as sophisticated as for a large project and may cover the requirements of a number of customers with a large set of deliverables to manage.

The Project Managers for small projects, field service support projects and the engineering change request and fulfilment requirements projects provide a clear focus and leadership role for these natural groups of projects, which clarifies accountability and facilitates good management of the organization.

The Project Manager, for product competitiveness improvement, has the task of reviewing established products, which have become cost or performance uncompetitive, of monitoring and reverse engineering competitor products, and then either managing product upgrade projects or sometimes passing sub-system work onto the Project Manager for smaller projects. He may procure specialist work-packages from the internal or external suppliers in the same way as the other Project Managers.

All of the Project Managers interface directly with their customers, and run regular customer review meetings. They have an agreed budget, built into the CAP financial plan.

Sub-process 3

The engineering administration and support process. This incorporates several important coordination and support roles, each having a small core resource and co-opting staff from specialist function groups and project teams for assistance and meeting duties on a part-time basis.

The Change Control Committee, chaired by the Engineering Director, and with commercial and project team membership, meets monthly to review all requests for changes in specification or to eliminate problems.

It assesses the needs, defines the necessary commercial responsibilities for paying for the changes, and approves modification package structures and timings. It receives the minutes of project review meetings, particularly the change action lists, and manages the FRACAS information database and audits FRACAS conformance procedures (see Support Methodology in Chapter 3).

The design change approval unit may just be a single individual who formally administers records of changes and the updating of product structure and configuration control documents. He services the change and configuration control committee (see Support Methodology Section 3).

The manufacturing change approval team meets monthly to examine all change requests from the point of view of manufacturing process impact, and signs off approved changes against a checklist once the required supporting elements are in place, such as training for operatives and availability of working drawings and tooling (see Support Methodology in Chapter 3).

The warranty returns data control role collects and verifies warranty returns, and passes them for action to the relevant small projects manager and the change control committee, and reports monthly on their completion and impact. It compiles statistics on in-service performance to feed back to the product design functions and the Engineering Director.

The IT CAD support unit manages the IT infrastructure shared by all the project teams and functions, including the FRACAS database and customer-related information, the CAD system and configuration control documentation and information support for Account Managers. The Engineering Director supervises the choice of the IT equipment and IT developments to meet the needs of the engineering and manufacturing process. He also supervises the introduction of best practice tools and methods, recruitment and training requirements and professional development experience records in collaboration with the Resource Manager to ensure good staff development and job rotation.

The technical documentation unit coordinates the provision of bid presentation paperwork, standard worksheets, data sheets and other necessary supporting items to the entire organization, e.g. operating manuals.

The bid team office is used when the company receives a significant number of requests for quotations each month. Staff are temporarily allocated from all areas to support the Customer Account Manager in small cross-functional team groups reporting to a Project Manager, coordinated by the Bid Office Manager, who provides financial analysis support for cost estimation and pricing. This provides a rapid response and a flexible bidding capability to maintain a flow of customer orders. The basis for this has been discussed earlier in this chapter.

In the above case example, it is imperative to take seriously the importance of resource management, job rotation, and the tracking and recording of experience gained in order to motivate and make the most effective use of people. A well-managed project organization structure of the kind described, will typically produce up to 35% more output with 15% fewer people than a traditional functional department organization, using project progress chasers. Staff respond well to clarity of role and responsibility definition, to regular training and to clear allocation of team authority and responsibility. One aspect of resource allocation, which is believed to have many advantages, is to create a balanced mix of team personalities. This has to be done pragmatically because of practical difficulties of competence assessment and assurance of availability of exactly the right mix of people. The recommendations of Belbin, described in the Support Tools and Techniques Section 5, identify nine team member roles and provide a helpful rough-cut guide to effective team building, i.e. the roles of: Specialist, Team-worker, Coordinator, Completer, Shaper, Evaluator, Plant, Resource Investigator, Implementer, more than one of which, to a degree, may be embodied in a single person. There needs also to be a combination of transactional and transformational leadership skills, as discussed in Chapter 1.

4.7 Configuration and change control

Figure 4.5 shows an overall change requirement generation, approval, recording and implementation support system. Generally, the elements are all required in any business with reasonably complex products and services, although some of them may be implemented simply and combined in one function in less complex and dynamic situations. It is generally very important for changes carried out to be post-auditable, and for configuration definitions to be up-to-date, particularly when products and services are modular with significant numbers of variants or models. This helps to ensure that important requirements, such as the supply of the correct spare parts, the carrying out of applicable maintenance procedures, and the supply of the correct product or service are achieved. The impact on operational effectiveness in every part of the business, from purchasing to after-service sales, by eliminating wasteful confusion while increasing productivity, is very beneficial in terms of greatly reduced costs and improved quality of service.

In simple terms, if every product standard module or sub-assembly is allocated a reference number and each component in the module, is allocated a sub-number suffix to the module reference number, and each has a specification, which is up-to-date, no problems of confusion should occur. When changes are approved and implemented, a version number suffix is appended to the part or module number, and a revised dated specification drawing issued with the correct number. All are recorded on the information system. Together, these will lead to ease of auditing of changes, and ensure the correct product, service or component is supplied. Similarly, all approved changes not yet implemented should be recorded separately, together with their planned implementation date, for ease of access (see Chapter 5).

The benefits are immense for projects which form part of a consortia project with many sub-contractors having a large number of purchased components, such as projects to develop and design a railway system or new aircraft. However, even quite small companies require a well-disciplined

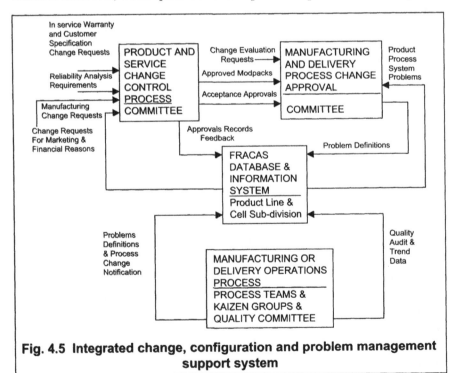

Fig. 4.5 Integrated change, configuration and problem management support system

configuration and change control system to minimise their operating costs and improve their quality of supply, implementation and service.

Recent studies, coupled with experiences in equipment manufacturing companies, have shown major potential improvements in work-flow management at reduced cost from the use of such simple effective systems. Some specific areas of benefit found were:

1. Provides easy, rapid access to 100% correct product information across collaborative, dispersed projects.
2. Much reduced time to produce product delivery documentation.
3. Product data and its component part status as a design evolves, and after completion, is easily accessible.
4. Much reduced non-value-added administrative work.
5. Very effective in supporting concurrent engineering team activity, which has dispersed team groups, and increasing productivity.
6. Provides considerable productivity and cost reduction benefit to the invoicing process, the procurement process and the aftermarket service support process.
7. Ensures the maintenance of sub-system and component part configuration integrity through the whole product or service life-cycle, i.e. development, design, manufacture, delivery, operational phases incorporating updates, upgrades and new products with common component parts, while eliminating the need for considerable administrative reconciliation effort.

A critical starting point, however, which also matches modern requirements for lowest cost for product design and service design, is for the project team to configure their initial top-level system view of the emerging product concept as an assembly of standard modules and sub-systems. This also brings considerable benefits to the product or service delivery process, since it enables high productivity, with reduced non-value-added activity. Auditable standard working routines can be designed, focused on delivery of each module and on the multi-module assembly process. A product or service assembly tree showing the service or product assembly configuration is an essential output of the PIP project activity. The logic of this is illustrated in Fig. 4.6.

A wider discussion of change control and problem management applicable to all kinds of businesses, not just engineering manufacturing businesses, is provided in the Support Methodology Section 5.

Note that variety in product specification can be catered for economically by the use of a mix of standard core modules and components with choices

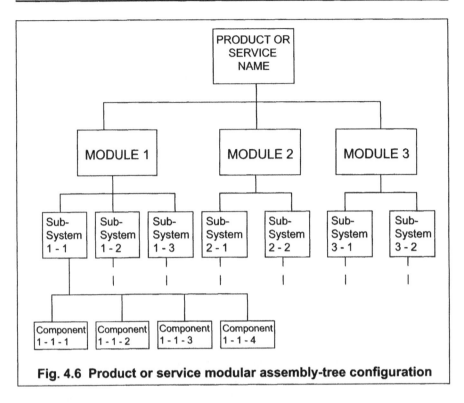

Fig. 4.6 Product or service modular assembly-tree configuration

from a set of option variant modules. The variant modules must be subject to configuration control, also shown in supplementary assembly tree charts. Sales staff can use these tree charts when negotiating a customer specification.

When setting up the necessary organizational mechanisms for configuration and change control, it is necessary to combine a cross-functional approval mechanism, which takes account of technical, commercial and cost issues, with an executive line management mechanism as outlined in the case study for a machinery supplier company, shown in Fig. 4.4.

The overall change management system shown in Fig. 4.5 will need to be flow-charted, and, when the design is completed, a standard operating procedure must be documented and staff must be trained. It is critically important for the operational procedures of the two key committees, the change control committee and the manufacturing change acceptance committee, to be defined and standardised and all staff trained in its operation. This implies the design of a standard agenda, a list of deliverable actions and a definition of the functional attendees, coupled with a clear definition of the roles and responsibilities of the committees, for communication to all staff.

Operational disciplines must be set up for the proper operation and control of the FRACAS information system and problem database, as shown in Fig. 4.5, particularly where the business operates modern team or cell-based delivery processes, where cell teams can find problems and solve many of them by themselves as part of a Kaizen continuous improvement procedure.

It is important that local computer terminals are used to allow such teams to keep the FRACAS database up-to-date with lists of problems solved and lists of problems outstanding. Many of these problems come from quality issues or issues related to the operation of equipment used in the delivery process, and need prompt and systematic management to a solution.

An example of a simple 13-point standard change management procedure statement based upon the best practice experiences of a number of engineering equipment design and manufacturing companies, is provided for illustration in Support Methodology Section 3.

In this procedure, the reference to a fast-track route relates to the classification of changes into the three groups: Runner, Repeater, Stranger.

Strangers involving sophisticated changes require a complex detailed control procedure, which can be slow in safety-critical product companies such as aerospace and automotive businesses. Runner problems, by comparison, which usually comprise the largest volume of change requests, often can be solved, checked and signed off quite simply. It is unproductive to clog up the system with large volumes of runners, which happens in many companies. Therefore, a fast track route is designed with a careful check and sign-off on completion, and all runners, plus a selection of repeaters, take this route. Considerable, and very beneficial, reductions in process lead-times result, leading to reduced cost and enhanced customer satisfaction.

4.8 Improving process effectiveness by the use of modern tools and techniques

In Chapter 1, an overall simplified flow-chart showing the main phases of a product introduction process, was provided in Figs 1.8a and b. There is a group of computer-based tools which can be used to improve process effectiveness in meeting objectives, and a typical set of these are shown on the flow-chart in Chapter 1, as well as being described in the Support Tools and Techniques sections of this book.

These tools become particularly powerful and effective when used by a cross-functional project team which is responsible for the whole project process. They lose their power when a traditional fragmented functional department structure is used because the opportunity to short circuit communications and closely integrate a cross-functional set of knowledge and experience becomes impeded. The tools are essentially team-based tools, which support structured brainstorming and ideas interaction.

Figure 4.7 shows how a set of co-located project teams can be grouped around a shared IT facility containing the toolkit and surrounded closely by the functional support groups in a physical realisation of the organisation model in Fig. 4.4.

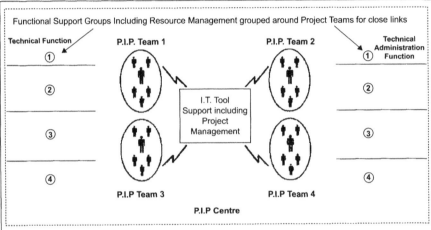

Functional Support Groups Including Resource Management grouped around Project Teams for close links

- Group projects into Runners, Repeaters, and Strangers
- Install engineering change control and manufacturing change control meetings for each team
- Each team is cross-functional

Fig. 4.7 Physical arrangement for the simultaneous engineering product introduction process

A number of tools, which make knowledge accessible to all team members are generic to all kinds of product and service development projects, for example:

- A product and process *data management system*. This can also include customer decision mapping and FRACAS data.
- *Failure Modes and Effects Analysis (FMEA)* to brainstorm potential problems with a new design, categorize them in pareto order of potential pain for the customer, and focus the team on their elimination before design finalisation. The problems can be grouped in relation to the product itself and the process for creating or delivering the product.

- *Design to target cost*, to systematically focus on each module and sub-system of a product or service, as it is being developed, and to estimate its cost in order to focus cost reduction exercises that achieve an acceptable cost to meet the target selling price requirement.
- *Quality function deployment*, to take the specification required to be met, including quality standards, and cascade their detailed implications into every specialised work-package in the product or service sub-system assembly tree in order to communicate directly the requirement to the particular project team members concerned.
- *Design for assembly and service delivery*, to take the modular assembly tree for a product or service, and carry out two very important operations to reduce cost and lead-times:
  - (a) to itemise the component parts and systematically eliminate all non-essential items;
  - (b) to carefully analyse the process for building the product or service and optimise the ease and reliability of performing this process, estimating the cost of each stage, on a 'first things first' basis, carefully flow-charted, best physical assembly route. Figure 4.8, summarises the 'design for assembly' (DFA) process for an engineering product. A service product delivered in modules is also amenable to the same logical process with considerable benefit.
- The intensive use of cross-company and sub-contractor *standard control charts* and bar diagram formats, accessible to all project teams for their project and the programme office (see Chapter 3 and its Support Methodology section).

Further background to the above topics is provided in the Support Tools and Techniques sections.

The combination of the above 'design for production' and assembly tools, with the use of cross-functional concurrent engineering project team organizations, has been shown to provide an extremely beneficial systematic team working discipline, with much reduced production lead-times, typically by a factor of between 3 and 10, and, 20–40% reduction in component parts. It also results in a more reliable and consistently higher quality product at much lower cost, which is easier to support in service. Software packages, such as the Team-Set product, developed by Lucas Industries, which integrate all the tools for team use, evolved in the 1990s, and were immediately applied, with the necessary training, by the better engineering companies, with considerable benefits. In such companies, it is now a standard element in their best practice methodologies, which is essential for competitiveness. The practices can be applied to both standard

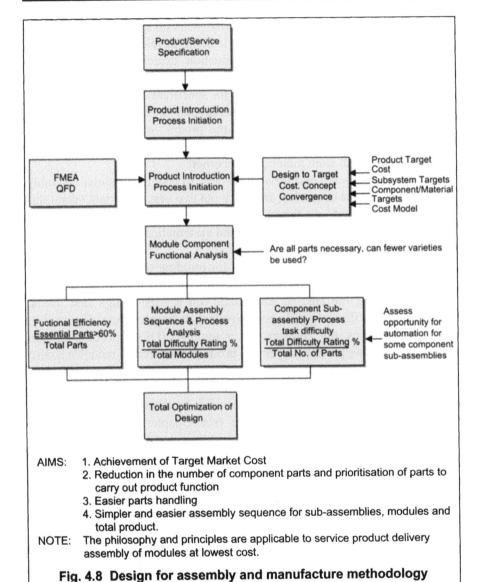

Fig. 4.8 Design for assembly and manufacture methodology

repetitive production products as well as to bespoke, one-off product development. In the latter case it applies a rigorous discipline to eliminate the casual re-work-centred, high cost, jobbing shop culture, and increases productivity. It also enforces a configuration control procedure. Here bespoke products tailored to individual customer needs, but within a product family of repeating product types, benefit considerably from the use of the tools and techniques. These enforce a hybrid modular approach to products and the partitioning of a core of standard modules or sub-assemblies and standard parts up to assembly level. There is a focus on parts for functionality and the elimination of unnecessary parts, supplemented by variation or option modules, which are partly standard and partly tailored to specific customer needs. The result is a more rapid and consistent quality of production and commissioning at significantly lower cost. It is often very revealing for a company, which makes tailored products or services, to analyse its part bespoke products when they may be surprised to find that there is a large percentage of runner or potentially standard components in their product.

4.9 Software product development

Software development is a very specialised functional activity where the work content and associated resource requirements are difficult to estimate by managers in advance, and where the monitoring of progress and productivity on a regular basis also has its difficulties. Part of the difficulty stems from the fact that managers, and other technical professionals associated with the software project, may not have any formal training in modern software engineering, and the application of measures of performance metrics. Software professionals, themselves, often have very narrow viewpoints. They may operate in a very individualistic and uncommunicative fashion, not carefully aligned to the business, and propagate the view that software development is a creative and 'impossible to plan' art; an art that cannot be managed in a predictive and disciplined way. This, of course, is not true as a comparison of best practice companies and less capable, less professional companies shows (see the final part of this chapter).

One result of this apparent amateurism is that software projects have gained a reputation for always being very late, in relation to meeting original project targets, and of being massively overspent. There is the intrinsic problem that managers cannot see and touch software in reviews, exercise common sense assessments and provide informed views, as well as they can with other types of product and service development.

Whether the software is being developed as a product in its own right or as part of another product such as a computer-controlled machine or a computer-based financial control and invoicing system, there is one very important element which must be properly taken account of. It is necessary to thoroughly analyse, understand and specify the needs of the business or machine process application which the software is intended to support.

Specialised software engineers and software programming technicians, who write the software code, generally do not have experience in, or understand, the field of the specific application for which the software is to be used.

To ensure success, high productivity and high quality of performance in software developments, a very disciplined and systematic approach is required, using all of the elements of procedure and tools, as discussed in this chapter and in Chapter 3. Specifically there are several mandatory requirements:

1. Set up a project team embodying a range of skills, including a thorough understanding of the needs of the application. Train the team as a group at the outset of the project, in common best application analysis and specification practices as well as the application practical requirements.
2. The Project Manager should be a systems engineer with overview experience and skill, who has expert knowledge of the application, e.g. the control of manufacturing machinery and the particular process carried out by the machinery, or the operation of particular business processes such as materials purchasing planning and scheduling or invoice processing.
3. Ensure that common software engineering standards are agreed upon. These should include the use of a common programming language and the use of standards for interfacing and communicating or networking which match the computers and machines which will host the software. It is usually essential for the project team to be supplied with identical computer work-stations with standard software. These are used for emulation and testing the developing software modules as well as providing the basis for an integrated data management network.
4. Insist upon the application of team tools, such as FMEA and QFD, to ensure that potential problems and causes of failure are carefully assessed at the outset, for preventative action by the team, and that the needs of the specification are broken down in detail to communicate to all members and functions within the team.
5. It is essential that complex software packages are built up in a modular way to match a carefully designed product architecture. These should be careful overall input–output definitions and matching inputs and outputs at the interfaces between sub–system modules, the users and the communication interfaces with their critical time cycles to and from the application. This also helps with quality control, rectification, and after-sales subsequent maintenance and upgrading. It is easier to track down and fix a fault or bug in a module than in a totally entangled, single

complex set of lines of programming code. Upgrades and modifications may often then be carried out, by simply replacing a module.

A software system assembly block diagram should always be constructed at the start of the project, as in the example of Fig. 4.6. Where possible, industry standard modules or well-proven application modules should be included. This minimises follow-on support requirements

6. Ensure, at the outset, that the Systems Engineer and the Software Engineer members of the project team, are fully trained to use and apply modern tools for software metrics assessment, e.g. for work content estimation, optimization of the number of lines of code in a software work-package and software module integration methods, as well as in the systematic testing of software modules and complete software systems

Considerable development of best practices has gone on over the past twenty years, which has helped to dispel the myth that software engineering is an unstructured, 'impossible to plan', black art. Managers should now refuse to accept that software development is particularly different and that the development process is a black hole. They must work hard at creating a communicative team culture. Organizations, such as the US Carnegie Mellon University Software Institute, have developed very structured definition and operational procedures, including monitoring and testing practice, with the associated standards and training courses. One aspect of this involves an initial audit of the particular company software development project capabilities and cultures; the company is graded on what is called a software development process maturity staircase – with reference to modern best practices. Table 4.4 summarises the excellent practical Carnegie Mellon software maturity assessment approach.

Many important companies have been embarrassed, following such an audit, to find that, although in some areas of product development they are competent, in software development they have not progressed past the first level of maturity. To achieve full professional maturity requires a change project programme to be run, as described in Chapter 5, to design the software development process and its operating procedures, and train the participants in a set of best practices, including the operation of project and programme management. Follow-on regular audits of process integrity and quality are usually also required, as well as induction training for new recruits to teach them the standard best practices and programming languages used and develop communication skills.

Table 4.4. Software project management quality

Summary of the Software Engineering Process Maturity Level
Assessment Standard developed by the: Software Engineering Institute,
Mellor University, Pittsburgh, Pennsylvania.

Criteria assessed:

- Product development process capability
- Management commitment
- Planning and control and tracking methods and procedures
- Customer requirements specification capture methods
- Product quality assurance
- Technology utilisation
- Education and training support

Lower grades mean:

- Decreased productivity
- Decreased efficiency
- Increased costs and delays
- Risk of customer dissatisfaction

Levels of maturity:

5. Optimising
4. Managed
3. Defined
2. Repeatable
1. Initial, low capability, vulnerable

Assessment performance levels are from 1 to 5, with number 1 being the lowest.

4.10 The software development team process

Software development project team sizes may vary, depending upon the industry and the scale and newness of the task. Sizes range from three or four people in small companies to several hundred, as required for complex aircraft engine fuel system control projects with their extensive testing, sophisticated safety-critical operational needs, and the requirements for automatic fault diagnostics and multi-channel duplication in case of failures. Nevertheless, the basic principles discussed above still apply.

The team composition to carry out the software engineering process described below has to be multi-functional because of the range of skills required, and would typically consist of the following roles or competences with numbers depending on project size:

1. Project Manager. Must be 'hands-on' capable, preferably an experienced senior Process Engineer with expert knowledge of the process to which the software is to be applied, and trained in project and programme management methods.
2. Software Systems Engineer. Experienced in architecture specification for modular software suites, knowledgeable in the relevant programming methodologies, specification procedures and testing practices.
3. Process Engineers. These must be computer literate and knowledgeable about the process, and its control and management practice needs, for which the software is required.
4. Software Engineers. Capable of carrying out the detailed design and specification of major total software sub-systems, and of supervising focused groups of programmers.
5. Computer or Electronics Systems Engineers. To support infrastructure.
6. Software Programmers. Capable of programming sub-systems to meet their specification requirements.
7. System Test Engineers.
8. Administrative and secretarial support. Depending upon the size of the project.

In addition, there should be a review and approvals committee, involving both suppliers and users of the software, who will approve the specification, meet for monthly reviews, and also carry out a post-project audit and hand-over sign-off.

4.11 The software development process flow-chart

A project start-up workshop is an essential initial process step for the whole team, to familiarise them with the software specification and its deliverables, the business process application for which it is intended, as well as the standard procedures and methodologies to be used. The project should then follow a standard process with clearly-defined iterative phases or sub-processes, for effective concurrent engineering, with defined time and cost monitors and review point phase-gates.

The most commonly used, simplified definition of the overall process flow-chart, analogous to other practical applications in other fields, discussed previously in Chapter 2 and in this chapter, is the so-called V-diagram in Fig. 4.9. The use of a 'V' has become customary to communicate the principle of matching the initial specification to the final software capability across the top of the diagram.

In Fig. 4.9, in the first three process stages, work-packages are led by the Senior Software Systems Engineer, supported by Process Engineers, Software Engineers and the Test Engineers.

Programmers start detailed code writing from phase 4, in software subsystem module work-package groups, supervised by Software Systems Engineers and Process Engineers for the remaining stages through to phase 10.

The hardware–software integration, phase 9, often requires the involvement of Electronics Engineers or Computer Systems Engineers because of the many opportunities for reliability and efficiency trade-offs from meeting certain high speed requirements by 'hard-wiring' using standard hardware, to using associated machine code software elements to suit the particular computer hardware and its operating system. It may be necessary to use techniques such as software coefficient read-in or plug-in electronic chip options to enable flexible use of the software system for a wide variety of applications. There are often opportunities for good cost and performance gains in this area.

Phase 10 is completed using an augmented project team, including customer or user group staff, who also have to be trained for the implementation and operation of the software.

The steering committee should ensure, as described earlier in this chapter, that the following are put in place and effectively used:

1. A standard set of regular control meetings.
2. A configuration and change control procedure plus the associated documentation controls.
3. A project data information system, including all specification data and evolving software designs, fully accessible to the whole team. It should also include the FMEA and QFD databases.

4.12 Defining and delivering forward product strategy

In the final analysis the use of the best practices outlined in this chapter will only be successful in driving a company forward if the product and service strategy truly meets the needs of the market-place.

The CAP approach to three-year business development project planning requires disciplined attention to ensure that new products or product re-

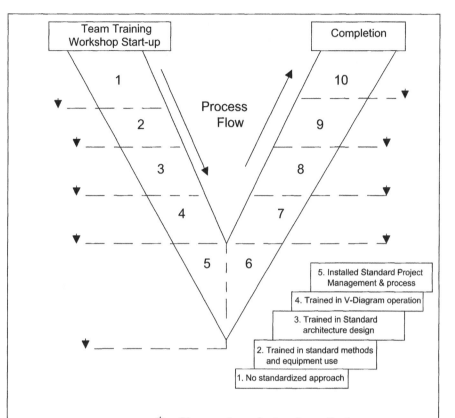

▼ = Phase-gate project review milestone

Stages

1) Application requirements specification
2) Top-level software input–output requirements specification for overall system performance, required deliverables and time cycle productivity
3) Sub-system/definition; I/O specification and modular architecture block diagram flow-chart definition
4) Sub-system coding – standard methodology
5) Sub-system test in-house and independent
6) Sub-system build evolution and test in-house and independent
7) System prototype build and test in-house and independent
8) System test, prove and safety integrity audit – in-house and independent
9) Hardware–Software integration and test
10) Deliver, install, test, train, hand-over and sign-off

Fig. 4.9 Standard software development process 'V-diagram'
(Ref: Facilitation of the Carnegie Mellon Development Process Maturity Standard)

lifeing updates to reshape the product life S-curve are delivered to a rigorous time scale. Being late to market can have disastrous consequences in terms of sales volumes of products. The company that is first to market with the right product specification climbs the experience curve early, finds ways of achieving volume economics early, generates rapidly growing cash-flow and makes it very difficult for competitors to catch up. Experience has shown that a company which gets a new product to market first, generally achieves the fastest growth and biggest market share.

A critical purpose of the project organizational and best practice methodologies, together with the integrated tools, described in this chapter, is to increase the speed and effectiveness, as well as the efficiency and productivity of the PIP.

Table 4.5. Common weaknesses in strategic plans

A majority of product development organizations have overloaded project plans. Typical bad practices are:

- Inefficient organization, specialist functional groups, poor communication of strategic needs.
- Engineers choose the most interesting technical topics – leads to too many and unnecessary projects.
- Poor engineering and manufacturing change control and poor grouping of changes.
- Failure to integrate manufacturing engineering.
- Failure to use best practice team support tools and utilise teamwork.
- Weak project management and review process.
- Failure to use technology route mapping to plan ahead and give strategic direction.
- Use of poor, imprecise specifications – leads to wasteful work and customer dissatisfaction.

In addition, strategic plans are not balanced to adequately represent all development needs and mix types, for example:

- Derivative products as variants on an existing platform product, which may be mature products.
- New core platform products.
- Breakthrough products – involve significant breakthrough in product and process concepts.
- R&D to fill gaps in the technology route maps to meet market needs
- Alliance and partnership projects to access technology elements.

Companies need to regularly audit review their product development portfolio for overloading mix, balance to meet market needs.

Table 4.6 New Product Project Categories – Achieving a Balanced Programme

Category 1   New platform product development project
Category 2   Significant adaptation/upgrade of an existing product
Category 3   Minor product modification mod-packs and specification
             change requests

A product development programme requires a mix of all categories for: a balanced short–medium–long-term, EVA generation profile delivered via a competitiveness improvement programme

An essential feature is to ensure that the strategic direction sub-process, the front end of the PIP process, shown in Fig. 4.1, is well executed and uses the necessary detailed assessments to ensure that all requirements are in place at the right time, to match the process milestone requirements. This is a fundamental responsibility of the senior management of a company because it leads to the long-term profitable survival and growth of the company.

For illustration, a number of common weaknesses in company strategic plans are summarised in Table 4.5. It is very important to ensure a balance in the portfolio of product introduction project activity through the correct mix of project categories, to achieve balanced EVA generation and long-term survival via new platform products to replace dying products, as shown in Table 4.6. It is also important to use benchmarking methods, based on studies of excellent companies, to guide target setting, as in Tables 4.7 to 4.9, and to regularly revisit and analyse the factors affecting product and service costs to prevent escalation, as summarised in Table 4.10.

A good, focused example of a powerful, practical, detailed product strategy forward planning technique, aimed at getting the right strategic requirements in the right place at the right time, is the use of an early stage multi-skilled, experienced team, possibly as a pre-bidding project, to construct technology route maps for the product and manufacturing process. The aim is to start by looking at the proposed end-product of the PIP, to be delivered a year or more ahead, as defined by careful market and customer analysis. This is followed by a 'right-to-left' project planning technique to identify the essential new items of technology, materials or methodology which will be required, with their timings, to be certain that the desired product specification can be achieved.

As an example for a three-year automotive suspension sub-system product development and design programme, a product technology route map is shown in Fig. 4.10.

TARGET DATES FOR ACHIEVEMENT →

	TECHNOLOGY R&D REQUIREMENTS	COMPONENT DEMONSTRATORS	PRODUCT SYSTEM DEMONSTRATORS	PLATFORM PRODUCT OPPORTUNITIES
MATERIALS	Ceramic coating (2/99) Metal matrix alloy (3/99)	Ceramic surface spool value (2/00) Micron tolerance needles (6/99)	Flexible test rig (4/00) Small vehicle prototype, Front wheels only, Turnable functionally (9/00)	Heavy duty adaptive suspension control unit (12/01) Fully functional and failsafe
MANUFACTURE	Silicon Micro-machining (1/00) Nanotechnology for critical parts (4/99) Precision Machining (2/99) Low melting point Core casting (3/99) Automated Assembly	Small smart electronics package with electro-optical interface (6/99) Motor hydraulic pump unit (2/00)	Heavy duty four wheel independent (12/00) Small vehicle fully integrated four corner suspension (2/01)	Simplified suspension levelling unit (5/01) Full four corner integration of adaptive suspension (10/01)
ACTUATION	Miniaturised smart solenoid capability in silicon (7/99) Constant pressure hydraulic multiplexing (7/99) Miniature power electronics (9/99) Switched reluctance motor (10/99)	Power electronics driver (03/00) Sensor feedback package (12/00) Optical data highway (12/99)	Data highway and control feedback flexible test rig (11/99)	
SENSING and CONTROL	Optical data transmission (10/99) Smart pressure sensor (2/99) Opto-electric interface (3/99)			

Fig. 4.10 Focused R&D – technology road map structure example

The logic of this route map is followed from right to left as follows:

1. List the new product or product variants at the right-hand side with the target delivery date.
2. Move left and list prototype demonstrations required for test and evaluation, with their delivery dates.
3. Move left and list the new types of component and sub-systems which are novel and which are required to be available with the necessary delivery dates, to achieve the programme.
4. Move left and list critical new technologies for system integration and materials and manufacturing processes, which have to be developed, with their essential delivery dates.

Once this route map is finalised, the Senior Management and the project team have to define clearly two categories:

1. Those technologies, sub-systems and components which will be critical core components, and which the company will be able to develop itself on time.
2. Those technologies, materials and components which are outside the resourcing and knowledge capability of the company, and which, therefore, must be outsourced from expert specialist suppliers yet to be defined.

The negotiation of timely outsourced supplies then becomes a critical purchasing/development work-package in the project plan.

This is a good example showing one way in which the CAP strategic forward development plans are systematically converted into application. The criticality and timing of key activities are assessed in advance and delivered on time to ensure that new products reach the market on time.

Tables 4.7 to 4.10 illustrate some very effective measures, which attempt to look under the surface of company organizations to find out the underlying detailed practices which contribute to excellent performance and effectiveness of the business process.

4.13 Summary

The importance is emphasised of every company having an agreed business-specific flow-chart. This should define the total process for developing and introducing new products and services to the market. This should link the CAP strategic direction process to the customer account development process and bidding process, the follow-on

Table 4.7 Comparison of world-class companies and others. Post market-need-definition, product introduction projects

	World-class companies	Average of others
Percentage overrun of project plan time	-5	30
Percentage overrun of project budget	-6	30
Number of specification change requests	4	140
Percentage use of standard components	75	26
Overall project duration	17.9 months	33 months

Table 4.8 Product introduction process – typical measures of performance

Productivity
- Man hours per project.
- Development cost as percentage of sales revenue.
- Sales revenue per development project man hour.
- Patents filed per project.
- Number of new platform products per annum.
- Number of product variants or module upgrades per annum.

Lead-time
- Concept definition to full production initiation.
- Percentage cumulative lateness against stage milestones.

Cost
- Achievement of target cost of finished product.
- Total cost of development project.

Quality
- No. change requests.
- Changes per drawing.
- Warranty claims cost as percentage of revenue.
- Parts per million manufacturing scrap/rejects/re-work.

Typical targets for a change to team-based engineering: 50% improvement in all measures of performance (MOPs)

Table 4.9 Organization characteristics of a best practice machinery company

- Considerable pre-bid specification diagnostics audit on customer site.
- Current care taken to involve customers in agreeing accurate specifications.
- Use of Programme Office concept – for new product and change projects.
- Standard programme and project management procedures.
- Projects categorized into Categories 1, 2, and 3.
- Standard project management software support system capable of multi-project consolidation, resource and financial control.
- Use of co-located project teams – customer or product focused, and use of standard team organization and standard control meetings.
- Residual functional support groups operate project management of work-packages in support of projects.
- Teams trained in standard modern methodologies.
- Design for TPM – involve service engineers.
- Target cost culture and focus on minimizing product parts count.
- Standard training programme for project managers linked to selection procedures.
- Bid office concept used for rapid turnaround of bids to meet standard risk and gross margin requirements.
- Application of 'machine in manufacturing system' principles.
- Common manufacturing systems engineering principles to allow all varieties of machine to be assembled at each factory location for global supply.
- Weekly, monthly, quarterly reviews involving Programme Office and using standard MOPs and standard gateway milestones.
- Careful planning and approval of strategic product development plan to achieve balance and feasibility – supported by team organization.

product introduction process and the set of projects needed to deliver the strategy over the chosen period, e.g. 3 years.

All practices, controls and methodologies should be encapsulated in simple flow-charted procedures and a standard project management support system.

To facilitate the application of management by projects and achieve the necessary gains in process productivity, lead-time reduction and capability, it will be necessary to use modern principles of organization design to create natural group process team and project team structures. Benchmark measures of performance should be applied to support the development of a performance culture.

The practices and procedures required are generically similar for both product and service development projects, as are the phase structures and control practices required, although small companies will perceive opportunities to combine roles and functions and simplify procedures for their smaller-scale projects.

It is necessary to categorise the workflow and associated information flow streams, in order to simplify the approaches used wherever possible, and remove bureaucracy and non-value-added activity by the use of runner, repeater and stranger categorisations.

If configuration control and change control systems are not carefully designed and implemented, considerable, lengthy, costly company-image-damaging inefficiency and confusion can result, both inside the project process and afterwards during installation and in service.

Table 4.10 True product cost assessment

Procedure

- Flow-chart total process from purchasing through product manufacturing.
- Include inspection, transport, storage, changeover times on flow-chart.
- Calculate activity cost of each NVA and VA element including materials costs and cost of capital, and show cost growth profile along process.
- Revisit actual purchased cost of materials.
- Add in any ongoing development amortisation costs from initiation.
- Allocate any support costs, e.g. purchasing, sales administration, which are accurately allocatable.
- Define allocation rules for shared overheads.
- Include cost–volume relationships, e.g. for purchased materials.
- Determine scrap, rework and in-service quality costs.
- Draw up a product cost–volume graph and check target costs and gross margin.
- Compare current price–volume payment terms.
- Revisit overall process flow-chart and find opportunities to implement activity cost reduction.
- Implement any changes including design for manufacture.

To be truly world-class, it is essential to use a generic set of supporting tools and methodologies to enhance the benefit of project teamwork, and to train all participants in their use. The result is delight for the customer and an extraordinarily high total quality of performance by all processes.

Further reading

Association for Project Management. *Project Risk Assessment and Management, 'PRAM' Guide,* 1997.

British Standards Institution, *Guide to Project Management,* BS 6078 – 1, 2000 (HM Stationery Office).

Kaplan, R. S. and Norton, D. P. *The Balanced Score Card,* 1996 (Harvard Business School Press).

Kotler, P. *Marketing Management,* 5th edition, 1984 (Prentice Hall International).

Parnaby, J. *et al., The Lucas Manufacturing Systems Engineering Handbook,* 2nd edition, 1989 (Lucas Industries Publishers).

For Chapter 5 go to page 297

Customer Account Development and Management

SM4.1 Overall summary framework and typical modern practice

The main elements or stages are:

1. Define the full product and/or service set available for sale and show any modular possible sub-division to facilitate delivery in stages or to facilitate pull-through after customer penetration by sale of an initial module.
2. List all current customers in order of potential revenue per account and strategic importance.
3. List all potential customers.
4. Categorise the customer list into groups to allow a clear focus on key accounts, e.g.

Group 1. Target strategic key accounts capable of high-value-added, wide, long-term, multi-product and service sales development and high revenues per account.

Group 2. Existing and potential customer accounts capable of narrower sales and lower revenue opportunities, which could economically be managed to contribute to a base load of sales. Medium levels of sales revenue potential.

Group 3. Fill-in, narrow, single service or sales opportunities. Low potential revenues per account. Useful for filling gaps in capacity utilisation. However, must recognise that operating too many small accounts can be inefficient and expensive.

After the initial classification and collection of information on customers and potential customers, and the assessment of potential business, targets should be set to focus the activities of the customer account and bidding teams on winning high-potential strategic orders.

SM4.1.1 Example

Win three new key strategic accounts this year and penetrate by selling each at least one module of a product or service. Develop a pull-through account development plan and strategy for each account to win an ultimate annual target sales of £5M per year.

SM4.1.1.1 Preparatory work checklist for forming and initiating a bid team

1. Brief the customer account development and bid project teams on each allocated account and the business implications for your company if the account is won. Train in the use of the standard networked team information support and decision mapping system. Locate the team in the bid office.
2. Draw up a time-based project plan for developing each account and set target MOPs. Define your goals and the customer goals. Map out the list of decisions required by customer personnel and your matching decisions.
3. Circulate agendas for standard meetings and define the meeting roles and attendees.
4. Insist on circulation of all account related reports and minutes in a standard format with actions listed.
5. Circulate on the team information network all communications to and from the customer and any outline proposals or commitments made.
6. Circulate draft proposals and draft specifications to the team for finalisation.
7. List the names and job roles of all customer personnel who can influence the decision for each purchased product or service and allocate responsibilities for each member of the account project team, e.g. who to interface with and when.
8. Circulate hazard and problem lists for team members to follow up and recovery plan development.
9. Build into a solution selling standard support framework.

SM4.1.1.2 Customer organizational decision map roles

1. *Owner*. Decision maker with overall control of direction of the purchase to meet the economic and other needs of his or her business, short-medium- and long-term.
2. *Evaluators*. Supporting specialist decision makers and advisers who

contribute to the decision, e.g. quality, information technology, technical, sales, operations, finance, maintenance functional staff.

3. *Implementers.* Supporting staff who will supervise start up and acceptance sign-off, operate, use or maintain the purchased product or service, and will be involved in the evaluation of the alternatives. Some of these may be hidden antagonists due to previous poor experiences with your products or service and will require special attention by the order-winning project team.

A scope contact list can be constructed once these people and their job roles are known in which the account order-winning project team members are allocated to interface with each customer decision maker, with defined objects.

A decision matrix can be constructed showing how, through team feedback, the attitudes of each group of decision makers are tracking as the order-winning project progresses in order to facilitate team communications on priority areas for actions, e.g.

- Who to influence?
- Who should support the task?
- What benefit or good news supportive information can be communicated?
- What other assistance may be needed or evidence of field service or other customer experience?
- What benefits should be emphasised?

The project team should regularly review and discuss the customer viewpoint:

- *Need.* What is the background to the customer's need for the product/service. Research this thoroughly? What perceived value will the product/service provide?
- *Customer/supplier compatibility.* Are your practices, procedures, pricing and contractual policies matching customer expectation? What are the internal politics?
- *Financing.* How will the customer pay, what is the magnitude of the budget and how long does it last? How will the customer assess the financial return?
- *Competition.* Who are the competitors? What is their pricing strategy, what is their history and track record? What are their products' advantages and disadvantages? What are their life-cycle costs? How well established are they?

SM4.1.1.3 Achieving the highest value added

Try not to become a commodity supplier, i.e. where price competition is the worst. The project team should continually search out the customer problems or pains and aim to provide the maximum perceived value and support to the customer. In this way the supplier becomes increasingly perceived as a value-adding and trusted partner whose advice and assistance is valued. Figure SM4.1 illustrates the various possible levels of value adding customer–supplier relationship, and the implications for pricing potential and competitor vulnerability. There is a great deal to be gained financially and in terms of long-term stability of business from the use of professional account and bid project team standard working practices aimed at increasing the scope of supply and its quality and durability over a long period.

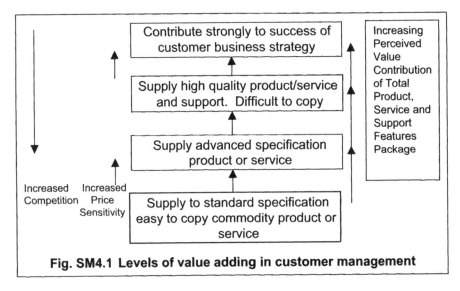

Fig. SM4.1 Levels of value adding in customer management

SM4.2 Summary

Customer account development and management is a natural team process, which is systematically managed using best project management practices and standardised working procedures to influence the customer decision making process. It results in a large increase in the percentage bid success rate and bids, which lead to an initial high quality order, leading to longer-term high value business. It leads to a broadening of the customer base through systematic winning of high-potential accounts and non-commodity product or service supply.

Goals chart – simplified example

Customer Goals	Our Goals	Customer Decision Possibilities	Our Decision Possibilities
Reduce costs	Achieve long-term partnership	Re-bid all key contracts	1. We supply components only
Reduce no. of Suppliers to be managed	Increase gross margin	Sub-contract management of whole system to one supplier	2. We supply a sub-system
Supplier to be TQM and ISO 9001 approved			3. We are sole supplier of product and all follow-on support including spares
Increase market share	Stabilize long-term order book	Quickly finalize short list of technically qualified suppliers	Target: Decision 3
Reduce inventory	Obtain good after-market sales possibility	Approve supplier capabilities to manage component sub-contract suppliers	In order to reduce customer costs and reduce supply chain logistics problems for customer
Short implementation lead-time	Avoid pure price competition		
Provide high quality in-service support			

Solution selling issues summary – simplified example

An important requirement is to understand the customer's problems and sell him or her a solution

A Our Issues

1. Value to us
   - Large potential annual sales value for fifteen years at £50M p.a. and 15% margin.
   - Would give us supply credibility to other potential key accounts.
   - Fits our competitiveness achievement plan strategy.

2. Inventory and mix
   - Can we economically handle the large number of parts and their overall assembly and manage component warranty issues?

   Funding
   - The cash flow profile through specification, development and pre-production stock building has to be feasible.

   Achieving sole-supplier role
   - An experienced fully functioned project team, trained and supported, is essential to win. Also, a focused customer manufacturing assembly cell and team is needed to give reliability of supply comfort and perceived dedication to customer with single point interfacing.

   Hitting customer key milestones
   - Approval to bid by 31st January, resources in place by end February, get customer sign-off of concept by 1st September, customer contract by 1st January.

B Customer issues

   - Customer relationships – due to past quality problems and high pricing of spares, customer Quality Manager and Finance Director are hostile. Customer cynicism we can meet time scales.
   - Competition – two other total supply competitors one of which is already a sub-system supplier.
   - Capability – must show our modern organizational approaches for quality management, product development and introduction, and modern Japanese manufacturing systems to get customers confidence that we can handle sole supply long-term.

Fig. SM4.2 Illustrative key support information spreadsheets

By carefully managing the bid project process and collecting information about all related aspects of a key customer account, highly informed direction of the bid team is achieved. Subjecting any adverse information feedback to rapid team corrective action ensures that major problems do not develop with the customer. All of the cross-functional skills and experience of the team is utilised to win the order through excellence of performance so delighting the customer.

An integrated computer spreadsheet-based up-to-date information system to support the team is required, such as that in Fig. SM4.2 utilising a QFD approach to goal cascading, incorporating in grouped structures all essential information to guide and control team activities and provide feedback and facilitate the careful sorting and follow-up of actions through all the stages of winning the order, i.e:

- Research and information collection, concept definition, structuring and refining, adding value to the bid, obtaining the decision, supporting the implementation, post-implementation evaluation.
- The developing attitudes of all customer personnel on the decision map are tracked through all of these stages to enable management by bid team members.

Basic important spreadsheets for supporting the process are shown in Fig. SM4.2. These spreadsheets should be regularly iterated and updated.

It's urgent

Problem

Company X's bid to write the software for us was priced on minimum cost. They offered to complete the work in 10 weeks from receipt of an order, including testing. They planned that if they were awarded the contract they would appoint the Systems Engineer who had prepared the proposals for their bid to be the full-time leader of the work, supported by a team of up to seven others who would be shared with other contracts, as this would be the most economic way of employing the company's resources.

Company X was awarded the contract, at the bid price and for delivery in 10 weeks. When signing the contract the Company X's Commercial Manager offered delivery of the work within eight weeks, expecting that impressive performance could attract further work from us. He informed the team leader that the work was now urgent. The team leader therefore asked what extra cost she could incur by taking five of the other members of the team off their commitments to other customers and by having to work them in parallel inefficiently. She calculated that this would add 25 per cent to the company's costs for the work. The offer to deliver in 8 weeks was withdrawn. After that no further invitations to bid were received from us.

Principles

- A bid needs planning and managing as a project. Team workloads and work-package contents should be analysed before offering delivery dates.
- Priorities should be decided in response to the customer's real objectives. If not clear and complete, those objectives should be queried and confirmed.

Lessons

- Bid on guesswork about a customer's wants only if this is accepted as an unavoidable part of a business strategy. Analyse the risks and possible consequences.
- Performance speaks louder than gestures.

Support Tools and Techniques Section 4

Management of many business projects can be improved by a careful application of a number of relatively simple, but very effective, techniques. Some of these techniques will be familiar to managers in engineering industries. Yet they are equally applicable to projects in other industries. This section provides an introduction to some of the commonly used techniques.

TT4.1 Balanced score card

The last twenty years have witnessed a very significant change in the business environment. The customer is now supreme and demands the delivery of high quality products and systems at low prices. There is a need for a high level of agility on the part of organizations. The employees need to be highly skilled as well as empowered to solve the problems. This often requires a different set of performance measures compared with the traditional measures of performance, developed during the twentieth century. Traditionally, many companies have relied very heavily on financial performance indicators that tell how an enterprise has performed in the past. These lag indicators provide relatively little information about the likely future performance and do not focus on the drivers of future success. Over the last fifteen years, leading companies have started to use non-financial measures of performance in addition to financial measures of performance. However, in overall terms, there has been a reluctance to simultaneously use operational and development measures of performance. The overall success of an enterprise can be measured by using a mix of leading and lagging indicators as part of an overall score card. The balanced score card, introduced by Kaplan, was a great step forward and provided a rational framework and checklist. It can be used by an organization to translate its overall vision into a set of measures of performance relating to four fundamental organizational performance perspectives: the financial perspective; the customer perspective; internal processes effectiveness perspective; and organization learning, innovation and development perspective. It is an excellent management tool in that it:

1. Identifies the business/company relevant financial and non-financial measures
2. Provides a balance between the short-term and the long-term.
3. Helps identify, from all relevant viewpoints, the current performance and the drivers of future performance.
4. Measures the drivers of current and future performance.
5. Helps align all business processes and functional areas of the enterprise to business and market needs.
6. Provides a quick but comprehensive view of the performance of the organization and facilitates exception reporting which should support decisions relating to the actions necessary to meet the performance targets set.
7. Can be cascaded all the way, from top to bottom, of an organization, thereby avoiding the use of isolated and unrelated measures of performance in different departments.

TT4.1.1 Performance dimensions

The performance dimensions must be related to the vision and strategy of the organization. The four main dimensions areas follow:

1. The financial perspective. This is closely related to the traditional financial measures of performance, typically indicated by: How well does the company look to its shareholders, i.e. shareholder value? How profitable is the company? What is the value added by the company? What is the return on capital employed? What is the rate of growth of turnover? What is the cash generation performance? etc.
2. The customer perspective. This assesses the position and performance of the company from the point of view of the customers. Typical measures of performance relate to the customer satisfaction levels, customer retention levels, product and service quality and growth rates, share of the market, satisfaction of customer needs and expectations as revealed by market research.
3. Internal Perspective. This relates to the efficiency and effectiveness of the internal business processes of the organizations. It helps identify the short- as well as the long-term core business processes in which the organization must excel in order to achieve high levels of performance in relation to the financial and customer perspectives, i.e. as viewed by the shareholders, the market-place and the customers. Critical operational measures of performance such as the time taken to process a customer order, level of work-in-progress, percentage of activities not

completed on due date etc. are often used to measure the internal perspective. The measures used must take account of the short- as well as the long-term objectives.

4. Organisational learning, innovation and development perspective. This perspective considers the ability to improve and create future value by focusing on learning, innovation and development issues, thereby making it possible to respond to new challenges and changes in the market-place. Thus the focus is on the quality of change management, continuous improvement, new processes, systems, technologies, as well as management philosophies to improve performance and deliver better value to shareholders as well as to the customers.

Figure TT4.1 illustrates the four perspectives of the Balanced Score Card.

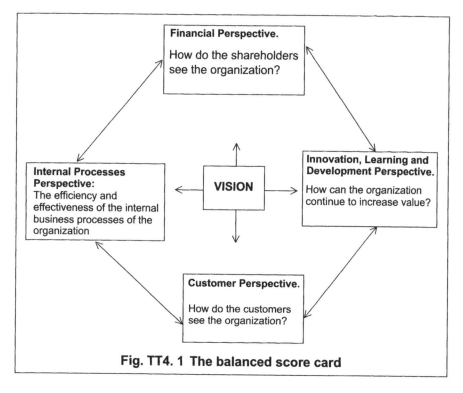

Fig. TT4. 1 The balanced score card

TT4.1.2 Application of the balanced score card approach to projects

Since all projects are undertaken in order to directly or indirectly improve the performance of an organization, it is important to consider the project contribution from all four perspectives when evaluating and prioritising projects. This is illustrated by considering a 'project' concerned with the implementation of a computer system for planning, monitoring and controlling all the projects carried out by the organization.

1. Financial perspective. All organizations use a variety of traditional financial measures of performance to assess the likely return. For example an effective computer-based project planning, monitoring and control system should help increase the number of projects delivering their specification and completed on time. This should, in turn, avoid the triggering of any penalty clauses thereby saving money. In other scenarios, better utilisation of all resources, in particular manpower, should also lead to considerable savings. A measure such as earned value is a critical measure of performance that monitors the progress of a project in terms of milestones delivered for money spent.

2. Customer perspective. Market research techniques, the likely improvement in customer satisfaction levels, and the quality of service given to customers can be used to assess the customer perspective. The Quality Function Deployment (QFD) approach, which relates the project deliverables specification to all levels in the project team, can be used to capture, make highly visible and prioritise the customer requirements. In some scenarios, the customer may be internal to the organization. The implementation of a computer-based project planning, monitoring and control system, which results in an increase in the number of projects completed on time, should increase the customer satisfaction levels, thereby improving the customer retention rate, sales growth and hence better return on the assets – thereby achieving measures of performance set from the customer perspective and, at the same time, improving the financial perspective.

3. Internal processes perspective. Any project will have an impact on the processes used by the organization. What will be the impact of the project on the critical internal business processes? Will some processes get better while others get worse? A computer-based project planning, monitoring and control system used, for example, for the operational delivery process, the new product introduction process or the customer account development process, should result in better scheduling, the ability to take account of other currently ongoing projects, better utilisation of the company resources and an increase in the number of projects completed on time. Furthermore it should increase the effectiveness of the processes concerned.

4. Innovation, learning and development perspective. All projects lead to lessons that can be learnt and used in subsequent projects. With the

emphasis on organizational learning and knowledge management, it is becoming increasingly important that the lessons learnt are documented and disseminated. A computer-based project planning, monitoring and control system used for all projects carried out in an organization should result in a sizeable database which can be explored and analysed using data mining techniques to assess the major causes of typical project problems such as higher than anticipated costs, delays in project completion, project risks etc. This should improve decision making and help with better planning, monitoring and control of future projects. As a result the performance of internal processes should improve and lead, in turn, to the improvement of customer and financial perspectives. Furthermore, the effective implementation of the computer-based project planning, monitoring and control system should involve considerable education and training, thereby providing opportunities for individual learning and development of new skills.

TT4.1.3 Summary

The balanced score card approach can be used at the strategic, organizational, as well as project, levels to consider the balance of performance across four perspectives, namely the financial perspective customer perspective, internal processes effectiveness perspective, and organisational/individual learning perspective. It must be emphasised that it is necessary to define appropriate measures of performance and targets in detail for each perspective. An effective balanced score card system should be linked to the strategic vision and the detailed objectives of the competitiveness achievement plan of the organization, as discussed in Chapter 1. It should provide readily available access to summarised information about the current performance as well as the drivers of future performance and the critical business success factors discussed in Chapter 1.

TT4.2 Best practices

Project management, in common with all types of activities in which an organization is engaged, can be improved by identifying and deploying appropriate best practices. This is a simple reflection of the fact that most organizations are not as good at managing projects as they think they are. Hence they can learn from the experiences of other companies. A 'best practice' can be defined as 'a practice that will lead to a superior performance.' Best practices are not static and hence need to be reviewed on a regular basis. In a highly dynamic global environment, today's best practices may become obsolete due to the impact of technology and management style as well as changing requirements – hence the need for an open-minded continuous improvement culture.

Best practices are related to bench-marking – which can be defined as the continuous search for and adaptation of significantly better practices which lead to superior performance by investigating the performance and practices of other organizations. Thus bench-marking goes beyond simple comparisons with competitors to understand the practices that lie behind the superior performance and adopting the practices for use in the organization. The term 'bench-mark' is the reference point against which the performance is measured. Bench-marking is the process of establishing bench-marks, using a combination of quantitative measures and judgement, the best performances against which comparisons can be made, hence the term 'best practices'. In the world of soccer, many people would regard Manchester United as the best and hence the bench-mark.

It is highly desirable that organizations are aware of the bench-mark since in the absence of such a reference point, they will not be aware of what they are up against and hence may not be able to compete in the long-term. Clearly bench-marks and best practices are closely related in that the bench-mark is the standard achieved by the adoption of best practices.

It is essential to check that the practice under observation is transferable directly or has the potential to be the best before it is adapted for use in the organization. This can be done in many different ways. For example if the same practice is used in many organizations and no better practice is found to exist, then it may be regarded as the best, or at least the starting point in the race to get ahead. Alternatively, experts can observe different practices and based on their knowledge identify the best practice. In many situations, it may be clear that the adoption of a new practice will lead to significant improvements, in comparison to the present practice, in which case the new practice should be assessed for transferability.

Bench-marking can take many different forms, the most common being:

- Strategic bench-marking. Assessment of the strategies of different organizations and their success.
- Competitive bench-marking. The comparison of the processes used by an organization against the processes used by direct competitors.
- Functional bench-marking. Investigation of the performance of similar core business functions in different industries.
- Internal bench-marking. Investigation of the performance of functions within different units of the same company.
- Generic bench-marking. Investigation of methods or technologies that

can be used in a variety of business processes.

- Best practice bench-marking. Investigation of business processes that integrate a number of specialist functions to achieve a common purpose.

TT4.2.1 Bench-marking process

Effective bench-marking requires a very considerable amount of planning and a high level of management commitment. The key steps in bench-marking can be summarised as:

1. Identify what to bench-mark.
2. Secure the commitment of senior management and involve all stakeholders.
3. Identify champion and team leader.
4. Select bench-marking team.
5. Educate and train the team.
6. Prepare draft bench-marking plan.
7. Identify and agree costs.
8. Obtain management approval.
9. Carry out internal assessment and strategic review.
10. Develop a data collection plan and decide on data collection, storage and analysis methods.
11. Analyse internal processes and identify measures.
12. Collect public domain information.
13. Analyse collected information to establish what other information needs to be collected.
14. Identify criteria for selecting bench-marking partners.
15. Identify potential partners.
16. Identify best practice organizations.
17. Obtain agreement of partner best practice organizations. Agree mutual benefits.
18. Plan the actual visits.
19. Conduct the bench-marking visits.
20. Compare own performance with the best practice performance.
21. Establish the performance gap.
22. Identify reasons for performance gap.
23. Predict future performance gaps.
24. Communicate bench-marking results.
25. Establish targets and prepare improvement plans.
26. Gain support and ownership for the targets and improvement plans.
27. Implement the improvement plans.

28. Measure performance.
29. Communicate progress.
30. Recalibrate bench-marks.

TT4.2.2 Best practices example

Many companies establish long-term partnerships with their suppliers to minimise costs while improving quality, reducing product cycle time, improving customer satisfaction, improving on-time delivery, cutting inventory and improving flexibility. This can be achieved only by implementing the relevant best practices associated with supply chain management. Some of the current best practices associated with supply chain management include:

- Developing appraisal criteria to select a partner.
- Selection of a supplier for long-term relationship.
- Creation of external centres of excellence.
- Setting up of clear and common set of objectives.
- Agreeing the style of relationship.
- Partners drawing strength from each other and creating win–win relationships.
- Removal of ambiguity and creation of trust.
- Management having the capacity to learn and apply lessons from partnership.
- Maintenance of a balance between trust and self interest.
- Capitalising on the Internet and intranets.
- High level of clear communication with suppliers.
- Working together for the design and development of a product or service.
- Working together to improve information and/or material flow.
- Cost sharing and building financial cooperation.
- Investing in training, learning and development.
- Continuously monitoring the results against objectives.
- Anticipating and managing alliance dynamics over time.

Chapter 5, Project Management Applied to the Change Process, gives other practical examples of bench-marking and best practices.

TT4.2.3 Summary

Bench-marking and identification of the best practices, followed by their adaptation/implementation and embedding into training courses has become essential for the survival and growth of organizations in a highly competitive global environment. Competitor analysis or identification of bench-marks is not enough. It is necessary to focus on, understand, adapt and implement the practices that help achieve the bench-mark. Furthermore, best practices can become obsolete over a period of time as a result of technological advancements, competition or the change in management philosophy. Hence it is necessary to review the best practices on a regular basis.

For best results, it is essential to examine the best practices of excellent companies in all sectors and not just the one in which the organization is currently operating. For example, a manufacturing company may be able to learn a great deal about best inventory management, material flow management and supply chain management from an excellent retail organization, such as Wal-Mart. A bank should be able to learn good practice in programme and project management to apply to large IT projects from large aircraft manufacturers who run large complex projects to develop new airliners. What is important is to identify typically up to ten measurable performance indicators in each of the four perspectives of the balanced score card. These should be related to the underlying business processes and the practices that underpin their performance.

TT4.3 Brainstorming

Successful projects frequently require innovative and creative thinking, involving the generation of new, useful and often unusual ideas to solve the problems. Brainstorming is a technique commonly used to focus on a problem and collect ideas from a group typically consisting of ten people. It is based on the premise that individuals can feed off the ideas generated by other members of the group in a quick-fire fashion to solve the defined problem or achieve the desired objective. It is often desirable to ask individuals to carry out individual brainstorming by defining a specific problem and come up with their own ideas. The individuals can then be brought together for a group brainstorming. Free association of ideas in a group and lateral thinking help generate new ideas. Each idea offered by a team member should lead to the generation of new ideas by other team members. All ideas put forward by the group are recorded without making any value judgements during the brainstorming process itself. Often the ideas that may appear to be very unusual or far fetched, when first considered, lead to creative solutions. All of the recorded ideas are subsequently evaluated.

An explanation of brainstorming can help members of task-forces, set up to focus on innovation, to become productive quickly.

TT4.3.1 Brainstorming rules

- There should be a minimum of five and a maximum of fifteen members in a group brainstorming session.
- The problem to be solved should be clearly defined.
- A free flow of ideas should be encouraged and the whole process should be conducted in a relaxed manner.
- During the idea generation stage there should be no discussion of specific suggested ideas. In particular, there should be no value judgements or filtering of ideas.
- All members of the group should be encouraged to participate.
- Association of ideas should be encouraged.

All ideas should be recorded, preferably written down, exactly as they are stated, so that all members of the group can see them. This provides an initial stimulus to subsequent creative discussion.

TT4.3.2 Brainstorming process

Typically the brainstorming process is carried out in a conference room with facilities to record ideas on a whiteboard, electronic board or wall charts so that all the participants can see the ideas as they are written down. The participants in the brainstorming session should have a broad range of experience relating to the problem as well as the disciplines associated with the problem. The brainstorming session leader, who may also act as the scribe, should define the problem clearly and set out the rules for the brainstorming session, in particular the need to avoid criticisms during the session. Often it is best to write down the problem so that all the participants can see it, thereby maintaining focus. The time period for the session should also be specified, typically thirty to forty five minutes, rarely exceeding 60 minutes. Each participant should be asked to contribute ideas in turn, recording each idea as it is generated. No chain of thought should be followed for too long thereby excluding other exciting ideas. All ideas, no matter how impractical, should be encouraged. This process should be continued until the flow of ideas stops.

The recorded ideas should be reviewed, clarified and sorted to draw up a raw list. Duplicate ideas should be eliminated and, if possible, a consensus should be established. Affinity diagramming, a technique for natural grouping of similar ideas, can be used for this purpose. The ideas should be prioritised for further evaluation and implementation.

TT4.3.3 Electronic brainstorming

The 1990s witnessed the emergence of electronic brainstorming whereby individuals make use of computers to interact and exchange ideas. A facilitator defines the problem and members are asked to contribute ideas anonymously. Anonymity can often lead to a better flow of ideas since individuals are not afraid of any criticisms; thereby creating a more relaxed atmosphere for the less experienced and introverts who may be reluctant to voice opinions and ideas in a public forum. The ideas can be recorded for later use. Also since individuals contribute ideas at their own pace, they have the time and opportunity to think and build on the ideas put forward by others. The organizational culture must of course be motivational to ensure a constructive and cooperative approach. This is the main challenge.

TT4.3.4 Application example

Brainstorming of problems associated with the lack of effective implementation of computer-aided manufacturing control systems resulted in the partial list shown in Fig. TT4.2.

Poor response time
Complexity of software
Complexity of procedures
Poor adherence to procedures
Poor quality of data
Lack of validation of input data
System complexity
Poor man–machine interface
Lack of disciplines
Open components inventory stores
Lack of knowledge of facilities in the system
Lack of help facilities
Poor ongoing education and training
Lack of adequate network capacity

Fig. TT4.2 Problems associated with the effective implementation of computer-aided manufacturing control systems

The raw list in Fig. TT4.2 can be grouped into the following affinity sets

• Hardware issues
  Lack of adequate network capacity
  Poor response time

- Software issues
    Poor response time
    Poor man–machine interface
    Complexity of software
    System complexity
    Lack of help facilities
    Lack of validation of input data

- Procedural issues
    Complexity of procedures
    Poor adherence to procedures
    Open components inventory stores
    Lack of disciplines
    Poor ongoing education and training

- Data-related issues
    Poor quality data
    Lack of validation of input data
    Lack of disciplines

- Human issues
    Poor adherence to procedures
    Poor ongoing education and training
    Poor man–machine interface
    Lack of help facilities
    Lack of knowledge of facilities in the system

It should be noted that some of the ideas appear in more than one affinity group. These affinity groups can then be used for further evaluation and action.

TT4.3.5 Summary

Brainstorming is a useful group-based approach to the generation of creative ideas for solving problems. It facilitates a free flow of ideas, without any criticisms and value judgements. Once generated the ideas can be sorted and prioritised for further evaluation and action through task-force projects, reference Chapter 3, or supported group improvement activity.

TT4.4 Cause and effect diagrams

Almost all projects run into problems at some point in time. In fact it would be true to say that many projects are not completed on time and within budget. This is a particular problem with many IT projects. When projects do run into problems, it is essential to get down to the real underlying causes. Cause and effect diagrams, also referred to as 'fishbone diagrams', provide a systematic method of looking at the effects, i.e. the symptoms of failures and the causes which lead to the effects. The cause and effect diagram is a particular form of input–output diagram used by systems engineers and was pioneered by Kaoru Ishikawa. Hence it is also referred to as the 'Ishikawa diagram'. It is a very useful tool for structuring teamwork in task-force activities. It is frequently used to help identify the root cause(s) of problems or the actions required to deliver the objectives of a project defined by the measures of performance set out in the competitiveness achievement programme.

A typical cause and effect diagram looks like the skeleton of a fish. The effect forms the main bone while the causes or connecting ideas form the smaller bones. Figure TT4.3 illustrates the general form of a fishbone diagram. The smaller bones, for example machinery, manpower, systems, and policies, represent the general factors that cause the effect. The causes are arranged in a hierarchy thereby showing the level of importance associated with individual causes.

TT4.4.1 Construction of cause and effect diagrams

The development of cause and effect diagrams requires very considerable skill and knowledge relating to the problem under consideration. It is therefore necessary to use a cross-functional team approach to the development of these diagrams with everyone making contributions in a structured manner.

The problem or target under consideration should be clearly specified and written at the end of a horizontal arrow. The main causes are written down against diagonal lines (or sub-bones), with arrows pointing towards the central arrow, on either side of the horizontal line. As shown in Fig. TT4.3, standard collective categories, such as methods, machinery, manpower, money, information, policies, procedures, systems and suppliers are used as the sub-bones of the problem to help organize the ideas. The effect can be analysed systematically, as part of a group discussion, or brainstorming, to identify all the potential causes of the problem in each category. As and when a cause is identified, it is recorded followed by identification of the causes at the next lower level. This process is followed until the causes at the lowest level are identified. As sub-causes are identified, they are attached as sub-sub-bones to the sub-bones and so on. This process is continued until the complete cause and effect diagram has been drawn and root causes of the problem have been identified. This information about root causes can be used to solve the problem under consideration by triggering an investigation of the potential causes in probability order. Often some of the causes appear under more than one category. These may represent the main causes of the problem that should be investigated for elimination or solution.

TT4.4.2 Summary

A cause and effect diagram is part of a concise structured method for identifying the root causes of a problem and handling the detail in an orderly way. Its development requires a high level of knowledge and experience relating to the problem under consideration. It is most effective when used by a team to identify the causes and achieve a consensus. If the cause and effect diagram becomes complex and hence difficult to comprehend, it should be decomposed into smaller diagrams linked together by an indented outline diagram.

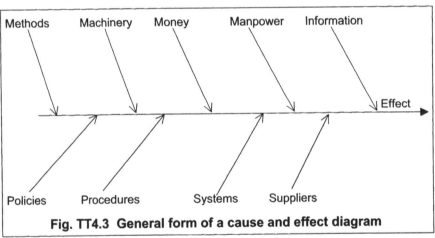

Fig. TT4.3 General form of a cause and effect diagram

TT4.5 Decision trees

All projects require a substantial amount of decision making over the life of a project. Decision trees, another manifestation of a form of input–output programme, represent an excellent, but simple, graphical tool for helping with the decision making process. Figure TT4.4 represents a simple decision tree. The decision tree approach is structured and makes it possible to take account of a large amount of information in a systematic manner. At each stage, or node, of a tree the alternative decisions, and the implications

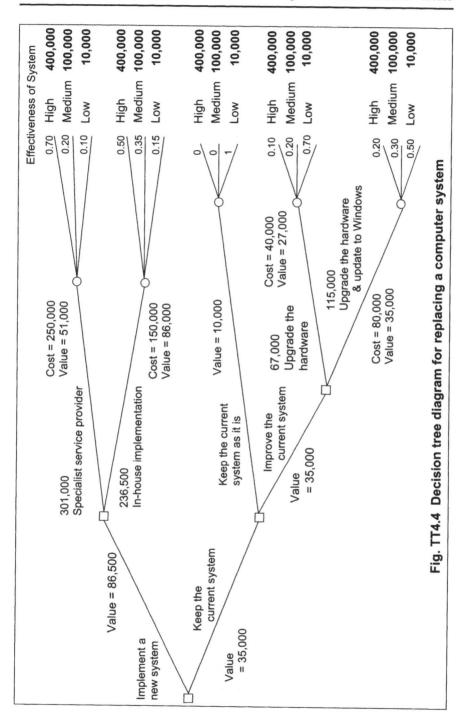

Fig. TT4.4 Decision tree diagram for replacing a computer system

associated with them, can be articulated and evaluated. This approach is particularly useful when assessing the risks associated with the alternative courses of action. For example, the decision to shut manufacture of goods at one location and transfer them to another location, possibly in a country where the labour costs are lower, has considerable implications that need to be evaluated. At one extreme the process may be entirely smooth. At the other extreme, employees on the location being shut down may react very angrily, refusing all cooperation with the management and making it impossible to transfer the manufacturing facilities, with a number of other in-between scenarios. Clearly the management needs to evaluate the main/alternative courses of action and their implications before making the final decision.

TT4.5.1 Drawing up a decision tree

The starting point of a decision tree is the decision to be made. Once this has been decided, a large piece of paper should be used, initially in the project team room, to record the various alternatives. A small square, representing the decision node, on the extreme left-hand side of the paper is used to represent the decision to be made. From this decision node straight lines, representing the branches of the tree, are drawn towards the right-hand side of the paper, with each branch representing the possible solution alternatives. The solution is written along the line.

Each of the solutions should be considered in turn. A solution may require further decisions in which case another square is drawn at the end of the branch. In many scenarios, the results of a particular solution may be uncertain and may not be under the control of the decision maker; in this case a circle is used to represent this uncertainty.

From each square node, tree branches are drawn representing the available options or solutions. Similarly from each circle node, tree branches, representing the possible uncertain results are drawn. Each branch of the tree should be annotated to record the option or outcome associated with the branch.

This process is repeated until all possible results associated with the original decision have been recorded.

TT4.5.2 Application example

This example demonstrates the options relating to the replacement of an existing computer-based manufacturing control system. The company concerned implemented a system in the early 1990s. When implemented the system represented the state of the art. The company has expanded considerably and so has the use of the system. The hardware has been upgraded on a number of occasions. The company management feels that the performance of the system does not compare favourably with the state of the art systems. The options available are to install a new system or to keep the current system. Thus the main decision to be made is whether the existing system should be replaced. The square node shown in Fig. TT4.4 can represent this. The new system can be implemented in-house by choosing a suitable package and using in-house personnel along with support from the system vendor. Alternatively the complete implementation can be sub-contracted to a specialist service provider. This is represented on the tree diagram. If the decision is made to keep the current system, there are two further options, namely keep the current system as it is or improve the current system. The latter option, namely improve the current system, leads to two further options, which are to upgrade the hardware only in order to improve the system response time, or to implement a new Windows-based version of the existing software which will necessitate a hardware upgrade. In all cases, there is an impact on the usability and effectiveness of the system and hence the financial benefits associated with it. The impact on system effectiveness may be high, medium or low depending upon the course of action chosen.

For the outcomes associated with each circle, it is necessary to assign a numerical value to each outcome. At the same time the probability of each outcome, associated with each circle, must also be defined. The fractional probabilities associated with the outcomes emanating from a circle node must add up to 1. These values are required to calculate the values associated with each branch of the tree and make the decision. Figure TT4.4 shows the complete decision tree including the financial benefit value of the outcomes and their probabilities, associated with the various options relating to the replacement of an existing computer-based manufacturing control system. The calculations associated with the decision tree are illustrated by considering the Specialist Service Provider Option. A high level of system effectiveness would have a financial value of £400,000. The total value of the high system effectiveness branch is calculated by multiplying the beneficial value and the probability of its occurrence, i.e. $400,000 \times 0.7 = £280,000$. This can be repeated for all outcomes; the medium system effectiveness branch of this node has a value of $100,000 \times 0.20 = £20,000$; the low system effectiveness branch of this node has a value of $10,000 \times 0.1 = £1,000$. The total value of this node is determined by adding up the values associated with all the branches emanating from it, leading to a total value of £301,000.

This process can be repeated for all branches of the tree. It can be seen that the financial benefit values associated with different decision nodes are:

Keep the current system as it is	=	£10,000
Upgrade the hardware	=	£67,000
Upgrade the hardware and upgrade the software to a Windows-based version	=	£115,000
In-house implementation of a new system	=	£236,500
Implementation of a new system via a specialist service provider	=	£301,000

Clearly there are costs associated with each of these options. On a-like-for like basis the costs of the different options are:

Specialist service provider	=	£250,000
In-house implementation	=	£150,000
Hardware upgrade	=	£40,000
Software upgrade to a Windows-based version along with hardware upgrade	=	£80,000

These can be used to calculate the value of the benefits associated with each option.

Specialist service provider	=	301,000 – 250,000	=	£51,000
In-house implementation	=	236,500 – 150,000	=	£86,500

Clearly of these two options, the decision would be to carry out in-house implementation that provides a financial benefit value of £86,500.

Similar calculations show that improving the current system by upgrading the software and hardware has a financial benefit value of £35,000, compared with a financial benefit value of £27,000 for the hardware upgrade only. Hence the decision in relation to this node would be to go for hardware and software upgrade. Comparison of this option with keeping the current system as it is, shows that improving the current system gives a bigger benefit with a financial value of £35,000. However, overall comparison at the stage of first node shows that the highest benefit of £86,500 would be obtained by the in-house implementation of a new system. Of course the final decision will have to take account of other criteria, for example the in-house availability of the competencies required for in-house implementation.

TT4.5.3 Summary

The decision tree is another effective decision making tool to catalyse the effectiveness of project teams. It can be used to consider all possible actions and outcomes. It combines the power of a quantitative analysis with graphic representation so that all possible outcomes can be viewed and analysed before making the final decision.

TT4.6 Failure modes and effects analysis (FMEA)

Most projects involve the design/re-design of a product, service, process or system. All products/systems/service operations have potential for failure at some point in their life. For example, the output from a chemical process may be subject to quality problems, a car brake may not operate effectively under certain circumstances, a rail track may develop defects if the maintenance processes and procedures are ineffective. Identification of potential failures of a product/service at the design stage, along with an assessment of the severity of failure and the possibility that the customer will be able to detect the failure, provides the opportunity to improve the reliability of the product/service by altering the design. Failure modes and effects analysis (FMEA) is a technique used, at the product design stage, for a systematic identification and evaluation of the potential failure modes and their effects on the performance of the product or output from the project. In this way it is possible to review the causes, the severity of effects and risks of the failure of a product or system. While FMEA is traditionally associated with manufactured products, in particular in defence, aerospace and automotive industries, it is equally applicable to service industries and can be used to identify the potential failures of service delivery operations. Detailed knowledge of the product/service is necessary to carry out the analysis. Once the potential failure modes, typically single point failures, have been analysed for their impact on the overall operation of the product/system, the product/service can be re-designed to eliminate the failure.

A suitably experienced cross-functional team should be used to develop the FMEA. A single specialist alone will not have the breadth of view to identify all the problems and the multitude of factors which may lead to them.

TT4.6.1 FMEA process

A typical FMEA involves the following actions:

1. All elements, which form part of the designed process, product or service, should be identified followed by a listing of the functions performed by each of the main elements.

2. Each function should be analysed in turn to assess what would happen if the function is not performed or is performed incorrectly. All conditions under which the system or service will be used should be considered. While data may exist for analysing the impact of normal conditions of use, it may be necessary to brainstorm for unusual or extreme conditions of use.

3. The potential effects of each failure should be analysed. What are the consequences of the failure? How will it affect the customers? How will the safety be jeopardised? Will this failure lead to other failures?

4. Assess the worst level of hazard or severity associated with each effect of failure identified at stage 3. The level of severity associated with an effect can be measured on a scale of 1 to 10 from minor severity, which will have little impact on the performance of the product/service provider, to catastrophic, resulting in serious injury or death or very serious consequences for the service provider.

5. Determine all the possible causes of each failure mode. These may relate to the design of the product/service or they may relate to operational issues. Whatever the problem, it is essential to look for real causes and not symptoms.

6. Assess the probability of occurrence of the failure. How likely is it that the failure will occur? On a scale of 1 to 10, this will range from remote to a very high level of probability that the failure will occur.

7. Assess the likelihood of detection of the failure. Will the failure reach the customer and if it does, will it be obvious to the customer or will it remain undetected? On a scale of 1 to 10, this will correspond to the failure being highly unlikely to be detected by the customer to the failure definitely reaching the customer and being totally obvious.

8. Calculate the risk priority number (RPN) by multiplying the ratings associated with the severity, probability of occurrence and the likelihood of detection of the failure. High RPNs indicate serious problems with high levels of risk. Table TT4.1 illustrates the calculation of the risk priority number.

9. Repeat the process for all failure modes. Prioritise the failure modes with high RPNs for the instigation of urgent action.

10. Identify corrective actions to eliminate the cause of the failure mode in the product or service. These include modification of design to eliminate the cause of failure and/or reduce the severity of effect. A variety of approaches can be used to prevent or control the problem. If this is not feasible then early warning signs to detect the onset of problems and likely failure should be incorporated in the design.

Table TT4.1 Calculation of risk priority number			
Rating	Level of Severity (R_S)	Probability of Occurrence (R_O)	Likelihood of Detection (R_D)
1	Minor	Remote	Highly unlikely
	Marginal	Low	Likely
	Critical	High	Very likely
10	Catastrophic	Very high	Totally obvious
Risk Priority Number (RPN) = $R_S \times R_O \times R_D$			

TT4.6.2 Application example

A multi-national is considering entry into the Internet system provider market. It has a good reputation in the market-place and it wishes to provide a reliable service for which it will make a charge but there will be free telephone access. Market research has shown that users expect a fault-free service. Systems Engineers at the company have identified five common failure modes, as follows:

- System overload.
- Server breakdown.
- Telecommunications network busy.
- Software problems.
- Help line busy.

Each of these has been looked at in detail and ratings have been allocated, as shown in Table TT4.2, to the probability of occurrence, severity of impact and the likelihood of detection. Risk priority numbers have been calculated for each failure mode.

Thus the failure modes can be prioritised as follows:

- Telecom network busy
- Help line busy
- Server breakdown
- System overload
- Software problems

To provide a high quality and reliable service, the company needs to focus attention on the number of telephone lines and the number of people manning help lines.

Table TT4.2 Main failure modes for an Internet service				
Failure Mode	Level of Severity	Probability Occurrence	Likelihood of Detection	Risk Priority Number
System overload	7	4	5	140
Server breakdown	8	2	10	160
Telecom network busy	6	7	8	336
Software problems	3	8	3	72
Help line busy	7	6	6	252

TT4.6.3 Summary

Failure modes and effects analysis (FMEA) is a very effective tool for predicting the response of a product/system/service operation to failures of any of its constituent elements. It helps identify the actions necessary to prevent the failure or at least minimise the chance of occurrence of the failure. For best results it should be carried out during the design of a product/service operation. However, this does not mean that FMEA should not be carried out at other times in the life of a product or service operation. Being a team activity its effectiveness depends on the skills and knowledge of the participants.

TT4.7 Force field analysis

In many scenarios, especially during the process of change management, there are positive forces that drive changes while negative forces resist/prevent change. Driving forces help achieve a change while resisting forces try to maintain the status quo thereby inhibiting the achievement of the change or the desired goal. Alternatively the forces may be slowing down the change. Effective project management requires that the project team have a good understanding of the driving as well as resisting/slowing down forces. Clearly it is essential that the driving forces are stronger than the resisting forces and that tactics are designed to overcome the resisting forces. Where resisting or slowing down forces are greater than the driving forces, change will occur only if the resisting forces are eliminated or at least minimised. The force field analysis technique can be used to assess the driving and resisting forces and then evolve a winning strategy, i.e. a performance culture.

TT4.7.1 Description

Force field analysis is a simple, yet powerful, diagrammatic technique that should be used when developing plans to obtain a holistic, i.e. total systems, view of the interests of all parties, the pros and cons, and the forces, which will drive as well as resist the decisions which may be made. This technique was developed in the 1950s by the social scientist, Kurt Lewin. Weighting of the pros and cons, driving/resisting forces, followed by an analysis of the situation, should make it possible to decide on the course of action. The analysis will indicate whether to continue with the plan/decision, increase the resources where they can help reduce the resisting forces, or abandon the plan. Application of this visual technique is relatively simple in that it only requires pen and paper. However, it is essential that the individuals carrying out the analysis have a good understanding and knowledge of the issue that needs to be resolved and the associated environment. It is often best to use a team from the environment in which the change is to be achieved to draw the force field diagram followed by analysis.

TT4.7.2 Development of the force field diagram

The development of the force field diagram should be carried out in the following steps:

1. Highlight the issue or goal as the header at the top of a page, which should be divided into two areas. Typically this will relate to a problem which needs to be resolved and hence the need for change or the need to achieve a defined objective.

2. The left-hand area should be labelled as the 'driving forces'.

3. The right-hand area should be labelled as the 'resisting forces'.

4. Analyse the issue or goal by brainstorming with the team and list all the driving and resisting forces in the two areas. Each member of the team should be asked to work individually first before analysing the issue as a team.

5. The forces should be grouped under common themes.

6. Right-hand arrows should indicate driving forces and left-hand arrows

should indicate resisting forces. Typical forces may be resources, actions, procedures, values, desires, etc.

7. Wherever possible weights should be assigned to each of the forces on a scale of 1 to 10. It should thus be possible to prioritise the forces.

8. The listed items should be analysed to assess how to increase the driving forces and reduce the strength of opposing forces. For effective and successful project management, it is essential to create an imbalance in favour of driving forces. Often it is best to reduce the strength of resisting forces rather than increasing the strength of driving forces. In many situations, these resisting forces only require proper attention to detail and discussion to obtain agreement and commitment.

TT4.7.3 Application example

Figure TT4.5 illustrates the force field analysis relating to the implementation of a new computer-based project planning, monitoring and control system. In this example, the sum total of driving forces is 36 while the resisting forces add up to 38. Clearly, pushing through the project may not lead to an effective implementation of the new computer-based system.

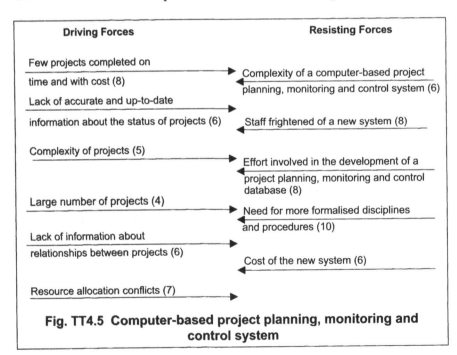

Driving Forces	Resisting Forces
Few projects completed on time and with cost (8)	Complexity of a computer-based project planning, monitoring and control system (6)
Lack of accurate and up-to-date information about the status of projects (6)	Staff frightened of a new system (8)
Complexity of projects (5)	Effort involved in the development of a project planning, monitoring and control database (8)
Large number of projects (4)	Need for more formalised disciplines and procedures (10)
Lack of information about relationships between projects (6)	Cost of the new system (6)
Resource allocation conflicts (7)	

Fig. TT4.5 Computer-based project planning, monitoring and control system

However, there are a number of options to change the balance. For example education and training should reduce the staff fear relating to the implementation of the system and help them to understand the project management procedures. It may reduce the strength of the resisting force 'staff frightened of a new system' from 8 to 4. Allocation of additional resources for purchasing the new system and setting up the database should create a new driving force of 6. Similarly the need to implement such a system to avoid lateness penalties should create another driving force with a value of 8. With this scenario the driving forces will add up to 50 while reducing the resisting forces to 34, thereby creating a very favourable scenario to proceed with the implementation of the new computer-based project planning, monitoring and control system.

TT4.7.4 Summary

Force field analysis can be used to assess the driving and resisting forces associated with an issue or goal to be achieved, and the changes that should be made to help achieve the goal. It can also be used for diagnosing situations, analysing the pros/cons and actions/reactions of a situation, strategy development, achievement of a vision and so on. All Programme Directors and Project Managers need to be familiar with this technique and become experienced in identifying and overcoming the resistances.

TT4.8 Project risk assessment and management

All projects involve a degree of risk. In fact risk is central to almost any activity. The more complex a project, the higher the degree of risk associated with it. The project may not be completed on time and within the anticipated project budget, thereby delaying or reducing benefits. The output from the project may not be of the quality required. A risk is anything that could result in the non-achievement of the goals but has not happened as yet. This may relate to time, cost, performance, technology, operation and development tasks associated with the product or service that will be the result of the project under consideration. While it is impossible to eliminate risks, they can be minimised through hazard recovery planning and kept within acceptable limits.

Risk assessment and management is the process of identifying, analysing, prioritising, avoiding, monitoring and controlling risks. A systematic approach to risk assessment and management should ensure that the impact of risks is minimised leading to a successful project outcome. It is an ongoing process that should be undertaken at the start and then repeated, at regular intervals, throughout the project to take account of changing conditions. Appropriate countermeasures should be implemented. The level of resource and attention devoted to hazard definition or identification and risk management will depend upon the scope and complexity of the project. In the case of complex and costly projects, it may be necessary to appoint a full-time Risk Manager who may have a team of people looking at different aspects of the project. In other cases, the Project Manager may handle risk management. For maximum impact, all project stakeholders should be involved in the assessment and minimisation of risks.

A typical risk has three elements: the fact that an event will happen which will prevent the achievement of the goal; the level of probability associated with the occurrence of the event; and finally the impact of the event if and when it takes place.

TT4.8.1 Risk identification

Risks can be identified by considering the major elements of a project and assessing the potential problems. Brainstorming technique can be used to identify likely risks. Experts can be asked to assess the likely risks. A checklist of all common risks associated with the type of project being undertaken can help with this process. The database of a computer-based project planning, monitoring and control system can be examined to highlight the risks associated with the projects previously carried out by the organization.

TT4.8.2 Risk prioritization

Risk identification will usually result in the identification of a number of risks for the project under consideration. Some may have a low probability of occurrence while others will have a high probability of occurrence. This probability can be on a scale of 0.01 to 1. Similarly the magnitude of problem or loss associated with an individual risk may be high or low. The magnitude of problem or loss can be assessed on a scale of 1 to 100. The overall magnitude of the likely impact of a risk can be evaluated by multiplying the probability of occurrence and the magnitude of loss associated with it. Clearly, this will result in values ranging from 0.01 to 100. These can be used to prioritise the risks. Any risk with a high probability of occurrence should also be prioritised for early consideration. It is thus possible to rank the risks from most to least dangerous.

Alternatively the probability of occurrence of an event may be graded simply as low, medium or high. Similarly the impact of the risk may also be regarded as low, medium or high. Whichever approach is used, it should lead to a prioritisation of risks. This then provides a helpful foundation for experienced project management to be applied to the choice of preventive measures or hazard recovery plans.

TT4.8.3 Managing the risks

Once the risks have been prioritised, the next step is to decide how to manage the risks. One response would be to avoid the risk by not carrying out the project. At the other extreme, the management may decide to accept the risk. This may, for example, be the case when using unproven, cutting edge technology. Often cutting edge technology is used by leaders in expectation of high levels of gains and capturing a large share of the market before their competitors introduce rival products in the market-place. The risk may also be avoided by eliminating it. For example, the use of well-proven technology will eliminate the risk associated with the use of cutting edge technology.

For many projects, the strategy adopted may be to reduce the risk. The risk can be reduced by minimising the probability of its occurrence and by reducing the actual impact of the event. In both cases, it would be necessary to devise and implement countermeasures. The countermeasures for reducing the risks should be devised by individuals with significant experience of managing these risks. These countermeasures may be pre-emptive, i.e. taking action before the event occurs reduces the probability of occurrence. Where this is not possible, contingency plans should be drawn up to deal with the occurrence of the event. Alternatively outsourcing the activity or insuring against the risk may transfer the risks.

A separate risk management plan should be developed for all high- and medium-level risks while low-level risks can be dealt with as part of routine management. Clearly the countermeasures associated with high-level risks should be identified and implemented before the project is approved and started. These countermeasures should be cost effective and easy to implement. Where this is not possible it may be best to modify the scope of the project at the approval stage. The contents of a risk management plan should include a description of the risk, the probability of its occurrence, the likely impact of the risk, the priority associated with it, the person or group responsible for managing the risk, the countermeasures designed to mitigate the impact of the risk and the costs of the countermeasures. It is essential to update the risk management plan as the project progresses.

The development of a risk management plan is only the first step in the long-term management of the risk. The risks will change over a period of time. Hence they need to be monitored and controlled, on a regular basis, as an essential element of project reviews. The monitoring, review and control should include the likelihood of occurrence of events and their impacts for risks identified at the start of the project, as well as any new threats which may have emerged. This may result in the need to revise the risk management plan. The regular monitoring and control of risks should be continued until the project has been completed successfully. On completion of the project, the risks encountered, and how they were dealt with, should be reviewed and documented with a view to learning appropriate lessons which can be taken into account when considering the likely risks associated with future projects.

TT4.8.4 Example – information technology project risks

The risk identification process is considered in relation to information technology (IT) projects. Very few IT projects are completed on time and at cost. Typical projects suffer from a variety of risks, the most common ones being:

1. Poor understanding of user requirements.
2. Continuing changes in user requirements.
3. Ineffective requirement change control process.
4. Inadequate experience of the application being developed.
5. Complexity of the system.
6. Poor real-time performance of the system.
7. Application of leading edge, but inadequately tested, system development tools.
8. Poor understanding of software development tools and techniques.
9. Poor configuration management.
10. Poor quality.
11. Poor project planning.
12. Poor project monitoring and control.
13. Poor communication.
14. Lack of adequately trained personnel.
15. Loss of key personnel.
16. Staff turnover.
17. Cost overrun.
18. Unrealistic project schedule.
19. Low level of user satisfaction.

20. Poor quality of user documentation.
21. Poor human–computer interface.
22. Poor operational management skills.
23. Poor cash management skills.

There will be many other risks, which can be added to the above checklist. In the context of an individual IT project, it will be necessary to identify the probability of occurrence and the impact of individual risks, followed by a prioritising of the risks, and the development of associated risk management plans. If, for example, there is a high level of risk of uncontrolled changes in system requirements, it will be necessary to implement an effective requirements change management process that should also incorporate a full analysis of the impact of the changes in requirements. Each risk has to be analysed and its effect mitigated by appropriate countermeasures.

TT4.8.5 Summary

Risk management is an essential and continually iterative element of any project. All risks should be identified and assessed for the probability of their occurrence and impact, followed by their prioritisation. Countermeasures and recovery planning should be implemented for high-level risks before the project is started. A risk management plan should be prepared for each high/medium-level risk. The risks, including any new threats, should be monitored and controlled throughout the life of the project to make effective use of the available project resources. All members of the project team should be involved in the effective management of the risks.

TT4.9 Quality function deployment

Quality function deployment (QFD) was developed at the Kobe Shipyard of Mitsubishi in Japan as a means of capturing the customer requirements and translating them into product characteristics, which subsequently drive the design, process and production processes throughout the supply chain to ensure that the customer requirements are satisfied. Since its original development, it has been used extensively in a wide variety of industries, in particular automotive and aerospace companies, as a systematic method of capturing real customer requirements for products as well as services and translating these requirements into specifications, for all stages and processes throughout every level of the organization. The translation is achieved through a series of matrices. Since the emphasis is on satisfying the customer requirements, the approach is often referred to as the 'voice of the customer'. In an overall sense quality function deployment can be regarded as a detailed technique for supporting the design of products or services to translate the voice of the customer into appropriate specifications at every stage and in every functionally specialised activity of the product or service design process. It complements the related, but more specialised and focused FMEA methodology.

While many of the early applications were in manufacturing companies, recent years have witnessed the application of the approach in a wide variety of industries. These applications include: software engineering; planning of a revised curriculum in a university environment to satisfy the needs of the industry, students as well as academic staff; strategic planning; construction industry; consultancy and so on. In the original, narrow, sense QFD focused on the design and quality issues. In a broad sense, QFD can be used to focus, more dominantly, on customer needs along with important issues associated with cost, reliability, technology, practices etc.

This widespread use of QFD is due to the fact that there is no single way of applying QFD. It can be adapted, as required, to suit the needs of the organization and the intended application. It can be regarded as a team-based systems engineering approach for synthesising innovative ideas and achieving a consensus, particularly in scenarios involving the need for trade-offs, to satisfy the customer requirements. It also makes it possible to summarise and display a large amount of information in the form of matrices.

TT4.9.1 QFD process

The traditional QFD approach involves four phases, as illustrated in Fig. TT4.6. Each phase has its own relationship matrix, referred to as the 'house of quality'.

In phase 1, the customer requirements are converted into the product or service parameters. Clearly it is very important to capture the real customer requirements as accurately as possible. A variety of approaches involving the use of market research, focus groups and sales representatives can be deployed to capture these customer requirements. The captured requirements should then be ranked in order of importance. Once captured, engineers, designers and product/service planners can convert these into the produce/service parameters. In many cases, especially in the case of service operations, this is the only phase that is put to real use. For example, in the case of organizations responsible for the maintenance of home central heating systems, the customer requirements might include: quick response to breakdowns; quick, one step fixing of problems; low cost; appointments scheduled as requested; appointments kept. Clearly it is essential to translate these customer requirements into appropriate measures of performance (MOPs) that also need to be prioritised. These MOPs can then be linked to develop additional matrices to link the voice of the customer to potential implementation strategies.

In phase 2, the product parameters are translated into critical part parameters. Phase 3 converts critical part parameters into critical process parameters. In phase 4, the critical process parameters are converted into production process or service delivery process requirements.

In each phase, the requirements are prioritised and fed into the next phase, thereby ensuring a continuity of information. Furthermore the voice of the customer is heard consistently at all stages of the process.

The most important part of the QFD approach is the 'relationship matrix', which is used to link the various parameters in the house of quality. Within the house of quality, the 'What's represent the requirements, i.e. the needs and expectations, while the 'How's represent the methods of satisfying the requirements. The relationships, if any, between the 'What's and 'How's are defined as strong, medium and weak. This is carried out in each phase of the process. This is very amenable to computer-based applications.

The advantages of the QFD approach include: high level of customer orientation; ability to organize large amounts of information in a logical, concise and easy to assimilate format; definition of relationships between parameters; prioritising of requirements; multi-disciplinary team approach; improving customer satisfaction levels; building quality into products/processes/services at the design stage; reducing product/service design and development time. However, there are some problems associated with the application of the approach. These include: the complexity of the approach; difficulties associated with the collection of the large amount of data that may be required and definition of the strengths of the relationships between the parameters; ambiguities associated with the 'voice of the customer'.

The detailed mechanics of each company's QFD system will vary depending upon the application. It is a team tool that should be used where it makes maximum impact. It can also be used to prioritise different projects in order to satisfy the needs of the customers as well as the company.

TT4.9.2 Application example

Figure TT4.7 shows part of the house of quality for a non-traditional application of the QFD approach. This relates to the development of an effective supply chain with the following seven objectives (What's):

- Improvement in quality.
- Reduction in costs.

- Reduction of product cycle time.
- Improvement in customer satisfaction level.
- Improvement in on-time delivery performance.
- Reduction in inventory.
- Increasing flexibility.

These objectives can be achieved by deploying a number of best practices (How's). In Fig. TT4.7, the relationships between the seven measures of performance, i.e. What's, and the 24 best practices (How's) are defined as strong, medium or weak.

TT4.9.3 Summary

QFD is a multi-disciplinary team-based approach for capturing the real requirements of customers and translating them into specifications at every stage of the design/development of a product or service. It is equally applicable to the design of products as well as service operations. It should be adapted to suit the requirements of the application.

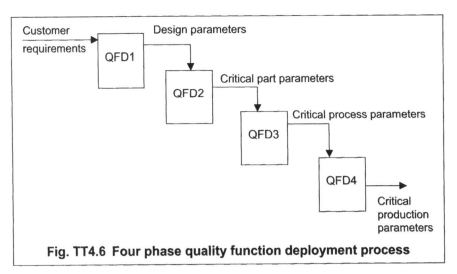

Fig. TT4.6 Four phase quality function deployment process

TT4.10 Chapter summary

Effective management of projects requires the application of a variety of tools and techniques. The tools and techniques highlighted in this chapter are relatively simple yet robust. They are relatively easy to apply and can help the managers achieve their business objectives by adding rigour to the decision making process.

Fig. TT4.7 Relationship between measures of performance and best practices

Key: Strong [S] · Medium [M] · Weak [W]

OVERVIEW groups and Best Practice 'How?'

BP	Overview group	Best Practice 'How?'
BP1	Choosing the first partners	Developing appraisal criteria to select a partner
BP2	Choosing the first partners	Selection of a supplier for long-term relationship
BP3	Defining what is required from the partnership	Working to achieve external centres of excellence
BP4	Defining what is required from the partnership	Setting up of clear and common set of objectives
BP5	Defining what is required from the partnership	Agreeing the style of relationship
BP6	Commitment to the partnership	Partners drawing strength & creating win–win situation
BP7	Commitment to the partnership	Removal of ambiguous relationship & creation of trust
BP8	Commitment to the partnership	Management having the capacity to learn & apply from partnership
BP9	Commitment to the partnership	Management to keep a balance between trust and self-interest
BP10	Commitment to the partnership	Implementing a proper structural form of collaboration
BP11	Flow of information	Looking at ways to capitalize on Internet & intranets
BP12	Flow of information	Establishing strong communications with suppliers
BP13	Flow of information	Correlation of information flow & merging of technologies
BP14	Building and making the partnership work	Working towards improving quality & encouraging quality certificates
BP15	Building and making the partnership work	Working together in improving the design process
BP16	Building and making the partnership work	Working towards improving the material flow, thus helping towards JIT
BP17	Building and making the partnership work	Focusing on quick and effective implementation of the results
BP18	Building and making the partnership work	Working towards cost sharing & building financial cooperation
BP19	Building and making the partnership work	Using purchasing cards as a new tool to foster partnerships
BP20	Building and making the partnership work	Investing in training, learning & development
BP21	Building and making the partnership work	Partners investing in a marketing programme
BP22	Refining & Developing	Continuously monitoring the results against objectives by setting targets
BP23	Refining & Developing	Working towards an insourcing programme
BP24	Refining & Developing	Anticipating & managing alliance dynamics over time

Measures of Performance (What?)

1. Improving quality
2. Reducing costs
3. Reducing product cycle time
4. Customer satisfaction level
5. On-time delivery performance
6. Cutting inventory
7. Flexibility

Further reading

Camp, R. C. *Benchmarking – The Search for Industry Best Practices that Lead to Superior Performance*, 1989 (ASQC Quality Press).

Daetz, D., Norman, R. and **Barnard, B.** *Customer Integration: The Quality Function Deployment (QFD) Leader's Guide for Decision Making*, 1995 (John Wiley).

DeBono, E. *Serious Creativity*, 1992 (HarperCollins).

Hiebler, R., Kelly, T. B. and **Ketteman, C.** *Best Practices – Building your Business with Customer-Focused Solutions*, 1998 (Simon and Schuster).

Ishikawa, K., Ishikawa, K. and **Lu, D. J.** *What Is Total Quality Control?: The Japanese Way*, 1988 (Prentice Hall).

Lewin, K. *Field Theory in Social Sciences*, 1951 (Harper and Row).

Nutt, P. C. *Why Decisions Fail*, 2002 (Berrett–Koehler Publishers).

Parnaby. J., *et al.*, *The Lucas Manufacturing Systems Engineering Handbook,* 2nd edition, 1989 (Lucas Industries Publishers).

Stamatis, D. H. *Failure Mode and Effect Analysis: FMEA from Theory to Execution*, 1995 (American Society for Quality).

Winston, W. L., Albright, S. C. and **Albright, C.** *Practical Management Science*, 2000 (Duxbury Press).

Optimization?

Problem

Ronnie B observed that they had dug the hole in the wrong corner of the field. It had to be in the opposite corner. Ronnie C commenced moving the hole by digging a new hole next to the wrong one. He put the spoil from the second hole into a wheelbarrow and then tipped it into the first hole. Ronnie B then dug a third hole next to the second one, filling another wheelbarrow with the spoil to tip into the second. Proceeding this way their chain of 34 holes got them to the intended position across the field.

Principles

- Objectives should be understood at all levels.
- Take an overview of any problem.
- Supervision is cheaper than wasted work.

Lesson

- It is easy to optimise the unnecessary. A passing efficiency expert might have observed that the Ronnie of B and C team would have been more effective if Ronnie B dug only half of each new hole, leaving room for Ronnie C to finish it throwing the soil from it straight into the previous hole. (A passing cost expert might have observed that they could therefore have disposed of one of the wheelbarrows.)

Reader's Guide

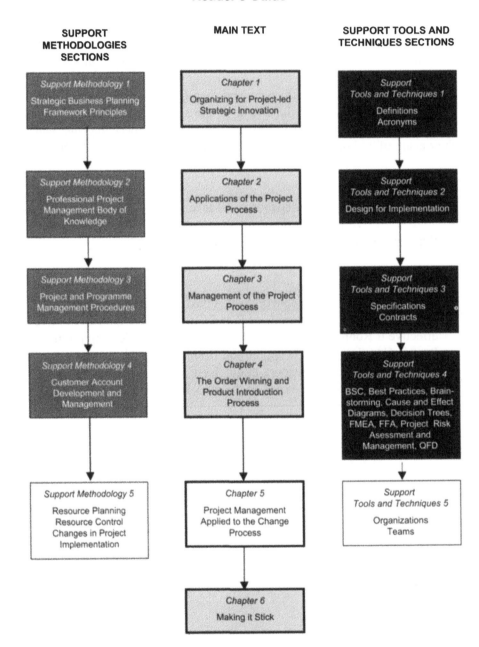

SUPPORT METHODOLOGIES SECTIONS

Support Methodology 1
Strategic Business Planning Framework Principles

Support Methodology 2
Professional Project Management Body of Knowledge

Support Methodology 3
Project and Programme Management Procedures

Support Methodology 4
Customer Account Development and Management

Support Methodology 5
Resource Planning
Resource Control
Changes in Project Implementation

MAIN TEXT

Chapter 1
Organizing for Project-led Strategic Innovation

Chapter 2
Applications of the Project Process

Chapter 3
Management of the Project Process

Chapter 4
The Order Winning and Product Introduction Process

Chapter 5
Project Management Applied to the Change Process

Chapter 6
Making it Stick

SUPPORT TOOLS AND TECHNIQUES SECTIONS

Support Tools and Techniques 1
Definitions
Acronyms

Support Tools and Techniques 2
Design for Implementation

Support Tools and Techniques 3
Specifications
Contracts

Support Tools and Techniques 4
BSC, Best Practices, Brain-storming, Cause and Effect Diagrams, Decision Trees, FMEA, FFA, Project Risk Asessment and Management, QFD

Support Tools and Techniques 5
Organizations
Teams

The underlying purpose of a change programme is usually to enhance the value-adding and shareholder value delivery capability of a business or organization. There is always a concurrent requirement to change the organization culture to one more supportive of innovation linked to employee motivation.

The field of change management has long been an area of frustration and difficulty. Machiavelli, the arch exponent of political manoeuvring and self-interested change manipulation, pointed out many years ago that the change agent had no friends, only enemies. This was, he explained, due to the fact that people on the receiving end are frightened of changes because of the potential impact on them personally; even people who may stand to benefit from change, oppose it because they do not know at the outset or understand the benefits to themselves. They are cautious and would like to stay with the status quo, which they have learned to live with.

Business literature and company annual report statements abound with examples of innovation initiatives or promises which have not been delivered, ranging from failed mergers of companies to unfulfilled sales growth promises and company total quality restructuring programmes which are aborted. Company directors are sometimes very nervous of publicising ambitious performance improvement initiatives because of a lack of relevant expertise, and related lack of confidence, that they can get their organization to reliably deliver. They, therefore, often focus on short-term easy target cost cutting initiatives such as head count reductions and cutting out longer-term value-adding capabilities such as R&D, training and new technology capital investment. Anything more ambitious is seen to be on the too-risky list and career and bonus threatening. They are also aware of the difficulty of persuading city analysts and shareholders to be patient and support a change programme. They fear these people will not support long-term competitiveness improvement programmes because they need to see good short-term returns from buying and selling shares when cost cuts result in short-term profit improvements.

Another problem is that some company Boards of Directors have a tendency to keep promoting additional new initiatives but without strong project management underpinning to ensure delivery of targets. As each previous initiative fails to deliver the promised innovation, a new one is started. This has led to buzz-word innovation and spin doctoring of company reports on innovation activities, with a trail of ill-conceived, supposedly world beating programmes which did not perform. Isolated new IT systems initiatives which often fail to be completed or deliver all the promised benefits are succeeded by others such as management by objectives, TQM, six sigma, business process re-engineering, team work, empowerment and Kaizen. The two unfortunate by-products of such an amateur approach are:

1. Disillusion and demotivation of employees who see the Boards as incompetent flavour of the month followers, chopping and changing their requirements.
2. A proliferation of confusing sales promotions by management consultants who keep changing the labels of their successive service product offerings, knowing that TQM, six sigma and business process engineering are very similar, while offering an even better 'promised land' to increasingly disgruntled and cynical customers. They also have their own brand of cynicism over the lack of capability in their customers to do the obvious and to complete programmes. An associated phenomenon which exists is a plethora of simultaneously rising or falling consultancy gurus depending upon which phase of the innovation era they have latched on to.

Rising above all of this cacophony of clamour for attention, there is no question that a clear message emerges. Designing and delivering lasting performance benefits through a business performance change programme is very demanding in reality. A well-run competitiveness achievement programme can take three years of persistent, intelligent, educated effort before a strong foundation for growth and performance improvement is created.

The problem is that few senior managers have taken enough time to become properly educated in the principles of change management and modern organization design, compared with the time they devoted to learning their speciality such as engineering, accountancy or marketing.

The principles of change project management are common sense and straightforward to learn. There is a core generic set of supporting methodologies and organizational practices to learn which are not difficult to find out about and apply. What is essential is for management at all levels to generate the will and commitment to get started and devote the necessary time, training effort and proper leadership.

5.1 Getting started – tactics and psychology

Initiating a change process requires careful tactics since it cannot be assumed that everyone in the organization believes in and supports the need for change. Many people may not be aware that performance of the company falls well short of excellent if they are inward looking and do not have the skills or opportunity to systematically compare performance in their part of the company with others and with competitors.

In advance of a formal start to a change programme, there are three useful steps to make it clear to the whole company that there is both a problem and an opportunity:

1. Initiate and visibly promote a competitor bench-marking analysis. An application of the approach to the product introduction process was introduced in Chapter 4. This requires careful preparation to ensure that it is professionally carried out. Information on competitors and best practice company financial performance, product/service performance, company practices etc., should be collected by a trained cross-functional, senior task-force team. The information can be gathered from company annual reports, magazine/newspaper articles, internal company magazines, customers and suppliers of equipment and services. The team should process the information and convert it to a set of financial and non-financial performance measures for a gap analysis comparison with their own company. Such a study should not just be confined to competitors but should be extended to competitive common business processes operated by other companies in other fields, e.g. distribution logistics, order winning, product introduction, service delivery, and supplier development processes, where these companies are known to be very good performers.

   The end results of such a comparison, combined with any significant emotional events such as failures to achieve internal budgeted performance, can then provide a driving force and a basis for a communication seminar to a wide cross-section of managers and supervisors to draw attention to gaps in performance and to agree the need for change and the first steps required. A communication seminar will usefully introduce the practice of running Executive Workshops for training and help develop expert leadership skills, on a regular basis.

   A sample overview bench-marking comparison from the automotive industry is shown in Table 5.1. In practice, it is surprising how much useful underpinning data can be collected by a trained, cross-functional task-force team in a few weeks. This initial exercise can be followed by ongoing bench-marking exercises by business management teams supported by task-force project teams.

2. Enlist volunteer managers from different business areas of the company to carry out short pilot projects to look for and exploit initial sources of problems and opportunities to improve performance against bench-marks. The business senior executive team should be involved in the selection and review of these pilots and their owners must be carefully chosen to enhance the probability of success. This is a key aid to the consensus winning process on the need for rapid change and the process for systematically widening involvement in change. Even though these are early pilots, as much of the best practice project management principles as possible should be applied to generate success in implementation of changes.

These pilot projects preferably should not target major total restructuring of business processes in the first instance since these are likely to be very risky, demanding tasks for an organization immature in relation to new best practices application and change management. The bigger challenges come later building on successful pilot project foundations.

3. One very effective and highly motivating approach for demonstrating that major improvements are feasible is to focus on the elimination of wasteful non-value-adding (NVA) activity; in particular modular parts of business processes, as a step towards world-class levels of performance. A pilot project, under the focused initiative of 'War on Waste Projects', is difficult to argue against in the same way that people cannot dispute the importance of improved quality of products or services. This tactic helps to budge 'immovable objects' in a management team.

Waste is the collective label for all activities in parts of operations and support processes such as sales departments, general offices, manufacturing areas or service delivery units, which do not add value. These unnecessary activities would not be perceived by customers as adding value to a product or service and they are not prepared to pay for their cost in the price of the product.

Classical examples of NVA activities which incur costs, but do not add value are:

(a) Holding and managing excessive inventories of work in process which tie up cash, incur interest charges and slow down work flow (*flow-chart symbol* $\triangle$).

(b) Transporting materials, including paper, between departments and functions, increased in cost and aggravated by poor flow-path design. This incurs overhead costs, including the cost of IT systems for circulating documents which would not be required if the processes were redesigned and simplified (*flow-chart symbol* ➔).

(c) Inspecting faulty work as a preliminary to re-working work in process. This incurs extra cost compared with the comparator zero-base case of a right-first-time, zero defects policy (*flow-chart symbol* ☐).

(d) Delays, incurred at points dispersed through a process, which extend the lead-time of the whole process and also interfere with the effective operation of dependent processes. Time and effort is wasted, and confusion is caused; the delay increases operating costs which a simplified flow system design could eliminate (*flow-chart symbol* D).

Note that value-adding operations on work flow-charts – which add value to materials or information by processing them, or enhance elements of service provided – are given a single *flow-chart symbol* ◯.

It is a straightforward matter to train project teams to analyse and design business processes by drawing flow-charts in two complementary stages (see Figs 5.1 and 5.2).

1. Draw an overall input–output diagram for the office or manufacturing site area under scrutiny, listing all inputs received and all outputs provided, and ensuring that items in each of these two groups are all necessary and are provided. Such validation usually creates a lot of surprises. In addition, the links back from input–output charts to input provider and output receiver areas should be traced to check the integrity of the sub-system under examination and that all inputs and outputs are necessary.

2. Walk the office or site area under scrutiny, trace the work flows and information or paper flows (plotting these on a flow-chart) and list all activities with the appropriate non-value-adding or value-adding symbol. Calculate the ratio of value-adding to non-value-adding operations. Based upon practical experience, this will probably show that 60–80% of all activities are non-value adding. The following typical example statistics are averages of many projects in a number of different businesses:

- Wasteful operations in the service delivery operations process – 65%
- Wasteful operations in the service development process – 75%
- Wasteful operations in the support administration process – 65%

The prime task then becomes very focused and obvious, i.e. to reorganise and simplify the flow process to eliminate all NVA activities.

5.1.1 Weekly reviews – to control and drive progress

In the pilot project weekly progress review meetings, the theme to be emphasised is:

First simplify:
- Operations
- Paperwork
- Work areas and work flows
- ˙Practices and procedures, standardising on best practices

Before automating these automation is achieved by two methods
1. Team training to carry out carefully designed standard working procedures.
2. By use of automated equipment and IT in suitable selected areas.

In many businesses these reviews make it obvious that too many people are employed in costly NVA activity for which the customer will not willingly pay. If more efficient and effective competitors offer lower prices then the others will not survive.

The principles to apply in simplification are:
1. The project team should redesign and rearrange the work flow in the area of focus to put people closer together, grouped as a team with total process ownership, around the flow-chart to eliminate wasteful activity.
2. Eliminate paperwork by combining or eliminating badly designed forms or reports that are not needed.
3. From the input–output analysis of work flow between work areas, count the number of losses of ownership where work and information flow crosses boundaries. Reduce these to less than 10 per cent by cross-role team training or personnel transfer to the new flow-chart owner team. This then allows the process team to complete their work quickly without waiting and develops an ownership culture combining authority to act with responsibility to deliver.
4. Design a set of measures of performance for the redesigned team process which are competitive, and monitor these on a daily, weekly and monthly basis with total visibility to the team and others.

When these pilot projects are completed, arrange for the project team to communicate their results to a wide internal audience in a formal presentation and review session. Typically they should present quantified results as follows, related to their 50% improvement target set

- Reduction in process lead-time due to shorter, simpler work flows with less to and from movements.
- Reduction in work in process.
- Increased process quality, i.e. zero work defects.
- Reduction in staff required, i.e. productivity increase.
- Reduction in percentage non-value-adding activities.
- Reductions in unnecessary paperwork and data circulation.
- Changes in work practice.
- Reduced operating cost.

To illustrate the methodologies and types of result achieved by such sharply focused demonstrator pilot projects, the following figures and typical examples are provided. Figure 5.1 illustrates in simplified format, the basic flow-charting tools for project teams to use. Figure 5.2 shows the results of a project to eliminate non-value-adding activity via the analysis of several sub-process flow-charts associated with the administration of equipment procurement and order winning bid process administration.

Figure 5.3 shows the results of a short project aimed at reducing the stock levels in a manufacturing process. Here a small project team measured the

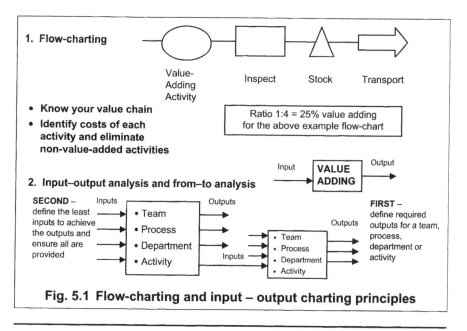

Fig. 5.1 Flow-charting and input – output charting principles

Principles illustrated:

- A simple representation of a complex set of office-based sub-systems

- Analysis shows:

  { 39% VA
  { 61% NVA

- Indication of where the long lead-times are coming from

Activity	Plant Ordering Systems		Office System for Layout Drawings Production		Cost Recording Paperwork Flow		SUB-PROCESS Modification Notes		Drawing Ordering System		Equipment Ordering System		Consumables Requisition		Capital Equipment Servicing	
◯	11	37%	9	28%	3	33%	11	47%	12	52%	9	47%	7	39%	18	30%
▢	1		4				2		1		1		2		5	
⇧	9	63%	10	72%	5	67%	1	53%		48%		53%	3	61%	10	70%
△	2		5		1		3		4		4		4		14	
D	7		4				6		6		5		2		13	
Total	30	100%	32	100%	9	100%	23	100%	23	100%	19	100%	18	100%	60	100%

Fig. 5.2 Results of a flow-charting project

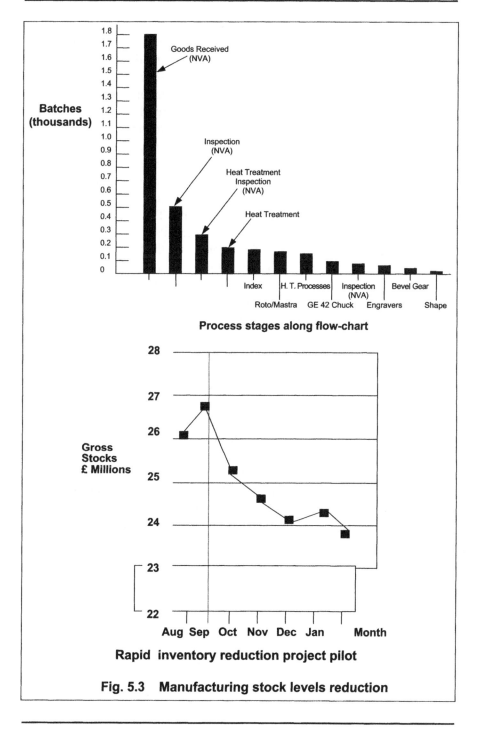

Fig. 5.3   Manufacturing stock levels reduction

levels of work in progress at each work station and then plotted these on a pareto diagram in order of magnitude. With the help of the operating staff, they tackled these intermediate pools of stock one at a time, found the root cause and eliminated this. For example, in the purchased goods received inspection area they discovered that a small inspection team could work faster if a Support Engineer worked with them to resolve problems on the spot and shorten communication delays. They also found that every type of purchased item was being inspected, even simple items, which did not need to be inspected, and this created delay from heavy workloads. By eliminating these problems, items passed through the goods received area much more quickly. This, in turn, prevented hold-ups further downstream caused by waiting for parts to complete work. The result was a rapid reduction in stock plus short-term cash flow benefits.

A final example given in Table 5.2 summarises the benefits from a pilot project aimed at reducing the large numbers of paper forms used in a pharmaceuticals production and distribution company. All forms were collected, counted and assessed for their purpose; then the work involved in completing, checking and circulating the forms inside and outside of the company to customers and suppliers was quantified and costed. It was discovered that the cumulative work required from all sources to complete one of the forms took three man-hours on average. By careful redesign of forms to eliminate duplication and overlap, simplification to reduce work content, combination of forms, elimination of unnecessary forms and by talking to customers and suppliers to simplify their requirements, it was possible to totally redesign the set of forms. Forms were grouped to match ownership by new groupings of process activity teams in the facility. Large savings resulted. On implementation, a further large saving resulted from putting 60% of the remaining paperwork onto a networked PC system at low implementation cost. The project achieved cash flow neutrality when only a third complete, and was then cash generating.

Table 5.2 Reduction in control paperwork		
Item	Before	After
Number of forms	143	32
Average man-hours per form	3	1.25
No. of sub-process department interfaces	19	8
No. of forms per supplier	10	3
No. of forms per customer	14	3

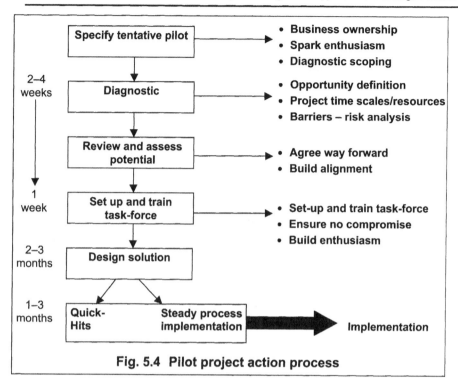

Fig. 5.4 Pilot project action process

Finally, to summarise the piloting project process and indicate the scope of the project management task required to ensure success, Fig. 5.4 provides a flow-chart incorporating the time phased main activities.

5.2 The second and most demanding stage – running major change programmes

Successful completion of a number of short pilot projects across several core processes makes life much easier for leaders of stage 2.

A prime tactical action at the end of the first stage pilot demonstration is to demonstrate that such prioritised projects are cash neutral at least, and therefore all businesses can afford to run change projects. This takes away excuses from any senior managers who are resisting change.

If the pilot demonstration project stage described so far is well managed and promoted, the results widely communicated, and the areas which have been improved made to look modern and attractive, the stage is set for a full-scale change programme launch, led by top management. The business audience will have been conditioned to appreciate that there is much improvement possible. They will have been surprised and probably embarrassed by such a systematic demonstration of their own inefficiency and lack of competitiveness. They will be ready to take on ownership for their part of a coordinated and systematic step-by-step change process.

At this stage, the creation of a fully integrated, two to three-year business-wide rolling CAP programme will be required with extensive preparation, supported by the Programme Office. It is necessary to train business unit teams in the methodology of CAP preparation as well as the methodologies associated with the design of effective organizations and the widespread empowered application of the 'management by projects' disciplines.

The prime purpose of CAP change programmes is to run substantial transformational projects to create a step change in business process effectiveness and business performance. These projects generally result in very significant restructuring of the organization, the roles of all staff and the practices employed. A transformational project creates a new more effective prototype business organization structure, which then provides a driveable platform for continuous improvement by staff trained in the new operational disciplines. A transformational project is a considerable task requiring longer-term management persistence and determination to see it

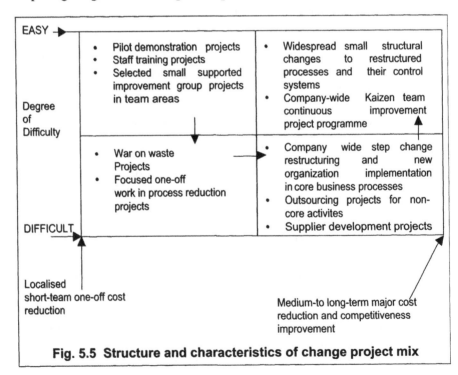

Fig. 5.5 Structure and characteristics of change project mix

through. In terms of tactics, therefore, experience has shown it is important to follow a set of pragmatic principles.

1. Choose priority areas carefully based upon up-front diagnostic projects and world class bench-marking to assess potential and set clear targets.
2. Train the project teams to apply modern techniques and methodologies but guard against paralysis by analysis. It is better to create a prototype structure for a key process and run it into operation quickly with a trained operational team operating with new flexible job structures and then lead them to refine and improve their process against measured operational targets.
3. Recognise the importance of the need to keep shareholders and stockmarket analysts happy. Aim for a programme divided into modules, prioritised in order of potential gains, to achieve cash neutrality at least in terms of its costs in the early stages, which preferably can be demonstrated to become cash positive very quickly.

These imply that senior management must be educated to understand all aspects and take a very close interest in directing and reviewing the programme. It also means that running a carefully chosen mix of types of project is important if the maximum speed of achievement is to be achieved. Follow each modular restructuring transition project with a well-managed programme of highly focused small continuous improvement projects to extract major benefits, while starting up the next major project.

Figure 5.5 illustrates, on a Boston chart, the logic underlying the project choices and mix, and the relative degrees of difficulty related to time required.

5.2.1 Supporting framework for a robust change programme

Once the company has completed the first stage of preparing the culture to accept the need for change and to embark on an action process, the hard work of managing major company wide innovation requires the building of a carefully detailed infrastructure of supportive best practices. The scene is set, the management team now perceive the opportunity for improvement and must put supporting structures in place.

The framework of directional elements to guide company-wide improvement has the following interlocking links of a CAP implementation:

1. Market strategy, product/service policy, delivery strategy.
2. Wide communication of the framework and a demand for a step change.
3. Studies of other organizations.
4. Application of business process concepts to map out a new more effective organization structure.
5. Insistence on simplification before automation through the systematic elimination of complexities.
6. Accent the focus on value-adding activity in all business processes.
7. Application of best practice principles, tools, methodologies and systems.
8. Improved effectiveness targets for the core business.

Thoroughness in preparation and communication is essential for two main reasons:

(a) The need for attention to detail in the analysis, design and implementation stages of the change programme and the need to train all task-force project teams to apply expert detailed best practical methodologies to ensure a professional result.
(b) The need to take a fresh look at the way the whole business operates and persuade all staff to open their minds to inadequacies and to new ways of operating.

It should be apparent by now why the creation of an executive line management organization structure to manage change, as described in Chapter 1, is so essential to success. The size, duration and complexity of the task requires this. The levels of professionalism required, clarity and consistency of leadership and direction demand it. The Programme Office role whether carried out by one person in a small business or by a team in a large business in providing guidance, support and also the monitoring role is of particular importance.

It is a real challenge when setting up a full company-wide programme of change, to define and communicate a long-lasting single initiative framework to link all projects over a long time period with sustained commitment.

For a typical commercial business the approach might proceed broadly as follows:

A typical first step is for the top executive team to develop a vision statement and a mission statement for discussion with the workforce. These

---

Table 5.3 The total quality organization

1. Achieves a high quality international standard of performance in all functions and cross-functional business processes.
2. Has a clear understanding of and focus on the needs of its market.
3. Has a clear view of the improvements required in its overall measures of performance and ensures that these measures are cascaded into locally relevant terms to all levels in its business processes.
4. Operates the simplest possible structures and procedures.
5. Continually scrutinises all processes for the elimination of non-value-adding activities and waste.
6. Has a balanced and integrated mix of operations and development functions, ensuring good attention to short-, medium- and long-term requirements for excellence in process operations, product and service development, and process development.
7. Uses well-trained and managed multi-disciplinary team practices for operational effectiveness, development, and change, and to ensure flexibility, adaptiveness and speed of action.
8. Understands its competition in detail.
9. Operates good communication procedures and visibly acknowledges good work.
10. Achieves low operating costs to match targeted competitive product and service costs while maintaining value-adding and development competencies.

---

will be fairly short and generic using statements such as 'We want to be number 1 in our chosen market-place'. They will emphasise the needs of all stakeholders, including the shareholders, staff, and customers, with training and development support to achieve excellence in core competencies being mentioned, and the aim to 'delight all customers' with a high total quality of performance in all activities and business processes. These help to give simple, clear top-level guidance to all, on the intentions of the company.

Such simple top-level statements are easy to understand. Clearly, however, it is also necessary to develop quickly a more detailed statement of content capable in practice of serving two aims:

(a) Providing guidance to all involved in the integrated set of elements which must be brought together for success, i.e. giving a total systems view.
(b) Enabling people at all levels to identify the probable areas that will be the focus of improvement project activity.

A particularly powerful and easy to understand means of providing such a practical signpost is to declare the aim of creating a 'Total Quality Organization' which achieves a world-class competitive performance in all that it does. The total quality organization is then defined, a typical example is shown in Table 5.3.

The definition in Table 5.3 is sufficiently detailed to allow team leaders to run brainstorming sessions with their teams to solicit creative and practical suggestions for project proposals to support any one or more of the ten requirements for becoming a total quality organization.

Figure 5.6 shows a second device to facilitate rapid understanding and self-generating commitment to the change programme. Creating pictures in the mind emphasises a practical step-by-step way to achieving excellence.

Figure 5.6 illustrates how a major step change in competitiveness is built up as a sequence of smaller steps in which new business processes are designed and implemented in modular steps by task-force projects to create natural group team-operated segments of each process. Continuous improvement team projects follow each step change.

These steps are carried out in a priority order as identified by an initial diagnostic opportunity audit of the company following a first stage training exercise delivered via executive workshops.

The methodology used for designing each module is that of the five-step systems engineering approach. This is summarised in Case Example 1, Chapter 1, i.e.:

1. Collect the data.
2. Analyse the data and extract structure and patterns for action.
3. Steady state system design.
4. Dynamic design.
5. Monitoring and control system design and integration.

In each case, 'paralysis by analysis' is avoided by rapidly creating and implementing a sound but rough-cut design, with areas for further work being made clear. A natural team group cellular architecture is set up and the new operational team is trained to progressively improve on their process performance using Kaizen continuous improvement methods.

In this way, change spreads across different parts of the company in a managed, systematic and modular fashion and Kaizen group activity is initiated each time a sound team architecture is put in place to make it effective. The number of people involved in the changes as part of their job role, rapidly increases, and change fans out across the company so becoming increasingly self-sustainable and less dependent on the initial small group of senior managers who started it off.

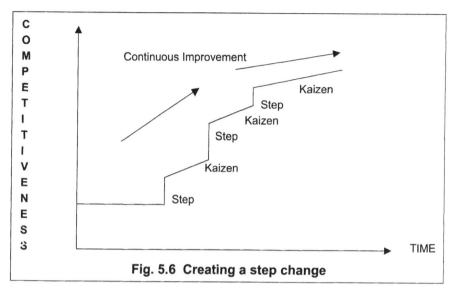

Fig. 5.6 Creating a step change

5.2.2 Defining the process map and the proposed organizational model

It is important to have a guidance plan fairly early in the change programme for the targeted organizational architecture before too many projects are established; this avoids confusion from sudden changes and eliminates the risk of making errors. In the early stages the organizational model will be flexible and its tighter definition will be an iterative process as more data and facts become available from the initial priority task-force team activity.

Here again, it will be necessary to progress in detail beyond general statements such as broad aim of simplification, reducing job levels and layers, and creating teamwork with the minimum number of divisive over-specialist job titles.

The best way to execute the task in an expert manner while achieving good communication, buy-in and broad involvement of staff is to run an early executive training workshop for the top team on the topic of design of effective organizations. The workshop should cover the following typical set of topics:

- Example critical success factor competitive bench-marks.
- Case studies of other companies.
- Defining product units and support units, i.e. a cellular customer–supplier structure.
- Exploiting synergies across an organization.

- Using 'make versus buy' analysis as a basis for outsourcing strategy.
- Defining core competencies of the organization.
- Defining general purpose competencies which can be outsourced.
- Staff roles, line roles, integration of functional specialist centres of excellence with cross-functional team activities.
- Designing effective teams by generic job and team role specification.
- Defining the natural team groups to match core business processes and their modules or cells.
- Organization chart definition.
- Flexible resource management and human resources (HR) personal development planning.
- Business process design tools.

The output from the workshop syndicate group sessions should be a first rough-cut sketch of the main features required of a modern organization, together with a list of primary analysis tasks required to add shape and detail, e.g. by putting task-force resource groups together from across the organization to exploit synergies in such areas as purchasing, IT support, distribution logistics. Another typical key task would be to calibrate the organization core competencies in terms of their level of capability versus world-class standards as a preliminary to carrying out an outsourcing opportunity analysis.

Once the top team, together with the Programme Director and Change Manager, have sketched out a broad outline, an early multi-disciplinary task-force project of typically four to six weeks duration (after workshop training and briefing and target setting by the Chief Executive and his or her team), can carry out a more detailed organizational and business process map design for review and decision by the top team in a joint workshop.

After this, the major change programme can roll out rapidly, with multi-disciplinary task-force project teams in succession following the list of priority projects agreed with top management. Once again, this type of planning and initiation process, with broad personnel involvement, exposes individual reactions in workshop and review sessions, creates commitment, will help to mitigate resistance to change and obstructive company politics as well as contributing to the development of an educated performance achievement team culture at all levels.

Some of the main basic practical concepts of organizational and business process model definition for the company or organization under scrutiny are:

1. Definition of the natural product or service groups in a business and their shared support processes. Identification of the list of business processes

in each business using the typical list given in Chapter 1, Table 1.3. Their categorisation according to core, non-core, and special or non-special categories, as well as an assessment of how far each is from world-class operation

2. By looking into the organization as a customer would, from the market interface, definition of the different product or service groups which require clear identities from the point of view of the customer. Some product groups may offer a one-off bespoke project type service and others may deliver standard products in volume, or provide after-sales service. These differences create a need for differences in organizational structure in the real world of business and markets to ensure customer friendliness.

3. Definition of the internal support units which serve internal customers, including dedicated team groups or cells which underpin product groups.

Some simplified case examples may help to clarify all of the points discussed above.

5.2.2.1 Macro-level business process model for a Facilities Management (FM) company

(a) Customer account development process.
(b) Bidding and order-winning process.
(c) FM service development, design and best practice improvement process.
(d) Sub-contract supplier and partner management process.
(e) Service delivery process and start-up project management.
(f) Service quality and safety audit and monitoring process.
(g) Risk definition and audit process.
(h) Procurement process.
(i) Specialist functional needs support process.
(j) Financial management and administration process.
(k) Corporate governance process.
(l) Corporate leadership CAP strategy planning, review, approval and programme management process.
(m) HR development and training support process.
(n) Infrastructure support management process.

Mission statement and supporting strategic aims

'The company intends, through change management and managed continuous improvement, to be a leader in the delivery of high quality value-adding supporting services and related products, to customers involved in infrastructure provision.

The company will integrate its supply chain through close involvement of suppliers in service specification and development.

It will deliver competitive services which delight the customer through the application of world's best practices which improve its core business processes and create excellence in its core competences.

It will lead in the continuous development and training of its employees and the selection of sub-contract resources.

Through continued entrepreneurial actions, the creation of a total quality organization, and professional development of services to meet the emerging needs of its chosen markets, the company intends to grow shareholder value and achieve upper decile financial performance, so providing long-term stability for all stakeholders.'

5.2.2.2 Redesign of the service delivery process for a clearing bank

(a) Service delivery flow process analysis, Fig. 5.7, for clearing large volume requests for payments.

(b) Clearing centre process redesign, Fig. 5.8, reduced from twenty specialist departments into 5 natural team groups, by flow-chart design. Work flow had followed a very complex zig-zag path through the specialist departments with consequential high content of non-value-added activity, poor communication delays and long lead-times. Payment requests were required to be checked and either paid or rejected by labour-intensive reference to file data.

(c) Capacity management and resource scheduling redesigned, i.e. resource levels, shift patterns and core team numbers to suit demand cycle forecast patterns.

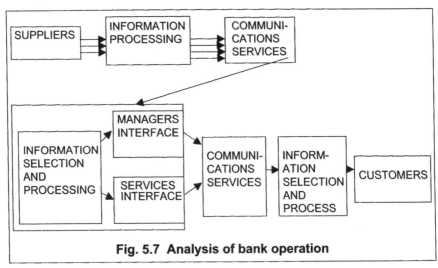

Fig. 5.7 Analysis of bank operation

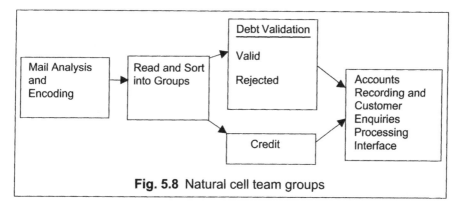

Fig. 5.8 Natural cell team groups

(d) Organization structure redesign around business processes. Six organization levels reduced to three with team leaders for cross-functional natural group sub-processes, each team's members co-located.

(e) Overall benefits:
- over 20% reduction in operating costs,
- less than 1 year payback,
- better control and planning,
- 100% planned schedule achievement,
- 70% reduction in process lead-time.

5.2.2.3 Simplification of a hardware equipment distributor delivery process

Three natural group units covering the order winning to delivery process activities were created from ten departments after flow chart analysis, each with trained teams capable of flexible cross skill working. The net result was a 50% reduction in stock, an 80% reduction in average process lead-time and a 40% reduction in staff employed. Figure 5.9 shows the modular framework.

5.2.2.4 Re-organization and restructuring of an international engineering automation component manufacturing business

Following an extensive acquisition programme, a portfolio of ten stand-alone fully functioned businesses was built up, each averaging £15M p.a. turnover and spread over twenty one sites in the UK, Europe and USA.

To achieve CAP strategic objectives, it was decided to set up a multi-project, two-year change programme to restructure and integrate this group into a single business. A 50% improvement in performance target for a set of chosen business ratios was specified. This was met by a combination of

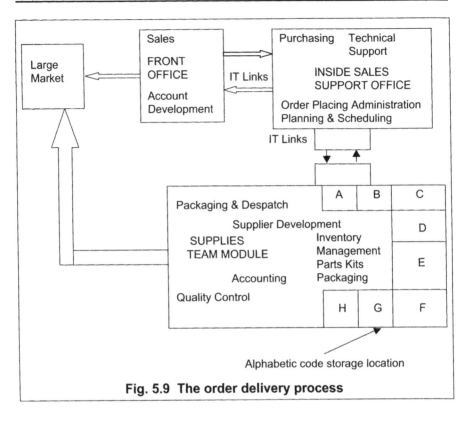

Fig. 5.9 The order delivery process

exploiting synergies and introducing a modern, low waste, business process organization supported by operational methodologies based upon those of the Toyota production system.

The core business processes of major importance and potential for improvement were chosen as:

- The new product development process.
- The applications engineering process for tailoring a range of platform products to customer order requirements.
- The sales and market development process.
- The manufacturing operations process.
- The procurement and supply chain management process.

Some specific core process competencies requiring focus were:

- The major customer account development and bidding process, to be organized as a cross-function project team activity, led by customer account Project Managers.
- Manufacturing. It was decided to concentrate on the high technology

know-how-dependent value-adding areas of design for manufacturing, manufacturing assembly and testing, and to outsource offshore, commodity component supply, retaining only a few critical know-how-dependent core components for in-house manufacture.

Basic features designed for the new restructured organization were:

1. Grouping management and teams around three distinct product business unit groups or modules interfacing directly to the market. Each incorporated project managers and product-specific applications support technical staff, as well as commercial staff, to support contract proposals preparation and pricing quotations.
2. Shared sales resource, but with specialist technical support attached, and supported by a despatch and distribution capability for delivering a range of standard products to a large distributed customer base.
3. Shared procurement via a single supplies module as in Fig. 5.9, operated by a cross-functional team that also included engineers to facilitate supplier development and supply chain management. The supplies module was responsible for all supplies scheduling to match the sales plan, the planning and integration of external component supplies with internally manufactured supplies, and the creation of kits for feeding just in time to its internal customer, the manufacturing assembly and test process.
4. A shared manufacturing operations process unit with a single large critical mass operational management and manufacturing systems engineering support team but with product assembly carried out in product group-specific cells, with a clear dotted line back to the product groups and the market-place.
5. A shared R&D process unit with a strong critical mass of technical staff and equipment, which also supplied technical resources to project teams run by the product group units to translate development output into customer-specific products.
6. A centralized support and administration process for synergistic provision of shared services such as IT support development.
7. A 60% reduction in the number of separate sites with the elimination of many overhead costs in a single integrated company organization.

Initial benefits achieved prior to commencing Kaizen continuous improvement were as follows:

- sales per employee ratio increased by a factor of 2.5,
- average lead-times reduced by 60% across all business processes,

- 40% cost base reduction and 15% reduction in purchasing costs,
- stock turnover ratio doubled,
- rate of development of new products increased by 30%,
- headcount reduced by 40%.

The methodologies summarised briefly for illustration in this manufacturing industry case example are generic and typical of the needs of all manufacturing businesses. The use of a multi-disciplinary task-force project change programme represents the only cost effective delivery mechanism for making change happen quickly due to the breadth of knowledge and many threads that must be brought together professionally.

5.2.3 Summary of key concepts

From the above illustrative case examples and preceding text a number of key concepts for consideration by change project teams when designing modern new effective organizations, can be summarised as follows:

- Design to meet the strategic requirements and future targets of the CAP.
- Achieving competitive advantage and cost reduction through synergy via sharing of resources, both tangible, e.g. headcount reduction and intangible, e.g. access to critical mass know-how groupings.
- Cross-boundary and cross-functional management of processes.
- Organizing for team work – the natural cross-functional process team group concept with locally relevant measures of performance.
- Ensure a product group market focus at the customer interface to make it easy for the customer to identify with his supplier in a multi-product company.
- Flatter, simpler job structures by role design and training.
- Improved capability for high value-added new product and service development.
- Cost base reduction and leanness creation but with enhanced development and value-adding capability for sales growth support.
- Definition of identities and scope of ownership for business units, product units and support cell groups.
- Achievement of critical mass in support process competencies.
- Core business process definitions for operations and development teams.

5.2.4 The natural group team building block of an effective organization

The concept of a natural group team, which has full ownership of all the functions of a process or a sub-module of a process, and which has defined suppliers and customers, has been introduced in several contexts so far. This is a critically important foundation element of the modern process team organization that requires a lot of attention to detail at the design stage, from the task-force project team.

The important requirements that are based on best practice experience are:

1. A natural group team is grouped around a newly designed flow-chart constructed by simplifying the original flow of materials and information. This is achieved by removing all non-value-added work activity and eliminating all losses of ownership caused by the flow zig-zagging repetitively across the original boundaries of separate functional skill groups. The target should be for a natural group team to possess in their multiple skills and facilities more than 95% of the functional facilities required to carry out the set of tasks they are responsible for. Empowerment of independent action directed by MOPs is the result.

2. Where a group cannot possess all the capability, e.g. where a specialised piece of expensive equipment needs to be shared by others, then they should be in control of the 'gateway' in their cell which is the controlled route by which the work leaves to be processed by the separate facility and returns. They should plan and schedule such departures and returns via the gateway using the Kanban principle to maintain control of 'just-in-time' operation.

3. A natural group should have a clear role and, by design, should have clear customers and suppliers, both internal or external, to their 'business'. They should set measures of performance expected from their suppliers, and should agree measures of their own performance with their customers for weekly review.

4. Measures of performance normally fit into five generic headings, i.e. productivity or unit cost, lead-time, work in progress turnover rate, percentage planned delivery schedule achievement measured by work item number and performance quality standard achieved.

5. When the natural group process is first designed, the team allocated should be given training in the operation of their module and in the understanding of their targets set and the controls for meeting these.

6. The minimum number of job titles should be used for the team. There should be some degree of cross-role training on start-up; this should be augmented by a follow-on training process. Generic job roles are:

   (a) Leader
   (b) Planner/Controller
   (c) Doer

   (d) Work mover

   (e) Support infrastructure repairer and maintainer

However, these can often be further reduced by combination, e.g. role (a) with (b), (b) with (e) and (c) with (d).

7. One best practice example of a support training structure is a five-star approach. Here, when all team members are given basic training in the operation of the new natural group or cell they are awarded one star. Basic training includes use of the standard operational handbook, the cell flow chart and awareness of the remaining non-value-added activity identified, together with common topics such as safety.

   Progressively, as they are subsequently trained in other relevant topics, the team members are awarded additional stars up to five. Typically, these topics are:

- Carrying out other job roles in the group.
- Self-certification of work and process capability monitoring.
- The problem definition and problem solution techniques to support Kaizen continuous improvement.
- Training others.
- Team leading.
- Specific methodologies such as the Japanese five-S's, i.e.
  - Seiton. Efficient and systematic organization of the workplace.
  - Seiso. Always leaving the workplace tidy.
  - Seiri. Careful separation of essential and non-essential activities and planning the work to eliminate accordingly.
  - Shitsuke. Conformance to standard operational frameworks, disciplines, and working procedures.
  - Seiketsu. Continuous improvement of effectiveness.

This approach can be readily translated to suit all types of team activity from professional staff to administration staff and manufacturing operations.

8. When creating a team it is helpful to apply the principles of the Belbin methodology to aid team effectiveness. This relates to such matters as the matching of personality types in a well-founded team ranging from 'leader' to 'challenger' and 'task finisher'.

The total support system required, designed by a change project task-force for an effective natural group team process unit is shown in Fig. 5.10.

Two illustrative examples related to natural group design are given in Figs 5.11 and 5.12 for a supply chain process module managing procurement and for customer–supplier team relationships definition.

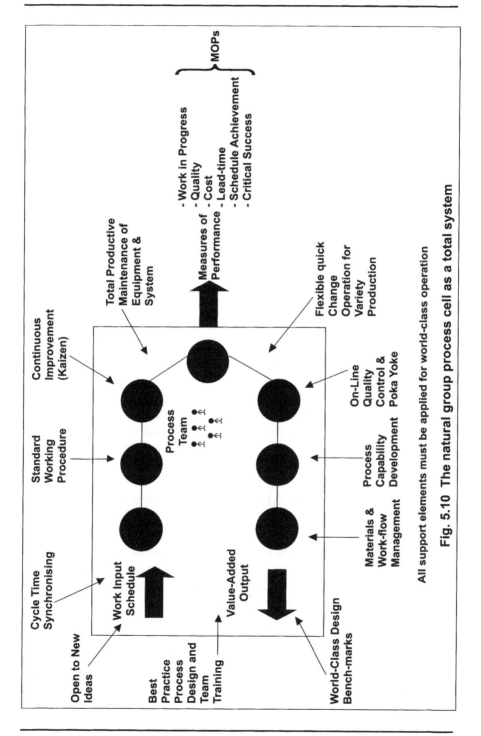

Fig. 5.10 The natural group process cell as a total system

All support elements must be applied for world-class operation

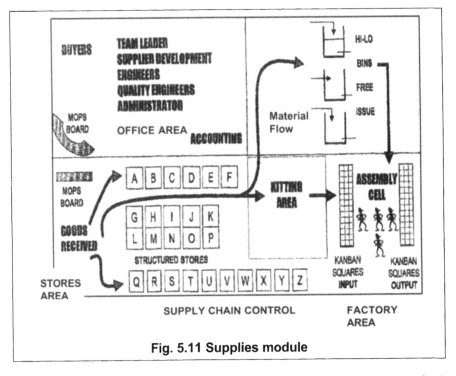

Fig. 5.11 Supplies module

These illustrate the detailed approach to business process design required of the change project task-force charged with its application. This further reinforces the need for every task-force to be multi-disciplinary and to be provided with a training workshop at the start of their task, as well as ongoing support and review by the Programme Office experts and the steering committee.

The first example in Figs 5.11 and 5.12, which applies to the supplies module process, can be seen to have similarities to the distribution process design, which featured in the case examples described earlier in this chapter.

In practical process redesign a major business process, such as the manufacturing delivery operations process, realistically must be divided into sub-process natural group team modules for practical implementation. A big process consists of a linked chain of modules, carefully matched at interfaces.

A major advantage of creating the organization as a set of natural group team groups is that it creates a much smaller number of focused and accountable resource units to be managed, planned, scheduled, monitored and controlled than the alternative highly fragmented vertical functional organization. It also embeds the customer-supplier measure of performance and achievement philosophy illustrated in Fig. 5.12.

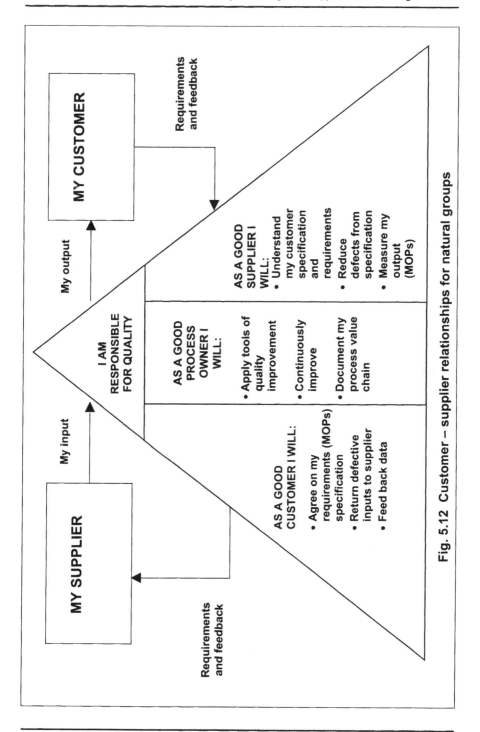

Fig. 5.12 Customer – supplier relationships for natural groups

5.2.5 Material, work and information flows in business processes

Process flow-chart work analysis, prior to creating an organization structure based on co-located natural group teams, is a very powerful way of creating a high-productivity, short lead-time, business process organization.

However, in modern organizations, whether in manufacturing companies such as automotive component manufacturers, or service companies such as the clearing bank example discussed previously in this chapter, the flows can be very complex, involving a large variety of materials and information. Some items flow through regularly and continuously, and others, often in high variety, flow irregularly or cyclically. Often, to design a single natural group to be able to handle all varieties and all frequencies of flow, can be uneconomic because of the difficulty of ensuring a relatively constant workload for the teams, resulting in over-manning or under-manning from time to time. Also, the skills required to handle all of the different varieties of product or service may turn out to be too sophisticated and demanding for a single team.

The control systems required for planning and controlling the required work schedules can also become too complex if variety and frequency flows are too high.

A useful method for overcoming these difficulties is to categorise the component parts of mixed high variety work flows into three groups during the flow analysis, i.e.:

1. Regular Runners
2. Repeaters
3. Strangers

It is possible for a team to become very familiar with, and occasionally expert in, handling regular Runners. The Repeaters, if there are enough of them, can be handled by a separate team or, depending upon capacity, can be systematically grouped and added to the work schedule of a Runners team, possibly requiring advanced warning to allow the team to refresh their skills and support tools required to handle them efficiently.

A stranger often requires a temporary project team to be set up, trained and equipped with the relevant support tools and facilities.

Adding Repeaters and Strangers to the workload of a Runners team creates confusion, requires different control techniques and, if the team has to stop and start due to the need to search for materials and information, productivity reduces dramatically and, usually, quality of performance also reduces. Hence, careful design to eliminate this can give major cost reduction benefits. It also makes the choice of MOPs, other than percentage delivery schedule achievement, more difficult to specify.

The following illustrative situations will clarify the problem.

1. In the automotive industry, motorcar models currently available require continuous high volume supplies of the many component parts involved in their assembly. Designing natural group team component manufacturing cells provides the optimum solution. For such cells only a very simple user-pull form of material flow control applied by Toyota, called 'Kanban' is needed, in which use of a component in production causes a pull signal for a replacement, i.e. via an empty container or storage square marked on the floor. Simple computer support for sales order processing, 'make versus buy' component requirements listing, stock monitoring and monthly scheduling are needed.

   The operators become highly skilled at the repetitive tasks, even when a high variety of regular Runners is produced, and special purpose automated support equipment can be justified because of the high throughput. However, past models of motorcar still in service around the world also require component parts for repair and servicing and these parts are usually different from those of current models. Their volumes required reduce over time and the flow is usually very erratic and can be classed as Repeater flows, due to erratic demand compounded by the activities of many alternative suppliers who repair or copy component parts.

   Therefore, the after-market supply team has a much less predictable task, manufactures spare parts in small batches of high variety, requires a wider range of skills and product reference data or instructions, and needs a more sophisticated forecasting, planning, scheduling and control system called MRPII, or a pseudo-Kanban form of planned 'push' batch supply called 'period flow control' in which batches of work move at timed intervals with support information attached to guide the team.

2. In a number of industries, a very complex new product or service is developed using a very large multi-skill project team. In the process of developing the product or service, the specification is prone to change due to the customer asking for changes or certain aspects of the design being found to be unsatisfactory when tested. Industry examples are the aerospace industry when a new aircraft or aircraft sub-system is developed, designed and tested to meet stringent government agency approvals; the construction industry when a new office block is being

designed and built; banking and insurance when major new one-off IT systems are being designed and installed.

The disciplined management, execution and approval of product change requests is an extremely important activity and, if not done well, can lead to very high cost over-runs, project delays and arguments with customers over who should pay for the changes and at what cost.

The best practice approach is to set up a change control committee of interested parties including the Project Manager, the customer and the heads of the specialist functional groups involved. This committee assesses the justification for changes requested and groups them into Runner, Repeater and Stranger categories. They also confirm the reason for the change and obtain estimates for, and agree the responsibility for, the costs, taking account of the commercial agreement.

The Runner–Repeater–Stranger classification therefore can enable the most effective mode of organization and management to be used. If the whole work flow process is charted it is found that large, complex Strangers require a focused project team to carry them out, involving standard meeting structures, cross-functional approval mechanisms and very comprehensive detailed cost and resource estimation.

In contrast, the Runners, of which there are usually many, may often be smaller tasks. If so, they may require only a single specialist to carry them out and, therefore, they can short circuit much of the necessary heavier bureaucratic approval procedures required for the Strangers, particularly in safety-critical situations, as in the aerospace industry. They follow a simpler work flow-chart. Control by Kanban is simple and effective.

The Repeater tasks are usually intermediate in both number and complexity requiring a small group of specialist skills for their execution. Therefore, they again follow a sub-set of the flow process used for Strangers. They do not require all of the checks, balances and activities of the full change process work flow chart. It is helpful and effective, therefore, when finalising the process flow-chart for the specification change process to identify and distinguish the two shortcut routes for Runner and Repeater assignments since Repeater's flow can be simply controlled in a manufacturing process for example, by temporary Kanbans, and in product or service change control, it is possible to define the coordination and responsibilities as follows:

(a) *Strangers*. Full-time Project Manager and core team assigned. Approval by specification change committee. A full set of procedures, including the necessary testing, auditing, commercial, and cost estimating approval.

(b) *Runners.* A dedicated Project Coordinator manages all approved Runner changes with regular reviews and allocates them to the relevant specialist in specialist-functional departments as a defined work-package with an agreed labour time cost allocation. Note that some of these may be focused specialist work-packages required by Stranger projects.

(c) *Repeaters.* These may require full- or part-time work from a cross-functional team of related specialists. A full-time Project Manager is required with some administrative support for planning and scheduling. He or she manages the Repeaters as whole work-packages on a project bar diagram plan, ensures good communication between full- and part-time team members and manages the transfer of work as the work-package progresses along its planned route.

By adopting such an organizational approach for each of the three processes, confusion and clogging-up of the overall change process is avoided. Ownership responsibility and clarity of management are ensured and the following critical needs are satisfied:

1. There is full visibility of progress, regularly reported and reviewed for each approved assignment.
2. Responsibility, accountability and authority for progress to the planned master schedule are maintained.
3. Every assignment is carefully planned and controlled to meet the cost and time milestones required for the overall project.

The base principles summarised above are necessary for all processes. The overall process is simplified, the degree of bureaucracy is reduced, small projects do not become lost in the system, and overall control becomes much improved and easier to automate using information technology.

5.3 Company transitional change programme leadership and direction to create a value growth achievement culture direction

Managing company-wide change programmes places heavy demands on the management team, and creates many stresses; the whole change process must be well designed and organised. An effective organization reinforces the essential principle of there being no compromise allowed in the change project process when it comes to the important requirement of creating a world-class competitive total quality organization in a required time scale.

It also reinforces the important role of the programme office in facilitating and auditing progress.

There are three main interlocking segments in the change programme process:

1. The setting of targets to be achieved by each task-force project team based upon the top-level objectives on which the CAP is based. The performance bench-marks are required to be cascaded to every level in the organization and then further expanded into sets of MOPs for each task-force project for the business process redesign task-force teams to achieve. The process operating teams have then to run the processes to meet the bench-marks and then continuously improve.
2. The start-up ritual involving management in task-force training and MOPs setting, the follow-on regular reviews of progress, implementation approval and communication, in general, using every channel to reach all parts of the organization.
3. The operation and communication of a standard no-compromise task-force delivery and hand-over process, and training of all involved. This is discussed in the final section of this chapter.
4. The definition of the set of projects to be carried out, their priority sequencing and construction of the project plans using a standard project planning system, as discussed in Chapter 3, and its Support Methodology section. A useful operating principle here is to insist on no more than two major projects at a time to avoid resource over-load and organizational risks from disturbance and loss of focus. The final section of this chapter shows a typical example of task-force project phasing, interlinked with quick-hit activities.

5.3.1 Background to value management and bench-marking

Setting targets for value creation and identifying best project practices and value drivers, empowers project and process operational teams, within a carefully specified framework of constraints, to deliver increased values.

In essence, it is necessary to identify and enhance the activities that create value and eliminate those that destroy it. Therefore, it is a fundamentally important strategic task for a CAP to find and implement value creation project programmes faster than competitors.

The three foundation elements are:

1. Value opportunity measurement and calibration.

2. Value generation management, e.g. via change and transition projects.
3. Value improvement related incentives to reward management.

These lead to the two important tasks required of a management team and its supporting change programme activity:

(a)   improvement target setting, e.g. via bench-marking using financial and non-financial targets;
(b)   the identification of all value generation drivers, positive and negative.

In turn, these support the creation of an integrated hierarchy of target measures across every organizational level supporting strategy and facilitating communication and performance improvement monitoring and audits.

A reward strategy related to achievement of targets can then be related to each natural group of involved employees from the Board executives down to operational cell teams. This provides a carefully linked incentive element to drive the creation of a performance culture throughout the organization.

In this way, CAP strategy and change programme priorities and management CAP strategies become carefully aligned and matched to the time-dependent milestones for annual and medium- to long-term financial investment budget approval, supported by forward value growth requirements and their time scale tracking.

There is close alignment also between shareholder and employee interests with a resulting benefit for employee motivation and an understanding of the links between investor expectations and financial and non-financial goals.

The critical management requirement is to align the interests of all teams in a business to the CAP strategy and the success of the change programme of projects by creating distributed ownership of the action plans using the simplest set of reliable and relevant measures in every part of the organization. For example: an office process cell for purchasing management can have a display board with measures of performance on commodity group buyers and suppliers relating to economic value added (EVA) from purchase cost reduction, delivery performance, just-in-time stock control and delivered quality; a sales front office cell might display value of orders received versus budget, percentage of bids or quotes sent out on time, number of new customers and EVA contribution per month; a manufacturing cell would display percentage delivered on time, quality in parts per million, stock turnover ratio and EVA contribution from costs below target. Such information provides a focus for a 10 minute daily stand-up review and communications meeting with the team leader in the office cell or delivery process cell, which as a result focuses clearly on the real-time requirements of the business strategy as reflected in the targets set for the specific process teams.

There are two very serious requirements that result for the organization:

1. Communication and training capabilities enhancement and their execution, updating and development must become excellent.
2. Remuneration practices must be carefully and very practically designed in detail and regularly updated to ensure they truly align with target setting at all levels, and so that they cannot be abused by unscrupulous senior management and that sanctions for non-achievement are adhered to.

The total systems approach to business process effectiveness improvement and CAP framework setting requires every element involved to be integrated with the others with integrity.

There have been many examples of executive directors of companies being rewarded extravagantly where a stand-back examination of the overall performance of their business showed that this was not justified.

Remuneration committees, non-executive directors and major shareholders must ensure that professionalism and attention to detail are of the highest order, and that determined action and penalties against exploitation, coupled with adherence to sanctions, is imposed. This is particularly important where setting out the properties of a reward derived from short-, medium- and long-term improvement in shareholder value are concerned. Short-termist management can wreck the capability of a business to generate medium- to long-term value, e.g. by cutting out capital expenditure for forward development, training expenditure and change projects, while increasing their short-term rewards through bonuses related to short-term cash flows.

A goal setting approach, which balances shareholder and management expectations is essential.

The bench-mark measure, mentioned earlier, that has been applied in some companies with both good and very bad experiences, is the measure of economic value added (EVA). This focuses on measuring the return on capital employed in excess of that required to finance the capital. In simple terms, if the interest which would be paid, on a sum equal to the capital invested in all areas of the business from work in progress to equipment and facilities, is greater than the return on capital generated by the business profits and consequential cash generated, the EVA is negative and the shareholders have lost out. EVA targets can be sub-divided for local ownership by allocation to specific business processes or cell units, as well as being measured for the whole company.

In principle, short-termism can be prevented by retaining in the company a proportion of the management bonus from EVA, generated from the annual performance of the business, and offsetting it by any negative EVA generated on a sliding scale for the subsequent four years. A 5-year incentive horizon can be created to protect the future.

This requires remuneration committees to be very carefully trained and advised professionally. Major shareholders should also understand the finer points of an EVA-based incentive scheme and avoid the dangers. It also requires major shareholders to be more proactive in meeting regularly with non-executive directors, not just with the Chairman and the Chief Executive or Finance Director.

5.3.2 Bench-marking applied (see Support Tools and Techniques Section 4)

World-class bench-marks are generally very demanding or stretching, if not for all parts of business processes at least for major portions. It is the demanding of conformance with stretch targets by top management, such as 50 per cent improvement targets, which pressures project task-forces to apply new approaches to organization design. These encompass typically the elimination of waste, use of modern methodologies and support tools and application of optimal standard working procedures to new process designs. Selective outsourcing of specific non-core elements, sub-processes and services to specialist contractors with competitive performances and cost bases may form part of the solution.

Bench-marks should relate to practical measures, which are easy to relate to customer requirements, either internal or external customers of a process. Some bench-marks can be integrated as part of personal objective remuneration incentive bonus criteria for individuals, to help achieve the necessary change, and enable business CAP bench-marks to be met. For example, an individual set of objectives for a senior manager's annual bonus scheme is often structured into two equally weighted sections as follows in the practical example below.

5.3.3 Practical example of a management performance incentive scheme

A Financial bench-mark objectives (short-term):
- return on sales or operating profit as a percentage of sales;
- cash generated per unit sales revenue;
- return on capital employed (ROCE).

B Non-financial personal objectives of a development nature (medium- to long-term):
- deliver two task-force change projects;
- develop and introduce to the market one new platform product or service;
- install a training scheme in modern best practices to support change and the subsequent standard working operation of new process designs;
- improve product or service quality delivered by 10 per cent and reduce the cost of quality by 20 per cent;
- introduce a pilot Kaizen programme;
- bench-mark the two leading competitors;
- introduce an intranet for best practice experience and knowledge transfer, enabling easy reference across the organization.

With this approach, managers are motivated in three important aspects:

1. To systematically deliver the changes needed to meet the CAP requirements.
2. To achieve a balanced approach to operations issues and development issues, so supporting short-, medium- and long-term value growth.
3. To carry out essential performance improvement sustained over a lengthy period of time, creating a performance culture and providing a logical base of activities aligned to CAP strategy. This contributes to eventual shareholder value growth, which can be communicated with conviction to external financial investment analysts and shareholders.

The financial objectives in the above example are often expressed differently to the traditional individual profit, cash and ROCE terms in order to link these to value creation, e.g. the use of EVA.

In addition, so that the managers are strongly motivated to ensure long-term value growth is achieved, there are two common additional incentives used:

1. The award of options to purchase a block of shares at today's prices at a time several years in the future. If the share price grows, the manager is able to sell and achieve a capital gain.
2. A long-term performance incentive scheme in which shares are allocated each year for annual performance achieved, over several years, before they can be owned by the participants in the scheme. There is also often a supplementary requirement for managers to own a minimum number of shares.

There is a problem, however. The combination of such incentive schemes must have the aim of achieving short-, medium- and long-term value growth. The purpose is to resist the danger of asset stripping and rejection of innovation by managers who try to ensure short term bonuses are maximised. Such combinations often result in excessively complex MOPs systems, difficult to understand and monitor.

To combat the problem the relatively straightforward practical example of a two-section A & B annual bonus scheme can be carefully designed to include two ways to retain a dynamic innovation driver:

1. By including shareholder value growth MOPs in part A, financials.
2. By ensuring continuity from year to year in development projects, their implementation results profile, and in continuing support for innovation such as training.

5.3.4 *Value growth management and bench-marking*

When faced with the task of improving shareholder value generated by an organization, this inevitably leads to identification of the need for two main strands of well-ordered, disciplined change activity:

1. The redesign and restructuring of the organization to improve its effectiveness.
2. Acquisitions of other businesses that, when added to the organization, restructured, integrated and subjected to the exploitation of synergies along the value chain from the inbound logistics process through to the product or service development and operations delivery processes, create a step change in value. This is then followed by progressive further increased value adding from new products and services using the combined skills and knowledge added to the joint portfolio. Synergies come from such areas as combination of purchasing, distribution, administration, head offices, sales and marketing channels and operations facilities. This is part of a transition process aimed at integrated organizational design for improved effectiveness and reduced lead-times and costs of the processes.

In both of the above cases of organic-led growth and acquisition-led growth there are two essential common features:

1. The application of project and programme management practices to a change programme of targeted projects in the case of organic growth, and to a transition programme of projects in the case of acquisition-led growth.

2. The setting of target measures for performance improvement based upon bench-marking of good company practices and performance, for achievement by task-force teams or acquisition transition teams, following on from a due diligence diagnostic analysis of the status quo in the company at the outset.

In the case of an acquisition, it is good practice to adopt the following stepwise procedure:

1. Set up a diagnostic project team to bench-mark and carry out an analysis of current performance and practices in the target acquisition in order to identify potential sources of value enhancement and non-value-added activity elimination.
2. For each opportunity the following are tabulated:
   (a) The practical methodology required to apply known best practices and the calculated value of likely benefit and its time scale. Often, the benefit comes from a reduction in operating costs or growth in sales through synergy, so leading to a cash flow and a sales revenue growth benefit.
   (b) Estimates of the likely impact upon share price and its time scale and net present value.
   (c) A bar diagram adding the opportunity value from the sum of the value of all other identified opportunities.
3. Use the accumulative growth in value in step 2 from all identified opportunities to estimate the potential increase in the initial share price of the company. Compare this with the likely share price of the target acquisition at the point of acquisition, allowing for the probable 30–50% premium which would be required once a bid for the target became public.
4. If the gap between the likely share price at the time of purchase and the value from the potential growth in the parent share price, due to the planned release of transition project opportunities, is attractive enough, then proceed with the acquisition negotiation using an estimated maximum permissible share price as a guide to the maximum bid price.

If the acquisition is successful at a price that allows scope for share price increase through value extraction, this then triggers the need for a disciplined set of transition team projects to release the estimated value, e.g. via a target cost base reduction. The work done in the diagnostic audit will be very valuable for training the transition project team and setting bench-mark targets so that they have their project plan ready to implement on day one, when they move into the acquisition, in collaboration with the acquisition target management team.

5.3.5 *Practical bench-marking principles applied – summary*

The Support Tools and Techniques section of Chapter 4 provides a systematic framework for bench-marking as a basis for setting measures of performance (MOPs), based upon the four complementary groups of measures, which, together, provide a balanced score card:

- financial measures;
- customer-related measures (external and internal between natural process groups);
- business process effectiveness measures;
- growth through all forms of innovation, large and small.

These fall into two categories, i.e. financial and non-financial and, in turn,

1. Financial Objectives – 2yrs	2. Business Process Objectives	3. Customer-Related Objectives
• Improve sales per employee by 30% • Improve return on sales to 17% • Increase annual net cash-flow by 40% • Double capital turnover ratio • Reduce debtors to 10% of sales with creditors twice debtors	• Reduce lead-time of operations delivery • Reduce non-pay roll overheads by 25% • Improve account development process to add 40% more category A customers • Reduce lead-time for account or service development process by 40% over 3 years and introduce 2 new platform service products	• Achieve 25 parts per million quality performance for service delivery • Achieve 98% score in customer satisfaction survey • Achieve preferred partnership status with 40% of customers • Achieve brand image in top five supplier group

4. Growth

- Introduce modern best practice training programme for monitored personal development to grow staff capability
- Grow economic value added by 10% p.a.
- Grow shareholder total value added by 15% p.a.
- Achieve 15% p.a. sales growth and double sales in South America

Fig. 5.13 Balanced scorecard illustration

quantifiable and non-quantifiable.

It is important to recognise two very significant points:

1. To direct the efforts of all staff in an organization, internal measures of performance are required between supplier–customer natural groups at every level within the organization in locally relevant terms, as well as overall measures for a business or group of businesses.
2. Managers use assessments of the gaps between world-class bench-marks and their own unit performance to prioritise and set targets for the projects in a change programme aimed at closing the gap; they must use an effective communication system to motivate staff to close the gaps.

A simplified overall framework statement in balanced score card terms for a three-year horizon is shown in Fig. 5.13. A set of change projects to deliver the overall targets is needed.

Table 5.4 provides a case example to illustrate top-level initial bench-mark comparisons for a specific business.

Table 5.4 Electromechanical engineering manufacturing company comparisons		
Measure of performance	**Western**	**Japanese**
Ratio of indirect staff to directs	1.2	0.5
Sales per employee p.a.	£55k	£150k
Capital turnover ratio	2.5	4.7
Stock turnover ratio	5	20
Product cost ratio	100%	70%
New product introduction lead-time	100%	60%
Manufacturing lead-time	100%	35%
Ratio of engineers in product development to engineers in manufacturing development	1:0.1	1:0.8
Incidence of team structures, continuous improvement teams and Kaizen application	2%	90%

5.4 Organizing a Kaizen project programme

5.4.1 The Kaizen continuous improvement programme phase

Kaizen programmes follow on naturally from large company-wide projects used for strategic restructuring of major business processes. The restructuring projects will have reorganised the work-force into co-located natural team groups, each team grouped around a business process or sub-process cell flow-chart and having the necessary cross-functional skill set. The new process design, while making major improvements in terms of non-value-added activity elimination, lead-time reduction, work in process turnover rate, delivery schedule achievement and quality of performance, will, nevertheless, still have many opportunities for further improvement. In addition, there will be an ongoing requirement to adapt to future changes in needs.

This new team process organization, which results from a systematic redesign and reorganization around core processes, creates a much improved platform, with clear team ownership, for effective and rapid continuous improvement compared with the fragmented situation before the process was redesigned and reorganised.

The main reasons for this are:

1. In medium to large companies, prior to reorganization and re-grouping of the operational staff into coherent team cells, the process activity was often fragmented into functional specialist departments, and the people concerned with its operation were widely distributed, often with little personal contact and little awareness of and control over the factors which interacted with and affected their fragment of work. Because the supervision was also fragmented, they had no way to create integrated views of and optimal solutions to long-standing problems. Therefore problems, which required coordinated cause and effect data collection and corrective actions, could not easily be solved. Frustration and inefficiency resulted.

   Individuals involved in the previously functionally fragmented process could not be reasonably expected to have a clear view of the whole process and its relevant target MOPs. All they could see was their own specialist piece of work, and they had no general understanding to provide a base for a constructive problem solving dialogue with colleagues on process-wide problems.

   To expect such fragmented groups to reform on their own into cross-functional teams and carry out their own continuous improvement problem definition and solution activities, or to prioritise cross-functional problems in order, was not practical. Kaizen schemes introduced into such fragmented situations have a very high failure rate.

2. Once a process team is in place with clear ownership of the process, a high degree of empowerment to take initiatives, a set of process target MOPs to meet and cross-functional process training, the Kaizen process,

with some facilitating by expert systems engineers and management, becomes very effective and self-sustaining. The team has a common involvement in, and understanding of, the process and the cause and effect interactions within it, supported by the natural driving effect of their accountability for meeting the process performance targets.

It is not very difficult in this situation, after providing some basic training for the cell process team in simple problem definition and problem solution methodologies, to set up a sequenced continuous improvement programme of small-scale projects for the cell team to work on to improve their process performance step by step. The right time to initiate such a programme is during the hand-over training session, at the end of a step change project, when a new process team take full operational and forward development responsibility for a newly designed natural group process cell.

The logical point for a Manager to trigger the initiation of a Kaizen programme as has been mentioned earlier is when the first project module of a transformational change programme has been implemented, and the newly trained process module team is in place. They have much more opportunity to make improvements to their integrated process than in the original fragmented organization. This will be perceived as a logical step within some competitiveness achievement programme initiative, and it can

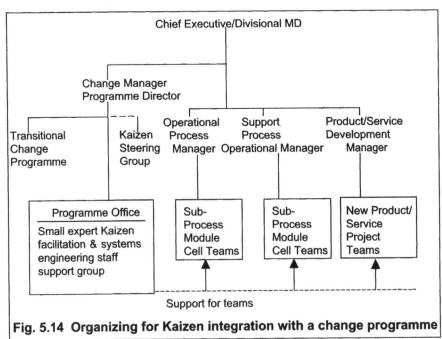

Fig. 5.14 Organizing for Kaizen integration with a change programme

justify sufficient attention in parallel with the progress of the other stages of the transformational change programme. It will be logical to provide some form of start-up communication ceremony in line with the need for management to regularly stimulate motivation and maintain momentum.

The organization necessary to support managed continuous improvement change needs to be created by a modification to the transitional change management organization. A typical outline organization structure is shown in Fig. 5.14.

5.4.2 Organizational support requirements

Other elements required to be in place prior to start-up to ensure right-first-time progress are as follows:

1. A *Steering Group* to support and review the activity and provide a regular review committee for the Change Manager. The Chairman of this committee should be a senior member of the Executive Committee, taking on the role of the Kaizen programme champion.

Steering Group responsibilities

- Provides visible senior management commitment.
- Provides direction on strategic priority and links to the CAP.
- Carries out regular audits and checks.
- Coordinates communication and a team recognition/reward scheme.
- Maintains visibility of the whole programme.
- Picks up important quick hit opportunities highlighted by project teams.
- Agrees the priority themes each year and the related targets.
- Provides resource and facilities.
- Maintains contact with the working level activities of the business and provides leadership.

2. Some *expert support resource* attached to the Programme Office to coach, train, and give assistance on request to the Kaizen problem solving target teams. It is very important that good project disciplines should be maintained, and all projects should be formally approved, with a clear specification and targets, and recorded on the Programme Office database. They can then be tracked by regular reviews and checked post-implementation, to evaluate the benefits. It is good practice to have the Programme Office and the business process managers maintain a tabular record, as in the example in Table 5.5, to ensure a visible high quality approach.

3. *Facilities* such as areas for daily stand-up meetings of teams, personal computers, small equipment and tools for testing ideas.

Table 5.5 Project support record

Approved Project List	Minimum start-up team training	Minimum time-tabled support time from Systems Engineers	Targeted benefits
Stock reduction	1 day	1 hour per day	60% reduction
Organize workplace	$^1/_2$ day	2 hours	50% 5S's score increase
Etc.			

4. A *recognition system* to help promote a continuous improvement culture and spread the involvement widely to the employees at all levels:
   - give recognition to individuals for achievements made,
   - provide an opportunity to say 'well done' to project teams and so generate confidence, capability, enthusiasm and controlled empowerment,
   - encourage the generation of ideas by every individual.

It is important that the forms of recognition and reward used are not divisive and do not lead to obstructive office or factory politics. Simple

Table 5.6 Project types and roles

Type	Constitution	Type of project	Review Responsibility	Who Implements	Who Trains
Supported Improvement Groups (SIGs)	Carefully selected Cross-Process Teams	Special exercises chosen by management of cross-business relevance	Steering Group	Small representative teams in areas of impact supported by SIG leader	Change Manager/ Programme Office
Continuous Improvement Teams (CITs)	2–3 Volunteer representatives from a Process or Cell Team	Small improvement projects associated with cell run by Team Leader	Process Manager or Process Team Leader	Local Process Team	Local Process Manager

small awards are usually quite sufficient. Examples are:
- tee shirts, pens,
- prizes for the maximum number of project opportunity suggestions,
- a team certificate for completion of each project,
- a special car park place for a period,
- visits to customers and suppliers,
- teams of the week, month and year awards.

5. *Clarity in definition* of the roles and requirements of the different kinds of project and their roles (see Table 5.6).
   - transition task-force change projects senior management
   - supported improvement groups initiated
   - continuous improvement (Kaizen) teams – process team and individual initiated.

6. *Integrated and cascaded plans* coordinated by the Change Manager to translate the CAP targets into local team targets (see Fig. 5.15).

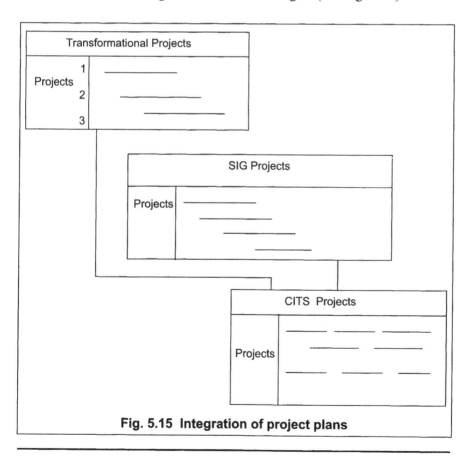

Fig. 5.15 Integration of project plans

7. A *formalised launch process* led by the Chief Executive. This is a most important element and the process should be carefully developed and agreed in advance of the start of the programme with all the support in place and activities professionally executed. A key aspect is to provide the necessary training and understanding for the management team to ensure they are able to effectively lead.

   A typical top-level process flow-chart for a Kaizen delivery process used by a number of companies is shown in Fig. 5.16.

8. *Training.* In addition to developing the executive workshop agendas, the Programme Office should also coordinate in advance the necessary support training material. This needs to cover the staged requirements of the process teams.

   Generic tools which are likely to be required to be learned to allow teams to be empowered are as follows:

   • data collection – bar charts, pareto diagrams, pie charts, trend monitoring graphs for opportunity definition;

   • cause and effect fishbone diagrams to support problem solution;

   • simple process flow-charting;

   • identifying and resolving the wasteful activities and applying the 5S's philosophy;

   • poka yoke (process fool-proofing) techniques;

   • statistical process control for process capability assessment to

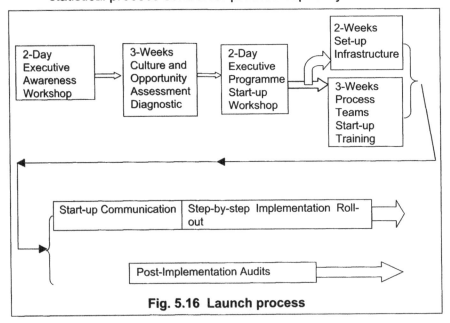

Fig. 5.16 Launch process

    meet all process targets by quantifying performance every day;
- paperwork simplification;
- standard meeting design;
- safety;
- total productive process system maintenance.

5.4.3 Total support system integrity

The Change Manager must ensure, with the support of the Programme Office, that all the necessary elements are in place and fully effective. This includes ensuring that the critical need for bottom-up, as distinct from top-down, action is fulfilled. The way in which responsibilities and accountabilities are

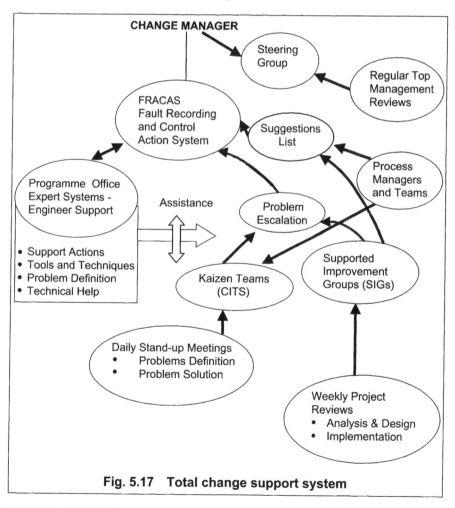

Fig. 5.17   Total change support system

accepted by team leaders must be specified. Also, it is important that process teams are properly trained and supported to facilitate empowerment to act within the constraints of a set of targets to meet, and subjected to regular reviews and audits. The total system is as shown in Fig. 5.17.

5.5 Practical project management of change programmes

Many company managements do not appreciate that it necessary to apply the same disciplined no-compromise management and review procedures to change project programmes as they have learned are needed for product and service development projects. With change programmes there is the additional dimension of cultural change and comprehensive communication requirements. This dimension, together with unknown consequences for individuals, of change programmes, makes the management of change projects much more demanding than other types of project.

The articulation of such concepts as 'first simplify and then automate', or the use of 'stretch targets' or the creation of new business process organization structures around the three core processes of order winning, product and service development and service delivery, with the associated elimination of the many fragmented office departments and application of the 'only three offices' concept, naturally leads to staff feelings of insecurity and many general concerns. Insecurity and resistance to change also results from a lack of understanding of the new methodologies involved in best practice change management.

To make progress in such an environment requires managers to pay particular attention, in the way that change projects are staffed and managed, to the following factors:

1. Continual widespread communication of policies including HR policies, activities and progress as well as the justification of a need for a strong disciplined no-compromise approach to change.
2. Training.
3. Progressively wider involvement, in either part-time or full-time roles, of staff from all levels and all areas.
4. The definition and explanation of the project process.
5. Actions to make change stick.

5.5.1 The change project process

A detailed flow-chart for the process is shown in Fig. 5.18, which includes all the very necessary important elements. Figure 5.18 is explained below.

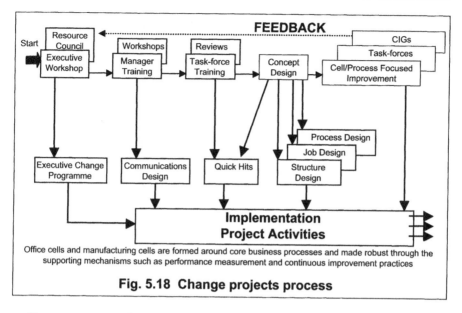

Fig. 5.18 Change projects process

To ensure coordinated leadership and management support for the Change Manager, a Steering Committee, sometimes called a Total Quality Council, is necessary. This will be composed of senior core managers who provide resources and should also be formally trained in an executive workshop. In the workshop they finalise the overall set of change projects plans in priority order to deliver the benefits of the business CAP. They then support the programme through attendance at weekly task-force reviews, agreement of targets, making of decisions on implementation and in the allocation of full- or part-time task-force members to the Change Programme Manager. They also manage the continual communication process and make all progress visible throughout the whole programme.

A typical list of topics for a three-day Executive Workshop is shown in Table 5.7, and this should include syndicate break out sessions to drive home the understanding of application of particular concepts via case examples etc.

The multi-function task-forces, after detailed workshop training, design the new structures and then, after agreement by the Steering Committee, manage the implementation, train the resulting natural group operating team and install the basic procedures for ongoing continuous improvement.

Steering Committee members implement quick-hits along the way by allocating these to their staff, so widening the involvement of all levels of staff as the projects progress and creating wider visible involvement in and ownership of implementation. Daily stand-up meetings together with weekly and monthly reviews are integrated with the process for good control.

Table 5.7 Example executive workshop agenda

1. Organization of a change programme – the 'no compromise' approach – syndicate group exercise.
2. Initiating task-forces, SIGs and quick-hits.
3. Bench-marking – case examples.
4. Summary of best practice from other industries
   • syndicate group exercise.
5. Effective organization design – agreeing the model concept:
   • exploring synergies,
   • business processes and modular implementation,
   • natural group team process concepts and their MOPs,
   • industry case examples,
   • syndicate group activity and debrief.
6. The task-force design process – the five-step approach.
7. Task-force project case study – a repair and overhaul business redesign.
8. Tools, techniques and methodologies:
   • flow-chart analysis and NVA,
   • input–output analysis,
   • war on waste projects,
   • syndicate group case study analysis.
9. Natural group organization in analysis examples:
   • the front office,
   • the supplies module,
   • the customer account and solution selling team.
10. Project and programme management and steering group change management organization
11. Syndicate group working session – defining the programme plan and setting targets.
12. Report back, review and approval session.

Note. Preliminary reading material including case examples to be circulated 2 weeks before the workshop plus a reference book list.

SIG groups are spun-off where timely, and the overall business activity is supported, including all training, project specification and results auditing, by the Programme Office.

As a focus for discussion, a concise aid to the process for setting up the change programme and defining the target business process organization modular structure is provided in Fig. 5.19. This is based upon modularising the organization around two core processes, the product introduction process (6 and 7 in Fig. 5.19) and the operational delivery process (13, 14 and 15), integrates some of the important, supporting infrastructure tools and starts with the basic initiation foundation elements 1–5.

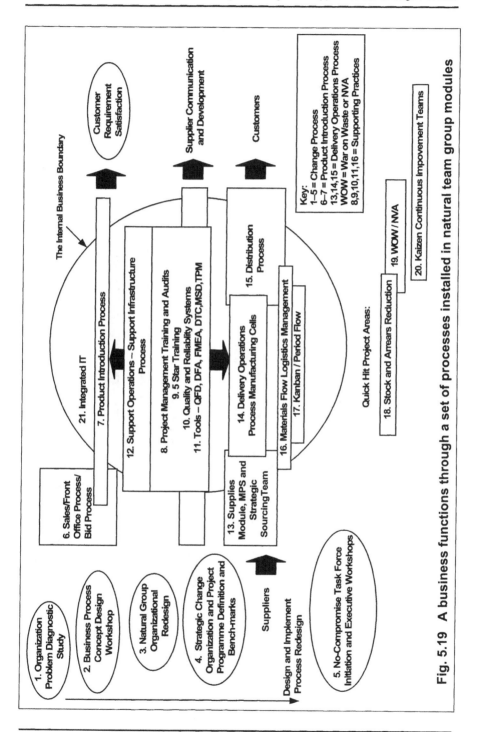

Fig. 5.19 A business functions through a set of processes installed in natural team group modules

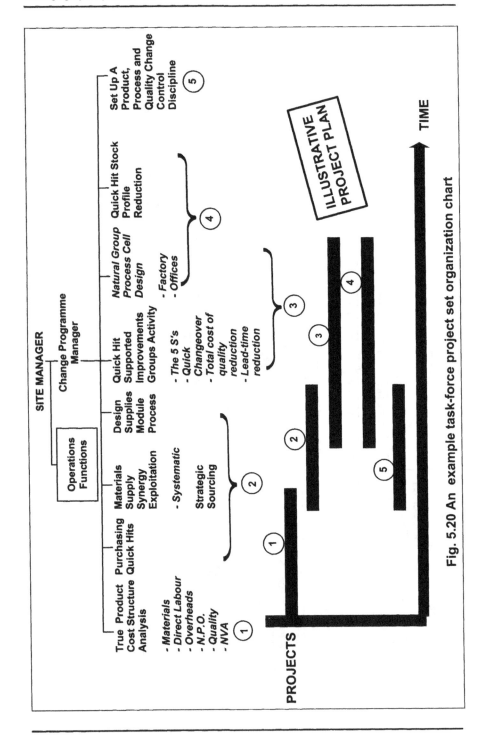

Fig. 5.20 An example task-force project set organization chart

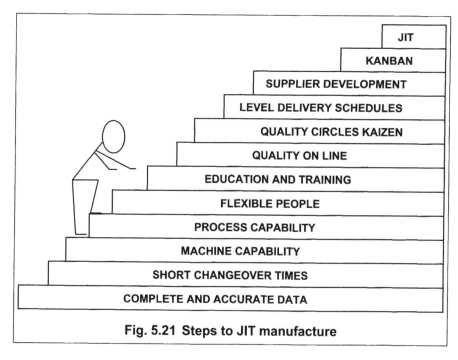

Fig. 5.21 Steps to JIT manufacture

Figure 5.20 shows a typical resulting total change programme set of projects to be initiated in an achievable time-phased order for an engineering manufacturing business. The figure shows mixtures of short quick-hit projects and mainstream task-force redesign projects in each area of focus, indicated by the brackets.

Table 5.8 Designing an effective organization

Some key concepts for consideration

- Competitive advantage through synergy and shared resources.
- Cross-boundary and cross-functional management.
- Organizing for teamwork.
- Product-group market focus.
- Flatter, simpler job structures.
- Improved new product introduction management.
- Reduced cost base.
- Integration of strategic planning.
- Definition of boundaries for business units.
- Critical mass.
- Cellular product group structures; natural groups.
- Core business process definitions – operations and development.
- Competitor positioning and competitor analysis.

When training and communicating with task-force teams and SIGs, it is important to pay careful attention to the necessarily more simple explanations of methods and principles. An example of an effective approach, using a hill climbing analogy for the completion of all supporting steps for just-in-time process operation achievement, is shown in Fig. 5.21.

A matrix of example objectives related to effective organization design is provided in Table 5.8.

5.5.2 People and leaders – the choice and development of the Change Project Manager

The professional development of Change Agents and Change Project Managers for any organization is now a very important requirement, which is essential to the delivery of competitiveness achievement programmes.

Table 5.9 summarises the change-related set of core competences of a Change Agent and Table 5.10 provides a Change Manager's checklist example.

Good Change Managers are well organized and systematic and strive to be very effective in making things happen. They often develop standard working practices for themselves and use personal checklists to maintain their effectiveness. A typical example is provided in Table 5.10.

Table 5.9 Change Agent – basic core competence

- Understands roles of senior management in supporting change.
- Knows competitiveness gaps and required strategy for business/customer.
- Can prioritise projects/tasks and write specifications and targets.
- Understands project start-up and support routines.
- Understands the basic tools and methodologies (ref. the Toyota Production System).
- Good communicator and supporter/networker.
- Understands project management and review disciplines.
- Can construct a project plan and sub-divide into tasks.
- Good communicator and presenter upwards and downwards (including reports).
- Understands how to set measures of performance and the essentials of making change stick, and involvement via a well-managed 'quick-hits' programme.

Plus: general knowledge of the relevant business process and its participant parts

---

> **Table 5.10 Change Manager checklist for task-force project programmes**
>
> - Has the list of opportunity/problem areas for task-force attack been prioritised – first things first: cost reduction, productivity, improved sales process, improved service, new service package etc?
> - Only two projects at a time – 'single initiative', avoid overloading?
> - Are the objectives, specification and targets clear for all task-force projects?
> - Task-force to be trained via structured workshop of 3 days minimum – best practices, project planning?
> - General Manager launches task-force and agrees project plan?
> - Senior management steering committee – to agree decision and implement?
> - Standard meeting structure in place?
>   - Daily stand-up meeting, weekly Change Manager review meeting, monthly steering committee review, implementation plan review and launch with hand-over sign-off and natural group training in place.
> - Projects categorised into category 1, category 2 for Programme Office, in top-level work-package schedule terms?
> - Full-time task-force leader, team minimum of two full-time core members allocated, plus part-time members?
> - Project owner defined and on steering committee?
> - Roll out on time with 'no-compromise' standard task-force process?
> - Communication structure defined?
> - Budget agreed and target benefits agreed?

5.6 Overall summary of Chapter 5

Change management is perceived as one of the more difficult challenges for many organizations. Senior managers must plan their tactics very carefully for introducing CAP implementation change programmes into organizations. Excellent and persistent broad communication of requirements and achievements is central.

The use of well-supported initial pilot demonstrators is very important with a managed progression, as a performance achievement culture develops, to a full task-force change project programme, which then transforms into a self-sustaining Kaizen continuous improvement strategy based upon a supportive foundation.

The change programme requires relevant stretch targets and MOPs to be defined using bench-marking practices and the projects must form the engine of a competitiveness achievement plan, subject to regular business review.

The organization structure requires a line change management process; this should include a budget, to be embedded, and a senior management steering group, supported by a Programme Office, which provides a training capability via management workshops, task-force workshops, and operational team training and facilitation. Education-led innovation and culture change is essential following a practical theme of 'train–do'.

Carefully managed integration of a wide range of projects, large and small, is applied to progressively widen the involvement of all levels of personnel and deliver early visible achievement from visibly promoted 'quick-hits'.

A target organization model is needed, based upon modern effective organizational practices using team structures focused on clear core business processes, sub-divided logically into modules to form natural self-sufficient groups of people. The aim is to create a competitive MOP-driven cascade of modules translating CAP targets into achieved performance, using the total integrated cell system concept of Fig. 5.10.

It is essential to take a realistic fresh look at the company organization, its processes, job roles and competences – its performance, its inadequacies and the wasteful non-value added activities, in a systematic way, using modern tools and techniques of material, work and information flow analysis. The aim should be to achieve total quality of performance through improved cost effectiveness of each business process team, as checked against world-class performance standards using the principle of the balanced score card. Unnecessary procedures and wasteful work have to be eliminated systematically while increasing the value-adding capability and ability to meet internal and external customer requirements by every natural group process team. Ensuring a clear customer interface and customer orientation is important, e.g. from the front office design.

It is also essential to eliminate weaknesses in the product and service portfolio, by being honest about inadequacies, asking the customer's opinion, reverse engineering competitor products and resolving problems in priority order using project teams.

The implementation of a supply chain delivery process development strategy and a product and service development strategy, should progress in tandem with equal management focus.

5.6.1 The essential ground rules for the change process

1. No compromise
   - Full-time commitment to what is worth doing well.

- Persistent application of the Change Manager led task-force project process principle.
- Task-forces to be allocated full- and part-time resource.
- First simplify then automate – do not just make the waste go around faster.
2. Clear objectives

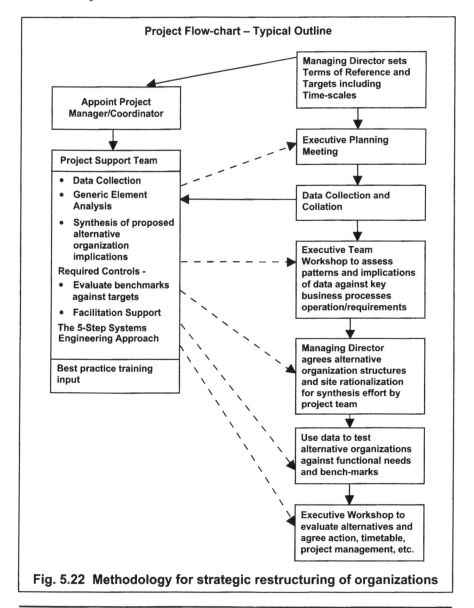

Project Flow-chart – Typical Outline

Managing Director sets Terms of Reference and Targets including Time-scales

Appoint Project Manager/Coordinator

Executive Planning Meeting

Project Support Team

- **Data Collection**
- **Generic Element Analysis**
- **Synthesis of proposed alternative organization implications**

Required Controls -

- **Evaluate benchmarks against targets**
- **Facilitation Support**

The 5-Step Systems Engineering Approach

Best practice training input

Data Collection and Collation

Executive Team Workshop to assess patterns and implications of data against key business processes operation/requirements

Managing Director agrees alternative organization structures and site rationalization for synthesis effort by project team

Use data to test alternative organizations against functional needs and bench-marks

Executive Workshop to evaluate alternatives and agree action, timetable, project management, etc.

Fig. 5.22 Methodology for strategic restructuring of organizations

- Interactive involvement of top management in target setting for task-force reviews, i.e. sound direction and coordination from the centre.
- Regular project reviews and audits with defined agendas, project owners, outputs and attendees.
- Regular to and fro information communication from all levels.
- Visible recognition of achievement.

3. A formalised training support programme for the creation of a learning

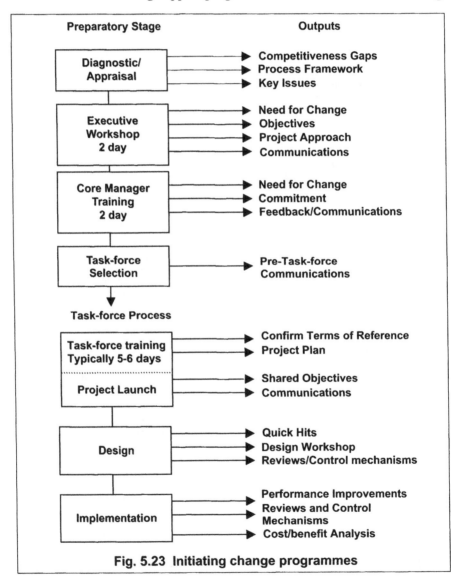

Fig. 5.23 Initiating change programmes

and doing organization.

4. Harness and focus the efforts of all of the people in the company – find them, train them, use them effectively in innovation, organise them into value-adding natural process cell teams in offices as well as factories.
5. Identify and strengthen value-adding competencies.
6. Make careful, managed, integrated and effective use of soft system methodologies and hard technologies to create a world-class business system.

When defining an organization model for a multi-product organization, the following architecture guidelines apply:

- create distinct product groups with clear market interface identities, and apply the five-step systems engineering design approach;
- inside each product-group module, use cellular or module team groups for business processes linked by input–output MOPs cascaded from the overall business CAP targets;
- provide cross-product group support process team modules where critical mass team synergies can be exploited due to common needs;
- apply the relevant control mechanisms to integrate.

Figures 5.22 to 5.24 summarise the overall process of initiating a change programme. The Appendix provides an example, based upon practical experience over several hundred strategic change projects, of a role specification for a Business Change Programme Manager.

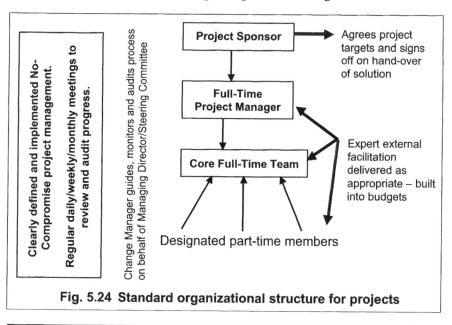

Fig. 5.24 Standard organizational structure for projects

Further Reading

Banner, D. K. and **Gagné, T. E.** *Designing Effective Organizations*, 1995 (Sage Publications).

Belbin, R. M. *Team Roles at Work*, 1996 (Butterworth-Heinemann).

Bicheno, J. *The Quality Co – A Guide for Service and Manufacturing*, 1998 (PICSIE Books).

Dieter, G. E. *Engineering Design: A Materials and Processing Approach!*, 2000 (McGraw Hill).

Dyer, C. E. (editor) *The Canon Production System*, 1987 (Productivity Press).

Hammer, M. and **Champy, J.** *Re-Engineering the Corporation*, 1994 (Harper Business).

Munro-Faure, L. and **Munro-Faure, M.** *Implementing Total Quality Management*, 1992 (Pitman/F.T.).

Parnaby, J. A Systems Approach to Introducing JIT Methodologies into Lucas Industries, *Int. J. Prod. Res.*, 1998, **26**, (3), 483–492.

Parnaby, J. *et al.*, *The Lucas Manufacturing Systems Engineering Handbook*, 2nd edition, 1989 (Lucas Industries Publishers).

Schonberger, R. J. *Japanese Manufacturing Techniques*, 1982 (Free Press).

Shingo, S. *Non-Stock Production*, 1988 (Productivity Press).

Slater, R. *Get Better or Get Beaten*, 1994 (Irwin Inc.).

Taguchi, G. *Introduction to Quality Engineering*, 1987 (Asian Productivity Association; UNIPUB New York).

Wearne, S. H. *Principles of Engineering Organization*, 2nd edition, 1993 (Thomas Telford Publishing).

Wearne, S. H. and **Wright, D.** Organizational risks of joint ventures, consortia and alliance partnerships, *Int. J. Project Business Risk Mgmt*, 1998. **2**, (1).

Womack, J. P. and **Jones, D. T.** *Lean Thinking*, 1996 (Simon and Schuster).

Appendix

Business change programme manager – role specification

Overall

To help the Managing Director and Business Executive Committee set up and professionally manage the business change programme, using a best practice project managed approach for systematically improving the methodologies, practices, procedures and business process of the organization to meet world-class standards of competitiveness and performance.

Scope of activity

Using bench-marking and customer opinion surveys to prioritise, sequence and manage a set of task-force and continuous improvement projects aimed at achieving a step change in performance and effectiveness of the following core business processes:

1. The service delivery process
2. The service design and development process
3. The customer account management and order-winning bidding process
4. The cask management process
5. The administrative and staff support process
6. The HR development process
7. The customer specification change process

Supporting requirements

1. To facilitate with the Managing Director and executive colleagues, the setting of clear vision, strategic direction and business process improvement targets for focusing the innovative work of short-term cross-functional task-force project teams.
2. To facilitate access to standard best practice methodologies and training materials in collaboration with group senior personnel, for use in task-force training workshops, and to gain from synergistic opportunities.
3. To coordinate the world's best practice bench-marking and the development of case studies of relevant high-performance service organizations, to facilitate the setting of clear business targets for communicating to each focused task-force.
4. To draw up an agreed rolling two-year programme of focused task-force projects of three–six months duration in priority order to systematically

improve business processes and practices using a modular approach to ensure visible, sound, steady progress and a world's best practice task-force change process.

5. To set up a parallel quick-hit programme to select sound short-term recommendations proposed by task-forces in their weekly reviews, for rapid implementation by managers and staff in the area of focus of each task-force and thereby to share managed involvement in change implementation over a wider group of personnel.
6. To agree with the Managing Director and Executive Committee a change programme task-force review committee to attend monthly task-force reviews, provide directional input to task-force training workshops, review and agree end of workshop project plans and ensure temporary task-forces are properly supported and aided by rapid management decision making on implementation proposals and facilitation of smooth hand-over of designed changes to operational personnel.
7. To implant a common 'war on waste' methodology across the business for facilitating the identification of all non-value-added activities and their systematic elimination, coupled with the introduction of world's best practices in order to reduce lead-times and reduce operating cost, increase productivity and improve the total quality of performance of every core business process, measured against world-class measures of performance.
8. To produce a monthly change programme progress report for discussion on the development agenda of the monthly business Executive Committee meeting.
9. To set up a communication programme for regularly informing, motivating and giving credit to all participants.

Characteristics governing choice of Change Programme Manager

The Change Manager's job is a very difficult one, often considerably more difficult than a routine operations line job. His change task-forces are all composed of staff temporarily allocated and trained for the short duration of their project. There is always considerable resistance to the discomfort of change and the impact on the job roles of people affected by the change, with the result that the Change Manager is always the subject of criticism and unpopularity. Therefore:

1. The Change Programme Manager role should be filled by a high calibre individual, typically 30–35 years old, who is the type of individual that his 'current Manager cannot spare'.

2. The role should be perceived as a typically two-year stint for personal development of a high potential individual at the end of which promotion to a senior line job is expected.

3. The Change Manager should be a team player with leadership skills, academically well-qualified to ensure he/she can absorb a modern set of best practice methodologies and techniques, and capable of understanding and helping to shape the strategic and commercial priorities for the whole business.

Essential discipline checklist – change management

1. Managing Director agrees with his executive, a priority order for projects and the targets for each.

2. Task-forces must have a minimum of two–three full-time members and part-time members should also be identified, together with their attendance requirements.

3. A training workshop should be used to start up each task-force project; the Managing Director should introduce the workshop, and close it by reviewing and agreeing the implementation plan.

4. A representative group of senior managers in each business should act as a steering committee to review progress monthly, and pick up quick-hits for intermediate parallel implementation to demonstrate steady progress.

5. There should be a communications meeting and a launch communication session for the total change programme and a two-weekly new sheet should be circulated.

6. The Change Manager should run the following review meetings:
   • Daily ten–minute stand-up meeting.
   • Weekly project review.
   • Monthly project review.

7. Change Managers from across businesses should meet monthly, as a Change Managers' club, to exchange ideas and methods and facilitate transfer of successful ideas.

8. Projects should follow two phases with quick-hits, running in parallel
   • Phase 1 – analysis, data collection and solution design.
   • Phase 2 – implementation of the new system or approach.

9. There should be a completion audit review against the original targets, and an acceptance sign-off by the project 'owner' for each project.

For Chapter 6 go to page 407

Support Methodology Section 5

SM5.1 Resource planning

SM5.1.1 Introduction

Planning of the use of time and resources is the centre of the project management process. It needs the ability to specify and apply appropriate techniques to plan, monitor and control work-packages, projects and programmes.

SM5.1.2 Definitions

Activity – A defined piece of work for a project.

Milestone – An important moment in the implementation of a project.

Planning – The process of identifying the means, resources and actions necessary to accomplish an objective (BS 6079).

Plans – The results of planning, an intended future course for action (Association for Project Management). The plans for a project usually include a schedule (see below) and budget.

Programme – A word not used here because it has at least two different meanings:

- A document showing the proposed dates for the work for a project – see 'Schedule' below.
- A set of related projects.

Note that 'program' means computer software, but in the USA is the spelling for 'programme' with both meanings stated above.

Resources – People, money, time, materials, equipment or information.

Schedule – A document showing a list of activities and dates. Information on the nature of each activity, its location, resources required and who is responsible for its satisfactory completion is usually given in separate documents, but all can be included in the schedule for a small project.

SM5.1.3 Need for planning

The process of planning must be as old as society. Consider what was needed in ancient times to grow crops, catch animals or build a Pyramid. All of these needed provisional decisions ahead of events and a basis for control and for learning to be better next time.

Costs and competition increasingly demand that projects are delivered on time despite their increasing complexity. Planning how to use resources is the basis for working economically and for monitoring progress and costs. More attention to planning also helps meet the increasing public requirements for safety.

The uses of planning are therefore to:

- Decide how to use resources to achieve maximum value.
- Recommend the dates for completion of all work.
- Explore the possible effects of uncertainties and risks.
- Establish the basis for assessing progress and trends.
- Provide information for learning to perform better next time.

These various uses of plans may have different users. They may therefore want different detail and different forms of plan.

SM5.1.4 Project definition

Planning has been defined as the process of identifying the means, resources and actions necessary to accomplish an objective. The objective of a project must thus be known in order to plan how to accomplish it. At the early stages of a project the objectives and information about resources and risks may be quite uncertain. Some planning can then be most helpful as a source of questions and ideas which help to define the best project. Planning how it might be carried out can affect the cost of a proposed project. Feasibility studies should therefore include some planning of the expected work, but at that stage have to be based upon uncertainties as to the scope of the project.

The questions asked about its objectives and risks can cause some re-thinking and exploration of alternative objectives, scope and plans. And the data used can change and new ideas arise as the project is being carried out. Planning is therefore often a repetitive process stage-by-stage through a project, as the promoters of the project learn the implications of their first ideas and the information changes.

SM5.1.5 Uncertainties and risks

All planning is uncertain, as it uses predictions to explore the future. Analysis of uncertainties and risks is therefore valuable at all stages of planning a project.

The techniques for risk analysis should be used to identify the events which could disrupt a plan, to explore alternatives to avoid or minimize risks, and to provide data for assessing probabilities of delay, extra cost or other potential threats which could stop a project.

SM5.1.6 Priorities

A project can have more than one objective and these can have conflicting demands. In particular there can be conflicts between the quality standards required, time for implementing the project and the cost of these. Quality and time cost money. These three variables are shown in Fig. SM5.1. As N. M. L. Barnes suggested, planning has to be based upon a decision where the project is in the triangle of these variables.

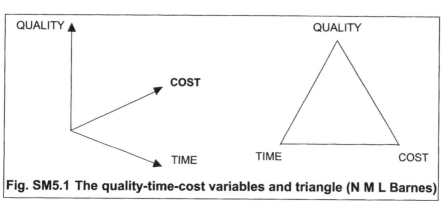

Fig. SM5.1 The quality-time-cost variables and triangle (N M L Barnes)

SM5.1.7 Cost and speed of project implementation

Most projects are sanctioned because they promise to deliver value in return for their cost. Public and commercial organizations have their criteria and procedures for assessing whether to invest in a project. Those criteria provide a basis for sanctioning normal projects, normal in the sense of being what a public service should provide or a business can expect to profit from. These criteria are essentially hurdles based upon comparing predicted cost and predicted benefit. The benefit is obtained from a project when the resulting service or product is delivered. Deciding the time to be allowed for its implementation is therefore important.

To be able to start to plan a project a decision is therefore needed whether to implement it at maximum speed and so use resources uneconomically – known sometimes as 'fast-track' or in the USA 'fast-trak'. Or whether to implement it at minimum cost – that is using resources as economically as possible and therefore more slowly. Or between the two. In theory, if the completed project is expected to earn a financial return, the total time to be allowed for its implementation should be decided after estimating the likely cost of the project over a range of possible speeds of work and selecting the time at which the net present value of extra income obtained earlier by faster completion equals its extra cost. The same criterion should apply to a project which is expected to provide a social benefit expressed in financial terms.

Fig. SM5.2 illustrates how total cost varies with the time allowed to implement a project. Some costs increase with the time taken, as indicated by the C_t curve in the diagram, for instance the financing cost of the use of resources. Other costs decrease, as indicated by the C_m curve, for instance the direct costs of resources. The sum of the two is shown by the total cost TC curve.

Continuous curves are a simplification in Fig. SM5.2. In practice the relationships may include step changes at choices in the number of people or the capacity of machines employed. In principle the relationship indicated between total cost and planned duration provides a basis for classifying projects in three distinct degrees of urgency:

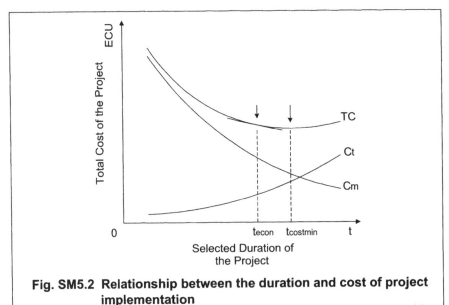

Fig. SM5.2 Relationship between the duration and cost of project implementation

1. *Minimum Initial Cost* – If the customer's requirement is to complete a project for minimum capital cost, its planned duration should be where TC is a minimum, the $t_{costmin}$ point shown in the diagram. Urgency is zero. This is the condition for investment in services which do not earn or save money or which are not credited financially for providing a benefit.
2. *Economic duration* – If a project is to produce goods or services which are expected to earn a financial return, greater expenditure than minimum cost is usually justified to try to achieve completion earlier than $t_{costmin}$. This point on the TC line is where its slope (shown by a tangent line) represents the discounted amount which is expected to be earned per week after completion (the slope of this line is negative, as it represents not cost but income per unit of time). Hence t_{econ} should be chosen as the planned duration of the project.
3. *Emergency* – If speed overrides all consideration of cost, any attention to optimizing the use of resources is irrelevant. Time is priceless. Only physical conditions and resources limit the speed of work. Costs are recorded for accounting, but not for control. This is typical of a life-threatening situation in which the resources available are insufficient to preserve life. Left uncontrolled the results become a disaster. These are the conditions requiring emergency planning systems.

Public and commercial projects therefore tend to vary in their priorities between time and cost.

The objectives of a project should state whether it is to be completed at minimum initial cost, or whether in a faster economic time or as emergency work, in order to guide the planning of the use of resources.

SM5.1.8 Urgency

As discussed above, a project sanctioned as an investment in services which will not earn money or financial credit should be planned to be completed in time $t_{costmin}$. If that project is also stated to be 'urgent', this must mean that there is some non-financial reason for deciding to use resources uneconomically so as to try to complete it faster than in time $t_{costmin}$.

Or a project sanctioned to produce goods or services which are expected to earn money should be planned to be completed in time t_{econ}. If this project is also stated to be 'urgent', this must mean that there is some non-financial reason for deciding to use resources uneconomically in order to try to complete it faster than in time t_{econ}.

Clearly the purpose of stating that any project is 'urgent' is much more likely to be understood and therefore achieved if expressed in terms of what extra can be spent per day it should save.

SM5.1.9 Changes of priorities

Priorities tend to change during all projects. The information used to plan at the start may change during project implementation. Ideas and problems arise, and markets, costs of resources, competition, new technology or legislation change.

Typically, projects are started after attention to cost compared to benefits. Yet as the work for such projects progresses, completion on time tends to become thought to be relatively more important. The importance of economy in the use of resources tends to become secondary to expedients adopted to save or recover time. Extra cost is then incurred to keep to time, often in the form of paying bonuses or paying the costs of overcoming what are claimed to be abnormal hindrances.

In contrast to this, projects initially authorised as really urgent tend to incur costs which lead to second thoughts. As a result, the priority may become less haste, more economy.

The economic speed calculated for planning a project should of course be changed if the expected future value of the project changes.

On all but brief and repeat projects, planning and re-planning should thus be continued stage-by-stage through all the work.

SM5.1.10 Project content

To be able to plan the resources needed we have to understand the pattern of work to be done stage-by-stage through a project.

Every project whether it is a change to a business, reorganization of a government department, launch of a new product, process, system or structure, large or small, proceeds through a chain of activities to achieve its objective. The same is characteristic of replacing, altering or discarding a product or a service.

Projects may differ greatly in their size, technical content, novelty, urgency and duration, but they also have much in common. They start with an initial study of ideas for a project, drawing on predictions of demand and using experience and data from previous projects to decide whether to spend more on obtaining better data to in turn to decide whether it is a benefit–cost positive. The minimum resources are used until the first studies show that it is worth spending more.

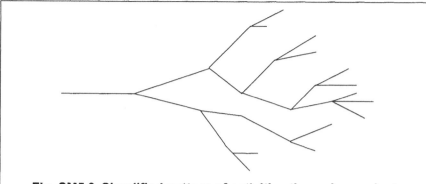

Fig. SM5.3 Simplified pattern of activities through a project
(This sketch follows the convention that time elapses from left to right)

The decision to proceed with a project leads to an increase in resources employed. Each stage as the project proceeds marks a change in the nature, complexity and speed of activities, types of resource, and importantly in the number of people and the rate of spend. The intensity of activities increases. Numbers rise to a maximum in implementing the project, usually drawing on specialists and others from other organizations, and then numbers fall off rapidly as it is completed.

The work for every project thus consists of a branching network of activities. A simplified picture is shown in Fig. SM5.3. The sequence proceeds from a few general and abstract activities to many smaller and increasingly simultaneous ones. Each line represents an activity in the sequence. Every activity is dependent upon the completion of prior ones. The freedom of choice decreases as a project proceeds to the large scale of interdependent detail.

Computer-based techniques to analyse the network of activities for projects have been developed to plan all stages of projects. Using them the durations of the activities are studied off the diagram in routines suitable for analysing sequential and cross-dependencies on a large scale using computers. In Fig. SM5.3 the lengths of lines representing each activity have been drawn in proportion to their typical durations, to indicate that the work content per activity tends to decrease to the end of the project. These trends are shown in Fig. SM5.4.

Continuous curves are shown in Fig. SM5.4 as this is typical of projects with a large number of activities rather than the few sketched in Fig. SM5.3.

The product of work content per activity multiplied by the number of simultaneous activities at each moment gives the rate of use of resources. This product follows a characteristic rise and fall in intensity of work.

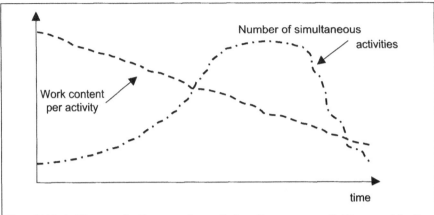

Fig. SM5.4 Change in the number of simultaneous activities and in the work content per activity during a project

Integrating this leads to the *S-curve* or *Ogee* relationship between the accumulated total work done and the elapse of time in the implementation of the project. This is depicted in Fig. SM5.5.

Records of the expenditure during projects demonstrate this characteristic S-curve form. The curvature and skew indicate the speed of the initial acceleration and the final deceleration. These vary depending upon the novelty of the work, the number of simultaneous activities, their interdependence and their durations. The work for every sub-project or work-package also tends to follow an S-curve.

S-curves are often plotted in terms of cost and time, as in Fig. SM5.5. Though the ordinate may be expressed in money terms, it can be a measure

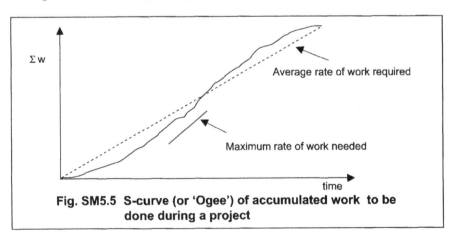

Fig. SM5.5 S-curve (or 'Ogee') of accumulated work to be done during a project

of the volume of work for a whole project or an activity, not just its cost, and is therefore a potentially useful way of showing the planned progress of a project.

SM5.1.11 Time is not linear

The S-curve as shown in Fig. SM5.5 indicates that to complete all the work on time the peak rate of work must be at least double the average rate of the total amount in the total time.

We may well plan to complete 50% of the work for a project by half-way through the time available. What matters for completion on time is that the work is by then proceeding at well above the average rate.

Just in case

Problem

40% of the budget for Stage II of developing the factory was for purchasing a new type of production machine, but the cost risks of purchasing it were low because its manufacturer had agreed a fixed price for it, including the testing of a prototype. The budgeted amounts for the services required for the machine, its installation and new building work were based upon the Stage I costs increased (following the 0.6 power rule) for the greater capacity of the project.

The Chief Manufacturing Engineer presented the budget for Stage II with a 20% addition for 'contingencies'. Asked to justify this he pointed out that Stage I had overrun its budget by that amount. The Managing Director (MD) stated that with the experience gained from Stage I no contingency should be needed. The Chief Manufacturing Engineer argued that the tests on the prototype of the novel machine could well show that output might exceed specification and to take advantage of this the capacity of the supporting services would have to be increased during the execution of the project. Or the services might need to be changed to suit problems or unexpected characteristics of the machine, and as in Stage I additional costs could be incurred in mistakes or interference between the services and building contractors. He showed his estimates of the possible cost of each of these. These contingencies the MD accepted. They amounted to a contingency addition of 10%. The MD agreed that within that limit the Stage II project was financially justified and should proceed.

Principles

- The lessons of the overrun of the past project should be known and agreed.
- The Project Manager (in this case the Chief Manufacturing Engineer) should budget for the 'known unknowns', i.e. specific amounts which may be needed for defined risks, ideally drawing on valid data bases.
- The customer (in this case the company) should budget for the 'unknown unknowns', i.e. the unforeseeable risks, using brainstorming to identify risks.
- Contingency amounts in project budgets should be specific in order to provide a basis for control of the project and for learning for future projects.

Comments

- There is no such thing as a risk-free project.
- Safe budgets can kill a project – if too expensive they shouldn't get approval.

SM5.2 Resource control

SM5.2.1 The control process

SM5.2.1.1 Objectives

Control of the allocation of resources based upon good project planning was discussed in Chapter 3. The word 'control' is used in its broadest sense to mean here the process of planning, implementing the plans, monitoring performance and costs, and taking action to achieve objectives.

The purpose of control is to see that the project delivers the maximum value in return for the resources consumed. By planning ahead, the control process ideally solves problems before they happen.

One characteristic of many projects is that the information used to select and plan the project changes during its implementation because of:

- Changes in the project environment of markets, corporate policy, society or law.
- Ideas and problems arising during project execution.

The effects of changes are not necessarily a problem in the sense that they are a threat to achieving project objectives. But they need to be controlled, as otherwise people can become uncertain about what is required, when and from who, and as a result lose commitment and confidence in the project.

Except for small, routine or emergency projects, control should therefore be a dynamic process based upon planning, reviewing and re-planning stage-by-stage through the project.

SM5.2.1.2 Control cycle

Figure SM5.6 is a general form of control diagram showing the principles also illustrated in diagrams in Chapter 3. The control process is shown as a sequence of steps with feedback. The core process from 'PROPOSE PROJECT' to 'HAND OVER PROJECT' is shown through the centre.

Added to the core process are the steps of assessing risks, monitoring the project environment and comparing performance with the plan which provide the basis for considering whether to review the plan. These are the feedforward and feedback processes which are usually needed to plan, monitor and manage all commercial and government projects to success.

Other models of the process vary in the detail and definitions of the steps. Some of the alternative models simplify the complexity of the links required to question objectives, explore alternatives, investigate risks, consult stakeholders, employ suppliers and the many other communications needed through a project. The core process may be all that is needed to control an emergency or repeat and short projects. Appropriate diagrammatic models of the control process can be a useful guide to defining where we are and where we should be in the control process. They can be particularly useful in deciding the purpose, scope and timing of progress reports and meetings (see Support Methodology, Chapter 3).

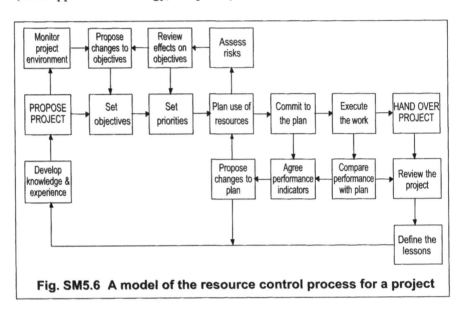

Fig. SM5.6 A model of the resource control process for a project

SM5.2.2 Monitoring

SM5.2.2.1 Performance indicators

The key performance indicators (KPIs) for a project should be established in the Project Execution Plan before authority is given to use resources.

Those KPIs should be chosen which represent the objectives of the project. Typically KPIs include quality specifications, milestone dates, completion time and earned value. All KPIs should be in terms of delivering useful output. Secondary indicators such as the quantities of resources available are important indicators of the potential to do work but they measure costs not performance.

SM5.2.2.2 The S-curve
S-curves are often used to plan and monitor the progress of activities and costs during a project or a contract. Similarly a supplier can use S-curves to

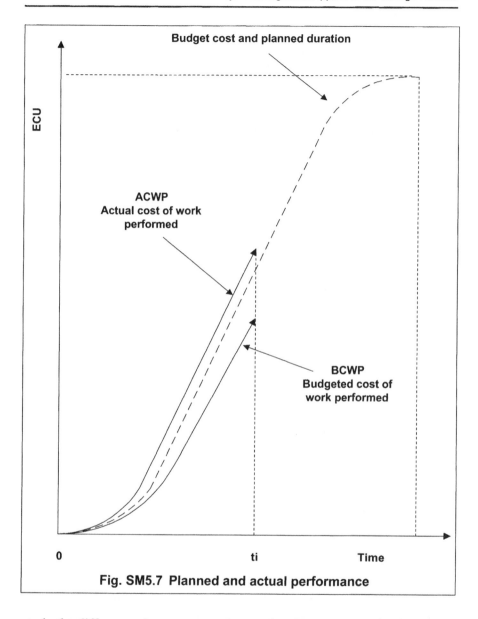

Fig. SM5.7 Planned and actual performance

study the differences between costs incurred and payment received over the duration of a contract.

An example for comparing planned and actual cost during the implementation of a project is shown in Fig. SM5.7.

In Fig. SM5.7 the broken line S-curve shows the budgeted-for costs up to a total on completion in the planned duration for the expected amount of work for a project or contract. The gradient of the line shows the rate of spend, and therefore indicates the rate at which resources must be used to complete the work in the planned time.

This S-curve indicates that having and using resources at the rate indicated by the straight line section of the 'Budget cost and planned duration' line is crucial to completion on time. Note that this rate of spend is at least double the average rate which would be calculated by dividing the budgeted total cost by the planned duration.

SM5.2.2.3 Deviations and trends

To be used in time to influence the remaining work, monitoring has to provide interim data so that we can infer from this data whether everything will be completed satisfactorily. Data is therefore required on:

- *Deviations* – What are the differences between the actual and the planned performance? (There are almost always some differences, good or bad, as the plan is based upon predictions.)
- *Rates of change* – Are the differences between the actual and the planned performance improving or deteriorating?
- *Accumulated deviation* – What is the difference between the total of work done to date compared with the planned total?

All three sets of control data are needed for critical and crucial activities. If deviations alone are considered, a serious trend may be missed. Or there may be over-reaction to trivial deviations or inaccurate data.

The two incomplete S-curves shown in Fig. SM5.7 indicate measures of the performance at time t_i in the work. In this example the actual cost of the work performed (ACWP) up to time t_i is greater than budgeted. Alone this data does not tell us that the work is also ahead of the plan. Maybe the cost estimates were wrong.

Also in Fig. SM5.7 the budgeted cost of the work actually performed (BCWP) at time t_i is less than planned. It indicates to us that the work is behind plan. Or that the plan was wrong.

The three curves therefore indicate that the work may be late and what has been done has cost more than expected, but they may also indicate that the estimates of time and cost for the work should be reviewed.

Continuous curves are shown in Fig. SM5.7, as that is how costs accumulate, but the data on costs is usually produced monthly and so all three curves may be plotted in steps.

Note that deviations from a budget are often called 'variances'.

SM5.2.3 Making a good start

Attention to costs and earned value alone is not enough to ensure completion on time. Completion of any work economically and on time depends upon good planning and then a good start to the first activities. The preparatory work at the start is typically small in cost compared to the total work. An S-curve plot of budgeted cost, actual cost and earned value therefore may not show up a poor start until too late to recover both budget and schedule. Checks and expediting should therefore be started early in an activity or contract, within the first 10% or so of the time for completion.

SM5.2.4 Cost of recovering time

If performance is poorer than expected, data is needed on output achieved to indicate possible limits to the recovery possible. If the data used in compiling in Fig. SM5.7 is correct, the slopes of the ACWP and BCWP lines indicate that performance and cost control have been poor since early in the work. Why they have been poor should be analysed in order to understand how to try to take action to recover from the situation.

Figure SM5.8 indicates the possible results from actions at time t_i to recover from the poor progress shown in Fig. SM5.7.

The chain dotted line in Fig. SM5.8 shows what may be the effects on progress and costs of accelerating the work. Perhaps time and cost will over-run by about 15%. But this assumes that the rate of work can be doubled from the best achieved so far. The reasons for the BCWP line being below plan must therefore be understood before deciding to accelerate the work. And whatever acceleration is practicable it is unlikely to use resources economically if applied in only the limited time remaining in the schedule. Recovery of lost time is rarely economic, even if possible, and adding people or other resources may delay work even further. For a supplier who is late it may therefore be cheaper to pay a liquidated damages liability for late delivery than incur the costs of recovering time.

The actual performance should be analysed in a form suitable not only for managing this project but also for improving the data bank for planning future projects.

Risk analysis provides a discipline for anticipating risks and deciding in advance how to avoid or minimize their possible effects. Uncertainties and changes are not necessarily bad for a project. Changes can be an opportunity to achieve more than expected. They can result in the project meeting an unpredictable need. Ideally any project needs to be what the users find they want when it is handed over. Performance is judged on how it meets the

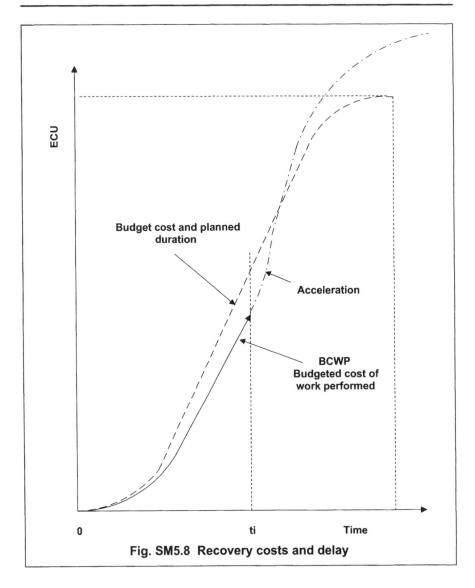

Fig. SM5.8 Recovery costs and delay

objectives at the time the work is complete. Completion of activities as first planned and to budget may not be satisfactory.

SM5.2.5 Lessons of control

- You cannot control the past. Everybody should learn from it.
- Plan, resource, analyse risks, motivate, monitor, review, give credit and improve.

- Start right.
- Be prepared to take advantage of good luck.
- Time is not linear.
- Place responsibility with those who control resources.
- Control where the problems may arise.

It's 90% complete

Problem

The usual supplier had said that providing five specials was no problem. Their engineer had come from a high-tech design organization. He would draft the details in the next six weeks, as shown in the bar chart programme he had prepared for this job. Production would follow as normal.

In a visit after five weeks the customer was told that the design work was 90% complete, happily ahead of programme, as he could see. Detail had yet to be checked, QA satisfied and manufacturing's needs implemented, but these should not be a problem. They were! The critical bar in the chart allowing six weeks for the design work had not allowed for these final 'non-productive' tasks.

Principles

- Study the implications of the delay and decide whether part delivery is useful.
- In the project planning stage agree an estimate of work in a process table, with detailed tasks and resource allocation.
- In the plan show the time and resources needed for all tasks, including manufacturing development and system checks.

Lesson

- Time is not linear. Learn that in any plan half the total time allowed for a task may be needed just for the final 20% of it.

SM5.3 Changes in project implementation

SM5.3.1 Changes to projects

SM5.3.1.1 Definitions

By *'change'* we mean an addition, deletion or alteration to the scope, nature, quantity, standards, timing or location of work for a project during its implementation. Projects are also the cause of changes in the wider sense that a new or improved service or product alters a business. As discussed earlier in Chapter 5, this effect of a project is usually part of its objectives and is a matter for decisions in project strategy and decisions on the business case. Here our concern are changes after sanctioning which can affect whether a project achieves its defined objectives.

The word *'variation'* is used in this book only for changes in the contractual scope etc. of a supplier's work for a customer. (Note that the word *'variance'* is used in project control to mean a difference between plan and performance, for instance where work has cost more (or less) than budgeted.)

SM5.3.1.2 Are changes a problem?

Changes to a project during its implementation are often stated to cause delays and extra costs, particularly when they lead to a contract variation. Not all changes are bad. They can be an advantage, to use new ideas, especially on a project started in order to develop and apply innovations during its implementation. They can also be an opportunity to improve a project or to overcome problems. To be able to control them to best meet the objectives of the project we need to understand why they occur.

SM5.3.1.3 Causes of changes

Table SM5.1 lists the causes of changes during the implementation of projects as stated by people working in various industries over the past ten years. The data was obtained in response to questions 'What is the greatest problem in project management?' and 'What is the cause of that problem?'.

Most of the causes of changes during projects listed in Table SM5.1 can be seen as due to:

- Markets and political conditions, exchange rates, material supplies and other input factors which change and continue to change.
- The conditions and resources for project implementation differ from the best predictions.
- The tendency of project sponsors to spend as little as possible on investigations before a project is sanctioned, as the cost and other resources

Table SM5.1 Causes of changes during project implementation

Poor communications
Culture and structure of organization, personalities
Pressure/time constraints preventing effective definitive design
Changing markets, customer demands, ideas
Company attitude, poor discipline
Innovative, immature technology
Contracts signed when scope is not frozen
Schedule-driven projects
Customers changing their minds
Conflicting requirements within the team, lack of experience
Getting contractors to 'buy into' plan
Insufficient front-end loading of the project
Changes from initial designs
New reservoir information, cost increase
Evolving relationship with customers and tasks from other projects
Lack of preparation, inadequate risk assessment
Poor scoping, lack of good chemical engineer
Lack of personal knowledge/experience, time pressures
Poor initial planning
Not enough discussion between all at start of project
Poor scope documents, scope changes, lack of resources, time
Not enough time at front end to finalise design
Projects are nebulous, company run by jargon spouting accountants
Scope of work unclear at start of project, changes in market, technology
Lack of understanding by project sponsors (Operations)
Developing situation in areas of new technology
Changes in design after commencing installation
Inadequate planning for business strategy
Individuals always have their own ideas on how to carry out their work
The nature of development work
The nature of the work
Unforeseen problems. Difficulty of scoping/defining tasks until start them
Being unable to see all the issues at the beginning
Lack of project management tools and understanding of workloads
Lack of understanding of senior players

used then appear to be wasted if the project does not go ahead or if it may be changed by any of the above. The same is characteristic of suppliers of goods and services before they have a contract. As a result, many problems are perceived and options considered only after the decision to go ahead and therefore at the expense of progress with the project.

- Project sponsors are tempted to make changes to incorporate new technology though this was not an objective of a project.
- Contract and internal procedures evolved to manage essential changes and variations have created an expectation that the specification and other decisions are open to being changed.

To understand how to anticipate and manage these changes they can be classified as:

- *Inherent in projects* – Changes due to markets, customer demands, evolving relationship with customers and tasks from other projects, immature technology, new information and the nature of development work may be classed as inherent risks in those projects.
- *Internal to the business* – Changes due to poor communications, culture and structure, personalities, company attitude, poor discipline, pressure and time constraints preventing effective definitive design, conflicting requirements within the team, lack of experience, poor initial planning and most of the rest of the list in Table SM5.1 may be classed as due to the organization undertaking the project.

The project sponsor has to accept changes inherent in a project and the Project Manager has to anticipate their effects. In what are called 'Mature Project Management' organizations, changes due to poor communications, culture, structure, company attitude, poor discipline, pressure and time constraints are managed out, stimulated by reviews of previous projects that have shown what the lack of action on them has cost.

SM5.3.1.4 Influence of changes

Research has shown that the cost and delay effects of changes during the implementation of a project tend to be under-estimated, for these reasons:

- Changes are often proposed as the solution to a problem when there is little time to decide whether they should be accepted. They are therefore not investigated thoroughly, and the alternative of living with the problem is not costed.
- Only the direct cost of a change may be obvious. The consequential costs of disrupting work and thereby disrupting relationships are difficult to estimate and tend to become apparent only later. But they can be much greater than the direct costs.
- Similarly the ultimate price of ordering contract variations tends to be underestimated.
- People tend to be optimistic about the success of adopting a new idea such as a change to a project.

Experienced Project Managers conclude that the potential advantages of making changes are nearly always over-estimated. Many changes therefore do not really serve the objectives of projects.

SM5.3.2 Control of changes

SM5.3.2.1 Anticipating changes
The lessons of successful projects provide the following recommendations on anticipating or at least minimizing the risk of unwanted changes:

1. Consider options in project scope, procurement and planning in the project feasibility study. Apply the lessons of previous projects. Even under pressures to limit expenditure, this is the time to use resources to consider alternatives and preferences.
2. List the possible reasons for later changes. Use risk analysis to assess the flexibility and margins to allow in the project size, budget and schedule.
3. Plan the project and decide all novel and uncertain detail before project sanctioning, so as to know *how* to proceed when the decision is made *whether* to go ahead with the project.
4. Involve and commit all downstream parties to the above decisions, motivating them to feel that they own the project definition and are personally responsible for the results.
5. If the project objective is development, proceed in stages and concentrate expenditure in the first stage on work which will reduce the uncertainties of whether and how to proceed further.
6. If the project is urgent, make final decisions before starting. Overlapping planning and implementation can cause greater delays than it promises to save.
7. If schedule or cost are important, establish a procedure to anticipate, assess and decide on possible changes.
8. Consider whether to set a policy that no changes shall be accepted unless imposed by new legislation or which offer an overwhelming and undoubted advantage to the project (for instance at least 2.5 times the financial rate of return or other base criterion for the sanctioning of a commercial project).
9. Maintain continuity of the senior staff, particularly those responsible for sponsoring and managing the project.

SM5.3.2.2 Configuration management
During the implementation of a project the volume of information on its form, size etc. becomes larger. It becomes more detailed and more

diffused as more people with different expertise undertake their specialist activities.

It is clearly desirable that everyone on a project should be basing their work on consistent information on its form, size and intended performance. The larger the project the more important it may be that there is system for compiling, controlling and communicating this information, and for controlling changes to it. For reasons of commercial or state security the system may also have to control who can see the information.

'*Configuration management*' is the term now used to mean the system therefore needed for compiling, controlling and communicating the information. The word '*configuration*' is used here in its ordinary sense to mean the information on the form, size, etc. of a project. It includes what are often known in engineering industries as the '*design parameters*'.

SM5.3.2.3 Change control procedure and configuration control

In the evolution of project management, 'configuration control' was the name given in the US defence industry for procedures instituted to review and document changes proposed to the functional and physical characteristics of large projects. These procedures were designed to control changes which had been seriously affecting the performance and delivery of military projects. As part of 'configuration management', the purpose was to deter unnecessary changes.

The costs of uncontrolled changes have led many organizations to set up formal procedures to control these changes. From this they have seen value in extending their system 'upstream' to anticipate changes. Establishing a configuration control system provides a basis for this. Aided by systematic questioning and checklists from other projects it should show up omissions in the project definition and avoid inconsistent specifications.

The procedure to control the potential effects of changes on cost or schedule can be simple. It needs to provide a basis for making decisions in time to minimize real problems yet deter the temptation to make a change rather than solve a problem. The procedure should therefore require anyone proposing a change to state:

- Who wants the change?
- Why?
- What are its potential advantages and consequences?
- What are the potential effects on schedule and budget?
- What are the alternatives?
- Is the change being proposed to overcome a hidden problem?
- What would be the consequences of refusing the change?

- What do the other stakeholders recommend about the proposed change?
- When and how should the change be best implemented?

On many projects many changes perhaps should not have been accepted, but some may be required for good reasons and perhaps to the advantage of a project. Formal systems to control changes should therefore be operated as an aid to success, not just as a deterrent. A specimen form for requesting a change is shown in Support Methodology – Section 3, Fig. SM3.7. It is quite simple and so should provide a disciplined basis for making decisions quickly when necessary.

Note that the form requires information on the 'zero action' option, the consequences of refusing the change.

Additions to the information required for a decision on a change should be limited. Providing information and reading it costs money. And any procedure that takes much time tends to be by-passed. Imposing any system of control which is not accepted as positively useful may cause real problems to be hidden until they are insoluble.

SM5.3.2.4 Pressure of time

Late completion is a recurrent fault of many projects, and changes to specification after project sanctioning are a recurrent cause of lateness. This is an old problem. It continues to be a risk of public and commercial projects, and in developed and underdeveloped countries. It can worsen the pressure for quick acceptance of proposed changes. The control of changes therefore needs to be both quick and be operated so as to serve the objectives of the project.

On the other hand, if a decision on a proposed change can be left until the end of the project or a milestone date, it may then be found to be unnecessary because the facts have changed. Or it may then be cheaper to implement it together with other changes.

SM5.3.2.5 Freezing the project

Some experienced people said that the recurrent lesson of their projects is that the scope should be complete and 'frozen' at the stage of approving a project. Some describe freezing as 'essential'. Clearly it isn't, as many projects are achieved without doing so.

The scope and schedule for a project can be frozen in a rigid way, but the concept and the phrase can mislead people on a project into thinking that they do not need to allow for irresistible forces for changes such as markets, mistakes or new data having specific effects on safety. Freezing in detail at the start is the policy to follow only if no reasons whatever will be accepted for changing decisions previously made, for instance on an emergency project where speed is the overriding basis for decisions.

The practical lesson of industrial and public projects is that flexibility and spare capacity are needed because of uncertainties during project implementation, but to use them successfully there must be a system which controls how and when they are used. Without control to discipline how they are used, flexibility and spare capacity may be mis-used to provide a cover for poor initial decisions.

Decisions may be irrevocable, but they are not irreversible. Changes can always be made, at the loss of time, money, morale and reputation. A project should therefore be planned to be flexible for the reasons accepted at project sanctioning.

SM5.3.2.6 Responsibility for the control of changes

The statements listed in Table SM5.1 show why changes may arise during a project. To be able to control changes we need to know where they come from. For this purpose the statements in Table SM5.1 can be classified as having three different sources:

A. *Corporate management* – for instance changes due to culture and structure, poor discipline, immature technology.
B. *Business environment* – for instance changes due to markets and customers' demands and changes to take advantage of new ideas and technology.
C. *Project management* – for instance changes due to contracts signed when scope not frozen, conflicting ideas within the project team, lack of preparation, inadequate risk assessment.

Clearly changes due to problems in Category A are a corporate rather than project responsibility. The control of changes in Category B should be the responsibility of the project sponsor (whoever is responsible for initiating the project or for bidding to a potential customer) and allowed for in the budget for the business case. The control of changes in Category C should be the responsibility of the Project Manager and allowed for in the budget for project execution.

Change control of large projects is often the function of a committee. If so, changes in categories A and B should be decided by the committee in consultation with the Project Manager. Changes in category C should be reported to the committee for information not decisions by them, to leave them time to concentrate on the changes which may affect the objectives and priorities of the project.

SM5.3.3 Crisis management

SM5.3.3.1 What is a crisis?

A crisis medically is 'when a change takes place which is decisive of recovery or death', and more generally 'a turning-point in progress' or 'a state of affairs in which a decisive change for better or worse is imminent' (OED). Any of these definitions describe crises experienced during some projects.

A crisis is therefore a time when it appears that objectives are no longer achievable. It may cause a major change to a project. One of the objectives of performance, quality, schedule or cost may have to be sacrificed. And in extremes safety, for instance to risk a life to save others.

If it threatens achievement of the project objectives, a crisis requires a decision on whether to proceed any further with the project. Up-to-date information on what can be done, how, how best, when and at what cost should be analysed. In effect the solution to a crisis is a replacement project, to be evaluated and from this to be abandoned or to proceed if justified.

People on a project may not know or agree that they are approaching a crisis. A person part-way through some work for the project may state confidently that it will be right on time. Others dependent on using the results may feel certain that what they will get will be seriously late or unfit to use. Ideally the Project Manager would be in regular and informal contact with everyone on the project and they would give early warnings of anxieties and doubts, but in bureaucratic organizations it may be difficult to get agreement that a crisis is approaching, particularly in time to minimize its effects. By the time a crisis is apparent a decision on it is therefore usually urgent and personal relationships may be deteriorating. All this can deter fact-finding.

SM5.3.3.2 Crisis control

If the facts justify it, immediate action on a crisis may be best in order to limit the damage, as in the classic instance of the Dutch boy using his finger to limit a leak in a dyke. Poor information can cause a false alarm, and the avoidable panic reduce confidence in the organization.

Managing a crisis should therefore proceed step-by-step logically, for instance:

1. What is really the problem?
2. Why is it urgent?
3. How does it affect achieving the project objectives?
4. Are the facts agreed?

5. What are the options?
6. Who agrees?
7. What is the best action?

and of course review the above and the results afterwards to learn the lessons for future Project Managers.

Planning and risk analysis from the start of a project should avoid or anticipate most potential causes of crises, but only so far as causes can be foreseen. It can enable the Project Manager to prepare for what H. S. Moody has called the 'known unknowns'. The 'unknown unknowns' cannot be foreseen. Time may not permit consultation with the project sponsor or other stakeholders when a crisis threatens the project. If so, the Project Manager needs to have (or take) the authority to define the crisis and to decide on actions on behalf of the project sponsor.

Feet on the ground

Problem

When the Company got the contract the Project Manager soon obtained from the Mechanical Engineering Section information that the main pressure vessel would require three foundation pedestals equally spaced at 120° and passed this detail, the expected floor loads etc. to the Civil Engineering Section.

On delivery of the vessel to the building it was found that it had been manufactured with four feet, following detailed design drawings that the vessel manufacturer had sent to the Mechanical Engineering Section. To replace the vessel with one with three feet would have caused six months delay. Instead, the Project Manager asked the Civil Engineers to rescue the project from the Mechanicals' mistake by adding new pedestals to fit four feet. The Civil Engineering Section Leader agreed to plan to make the change and said if the Project Manager could approve this extra cost that week he could probably get the construction contractor to do it for about £4000 at the same time as the contractor had to remedy a mistake. The budget given to the Project Manager by the Directors did not include any sum to pay for such additional work. He therefore requested authority from the Technical Director to incur the extra cost of the new pedestals. After reference through to the Financial Director the extra was approved. The contractor was then ordered to put in the additional pedestals. The price for them finally agreed with the contractor was £12,000.

Principles

- Place authority where risks arise.
- Define the authority of the Project Manager in relation to the project sponsor.
- Apply resources to check detail as soon as possible, to avoid such problems.
- Present facts, with supporting detail.

Lessons

- Understand how to manage those above you.
- Remote control is always inaccurate.

Support Tools and Techniques Section   5

TT5.1 Organizations

TT5.1.1 Structure and size

Organization is a means of enabling people to achieve more together than they could alone. Or it should be. How and how much to organize departments and project teams should therefore depend on how and how many people need to work together. How far to define a structure of jobs should be decided on the basis of the expertise needed and how people are dependent on each other in their work for each project. An organization structure should be designed to create the 'natural' team for a project, that is to link everyone who has the expertise and the authority for decisions on the objectives, scope, standards, design, economy, financing, timing, methods, safety, control and acceptability of a project. The structure should help to motivate people. It should convey facts, ideas and understanding. It should also feedback data useful for controlling projects and for improving future performance.

Sometimes everybody working on a small project can be located together. If so, they should be able to share information easily, and also understand each others' intentions and interests. More commonly, most of the people contributing to a project are employed in specialist functions. Many are usually in separate organizations and in them located in separate departments. As a result they may fail to keep others informed of new information and potential problems. Separated groups of people may also tend to interpret information differently. People employed in specialist functions are particularly likely to do so. They will tend to concentrate on their own work and its importance as they see it. Specialization by departments and individuals has the longer-term advantages that they can build up expertise and be spread economically over many projects. A disadvantage is that many specialists may be involved in only their part of a project. They may not know about or understand the needs of the project as a whole. And if treated as advisers rather than as members of project teams they may also tend to concentrate on quality rather than delivery times and budgets. A system of organization is therefore needed to link them together.

The need to plan these relationships and the information system does not mean that organizations should be bureaucratic. They should be flexible and informal in order to be able to perceive and solve problems and adapt to the changing needs stage-by-stage through projects.

TT5.1.2 Allocation of resources

The demands for the expertise of people and other resources required to carry out a project (or to alter one) are transitory. To be economic, these resources must be used as continuously as possible, i.e. on a series of projects. Continuity in the use of resources and the development of skills may not suit the order of their use that is ideal for a project. But the projects are the profit earners. An organization structure therefore has to serve two objectives:

- Achieving the sequence of activities essential to each project.
- Distributing the resources needed for all the projects.

Therefore most projects have to share resources. At the feasibility study stage alternative projects may be under consideration and competing for selection. Those selected are then likely to share design resources with others which may be otherwise unconnected, but therefore be in competition with them for the use of these resources. Similarly through all the subsequent stages in the cycle.

A project may therefore have a core team employed on it full-time for at least a peak of work, and the rest of the work for it may be 'sub-contracted' to specialised support functional departments within the company. Or bought from other companies. This requires planning, resource procurement and coordination by the Project Manager, stage-by-stage through the project.

TT5.1.3 Project teams

Typical of many projects is the formation of a project team by the temporary allocation of specialists from functional departments. An organizational problem is that most of the projects in hand in such a company are not large enough for people to be dedicated to only one project at a time. Attention to each project may therefore be interrupted by the needs of other projects or by delays from a customer or other parties. The consequent loss of continuity and risks to motivation and efficiency may be costly, especially if the people allocated to a project are not located together.

Very small projects may need some or all of the time of perhaps only one person plus some services from others, but their short time scale makes it difficult to predict when the services will be required. An organization therefore needs a system for setting priorities to employ people effectively.

The people allocated to a project need the expertise demanded by the nature of the projects, the problems and the risks, plus experience of applying this expertise to the type of customer and the range of work. Functional departments need to be reservoirs of specialist technical expertise, but with the flexibility and the ability to work on more than one project at once. Any one specialist may have several roles – leader of one or more projects, expert in a subject, and the person knowing most about a particular production system or client.

TT5.1.4 Dedicated project teams

One means of achieving attention to each project and its objectives is to dedicate people to a project from start to finish. The larger the project, the more it may be more practicable to do so. Putting together all the people and resources required for a project directly under a manager responsible only for meeting the objectives of that project to form what is known as a 'project task force' should concentrate attention and help motivate all to meet the customer's needs. It has disadvantages, one being that it requires people to work themselves out of a job by completing their stage of the work. Another is that skills and other resources are not shared between projects. This may be useful for limiting knowledge about a confidential project, but it can be wasteful at the time and fail to accumulate experience for future projects.

Choice of this system is clearly logical as a means of concentrating on objectives, as projects are the productive work and all other activities have value only as a contribution to a project. It puts together the people dependent upon information and decisions, and should therefore be coherent in reacting to demands and to new problems. Designating a separate project team involving all affected can also be a means of achieving an organizational transition, utilizing people's interest in the technical novelties or other features of a project to draw them into a changed system. It is the system that most tests the Project Managers, as each for his project has the range of responsibilities of a General Manager.

On the other hand the needs of a project for various skills etc., are only temporary and may fluctuate. Sharing of these needs between projects rather than having self-sufficient project groups may therefore be much more economical. Experience can then also be shared and reserves of resources drawn upon when required. A dedicated project team or 'task-force' located together is appropriate for a project which is urgent, important, complex or unique. Except in these conditions it is more logical to give preference to a system for sharing resources, adding to this a secondary means of linking the decisions for each project.

TT5.1.5 The project management role in a company structure

Whether formally called the Project Manager or not, the role is required to achieve leadership, championship of the project and continuity of knowledge of it. For small projects this can be part of the role of someone working on the project. For larger projects it can be nearly a full-time task and a separate role.

The structure of the company and its contracts with others provide the formal basis for generating and communicating authority and decisions. A project may also need its informal system for the Project Manager to obtain ideas, get early warnings of problems and check that information has been received and understood. This need varies according to the number of people employed on a project, the inter-dependence of their work, the extent of unexpected problems, whether they are located together and whether most are familiar with these conditions.

The simplest arrangement is to add the coordinating role to the tasks of a person already working on the project, and so not make communications more complicated.

TT5.1.6 Line-and-staff

If the size of a project makes its coordination a full-time task, a separate person can be given the role on behalf of the manager controlling the resources essential to that project, in a 'Staff Officer' position as indicated in Fig. TT5.1. The 'Line' manager remains formally in control of the resources. One person or a small team of people can be used in this position to provide temporary project management.

The important principle in this is that the 'Staff' position is not an additional level in the hierarchy. Its effectiveness may be limited by the role being that of coordinating the project-related activities of other people, rather than being their boss in the formal managerial system.

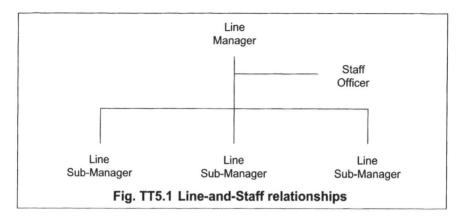

Fig. TT5.1 Line-and-Staff relationships

TT5.1.7 Matrix systems

Matrix systems of organization are found where the time of various specialists has to be shared between several projects, as in the systems illustrated in Chapter 1. The term 'matrix' is used in two ways. In what is called a 'weak' matrix the permanent staff are formally seen as in columns under leaders of each specialism and across the columns each project coordinator links the staff working on their project. The principle is shown in Fig. TT5.2. The people and other resources needed for the projects are based in three departments A, B, and C, each headed by a manager. Their work for each particular project is coordinated by a separate coordinator.

Figure TT5.2 shows what is known as a 'weak' matrix because the permanent managers of the specialist functions A, B and C are the line managers in the hierarchy of authority over resources.

The alternative of a 'strong' matrix is shown in Fig. TT5.3. In this, the resources are in 'task-forces' responsible to the Project Managers. The Project Managers are then the line managers. The role of the Functional Managers is to coordinate the use of the specialist resources, operating across the project teams to provide expert guidance and advise the top manager on the allocation of resources between the projects.

A matrix structure is a system for sharing resources between projects and concentrating the information about each project in its Project Manager. A matrix system is appropriate if people and other resources located in different functional departments have to be shared among a set of projects, but to be successful it requires planning of their allocation to each project and undivided authority and responsibility for standards, safety, costs and delivery.

Matrix systems can be more complex and organic, particularly in the extent of the formal authority of the Project Managers relative to that of the

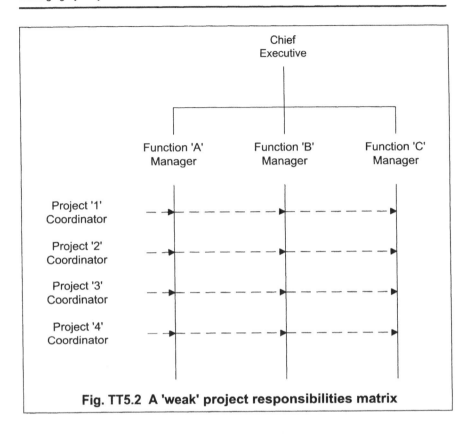

Fig. TT5.2 A 'weak' project responsibilities matrix

Functional Managers. The Project Managers and the Functional Managers should theoretically all influence decisions in a matrix system. In some cultures this leads to a common question – what is the authority of a Project Manager? In some organizations the Project Managers have been stated to be responsible for *quantitative* decisions affecting the cost and programme of the projects, whereas the Functional Managers are responsible for *qualitative* standards in allocating people and other resources to each project. If so, the Functional Managers have to act as consultants to members of their sections once allocated to a project. A matrix system thus provides opportunities to employ leaders with different skills and knowledge in these two types of managerial roles. In it responsibilities may be clear. In theory, authority should match responsibility.

TT5.1.8 Matrix management or internal contracts?

Observations of matrix systems indicate that there can be problems in them between the Project Managers and the Functional Managers about the

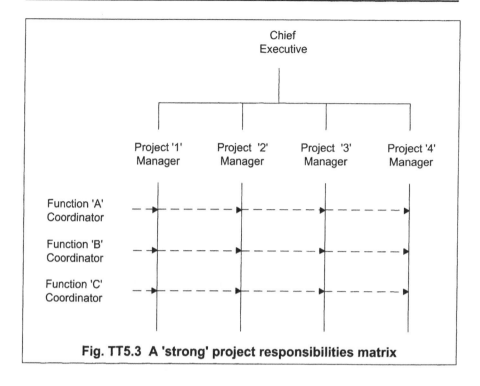

Fig. TT5.3 A 'strong' project responsibilities matrix

allocation of resources to a project and the quality, cost and timing of the work to be done by them. The Functional Managers should earlier have agreed on specifications, budgets and schedules for every project, but may have done so some time before a project starts and then only in sufficient detail to get a budget or a contract to proceed. This may not ensure that adequate resources are available when a project calls for them.

One means of avoiding most or all such problems is to treat the work for a project to be done by each specialist group of people as in effect a contractual commitment between their Functional Manager and the Project Manager. If the work was to be purchased by contract from another company there would normally be a prior process of investigating the potential supplier's capacity and understanding of the work required, followed by an invitation to offer to do it for a price and specified quality and delivery. Procedures for progress reporting, inspection, changes and resolving problems would also be established before they might be needed. The same are in effect needed within organizations, not through legally enforceable documents but by agreed definitions of what is expected of others rather than assuming that commitments are known, agreed and understood.

TT5.1.9 Final comments

The potential problems can be minimized if an organization structure is designed on the following principles:

- Least separation of the people working on a project.
- Those who control resources should be responsible for delivering the project.

Procuring

Problem

At the project progress meeting the Purchasing Department's representative stated confidently that Binary Unlimited would deliver the software as required. No, he hadn't spoken to them. That was the task of the Software Purchasing Section. The Software Purchasing Section Leader had checked with the Purchasing Officer who had visited Binary only recently. Did that Purchasing Officer know the work? Of course, she is experienced in procuring software. Was she the one who went through our requirements with Binary when they received the order? No, her predecessor looked after that at the start of the contract. The Project Manager asked for a further check. The Purchasing Department's representative undertook to pass this request to the Purchasing Director, but pointed out that his Department had to serve all projects and also was at present trying to settle the dispute with Trinary Ltd as to why they had not been given this order though lowest in price and stated as best by the software member of our project team.

The Project Manager commented that this was yet another example of Purchasing running policies that conflicted with their service to projects. On hearing this the Purchasing Director commented that here was another example of a project team demanding a service that conflicted with corporate interests to run an efficient expert procurement function.

The Chief Executive accepted the Purchasing Director's observation that since 75% of turnover was purchased out, purchasing was a major function. The Chief Executive also accepted that since the business now depended upon delivering projects, management's primary task should be to define and manage the project risks. The post of Projects Director was therefore created to plan all future commitments, anticipate procurement and other risks, and establish priorities in allocating resources. The

---

Purchasing Department was broken up and most of its staff allocated to project teams. Its Deputy Head was appointed Purchasing Manager with the tasks of providing advice to the six Project Managers and expert support to their purchasing staff. He was also made responsible to the new Projects Director for recommending the allocation of purchasing staff among the project teams and advising on their development needs.

Principles

- Projects are profit centres. Functions are cost centres. Functional departments are therefore a service to projects.
- The matrix was swung to achieve the natural project group. The previously strong position of the purchasing function was replaced by project authority over resources.
- A matrix system is at best only a framework for allocating resources and defining project responsibilities.

Lesson

- A system is only as good as the people in it, but changes of role can achieve changes in attitude and performance.

TT5.2 Teams

Successful, on time and within cost, completion of all but the simplest projects, requires a team approach. Many individuals, in all types of enterprises, in private as well as public sectors, are working on one or more projects at any one time. Hence an individual may be part of one or more project teams at any one time.

A team can be defined as more than one individual working together to achieve a defined goal. Effective team approach requires the bringing together and management of a group of individuals who share the same vision or goal and have the necessary skills and characteristics to achieve it. A project team which is always feuding or arguing rarely achieves its objectives. A project team is likely to be effective if the right person is in the right job. It is therefore essential to take great care in building a project team. The team members should possess the required functional competencies. Furthermore they should, between them, be able to perform all of the roles necessary in an effective and creative team.

Dr Meredith Belbin, based on research over a long period of time, has identified nine team roles in an effective team. Team role defines the behaviour and contribution of individuals when interacting with other members of the team. Each role has positive characteristics as well as any weaknesses that can be tolerated in an individual performing the role. The nine roles, as identified by Belbin, are coordinator, completer finisher, implementer, monitor evaluator, resource investigator, plant, shaper, specialist and team worker. These are now considered in turn.

Coordinator

As implied by the term, the coordinator is a stable individual who sets the agenda and coordinates the activities of the team to ensure that the agreed team objectives are achieved. Typically the coordinator is an extrovert with charisma and the ability to communicate with team members. Other traits include a high level of confidence and maturity, the ability to delegate, identify and make best use of the strengths and weaknesses of individuals, and facilitate decision making. In effect the coordinator performs the role of chairman by listening to the views of the team members, summing up the views of team members and making the decision about the way ahead. If this is the only task performed by an individual in a team, others may see the coordinator as someone who offloads personal work to team members.

Completer finisher

Most projects involve risks and things that can or indeed will go wrong. Completer finisher is someone who worries about what may go wrong and how to protect the team and the project from the likely effects. Typically a completer finisher is an introverted and conscientious individual with a tendency to worry unduly. Positive aspects of a completer finisher include the desire to ensure that everything is done to the expected standards and on time.

Implementer

In any project it is necessary to turn concepts and strategies into practical actions, manageable tasks and workable procedures. The major contribution of an implementer is to translate the team objectives into feasible plans. Implementer is seen as an organized and disciplined individual who is capable of working in a logical and efficient manner to organize and achieve the agreed plans. Some individuals with excellent implementer characteristics may be somewhat inflexible. However, such a trait can be tolerated in a well-balanced team.

Monitor evaluator
All projects involve a careful assessment of alternatives before arriving at the decision. Monitor evaluator has the role of ensuring that all the available options are considered. Thus the monitor evaluator requires the ability to assimilate large amounts of information relating to complex problems and dispassionately analyse them before making a strategic judgement. Typically monitor evaluators are introverted individuals with high IQs without a high level of ambition or the ability to inspire others. Monitor evaluators can perform a very useful role in an advisory capacity.

Plant
Every project requires individuals with bright and original ideas in order to solve problems and overcome difficulties. Plant is in effect an imaginative individual with radical ideas and suggestions, often involving lateral thinking. Typically plants tend to be very creative and dominant. They frequently possess very high IQs and are concerned with fundamental issues rather than detail. They help solve problems by making suggestions and generating new ideas. Frequently plants need careful handling since they do not easily accept criticism. Plants along with monitor evaluators have a very important role at the planning stage.

Resource investigator
Almost all projects involve a high level of interaction with individuals external to the team in order to achieve the project objectives. Resource investigators are the team members who are good at making outside contacts, exploring opportunities and developing ideas. Typically resource investigators tend to be extrovert, highly communicative, positive and frequently over-optimistic entrepreneurs with lots of external contacts. They also have the tendency to lose enthusiasm rather quickly but prevent stagnation of the team efforts.

Shaper
Every project needs individuals who can make things happen. Shapers are individuals who, in effect, direct the way in which the team effort is applied to achieve the project objectives. Typical shapers are dynamic and challenging individuals who often exude self-confidence and thrive on pressure. They create a sense of urgency and direct their nervous energy to overcome the obstacles in order to achieve the objectives. They also tend to be impatient and easily frustrated. As a result they can often upset other members of the team.

Specialist

Many projects require specialist technical skills and competencies. Specialists, by their very nature, focus on a narrow front thereby developing in-depth expertise and competency. Typically, specialists tend to be introverted, but highly dedicated and single-minded individuals with high IQ levels. They ensure that the project is completed to the highest technical standards.

Team worker

Every project team needs cooperative individuals who can support other members of the team and engender team spirit. Typically team workers tend to be extrovert but unassertive individuals who build on ideas and promote harmony within a team. They can carry out a wide variety of tasks at different times to achieve the project objectives.

TT5.2.1 Balancing team roles

The nine roles indicated above do not imply that a team must have at least nine members. In many situations the team will be much smaller and team members play more than one role. It may be necessary for individuals to assume team roles for which they are not ideally suited. For example, the coordinator may also be the implementer. The specialist may also be the completer finisher. However, it is essential that individuals are not asked to perform roles for which they are not suitable.

Identifying the correct composition of a project team and the right person for a given project task is perhaps the most challenging task of the team leader. Team members must have the competencies necessary to carry out all of the tasks to achieve the project goals. Indeed the primary reason for including an individual in a team is the functional competency they can bring with them. Functional expertise in a team, by itself, does not guarantee success. It is equally important that project teams have the correct balance of team roles, as identified by Belbin. Clearly some roles are more important than others depending on the nature of the project.

In a well-balanced project team, each member has 'task'-based roles as defined by competencies and 'team' roles as defined by the behaviour pattern. Teams balanced in terms of roles and competencies are often far more successful than teams with high levels of competency but without the roles balanced. For example, if a team has too many plants and no monitor evaluators or implementers, very few of the ideas will be developed to full fruition.

In a given situation some team roles are clearly more important than others. For example a team involved with the steady state operation of a smoothly running operation, with less need for innovation, may not have an essential requirement for plants. In contrast, a design project team without a plant, shaper, and monitor evaluator will not get very far. In fact a design project team requires all of the team roles as well as the task-related competencies to complete the project.

Computer-based systems are available to assess the characteristics of individuals and hence identify the team roles for which they are best suited.

TT5.2.2 Summary

A project team balanced not only in terms of the functional competencies, but also the team roles as identified by Belbin, is essential for successful completion of projects. A well-balanced team can capitalise on the strengths of the team members.

Line and Staff

Problem

The Pharmaceuticals Validations Manager and his four Section Managers accepted that they should be linked by each having a PC. They were always having arguments about lost messages, particularly those scribbled on their blackboards. Though shy of being computerized, the Section Managers saw that changing to linked PCs would enable them to post notes to each other as well as interact with the production planning system, check certification information and share resource and progress data.

The Validations Manager had a budget adequate for purchasing the system. But which of them should manage this little project? The Validations Manager was clearly the project sponsor, but too busy. Neither he nor any of the Section Managers had any computer expertise or project experience. Their strength was in managing immediate problems of operating the process validation process. They needed someone to provide advice and help them agree what they wanted from the PC system, and then write a specification, state the priorities, produce a project plan, review the budget and risks, request quotes for the system, supervise its purchase, testing and delivery, organize its installation, training, commissioning and hand-over, and finally review the results.

The Personnel Manager made a graduate trainee available for this work, attached to the Validations Manager, to act as a coordinator between the five managers to find out their expectations from the proposed system. From this the trainee produced a draft specification. Two of the five managers disagreed with the draft. Several meetings of all were needed to discuss revised drafts. The final draft was close to the original draft. It was formally signed off by the Validations Manager. With this agreed the trainee took on the role of project leader and proceeded to initiate the purchasing and installation of the system.

During training on the PCs three of the Section Managers questioned the displays and suggested changes. The coordinator argued against these changes. One change was strongly argued and was referred to the Validations Manager. He agreed that the change was not of value, and added that it should not have been referred to him.

Principles

- Create a project team, of all stakeholders, to own the project. Manage them through to the delivery of their project.
- Recognise that power in the 'Staff' role comes from being accepted as knowing what was best for the project.

Lessons

- Staff roles can be a test of personalities. They can be good experience, but are not a substitute for line responsibility.
- The trainee had become the Validations Manager's representative, acting in the 'Staff' role on his behalf as the 'Line' manager. This provided the leadership the project needed.

Reader's Guide

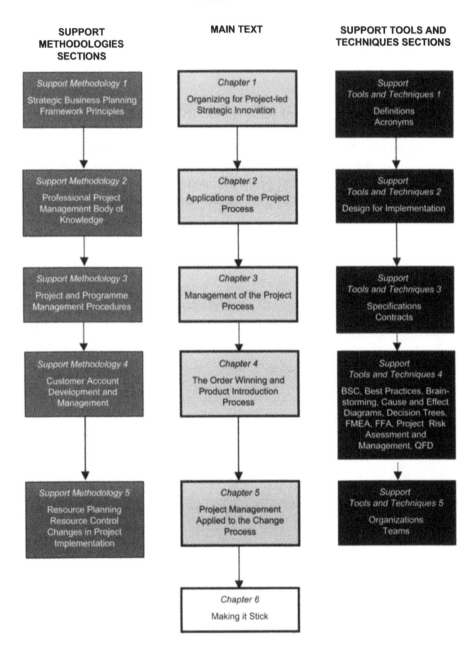

SUPPORT METHODOLOGIES SECTIONS	MAIN TEXT	SUPPORT TOOLS AND TECHNIQUES SECTIONS
Support Methodology 1 Strategic Business Planning Framework Principles	**Chapter 1** Organizing for Project-led Strategic Innovation	**Support Tools and Techniques 1** Definitions Acronyms
Support Methodology 2 Professional Project Management Body of Knowledge	**Chapter 2** Applications of the Project Process	**Support Tools and Techniques 2** Design for Implementation
Support Methodology 3 Project and Programme Management Procedures	**Chapter 3** Management of the Project Process	**Support Tools and Techniques 3** Specifications Contracts
Support Methodology 4 Customer Account Development and Management	**Chapter 4** The Order Winning and Product Introduction Process	**Support Tools and Techniques 4** BSC, Best Practices, Brain-storming, Cause and Effect Diagrams, Decision Trees, FMEA, FFA, Project Risk Asessment and Management, QFD
Support Methodology 5 Resource Planning Resource Control Changes in Project Implementation	**Chapter 5** Project Management Applied to the Change Process	**Support Tools and Techniques 5** Organizations Teams
	Chapter 6 Making it Stick	

Making it Stick

6

6.1 Making innovation and change stick

Seasoned managers, faced with innovation and the restructuring of businesses, to move away from uncompetitive status quo, know how difficult it is to change existing company cultures and how often failure to achieve sustained improvement can happen. The most often quoted example relates to companies cited in the best-selling management book *'In Search of Excellence'* as being leaders who, within a few years, were in financial difficulties, the most notable being Digital Equipment Corporation.

In many business companies or public organizations, it would now be accepted without question that to innovate by developing a new product or service requires a project management approach. Furthermore, the better companies will generally ensure that there is left in place, after the project team is disbanded, a well-defined product and service configuration definition showing carefully how these are assembled from their separate elements, i.e. an assembly tree. There will also be a carefully designed listing of the operational practices, showing how the product or service should be manufactured or delivered. Such good practice procedures help to ensure that the product and service performance intended by the Project Manager is made to stick long after the project team have departed. However, organizational culture can be very variable from company to company, and there are two very common problems.

1. As discussed in Chapters 1, 3, 4 and 5, the standards of professionalism in project management can vary from very poor to very good and, in some companies, what passes for project management is merely very inefficient progress chasing across specialist departments. Companies are often unaware of what truly world-class standards are, or how to transfer them permanently to their activities.
2. Even large, well-resourced companies often do not have good training schemes or systems in place to capture best practices from good projects so that when a project is completed and the project team disbands, their knowledge goes away with them. In such companies, a well-executed

project is often followed by a badly executed project, and the companies do not appear to understand why.

When, however, one examines experiences with change management activity in different companies, it is very usual to find that the use of highly disciplined and best practice project management practices in company change activities is not seen to be either normal or natural. Individual departmental management is often pressed by senior management, without any preparatory training, to make new sophisticated improvements in their operations as part of their normal day-to-day routine activities, using their own specialist resources and in the absence of knowledge of relevant world's best practice or project management support.

Their task is made even more difficult when their department is strongly affected by actions or inactions in other departments outside of their control. The use of cross-functional teams is often rendered difficult by inter-company barriers of a political nature, as well as because an efficient organization, as described in Chapter 1, and a well-communicated cooperative change programme have not been set up. In such circumstances, it is virtually impossible to systematically embed major improvements and make them stick.

For the above reasons, the problems of making change stick are common to both product development projects and competitiveness improvement change programmes, with the latter traditionally encountering the most severe difficulties. This is why the substantial and detailed coverage of best practice change programme requirements was provided in Chapter 5. Therefore, in the current chapter, the use of the phrase *'change and innovation'* projects is intended to encompass all types of project met in an enterprise.

The achievement of sustained competitive advantage from a CAP project programme requires considerable care in a number of aspects of detailed project implementation. The three most important elements to be embedded are:

1. Very wide-ranging and frequent internal communication, to clarify the need to innovate, to motivate, to develop a sense of urgency and of the consequences of the related *significant emotional event* for the company if the project is not successful.
2. Wide, carefully managed, progressive involvement of all of the employees.
3. Clear definition of competitiveness target specifications or objectives relevant to all levels in the organization. Regular publishing of audits of progress towards these.

If, as so often happens, only a small group of staff, possibly external consultants, are involved in the design and implementation of innovation and change, two serious limitations arise:

1. The culture of the organization vigorously resists change and employees defend the status quo due primarily to fear brought about by a lack of involvement plus the neglect of their useful practical knowledge, necessary to assure a successful outcome.
2. When the small management driving group, often including the Chief Executive, breaks up and inevitably moves on, the project championing is lost and the organization quickly reverts to its previous well-understood, comfortable operating practices.

The means to make change stick are commonsense, straightforward and easy to understand, but they have to be put in place progressively and will be summarised in turn.

6.1.1 Continuous mandatory training

The need for project-oriented training has been covered in previous chapters and the important messages are:

1. Involve in implementation the staff who will eventually have to run the delivered innovation, paying particular attention to selecting the operating team and making their training a part of the hand-over process from the design project task-force team. Leave some elements of the completed design for them to specify and therefore take ownership of. Provide the operations team with an operations handbook, including flow-charts, controls, MOPs and standard working routines for the process they are taking over, with residual NVA areas of possible improvement defined, and make it their responsibility to keep the handbook up to date as further changes are made.
2. Provide no-compromise, specific, project-related training for each type of innovation project team – Executive Steering Group, Project Task-Force, SIG team, Continuous Improvement Group – immediately before they start work. This ensures they have a good understanding of the requirements and how to deliver and maintain these. Apply the *train – do* philosophy rigorously, i.e. train them, set stretch targets and immediately launch their project.
3. Promote case studies of successful projects and make them available for general reference to widen organizational capability.

4. Use members of successful project teams to carry out diagnostic audits of other parts of the organization and then present their results to their colleagues as part of an awareness development programme.
5. Regularly send teams to other companies to investigate examples of good practice for them to then communicate on their return.
6. Run a regular internal programme of seminars within the company, within which task-force teams present their work and results to a mixed level audience from all parts of the company.
7. Write and circulate internal reference handbooks, packaging and covering best practice methodologies related to situation examples in the company and include case examples, profiles of projects and summaries of quick-hits achieved, together with the business target MOPs from the CAPs in the monthly company newspaper.
8. Install a five-star training programme for all office and factory staff to create multi-disciplinary flexibility.

6.1.2 Carry out senior manager spot audits on completed projects

Ask task-force project teams to provide an itemised check list of essential operational features and the target daily MOPs, for example for the new cell or process they have redesigned and implemented. It is then relatively straight-forward for senior managers to carry out random checks to discover if these features are still in place. Managers can then insist for good practice, that any discrepancies found must be rectified by the operational team within 48 hours.

Examples of features required, which can form elements of the checklist, are as follows:

- The '5s' items, see Chapter 5.
- The operation of the minimum number of standard meetings with agendas and action lists.
- The integrity of standard working practices, e.g. for customer account management, the application of decision mapping and opportunity classification and qualifying procedures.
- The state of the operational manual in terms of regular updating and formal approvals.
- The team job structure and job roles.
- Progress with 5-star training.
- The consistent operation of continuous improvement in terms of numbers of projects run and a number of suggestions made per month by the team.

- Improvements in the initial five-measures of performance, i.e. work-in-progress ratio, operating cost rates, productivity, cell throughput time, output schedule achievement.
- The state of the equipment infrastructure.
- The maintenance of the use of the standard project management system by new product project teams.

In general, all of the new business processes can be audited in this way whether operational, development or support processes. Similarly a checklist for testing a new product is possible.

6.1.3 Use of designed standard operating or working routines

This can be applied to the carrying out of a new service or the operation of a new piece of equipment or facility. For example providing standard working requirements for all of the job roles and operational requirements of a new natural group process cell in an office or a factory, in the form of a set of standard flow-charts, sometimes with estimated operational times and capacities and identified residual NVAs, it is possible for team leaders to be trained to use these to monitor performance. They can also be used to train replacement staff when members leave the team, so maintaining the knowledge base and the designed operational procedures.

The following are examples of the wide application of standard working operations, based upon the work flow-chart requirements of particular business development and delivery operations processes and the generic support processes discussed in Chapters 1 and 5.

1. The compilation of a financial accounting and risk management procedure manual covering financial control, process risk and corporate governance requirements and the use of this to support staff induction training.
2. The definition and utilization of a common set of modern human resource management and development practices to support the requirements of the CAP.
3. The use of carefully designed standard flow-charts defining all the work flow operations in each office or delivery process cell, and sub-sections relating to the job roles of each member of the team.

   For an invoicing cell team, for example, this would be required to show all the team tasks starting from a review of the original contract requirements, the original specification, change control approvals and concession agreements through to the order definition and payment terms.

6.1.4 Operational day-to-day practices adoption

- Regular skills audits of staff as a base for personal development planning.
- Reduction of the number of specialized job titles to reduce demarcation.
- Application of skills levelling by aligning the levels, grades and required skill elements across the HR structure.
- Training in teamwork skills – team roles, problem solving, problem definition, Kaizen.
- Design of a 5-star training course for directs and indirects, i.e. all staff.
- Project and programme management competence definition.
- The use of natural process team groups and the related HR practices and job structures.
- Routine application, improvement and support of standard working and Kaizen practices.
- Use of an integrated multi-level, top to bottom of the organization and back in 24 hours, communication network implementation.
- Definition of a modular training structure and training packages to support change project task-force programmes, matched to the skills levelling structure.
- Team incentivisation by performance against four or five natural group related MOPs.
- Competency-based selection, job design and training requirements definition – e.g. as for Project and Programme Managers defined in Chapter 1.
- Formalization of the task-force launch process, as described in Chapter 5.

6.1.5 Strategic practices adoption

- Embedding in the CAP a generic, across business training support strategy:
  - in-house modules for common needs;
  - externally provided modules for special needs.
- Graduate recruitment planning.
- Succession planning.
- Continuous professional development.
- Recruitment standards and policies.
- Job rotation planning and resource management.
- Incentive scheme standards for best practice.

1. The operation of a standard project and programme management system for all development and change projects based upon a standard work flow process chart and review milestones, as described in Chapter 3, and Support Methodology, Section 2. This would typically include the common use of the same eight standard control charts across the organization to improve communication and ensure thoroughness of professional management.

2. The implementation of a standard meeting structure with standard agendas, timings and attendance lists (see Appendix to Chapter 1), tailored to the particular business to facilitate minimum time wasting and maximum effective control for all business processes. A typical set, with variations for different business, consolidating some of the meetings for small businesses, might be:
   - a monthly Board process meeting (see Appendix to Chapter 1),
   - a quarterly CAP progress review meeting,
   - a monthly delivery process review meeting,
   - a monthly product and service development process meeting,
   - a weekly change projects review meeting,
   - a quarterly commercial, contracts and pricing policy meeting,
   - a monthly sales and customer account management meeting,
   - a quarterly product and service change approval control meeting for products and the delivery process,
   - a monthly Executive Committee review meeting (see Appendix to Chapter1):
     – operations review including financial review,
     – development review,
   - a monthly resource planning and HR policy review meeting,
   - a monthly cash management process meeting.

3. The careful communication of team roles for all organizational processes, such as described for the customer account development and product development process in Chapter 4, balancing focused team roles with the important work-package delivery roles of specialised support functions and other support staff groups.

6.1.6 Institutionalise Kaizen

A well-supported Kaizen continuous improvement programme in offices and factories following the completion of major change projects, can provide a strong support for making change and innovation stick.

The supporting pillars of Kaizen, each of which is relatively simple in concept, can together provide powerful support for ongoing performance improvement. These are:

1. Motivating the people in the business by paying attention to working conditions in the business.
2. Providing continuous communication to reinforce the need to improve quality, delivery and costs, and creating competitions for generating improvement suggestions by teams.
3. Supporting supervisors with good training to enhance their capabilities to lead their teams and focus on their six responsibilities for productivity, quality, effectiveness, morale, safety and continuous improvement.
4. Using all of the tools of continuous improvement to maintain performance.

6.1.7 Example case

A sample set of 'make it stick' elements for a manufacturing cell in an automotive manufacturing company taken from a particular task-force project is provided in Table 6.1.

6.1.8 The wider system influences

In this book we have concentrated primarily upon the processes internal to the particular business system although some of the case examples have related to supplier and customer processes. For any particular business whether in manufacture or service segments of industry, as has been demonstrated, there are generic similarities, and each business can be regarded as an integrated system of business processes, the associated control systems and utilising a CAP for driving the development and implementation of the business strategy.

There is, of course, a wider system viewpoint, which must be taken into account when creating a CAP to then regularly re-base it, to take account of changing external influences or shocks, which may impact upon business performance. Some of these are very obvious. Clearly, for example, if a market ceases to need the products or services from a business, or finds better quality and lower cost supplies, then the business will close down unless it introduces new products. If the legal environment and framework of national or international regulations change, then what have been sound, capable processes in a business may suddenly become incapable of matching the new requirements. A good example of this is the way in which emission control laws have provided a stimulus for energy saving product

Table 6.1 Standard 'make it stick' elements to match the total cell system concept

1. A cell handbook summarising the design flow-chart, controls and procedures.
2. A detailed cell audit checklist for monthly use by Supervisors.
3. A cell problem log and standard format for recording successes and failures.
4. A simple cell planning board or white board for control of material flow and week-ahead advance planning of the matching of tooling to materials flows.
5. Procedures for the cell level weekly scheduling team for Kanban or period flow control incorporating runners, repeaters, strangers, maintenance time and changeover time, capacity planning and gateway control to other cells.
6. Standard working sheets for each team member.
7. A FRACAS system for problems and changes recording, supported by a manufacturing change acceptance procedure.
8. A standardized continuous improvement procedure also incorporating Total Productive Maintenance.
9. Standard minimum variety generic job labels and flexible but clear definitions of duties.
10. A five-star training plan.
11. The minimum number of carefully designed, regular, disciplined, standard operational control meetings with standard agendas, e.g. for cell scheduling, for the supplies quality, for manufacturing change control, for continuous improvement procedures linked to FRACAS, for engineering change introduction control and target cost achievement.

development, of which adding necessary expensive equipment to power stations, and the major upsurge in new economical common rail diesel fuel system sales for cars are good examples. If the prices or availability of raw materials changes dramatically, if certain skills available in recruits, such as engineering, become in short supply, a business has to respond and change the way it operates to survive. One remorseless driver for change appears to be continuously changing customer expectations for product or service quality, functionality and, often, style or fashion.

Many businesses do not manufacture every component of their own product. For example, in the automotive industry, the vehicle manufacturer is likely to buy out from suppliers over 70% of the component parts, which make up the total car or truck. Therefore, the process capability of the suppliers to the vehicle manufacturer is of major importance and interest, and the vehicle manufacturer will continually monitor the performance of suppliers in a highly detailed manner. In this respect, the vehicle manufacturer, in order to make his own performance improvements stick, has no choice but to ensure that his suppliers are in turn, running their own CAP and change programme.

Vehicle manufacturers like many other types of company run supplier development projects with their key suppliers. An example of a best practice approach is the one introduced by Nissan in the UK. Its prime aim is to assure the total process capability of its suppliers to meet Nissan's requirement. It embodies all of the principles of the Total Quality approach, the six sigma version and, of course, the Toyota Production System, which is the original, fundamental basis for these. These are all effectively the same in principle, i.e. a set of measures of performance is defined for each supplier to meet, and the variability of each of the measured variables, sometimes specified in terms of statistical histograms or standard deviations, is tracked as an indication of the capability of the suppliers' processes to consistently achieve the customer requirements, see Fig. 6.1.

Process capability measured regularly and expressed in standard deviations or Cpk values, is central to the monitoring processes used by good companies.

Nissan specifies a maximum tolerable variance in overall quality of an assembled motor car, from all sources, in parts per million. Each supplier is then given his target measure as a share of this. If all suppliers deliver to target the assembled motor car will achieve the overall quality target. The Nissan approach to measures of performance showed considerable insight and was, however, much broader than merely focusing on only process quality. It also monitored other variables, some of which are essential to sustained development of the organization such as the methodologies, tools and techniques which the suppliers use. It is an excellent example of good practice as follows:

1. It set a target date by which quantified targets for MOPs were to be achieved.
2. It monitored five groups of variables each of which had a number (typically five) of sub-measures, which supported the total system requirement:

    Q – Quality, e.g. supplied product conformance to specification, including packaging.

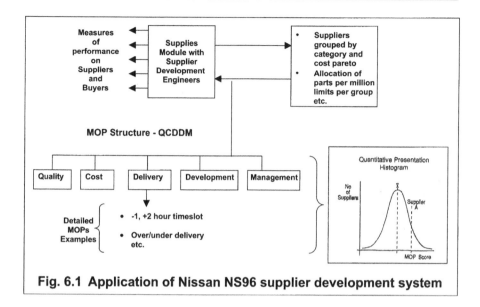

Fig. 6.1 Application of Nissan NS96 supplier development system

C – Cost, e.g. collaboration with Nissan engineers in achieving target product cost and making regular innovations to improve this.

D – Development, e.g. the quality of the supplier company development, innovation and change programme and its project management.

D – Delivery, e.g. delivery in a designated time slot, i.e. JIT delivery of the required total quantity and quantity per package.

M – Management, the quality of the supplier management, e.g. management of the interface with Nissan, management of specific problems, management of requested schedule changes, customer friendliness, management of internal processes and their external suppliers.

At the end of each month, Nissan supplied as feedback for continuous improvement a statistical report to each supplier giving the performance data on each of the five measures, and also showing a histogram of all suppliers' scores achievements with the mean, standard deviation and position above or below the mean for the particular supplier. These measures were displayed for all suppliers grouped by responsible Buyer in the Nissan Purchasing Office, and the supplier Managing Director had to attend the Purchasing Office for a review of performance each month.

If a supplier had persistent problems, a Nissan supplier development team would visit and hold a review meeting in order to define the problems clearly and to develop and agree a monitored action project plan for their solution. Regular follow-up review visits would be maintained until the problem was closed out. This is a classic 'make change stick' principle.

It will be clear that the Nissan approach ultimately reinforced the need for making beneficial change stick and the reviews created significant emotional events. These forced their suppliers to pay attention to all aspects of their organization, and the performance of its business processes and to install a change project programme to achieve total quality of performance. This again is an excellent example of an application of the fundamental principles of the Toyota Production System philosophy and the methodologies described in Chapter 5.

It will also be clear that, in relation to the very important business cultural requirement of persistently striving to sustain and make performance and competitiveness improvements stick, a management team and, particularly, those involved in change management must continually monitor and take account of their suppliers' and customers' business processes.

A well-designed customer account development process and associated information system, as discussed in Chapter 4, will allow changing customer requirements to be anticipated and actioned rapidly. It is also important to embed in the customer account management process an in-service quality management sub-process to audit the performance of products and services in service, and implement lessons learned via the product introduction process, as in Chapter 4.

A supplier development project embedded in the change programme will enable systematic and informed pressure to be put on suppliers to encourage them to set up a change project programme for applying the practices of management by projects and change project management.

These principles and practices are generic and readily transferable across all kinds of businesses, even though some originated directly in the automotive manufacturing industry.

In total, the probability that beneficial changes can be made to stick will be considerably enhanced by the dual approach of taking a total customer-oriented, systems engineering approach within a business, supplemented by a well-resourced wider systems approach to those external factors, which can have such an important impact upon competitiveness, growth and the delivery of shareholder value.

It is necessary for the Board and senior management of a business to recognise the need to employ, as a part of corporate governance, process risk management requirements and the principles of programme management, particularly in large multi-business-unit companies. They will also have to deploy regular audits to ensure that the wider view is being applied and also to ensure that change programmes are implementing strategic change requirements using best project management practices.

Many corporate efforts to transform businesses, after temporary success, have faded away. Management is often reluctant to accept the fact that successful change takes time and effort and cannot be rushed. As explained in Chapter 5, all the steps and phases have to be put in place, persistence is essential and, if any critical steps are omitted, there is a high risk of failure. There is a slow–quick approach to change and a quick–slow approach, of which the first is the successful one, i.e. patiently planning and communicating, then putting the full foundation in place first, results in rapid progress later.

Strategically using significant emotional events, creating a sense of urgency, supported by clear management team leadership and a clear vision, while taking the time to win the key people over and educate them to take initiatives, are all essential steps to achieving a sustained performance, as explained in Chapter 5. If individuals fail to respond and are perceived to be blocking progress after training and support, they have to go. The interests of customers and protecting the livelihood of the majority of the employees have to take priority in any business.

At each step, visibly spreading rapid benefit through quick-hits and institutionalising and standardising new practices, flexibly without bureaucracy, increasingly empowers an organization to move faster and to make quick decisions without the progress made slipping away.

Sharing out credit, emphasising the systematic approach and widely communicating steady progress are obviously necessary while, at the same time, recognising the need for new targets as the competition responds.

Above all, plans for succession and continuous leadership, with the same persistent, outward-looking performance culture devotion to ensure change sticks, are of critical importance. Too often, when the leadership changes, progress halts and benefits wither away. It is important to embed in all support staff processes the necessary supporting infrastructure elements. These are elements such as standard induction training courses, sustained innovation measures of performance in bonus schemes, intranets carrying best practice case studies, promotional criteria, selection procedures for Project Managers, and regular customer opinion audits and competitor analyses.

Careful balanced attention to short-, medium- and long-term requirements is good for shareholders, good for employees, and good for customers. Regrettably, this feature of clear commonsense does not appear to be all that common.

Your next problem

Problem

Principles

Lessons and 'Make it Stick' requirements list

Summary

- A problem defined is a problem already half solved.
- Time is the irrecoverable resource.
- Opinions come quicker that facts, but facts usually win.
- Distance distorts information.
- Look for what should be there, not just what is.
- All actions set an example.
- Finishing successfully demands hard work.
- Efficiency is being right first time.
- Be prepared for good luck.

Further Reading

Parnaby, J. *et al.*, *The Lucas Manufacturing Systems Engineering Handbook,* 2nd edition, 1989 (Lucas Industries Publishers).
Plant, R. *Managing Change* and *Making it Stick,* 1987 (Fontana).
Slater, R. *Get Better or Get Beaten,* 1994 (Irwin Inc.).

OVERALL REFERENCE BIBLIOGRAPHY

Relates to Core Chapters		Relates to Support Sections
1, 4, 5	**Monden, Y.** *The Toyota Production System*, 2nd edition, 1994 (Chapman Hall).	SM1, STT4, STT5
1, 3, 5	**Cooper, R.** and **Kaplan, R. S.** Profit priorities from activity based costing. *Harvard Business Review*, 1991, May–June, 130.	SM3
1, 3, 4, 5	**Drucker, P. F.** *Managing in Times of Great Change*, 1995 (Truman Tulley Books/Dutton).	STT5
1, 4	**Baylis, J. S.** *Marketing for Engineers*, 1989 (Peter Peregrinus Ltd; Institution of Electrical Engineers).	SM4
1, 4	**Miller, R. B.** and **Heiman, S. E.** *Conceptual Selling*, 1987 (Warner Books).	SM4
1, 4	**Parnaby, J.** Design of the new product introduction process to achieve world class benchmarks. *Proc. Instn Elec. Engrs*, 1995, paper 2191 A/A.	
1, 4	**Schonberger, R. J.** *Building a Chain of Customers*, 1990 (Hutchison Business Books).	SM4
1, 5	**Bhote, K. R.** *World Class Quality*, 1988 (American Management Association Membership Publications).	STT4
1, 5	**Christopher, W. F.** and **Thor, C. G.** *Handbook for Productivity Management and Improvement*, 1993 (Productivity Press).	STT5
1, 5	**Cox, J.** *The Goal*, 1989 (Gower Publishing Co.).	
1, 5	**Munro-Faure, L.** and **Munro-Faure, M.** *Implementing Total Quality Management*, 1992 (Pitman/F.T.).	SM1
1, 5	Open Systems Group, *Systems Behaviour*, 1981 (Harper & Rowe).	SM1
1, 5	**Parnaby, J.** Factory 2000 plus, *Int. J. Mfg Tech. Mgmt*, **4** (1/2), 158–169.	SM1

1, 5	**Probert, D.** *Developing a Make v Buy Strategy*, Manufacturing series, 1997 (Institution of Electrical Engineers).	SM1
1, 5	**Womack, J. P.** and **Jones, D. T.** *Lean Thinking*, 1996 (Simon and Schuster).	
1, 5, 6	**Dunlop, A. J.** and **Adelman, R.** *Mean Business*, 1997 (Fireside/Time Books).	
1, 5, 6	**Schonberger, R. J.** *Japanese Manufacturing Techniques*, 1982 (Free Press).	SM4
1, 5, 6	**Plant, R.** *Managing Change and Making it Stick*, 1987 (Fontana Paperbacks).	
2, 3	**Cooke-Davies, T.** Project management maturity models. *Project Manager Today*, 2002, May, 16–20.	SM3
2, 3, 4, 5	**Noble, P. J.** Quality assurance in the construction of process plants. *Engng Mgmt J.*, 1997, 169–176.	SM2, SM6
2, 3, 5	**Holt, P.** Proven methods deliver for the newest industries. *Project Management Today*, 2002, May, 10–14.	SM3
2, 5	**Wearne, S. H.** Management of urgent emergency engineering projects. *Proc. Instn Civil Engrs – Municipal Engng*, 2002, December, **151**, 255–263.	STT5
3, 4	**Davies, A., Miles, B.** and **Parnaby, J.** An integrated approach to quality engineering in support of design for manufacture. *Proc. Instn Mech. Engrs*, 1989, **202** (3), 53.	STT4
3, 4, 5	**Jurna, J. M.** and **Gryna, F. M.** *Quality Control Handbook*, 4th edition, 1988 (McGraw-Hill).	STT4
4, 5	**Douglass, M. E.** and **Douglass, D. N.** *Time Management Teams*, 1996 (Synergy Books Int., Malaysia).	
4, 5	**Price, F.** *Right First Time*, 1985 (Gower Publishing Co.).	
4, 5	**Bertodo, R. G.** Evolution of an engineering organisation. *Int. J. Tech. Mgmt*, 1998, **3** (6), 693–709.	

Index

Printed and bound by CPI Group (UK) Ltd, Croydon, CR0 4YY

23/04/2025

14660947-0003